Guide to Supporting Microsoft Private Clouds

Ron Carswell

COURSE TECHNOLOGY
CENGAGE Learning·

Australia • Brazil • Japan • Korea • Mexico • Singapore • Spain • United Kingdom • United States

COURSE TECHNOLOGY
CENGAGE Learning·

Guide to Supporting Microsoft Private Clouds

Ron Carswell

Vice President, Careers & Computing: Dave Garza

Editor-in-Chief: Marie Lee

Acquisitions Editor: Nick Lombardi

Director, Development – Careers and Computing: Marah Bellegarde

Product Development Manager: Leigh Hefferon

Product Manager: Natalie Pashoukos

Developmental Editor: Dan Seiter

Editorial Assistant: Sarah Pickering

Vice President, Marketing: Jennifer Ann Baker

Marketing Director: Deborah Yarnell

Production Director: Wendy A. Troeger

Production Manager: Andrew Crouth

Content Project Manager: Brooke Greenhouse

Art Director: GEX

Technology Project Manager: Joe Pliss

Media Editor: William Overocker

Cover Photo: ©iStockphoto.com/Alija

© 2014 Course Technology, Cengage Learning

For product information and technology assistance, contact us at
Cengage Learning Customer & Sales Support, 1-800-354-9706

For permission to use material from this text or product, submit all requests online at **cengage.com/permissions**
Further permissions questions can be emailed to
permissionrequest@cengage.com

Library of Congress Control Number: 2012951782

ISBN-13: 978-1-133-70366-2

ISBN-10: 1-133-70366-6

Course Technology
20 Channel Center Street
Boston, MA 02210
USA

Cengage Learning is a leading provider of customized learning solutions with office locations around the globe, including Singapore, the United Kingdom, Australia, Mexico, Brazil, and Japan. Locate your local office at: **international.cengage.com/region**

Cengage Learning products are represented in Canada by Nelson Education, Ltd.

For your lifelong learning solutions, visit **www.cengage.com/coursetechnology**

Purchase any of our products at your local college store or at our preferred online store **www.cengagebrain.com**

Visit our corporate website at **cengage.com**.

Printed in the United States of America
1 2 3 4 5 6 7 16 15 14 13 12

Brief Contents

Table of Contents

Preface

Welcome to *Guide to Supporting Microsoft Private Clouds*. This book prepares students to implement private clouds with Microsoft technology. The private cloud is a new model for delivering standardized information technology (IT) services on demand. Students learn how to build a private cloud environment and transform how IT services are delivered to an organization.

The research firm Forrester forecasts that the cloud computing market will grow from $40 billion in 2011 to $241 billion by 2020 in several dozen distinct market segments. Other forecasts call for significantly higher growth. Cloud services are expected to contribute to 14 million new jobs worldwide by 2015. "Making the move to the private cloud will be the next big step for forward-thinking businesses who want to maximize their information technology efficiency," said Scott Wiener, Senior Vice President of Information Technology for Yardi Systems.

Guide to Supporting Microsoft Private Clouds presents a structured approach for students, beginning with the development of foundational concepts. Figure 1 shows this progression.

Students create a virtual environment using Windows Server 2008 R2 SP1, the Hyper-V hypervisor, and Hyper-V Manager. In the next layer, students use System Center Virtual Machine Manager to coordinate the management of virtual machines on multiple host computers. Students develop the skills to implement three Microsoft technological approaches that deliver access to virtual machines in the private cloud:

- Self-Server Web portal provides a Web-based interface to virtual machines in the private cloud, which enables business groups to request and manage capacity for their applications.

- Virtual Desktop Infrastructure (VDI) gives users the freedom to access their Windows desktops on a computer of their choice. By using VDI, users can work almost anywhere inside or outside the organization's network.

- The Hyper-V cluster provides high availability—the implementation of operating systems technology in a private cloud that enables the takeover of processing by another computer if one computer fails. When a virtual machine has high availability, its downtime can be reduced.

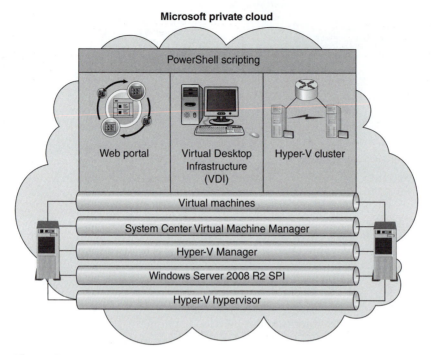

Figure 1 The Microsoft private cloud

Source: © Cengage Learning 2014

PowerShell is a new Windows command-line shell designed especially for server administrators. Students learn to automate tasks for the management of virtual machines in the private cloud.

Hardware Overview

Figure 2 shows the network diagram for a private cloud station to be shared by three students.

This approach reduces costs to the school while promoting teamwork among students. Lab activities are designed to distribute the tasks of configuring and testing the cloud station among the three students. Two clustered servers deliver virtual machines to potential users. Four switches provide for the heartbeat, management, private virtual machine, and storage networks. A firewall on the private VM network isolates the virtual machines while providing NAT services. A third server provides support for a number of required roles: virtual machine management, Active Directory for account management, a Web portal for student virtual machine access, and a storage server to provide storage for the virtual machine files.

To cluster the two servers for a cloud station, identical hardware must be used on both servers.

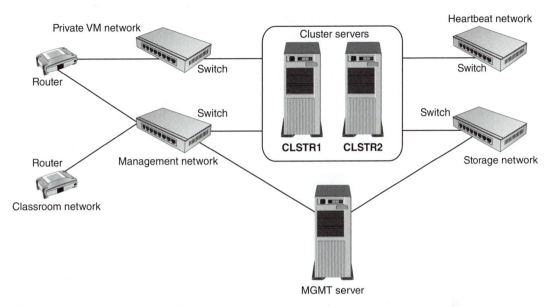

Figure 2 Network diagram for private cloud

Source: © Cengage Learning 2014

Two clustered servers per cloud station	
Processor	64-bit processor, 2.00 GHz required, 2.60 GHz recommended, hardware virtualization required
Memory	4 GB required, 6 GB recommended
Hard drive	250 GB 7.2K RPM SATA 3.5
DVD	16X DVD
Network (4 NICs)	On-board single gigabit network adapter Three single-port NICs

Source: © Cengage Learning 2014

The management server requires only two network adapters. An additional hard drive is required for storage and backup activities.

One management server per cloud station	
Processor	64-bit processor, 2.00 GHz required, 2.60 GHz recommended, hardware virtualization required
Memory	4 GB required, 6 GB recommended
Hard drives (2)	250 GB 7.2K RPM SATA 3.5, 1 TB 7.2K RPM SATA 3.5
DVD	16X DVD
Network (2 NICs)	On-board single gigabit network adapter One single-port NIC

Source: © Cengage Learning 2014

To provide for network connectivity, four network switches and a VPM firewall are required. For additional information about hardware requirements, refer to Appendix A.

Software Overview

The two clustered servers require Windows Server 2008 R2 SP1 Enterprise edition with the appropriate roles. The third server also supports virtual machines for Windows Storage Server 2008 R2 and a Windows 7 client.

Clustered servers	
Operating system	Windows Server 2008 R2 SP1 Enterprise edition
Roles	Hyper-V Manager Failover Cluster Management Cluster Shared Volumes
Agents	Virtual Machine Manager iSCSI configuration
Management server	
Operating system	Windows Server 2008 R2 SP1 Enterprise edition Windows Storage Server 2008 R2 System Center Virtual Machine Manager 2008 R2 SP1 Windows 7 Enterprise client Microsoft Office
Roles	Hyper-V Manager Failover Cluster Management Active Directory Services DNS Internet Information Server Web portal iSCSI Software Target 3.3

Intended Audience

Guide to Supporting Microsoft Private Clouds is intended as a capstone course for students who are getting started in IT and for users who have experience with Windows Server 2008 in a corporate environment. To best understand the material in this book, students should have previously installed and configured Windows Server 2008.

Chapter Descriptions

This book contains the following 10 chapters and two appendices:

- **Chapter 1,** *Introduction to the Private Cloud,* illustrates the transition to cloud computing and its architecture. Chapter 1 also summarizes hardware and software requirements for cloud computing.

- **Chapter 2**, *Creating and Managing Virtual Machines*, helps you work with the Hyper-V hypervisor and develop a virtualized environment that the guest operating system perceives to be a physical computer. Within this environment, virtual hard disks work like hard disks and virtual network switches work like network adapters.
- **Chapter 3**, *Configuring the Hyper-V Environment*, builds on the first two chapters and teaches skills for using the Hyper-V environment effectively.
- **Chapter 4**, *Installing and Using Virtual Machine Manager*, builds on your knowledge of Hyper-V to help you install and configure VMM. Chapter 4 equips students to use Hyper-V to manage a group of host computers and their virtual machines.
- **Chapter 5**, *Working with Virtual Machines*, explains how to work with the VMM library, which is a prerequisite for rapidly provisioning virtual machines in private clouds to meet increased application demand.
- **Chapter 6**, *Installing and Using the Self-Service Portal*, explains how to use the self-service portal, which provides a Web-based interface to virtual machines within an Infrastructure as a Service (IaaS) model of a private cloud.
- **Chapter 7**, *Using the Virtual Desktop Infrastructure*, shows you how to use the VDI, which provides the freedom to access Windows desktops on a computer of your choice.
- **Chapter 8**, *Implementing High Availability*, explains how to implement operating systems technology in a private cloud that provides high availability for mission-critical applications.
- **Chapter 9**, *Managing High-Availability Clusters*, explains skills needed for day-to-day management of software that supports the private cloud.
- **Chapter 10**, *Managing the Private Cloud with PowerShell*, explains how to use PowerShell, a new Windows command-line shell designed especially for server administrators.
- **Appendix A**, *Author's Configuration*, is an overview of the hardware and software used in the text.
- **Appendix B**, *Configuring Support Hardware and Software*, provides instructions to configure the specialized hardware and software used in the text.

Features and Approach

Guide to Supporting Microsoft Private Clouds differs from other books about private clouds. This text provides the skills to create a working private cloud. Each chapter builds on the previous chapter using a structured, linear approach.

- **Chapter objectives**—Each chapter begins with a list of the concepts to be mastered. This list provides a quick reference to the chapter's contents and can be a useful study aid.
- **Activities**—Activities are incorporated throughout the text to give you a strong foundation for carrying out tasks in the real world. Because the activities build on each other, you should complete the activities in each chapter before moving to the end-of-chapter materials and subsequent chapters.

- **Chapter summaries**—Each chapter ends with a summary of concepts introduced in the chapter. These summaries provide a helpful way to recap and revisit the chapter's ideas.

- **Key terms**—All boldfaced terms introduced in a chapter are listed alphabetically after the chapter summary. Use this list to check your understanding of the terms.

- **Review questions**—The end-of-chapter assessment begins with a set of questions that reinforce the ideas introduced in the chapter. Answering these questions helps ensure that you have mastered important concepts.

- **Case projects**—Each chapter closes with a section that asks you to evaluate real-world situations and decide on a course of action. This valuable tool helps you sharpen your decision-making and troubleshooting skills, which are important in IT.

Text and Graphic Conventions

Additional information and exercises are included in this book to help you better understand the chapter discussions. Icons throughout the text alert you to these additional materials:

Tips offer extra information on resources, problem solving, and time-saving shortcuts.

Notes present additional helpful material for the subject being discussed.

The Caution icon identifies important information about potential mistakes or hazards.

Hands-on icons precede each activity in this book.

Case Project icons mark the end-of-chapter case projects. These scenario-based assignments ask you to independently apply what you learned in the chapter.

Instructor's Resources

The following supplemental materials are available when this book is used in a classroom setting. All of these supplements are provided to the instructor on the Cengage Web site (*www.cengage.com*) and on a single CD-ROM (ISBN: 978-1-13372-836-8).

Electronic Instructor's Manual. The Instructor's Manual that accompanies this book includes additional material to assist in class preparation, including suggestions for classroom activities, discussion topics, and additional projects.

Solutions. Solutions are provided for review questions and for case projects when applicable.

ExamView®. This book is accompanied by ExamView, a powerful testing software package that allows instructors to create and administer printed, computer-based, and Internet exams. ExamView includes hundreds of questions that correspond to the topics covered in this text, enabling students to generate detailed study guides that include page references for further review. The computer-based and Internet testing components allow students to take exams at their computers and save time by grading each exam automatically.

PowerPoint presentations. This book comes with Microsoft PowerPoint slides for each chapter. These slides can be used as a teaching aid for classroom presentation, made available to students on a network for chapter review, or printed for classroom distribution. Instructors can also add their own slides to cover additional topics they introduce to the class.

Figure files. All of the figures and tables in the book are reproduced on the Instructor's Resource CD in bitmap format. Like the PowerPoint presentations, these files can be used as a teaching aid in class, made available to students for review, or printed for classroom distribution.

Errata and Book Support

We have made every effort to ensure the accuracy of this textbook. Any errors reported since publication are listed on the Cengage Learning Web site at *www.cengage.com*. To find the list after accessing the site, enter "Guide to Supporting Microsoft Private Clouds" in the Search Products box.

The Author Wants to Hear From You

If you are working with this book in the classroom and you need a tip or a question answered, you can send an e-mail to the author at *carswellprivatecloud@gmail.com*.

Acknowledgments

This text is a product of many talented people. First, I want to give a well-deserved pat on the back to the staff at Cengage, especially my product manager, Natalie Pashoukos, for her patience and help. And, of course, thanks to my developmental editor, Dan Seiter, for providing the inspiration to mold thoughts clearly and concisely. I also thank the technical editor, Marianne Snow, for the numerous hours she devoted to proofing the text and testing each lab activity. Her insight, from a student perspective, enhanced the quality of this text. And, last but not least, I thank my wife Coleen for the hours I spent away in the "man cave" with the private cloud.

About the Author

Ron Carswell has more than 20 years of computer experience in large and small organizations. Ron holds a bachelor's degree in Business Administration from the University of Texas and a master's degree in Business Administration from Baylor University. He has received the A+, N+, CTT+, MCSA, MCSE, and MCDST certifications. He is a professor emeritus at San Antonio College, where he teaches MCITP certification courses. Ron is the lead principal investigator for a National Science Foundation (NSF) grant at San Antonio College to create an Enhanced Skills Certificate in server virtualization, which increases the number of technicians who enter the IT workforce with competencies in server virtualization and cloud computing. He has eight books to his credit. His last textbook was *Parallel Operating Systems with Windows and Linux, Version 2.*

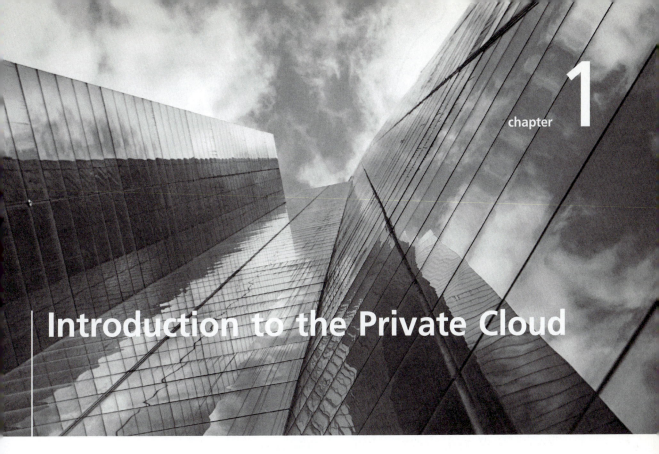

chapter 1

Introduction to the Private Cloud

After reading this chapter and completing the exercises, you will be able to:

- Describe the architecture of a private cloud
- Identify the hardware requirements for a private cloud
- Describe the software requirements for a private cloud
- Install the management server

This textbook explains how to implement a private cloud—a computing platform that operates behind a private organization's firewall under the control of the Information Technology (IT) department. **Cloud computing** is the use of multiple server computers on a digital network that work together as if they were one computer.

Cloud Architecture

In this section, you will learn about the transition to cloud computing and its architecture. The section includes information about public cloud offerings.

Making the Transition to Cloud Computing

In the past, a document could not be created without application software installed on the user's computer. A license for each application was purchased from a software vendor, which permitted the application to be installed on one computer system. The introduction of local area networks (LANs) led to the creation of the **client/server model**, as shown in Figure 1-1. In this model, server computers with enhanced capabilities and large storage devices could be used to store data for multiple users. To enable the client to access data stored on the server, a network-aware version of the application was installed on client computers; the application used the client system's memory and CPU for processing. Rather than storing documents and other data files on the clients, the files were stored on data servers. This model also required the purchase of multi-user licenses.

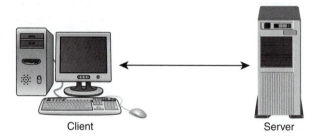

Client   Server

Figure 1-1 Client/server model

© *Cengage Learning 2014*

Figure 1-2 illustrates the basic concept of cloud computing, which represents a major transition from the client/server model. Cloud computing provides applications from a server that are executed and managed by a client's Web browser. No applications are required on the client computer. Cloud service providers have complete control over the browser-based applications, eliminating the need for version upgrades or license management on client computers. The term **Software as a Service (SaaS)** is sometimes used to describe the application programs offered through cloud computing services. These services, or the aggregation of all existing cloud services, are sometimes simply called *the cloud*.

Figure 1-2 Cloud computing

© Cengage Learning 2014

Any computer or Web-friendly device connected to the Internet can access the same pool of computing power, applications, and files in a cloud computing environment, as shown in Figure 1-3. You can remotely store and access personal files that contain music, pictures, videos, and documents. You can also perform word-processing tasks on a remote server. Data is centrally stored, so you do not need to use a storage medium such as a thumb drive. As an employee of a private company, you can also use the company's customized cloud e-mail servers, such as Microsoft Exchange.

Figure 1-3 Cloud computing using Web devices

© Cengage Learning 2014

A traditional Web application runs on a single computer or a group of privately owned computers. Such computers are powerful enough to serve a certain number of requests per minute and can provide an acceptable response time for Web requests. If a Web site or Web application suddenly becomes more popular, the increased traffic can overwhelm a Web server, and the response time of the requested pages will increase from the overload. On the other hand, much of the server's capacity is unused when demand is low.

By contrast, if the Web site or Web application is hosted in a public cloud, additional processing and computing power is available within the cloud. If a Web site suddenly becomes more popular, the cloud can automatically direct more individual computers to serve pages for the site. If the site loses popularity, the cloud will scale down the number of servers to reduce the cost of service. The Web site might share the cloud servers with thousands of other Web sites of varying sizes and memory. Cloud computing is popular for its "pay-as-you-go" pricing model.

A private cloud is designed to offer the same features and benefits of public cloud systems, and it removes a number of objections to the cloud computing model, including control over enterprise and customer data, worries about security, and issues of regulatory compliance.

Figure 1-4 shows a hybrid cloud in which the public cloud supplements the power of the private cloud. The hybrid cloud approach is effective when the private cloud is not capable of scaling to meet the needs of an infrequent event, such as increased online sales on "Black Friday," the day after Thanksgiving in the United States. In such cases, the private cloud will offload sales transactions for the peak sales period to a public cloud.

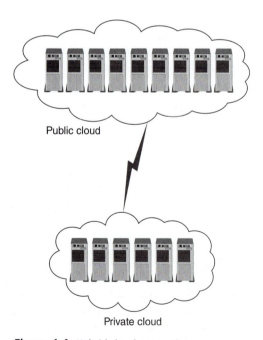

Public cloud

Private cloud

Figure 1-4 Hybrid cloud computing

© Cengage Learning 2014

Server Virtualization

Virtualization is the use of software to simulate a physical computing environment and the use of virtual hardware on which you can install a number of operating systems (OSs) and interact with them. With virtualization technology, you can run a range of OSs on top of the host operating system.

Figure 1-5 provides a high-level overview of how server virtualization is used to deploy a hypervisor. The **hypervisor** allows multiple operating systems, called **guests,** to run concurrently on a **host** computer. In the figure, the base layer represents the hardware within the physical computer, including the system board, memory, disk, network, and other hardware components. The hypervisor is so named because it is conceptually one level higher than a supervisory program. The hypervisor presents a virtual operating platform to the guest operating systems and manages their execution. Multiple instances of different operating systems can share the virtualized hardware resources. Hypervisors are installed on dedicated server hardware that exists only to run guest operating systems.

Windows Server 2008 R2 Enterprise	Windows 7 Client	Windows Storage Server 2008 R2
Hypervisor		

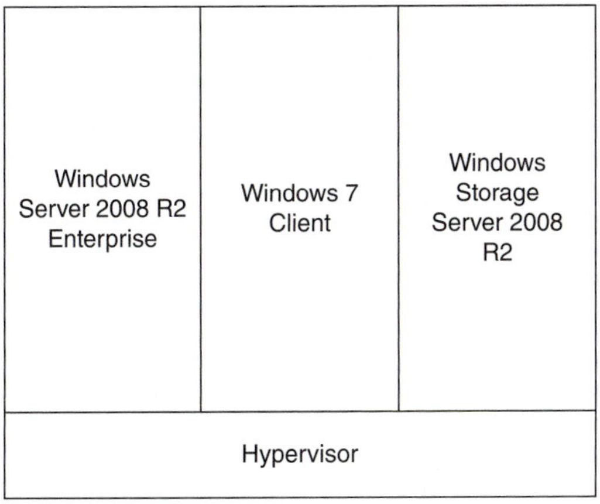

Figure 1-5 Hypervisor virtualization technology

© Cengage Learning 2014

A **standard hardware system environment,** which imitates the function of a computer system, is provided within each virtual machine for each guest OS. The OS and software within each virtual machine are unaware of the other virtual machines and have full access to the virtual platform.

If you need to install a new OS in a traditional system, you must purchase a new computer, install an additional hard drive, create a partition on the existing hard drive, or remove and replace your existing OS. Virtualization permits the installation of a new OS on an existing computer system without disrupting the previous OS. Because each virtual machine uses the same standard hardware, you can save time by copying a standard system image for use by this virtual machine. The **system image** contains the operating system and related files, installed applications, and configuration preferences. This standard image would be available in a library of previously installed virtual machines.

Server virtualization in cloud computing enables **rapid provisioning**—the addition of virtual machines to meet increased demands for processing online requests. Recall that additional processing and computing power are available within the cloud. If a Web site suddenly becomes more popular, additional virtual machines can be deployed rapidly within the cloud.

Storage Virtualization

Within a network, a file server is a computer that has the primary purpose of providing a location for **shared disk access**. Figure 1-6 illustrates the shared storage of computer files that can be accessed by workstations attached to the computer network. The term *server* highlights its role in the client/server scheme, in which clients are workstations accessing the shared storage. A file server is not intended to run applications for its clients.

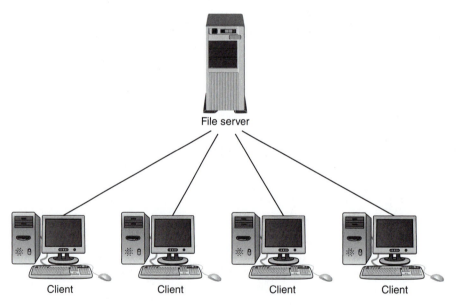

Figure 1-6 File server shared access

© *Cengage Learning 2014*

Network-attached storage (NAS) is file-level data storage on a computer network that provides data access to clients. Unlike a general-purpose file server, a NAS is a specialized computer built specifically for serving files. NAS systems usually contain two or more hard drives that are combined and arranged in **Redundant Array Independent Disk (RAID)** arrays. See Figure 1-7.

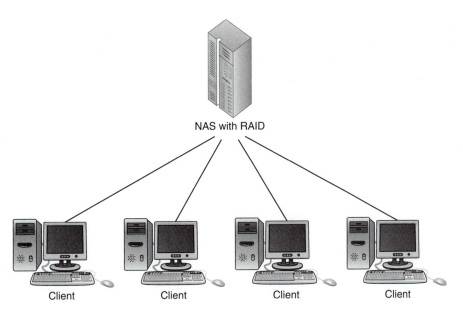

Figure 1-7 NAS with RAID

© Cengage Learning 2014

Multiple disk drives can work together as a team to form a disk array (see Figure 1-8). Data that is frequently needed is retrieved from a cache. The temporary memory of the cache is faster than the magnetic disks. Redundant components such as RAID, processing modules, and power supplies increase availability.

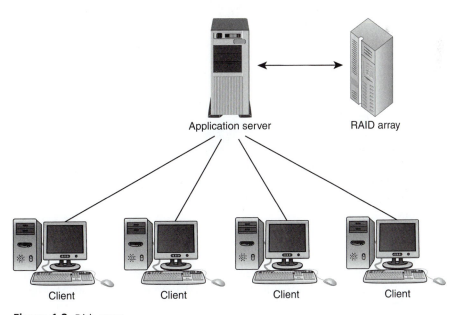

Figure 1-8 Disk array

© Cengage Learning 2014

Disk arrays also can be consolidated into a **storage area network (SAN)**. A SAN, as shown in Figure 1-9, connects multiple servers so that all data appears to be stored to a single source. This approach is much easier than managing individual disks on multiple servers. Using a SAN, system administration tasks such as disk replacement and routine backups are easier to manage and schedule. In some SANs, disk arrays can be automated to copy data to other disks for backup without requiring processing at the servers.

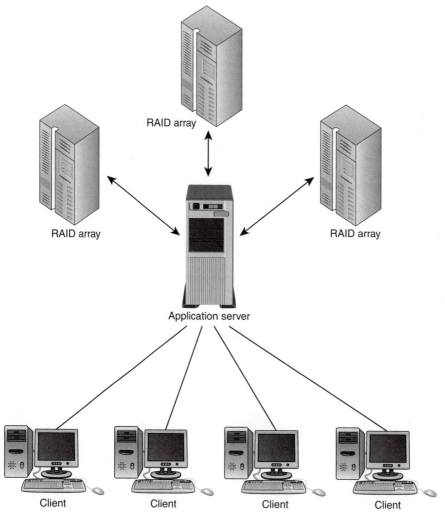

Figure 1-9 SAN

© Cengage Learning 2014

A SAN uses the principle of **storage virtualization,** which handles storage as a unified whole. In this system, the locations of available physical media are not important. Storage virtualization enables virtual machines to use data from a unified storage entity rather than individual disks, which permits more flexibility in the management of storage. A **logical unit number (LUN)** is a unique identifier used to designate a unit of storage. Although a LUN represents a single client connection, the connection can be made to part of a hard disk, a whole hard drive, or even multiple hard drives. As storage requirements change, LUNs can be adjusted in size, which makes storage easier to manage. Storage virtualization works well for migrating LUNs from one disk array to another without downtime (see Figure 1-10).

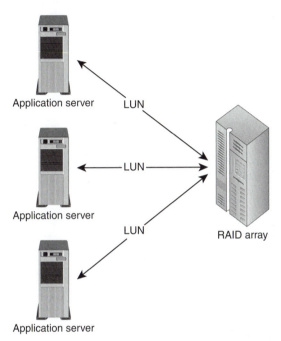

Figure 1-10 Virtualized storage

© Cengage Learning 2014

You can use **thin provisioning** with storage virtualization. In this approach, you can create LUNs for new servers in the system but assign more disk space on those servers than the actual amount of space configured for the SAN. For instance, a Windows 2008 server that hosts your database may appear to have 100 GB allocated for data storage when only a small percentage of that capacity is actually allocated. Over time, up to 10 GB might be used as the database file is populated. If so, you can save up to 90 GB of disk space but still be able to store more data on the LUN without taking further action.

Virtual storage is not the same as storage virtualization. Virtual storage refers to extending a computer's internal memory.

Network Virtualization

A **virtual LAN (VLAN)** is a group of PCs, servers, and switches that appear to be connected to a single, logical network segment, even though they may not be. The resources and servers of other users on the physical network are invisible to other VLAN members. However, there is much more to network virtualization than just VLANs.

In network virtualization, a computer network's resources and client/server system are combined and put on a virtual network. This network treats all hardware and software as a single collection of resources that can be accessed regardless of physical boundaries. This globalized approach requires using routers and switches to perform more services, such as access control, path isolation, and edge services. Internet Protocol Security (IPSec) is an example of an edge service that secures IP communications by authenticating and encrypting each IP packet of a communication session. Routers and switches support globalization, as shown in Figure 1-11.

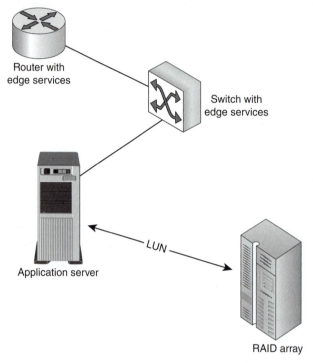

Figure 1-11 Virtualized networks

© *Cengage Learning 2014*

Clustering

Clustering means connecting multiple computers to make them work as a unified system (see Figure 1-12). Clustering increases a computer system's load balancing and redundancy.

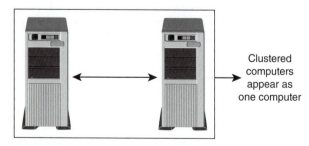

Figure 1-12 Clustered computers

© *Cengage Learning 2014*

Load balancing distributes processing across multiple servers, which is important when you do not know how many requests to expect for a group of servers or when the requests will arrive. Load balancing might allocate incoming requests evenly to all servers or it might send requests to the next available server.

Redundancy is the ability of a cluster to respond gracefully to an unexpected hardware or software failure. **Failover** is the capability to switch to a redundant or standby server automatically when the active server fails. Failover automation occurs using a "heartbeat" network of two servers. Essentially, the second server monitors the main server, and will immediately begin executing the functions of the main server if it detects a failure.

Role-Based Security

In addition to file-based security permissions, virtualization requires a new approach called **role-based security** that provides finer control over permissions in a virtualized environment. In this approach, groups of virtual machine instances determine which machines are available for particular user tasks. Administrators specify the operations that a user can perform for a group in which the user has membership. For example, when a user starts a virtual machine, a check is made to verify that the user has permission to do so.

For a specific example of role-based security, consider the **self-service user role**. Members of this role can manage their virtual machines under certain controls. The user is given a simplified view of his virtual machines and the tasks he can execute with them. These operations might include creating virtual machines that use particular templates and ISO image files. The role also can be used with a quota to limit the number of virtual machines that are available to a user.

Examples of Cloud Computing Services

Three types of services are available from a cloud service provider:

- *Infrastructure as a Service (IaaS)*—In this approach, the service provider pays for servers, network equipment, storage, and backups. Customers pay only for the service, which allows them to build applications on the cloud without using their own company's computer resources. Amazon offers IaaS; the company characterizes its service as Amazon Elastic Compute Cloud (Amazon EC2), "a Web service that provides resizable comput[ing] capacity in the cloud." Rapid provisioning contributes to Amazon's ability to scale up by adding virtual machines to meet increased demand.

- *Platform as a Service (PaaS)*—The service provider offers business solutions for users. For example, Salesforce.com distributes business software on a subscription basis and is best known for its Customer Relationship Management (CRM) products. CRM aids sales personnel by tracking customers and sales while providing analytical reports.

- *Software as a Service (SaaS)*—Customers pay to use the service provider's software, particularly application software. An example of SaaS is Google Apps, which provides a wide range of office applications such as mail, word processing, spreadsheets, and presentations from the Web.

Computer Hardware Requirements

Virtualization requires specific hardware to make the host computer's operating systems function properly. This section provides hardware requirements for three servers, networks, and storage that will be needed for each student team.

Figure 1-13 provides an overview of hardware requirements. The private cloud implementation for each student team requires three servers. The cluster consists of two servers (CLSTR1 and CLSTR2) that provide fault tolerance for the virtual machines. A third server (MGMT) manages the virtual machines in the private cloud. Around the periphery are network switches and routers that support the four required networks (Heartbeat, Storage, Management, and Private VM).

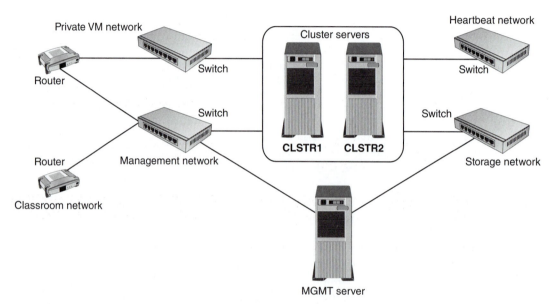

Figure 1-13 Hardware diagram for private cloud

© Cengage Learning 2014

A router within the private virtual machine (VM) network provides DHCP support and NAT support for the virtual machines running in the private cloud. **Dynamic Host Configuration Protocol (DHCP)** and **Network Address Translation (NAT)** are required for the network. DHCP assigns dynamic IP configurations to devices on a network. NAT enables networks to use one set of IP addresses for internal traffic and a second set of addresses for external traffic. A second router, the classroom router, provides NAT support for each team's set of three servers.

Processor Requirements

X86 virtualization allows multiple operating systems to simultaneously share processor resources safely and efficiently. This virtualization is used to simulate a complete hardware environment, or virtual machine, in which an unmodified guest operating system executes in complete isolation using the same instruction set as the host machine. Hardware-assisted virtualization was added to most x86 processors (Intel VT-x or AMD-V) in 2006.

To use hardware virtualization, the VT-x or AMD-V option must be enabled in the BIOS. You can access the BIOS settings menu by pressing the appropriate key (F2 or Delete) as the startup flash screen is displayed. The BIOS settings for Intel VT or AMD-V are usually in the Chipset or Security menu.

A multi-core processor is a single computing component with two or more independent actual processors (called *cores*). A **dual-core processor** has two cores, a **quad-core processor** contains four cores, and a **hexa-core processor** contains six. Performance improves when cores are shared between virtual machines.

Memory Requirements

The amount of memory required for effective processing is determined by the number of virtual machines that will run concurrently. Running Windows Server 2008 R2 SP1 requires at least 512 MB of RAM; 1 GB of RAM is suggested. To start the Hyper-V hypervisor, you need almost 300 MB of memory. A good standard for determining the memory overhead of each virtual machine is to start with 32 MB for the first 1 GB of virtual RAM, and then add 8 MB for each additional GB of virtual RAM. Use this standard when calculating how many virtual machines to host on a physical server.

Table 1-1 provides estimates for the number of virtual machines that can run concurrently, assuming an average memory requirement of 768 MB for the lab activities in this textbook.

Memory	Hypervisor	Parent Partition	Number of Virtual Machines
4 GB	300 MB	1,096 MB	3
8 GB	300 MB	1,256 MB	8
12 GB	300 MB	1,384 MB	12
16 GB	300 MB	1,512 MB	16

Table 1-1 Estimated memory needed to run virtual machines

© Cengage Learning 2014

To complete the lab activities in this textbook, 4 GB of memory is required and 8 GB is recommended. If you have the opportunity, use host computers with as much memory as you can afford.

Networking Requirements

The number of network adapter cards you need is determined by the minimum number of networks required for the creation of private clouds. To complete the lab activities in this textbook, the following networks are required. (Color-coded cables are recommended to make device connection easier.)

- *Management*—Monitor and manage the host computers and virtual machines in the cluster. Blue cables are recommended.

- *Storage*—Provide shared storage for the virtual machines in the cluster. Green cables are recommended.
- *Heartbeat*—Communicate between the host computers in the cluster. Red cables are recommended.
- *Private virtual machine*—Communicate between virtual machines running on each host computer and the Internet. Yellow cables are recommended.

Most computers have one or perhaps two network adapters, but you will need a total of four adapters.

Three gigabit Ethernet switches are required for three of the networks. A fourth gigabit Ethernet switch for the private virtual machine network requires support for VLANs. An Internet-style router that supports DHCP and NAT is required for the private virtual machine network.

Storage Requirements

As you learned earlier, a SAN is a dedicated network that provides access to consolidated data storage. The **Internet Small Computer System Interface (iSCSI)** is an IP-based storage networking standard for linking host computers to data storage facilities. The protocol allows clients, called initiators, to send SCSI commands to SCSI storage arrays. The iSCSI protocol supports the storage requirements for the lab activities in this textbook. You will learn more about iSCSI in Chapter 8.

The disk controller in your host computer uses block-level access to read and write to the disks that are attached internally within the computer. In a SAN, where disks are external to the servers, read/write access is also at the block level. When connected to a SAN, disks appear to the operating system as resident (installed locally) to the computer. These devices can be partitioned and formatted with Windows Server 2008 tools.

To conserve costs, this textbook uses Microsoft Storage Server 2008 R2 to provide an iSCSI-based SAN. For detailed information about the hardware used in this book, refer to Appendix A.

Computer Software Requirements

Windows Server 2008 R2 SP1 Enterprise Edition will be installed on each of the three servers. On the management server, you will install Hyper-V, Active Directory Domain Services (AD DS), Domain Name Service (DNS), and Windows Server Failover Clustering. **Windows Server Failover Clustering** is designed to allow servers to work together as a computer cluster, which provides failover and increased availability of applications. Windows Storage Server 2008 R2 Enterprise Edition will be installed in a virtual machine to support iSCSI block mode storage for the cluster servers. Windows 7 Enterprise Edition will be installed in a virtual machine to provide access to virtual desktops. Hyper-V and Windows Server Failover Clustering will be installed on the two cluster servers.

In Chapter 4, **System Center Virtual Machine Manager** (VMM) 2008 R2 SP1 will be installed on the management server to manage the virtual machines running on the cluster servers.

The lab activities in this textbook are designed to be completed by three-member teams. A likely scenario might have the first team member leading during the first set of steps as the other two team members watch and assist. The second team member should complete the next set of steps and the third team member should complete the remaining steps. The step assignments for team members are provided in the Description section of each lab activity.

Activity 1-1: Taking Inventory of Private Cloud Devices

Time Required: 10 minutes

Objective: Identify the computers and devices needed to build a private cloud and confirm that they are available.

Description: In this activity, you will identify the items provided by your instructor and verify that all are available. If you are missing an item or cannot identify one, contact your instructor. The first team member should lead in this activity as the other two team members watch and assist.

1. Using Table 1-2, complete the inventory and place checks in the Mark column to indicate that the components are available.

Mark	Quantity	Item Description
	2	Cluster servers with four RJ45 network connections
	1	Management server with two RJ45 network connections
	3	5-port network gigabit switches with power supplies
	1	5-port network gigabit VLAN switch with power supply
	1	WAN/LAN router with power supply
	4	Blue network cables
	3	Green network cables
	2	Red network cables
	4	Yellow network cables
	1	LCD panel
	1	KVM switch with 3 cable sets (if required, a power supply)
	1	Keyboard
	1	Mouse
	2	6-outlet power strips

Table 1-2 Component inventory worksheet

Do not place network cables in the servers or switches until you are instructed to do so in future activities.

Activity 1-2: Cabling the Management Server

Time Required: 10 minutes

Objective: Cable the management server and start populating the management network.

Description: In this activity, you will prepare the management server for the software installation in Activity 1-3. First, you will connect the KVM switch to the management server. Next, you will connect the management server to the 5-port network switch, and then you will connect this switch to the classroom router. Use blue cables for these network connections. Pay attention to the steps to make future activities easier. The second team member should lead in this activity as the other team members watch and assist.

Do not place network cables in the servers or switches until you are instructed to do so in each activity.

1. Locate the management server.

2. Cable the KVM switch to the management server using port 1.

3. If required, place the USB connectors for the keyboard and mouse in the KVM switch.

4. If required, cable the power supply to the KVM switch, and plug the power supply into the power strip.

5. Connect a blue cable between the top RJ45 connector on the management server and port 1 of a 5-port network switch.

6. Connect a blue cable between port 5 of the 5-port network switch and the classroom router.

Ask your instructor for specific details about the network in your classroom. In this textbook, the classroom router isolates the host computers from the college's network infrastructure while providing Internet access. If you plan to build a private cloud at home to practice, see Appendix B, which explains how to set up your home router as the "classroom router."

7. Connect a power cable between the management server and the power strip.

Installing the Management Server

As you progress through this textbook, you will put in place the software to build a private cloud. In this chapter, you start building the management server. In Chapter 2, you start on the two future clustered servers.

Windows Server 2008 R2 SP1 is a multipurpose server designed to increase the reliability and flexibility of your server and private cloud infrastructure. It provides you with powerful tools to build private clouds.

You will install the following roles to manage and support your private cloud environment:

- **Active Directory Domain Services (AD DS)** is the central location for configuration information, authentication requests, and information about the resources stored in your private cloud.
- **Domain Name Service (DNS)** is used in TCP/IP networks for naming computers and network services within a hierarchy of domains. DNS locates computers and services through user-friendly names.
- **Hyper-V** provides a scalable, reliable, and highly available virtualization platform.

Activity 1-3: Installing the Operating System on the Management Server

Time Required: 30 minutes

Objective: Install Windows Server 2008 R2 SP1.

Description: In this activity, you will install Windows Server 2008 on the management server. Pay attention to the sequence of steps to make future activities easier. The third team member should lead during Steps 1 through 15 as the other team members watch and assist. The first team member should complete Steps 16 through 25, and the second team member should complete Steps 26 through 33. The third team member should verify the configuration in Steps 34 through 38.

1. Locate the management server that you cabled in Activity 1-2.

2. Turn on the management server and switch the KVM switch to port 1.

3. Insert the Windows Server 2008 R2 SP1 DVD and press the **Reset** button.

4. If the Select CD-ROM Boot Type message appears, enter **1** and then press **Enter**.

5. When prompted to press any key to boot from the CD or DVD, press the **Spacebar**.

6. Wait for Windows to load files. When the regional settings window appears, verify the selections for language, time, currency, and keyboard. Make corrections as needed, and then click **Next**.

7. Click the **Install now** link.

8. To indicate which version to install, click **Windows Server 2008 R2 Enterprise (Full Installation)**, and then click **Next**.

9. When the license terms appear, check **I accept the license terms**, and then click **Next**.

10. Click the **Custom (advanced)** icon.

If a previous partition exists for Disk 0, click Drive options (advanced), click Delete, and then click OK.

11. Click **Disk 0 Unallocated Space,** and then click **Next.**

12. Wait for Windows to copy and expand files, install features and updates, and restart the computer to complete the installation.

13. Wait while Windows prepares to start for the first time and then prepares the computer for use.

14. If the Select CD-ROM Boot Type message appears, remove the DVD, enter **1,** and then press **Enter.**

15. Remove the Windows Server 2008 R2 SP1 DVD.

16. When prompted that the user password must be changed before logging on for the first time, click **OK.** Enter **P@ssw0rd** in the New password text box, press **Tab,** enter **P@ssw0rd** in the Confirm password text box, press **Enter,** and then click **OK.**

 When the Set Network Location window appears, click Work and then click Close.

17. To set the time zone, click the **Set time zone** link. If necessary, click the **Change time zone** button, click the appropriate time zone, click the **Change date and time** button, change the time, and then click **OK** twice.

 It is very important that you use the correct IP addresses for your classroom network. Ask your instructor if an alternative IP addressing scheme will be used in your classroom.

18. To determine the IP configuration for your management (MGMT) computer, locate the team number assigned by your instructor in Table 1-3. This row contains the IP configuration.

Team#	IP Address	Subnet Mask	Default Gateway	DNS Server Address
1	192.168.0.111	255.255.255.0	192.168.0.1	192.168.0.1
2	192.168.0.121	255.255.255.0	192.168.0.1	192.168.0.1
3	192.168.0.131	255.255.255.0	192.168.0.1	192.168.0.1
4	192.168.0.141	255.255.255.0	192.168.0.1	192.168.0.1
5	192.168.0.151	255.255.255.0	192.168.0.1	192.168.0.1
6	192.168.0.161	255.255.255.0	192.168.0.1	192.168.0.1

Table 1-3 IP configurations for management (MGMT) server

© Cengage Learning 2014

19. To view the local area connections, click **Configure networking.**

20. To disable the local area connection(s) that are currently not being used, right-click the message that a local area connection's network cable is unplugged. Then click **Disable.**

21. Repeat Step 20 for any remaining local area connection(s) that display the same message.

22. To enter the IP configuration, right-click the active local area connection. Click **Properties**, clear the **Internet Protocol Version 6 (TCP/IPv6)** check box, click **Internet Protocol Version 4 (TCP/IPv4)**, and then click **Properties**. Click **Use the following IP address**, enter the IP address you identified in Step 18 in the IP address text box, and then press **Tab** twice; the subnet mask will appear in the Subnet mask text box. Next, enter the default gateway you identified in Step 18, press **Tab** twice, and enter the preferred DNS server from Step 18. Click **OK**, click **Close**, and then close the Network Connections window.

 It is very important that you use the correct computer names. Failure to do so will make future lab activities difficult!

23. To determine the computer name for your MGMT computer, locate the team number assigned by your instructor in Table 1-4. This row contains the computer name.

Team#	Management Server Name
1	TEAM1-MGMT
2	TEAM2-MGMT
3	TEAM3-MGMT
4	TEAM4-MGMT
5	TEAM5-MGMT
6	TEAM6-MGMT

Table 1-4 Computer names for MGMT server

© Cengage Learning 2014

24. To enter the computer name, click **Provide computer name and domain**, click the **Change** button, and enter the computer name you located in the previous step in the Computer name text box. Click **OK** twice, click **Close**, and then click the **Restart Now** button.

25. Wait for the MGMT computer to restart.

26. Press **Ctrl+Alt+Delete** and log on to your MGMT server with a username of **Administrator** and a password of **P@ssw0rd**. Minimize the Initial Configuration Tasks window.

27. To set the screen resolution, right-click the desktop, click **Screen resolution**, click the **Resolution** arrow, and click **1280 × 1024** or a higher resolution of your choice. Click **Apply**, review the resolution, click **Keep changes**, and then click **OK**.

28. To place the Computer icon on the desktop, click **Start**, right-click **Computer**, and then click **Show on Desktop**.

29. To rename the Computer icon with the computer name, right-click the **Computer** icon, click **Rename**, and enter an appropriate name for your MGMT computer, such as TEAM1-MGMT. Press **Enter** when you finish.

30. To maximize the Initial Configuration Tasks window, click the **Initial Configuration Tasks** icon on the taskbar. This icon depicts a server with a wrench.

31. To switch to the Server Manager window, click **Do not show this window at logon,** and then close the window.

32. If your school uses volume keys, click **Activate Windows,** ask your instructor to enter the product key, and press **Enter.** If your school does not use volume keys, click **Activate Windows,** enter the product key provided by your instructor, and press **Enter.** When you finish, click **Close.**

If Windows is not activated, contact your instructor.

33. If the Server Manager window is not displayed, click the **Server Manager** icon on the taskbar. This icon depicts a gray server with a toolbox.

34. Verify that the full computer name is the one you entered.

35. If necessary, click **Change System Properties,** click **Change,** enter the correct computer name in the Computer name text box, click **OK** twice, click **Close,** and then click the **Restart Now** button. Wait for the MGMT computer to restart. Press **Ctrl+Alt+Delete** and log on to your MGMT server with a username of **Administrator** and a password of **P@ssw0rd.**

36. To verify that the IP configuration is correct, click **View Network Connections,** right-click the enabled local area connection, click **Status,** and then click **Details.** Match the IP configuration to the proper settings in Table 1-3. Click **Close,** and then close the Network Connections window.

37. If necessary, click **View Network Connections,** right-click the enabled local area connection, click **Properties,** and re-enter the IP configuration. If you need help, see Step 22 of this activity.

38. To set the administrator password properties, click **Start,** point to **Administrative Tools,** and click **Computer Management.** Expand **Local Users and Groups,** click **Users,** right-click **Administrator,** and click **Properties.** Click the **User cannot change password** check box, click the **Password never expires** check box, and then click **OK.** Close the Computer Management window.

39. Remain logged on for future lab activities.

Active Directory Domain Services

AD DS provides a distributed database that stores and manages information about network resources. You can use AD DS to organize elements of a network, such as users, computers, and other devices, into a hierarchical structure. This structure includes the Active Directory **forest, domains** in the forest, and **organizational units** (OUs) in each domain. A server that runs AD DS is called a **domain controller.**

Security is integrated with AD DS through **logon authentication** and access control to resources in the directory. Using a single network logon, you can manage the AD DS directory data and organization throughout your network. Authorized users can also use a single network logon to access resources anywhere in the network.

Policy-based administration expands the role of AD DS to centralize the management of computers. Similar to how permissions are used to control access to computing resources, **Group Policy** defines the settings and allowed actions for users and computers.

The AD DS server role requires DNS to be running so that network resources and services can be located. For example, the AD DS structure uses DNS domain names for forests and domains.

Domain Name Service

With the DNS server role, you provide a name resolution process that enables users to locate network computers by querying for a user-friendly name instead of an IP address. A computer that runs the DNS server role can host the records of a DNS database and use the records to resolve DNS name queries sent by DNS client computers. These queries can include requests such as the names of Web sites, network computers, or computers on the Internet. The local DNS server will forward name queries for computers on the Internet.

Activity 1-4: Installing AD DS on the Management Server

Time Required: 30 minutes

Objective: Install Active Directory Domain Services and Domain Name Service.

Description: In this activity, you will install Windows Server 2008 R2 AD DS and DNS on the management server. DNS is installed as part of the AD DS role installation. The first team member should lead during Steps 1 through 15 as the other team members watch and assist. The second team member should complete Steps 16 through 20.

1. If necessary, switch the KVM switch to port 1.

2. If necessary, log on to your MGMT server with a username of **Administrator** and a password of **P@ssw0rd**.

3. Click the **Roles** entry in the left pane and then click the **Add Roles** link in the far right pane.

4. To add the AD DS role, click **Server Roles**, click **Active Directory Domain Services**, click **Add Required Features**, and click **Next**. Read the notes, click **Next**, and then click **Install**.

5. Wait for the role to be added.

6. Click **Close this wizard and launch the Active Directory Domain Services Installation Wizard (dcpromo.exe)**.

7. Click **Next** twice, click **Create a new domain in a new forest**, and click **Next**. Enter *Team1*.**local** in the FQDN of the forest root domain text box; substitute your team name for *Team1*. When you finish, click **Next**.

8. Wait for the names to be verified.

9. Click the **Forest functional level** arrow, click **Windows Server 2008 R2,** and then click **Next.**

10. Wait for the DNS configuration to be examined and then click **Next.**

 Do not uncheck the DNS server check box. If you do, DNS and Active Directory will not work.

11. Click **Yes,** click **Next,** enter **P@ssw0rd** in the New password text box, press **Tab,** enter **P@ssw0rd** in the Confirm password text box, and then click **Next.**

12. Review the summary and then click **Next.**

13. Wait for the AD DS and DNS to be installed and then click **Finish.**

14. Click **Restart Now.**

15. Wait for the MGMT computer to restart.

16. Log on to your MGMT server with a username of *Team1***Administrator,** substituting your team name for *Team1.* Enter a password of **P@ssw0rd.**

17. Verify that the full computer name is *TEAM1*-MGMT.*Team1*.local, substituting your team names for *TEAM1* and *Team1.* Notify your instructor if the name is not correct.

18. Expand **Roles,** click **Active Directory Domain Services,** and verify that no errors or warnings appear for the events. If you see any events that are not merely informational, notify your instructor.

19. Click **DNS Server** and verify that no errors or warnings appear for the events. If you see any events that are not merely informational, notify your instructor.

20. Remain logged on for future lab activities.

Hyper-V Hypervisor

The Windows Server 2008 R2 hypervisor enables you to create a virtualized server computing environment. You can use this environment to implement a private cloud of guest virtual machines, and then use Hyper-V to manage the virtual machines and their resources. Each guest runs in an isolated execution environment, which allows you to run multiple operating systems simultaneously on one physical computer.

The Hyper-V role in Windows Server 2008 R2 SP1 consists of several components, including the following:

- Hypervisor
- Parent and child partitions
- Virtual machines and guest operating systems
- Synthetic and emulated devices
- Integration services

The Hyper-V hypervisor is the core component of Hyper-V, and is responsible for creating and managing isolated execution environments called partitions. The hypervisor sits directly on the hardware and controls access from the partitions to the physical processors, as shown in Figure 1-14.

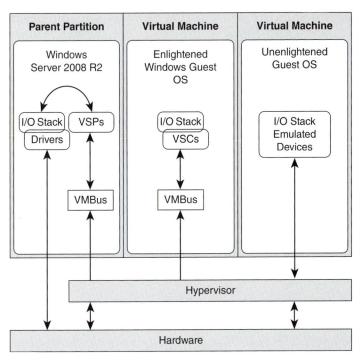

Figure 1-14 Hyper-V high-level architecture

© *Cengage Learning 2014*

When the Hyper-V role is enabled in Windows Server 2008 R2, the hypervisor uses the virtualization extensions built into the processors to place itself "under" Windows Server 2008 R2, giving it greater control of the physical hardware. When the Hyper-V hypervisor loads for the first time, it creates a partition called the **parent partition**. This parent partition, the first virtual machine, hosts the Windows Server 2008 R2 operating system that was running on the hardware before the Hyper-V role was enabled.

The parent partition is important for two main reasons:

- It controls all hardware devices, such as network adapters, hard disks, keyboards, mice, and graphics adapters, and is responsible for allocating physical memory to the partitions.

- It directs the hypervisor to create and delete **child partitions**. This activity is actually performed by the virtualization stack that runs in the parent partition.

Unlike the parent partition, child partitions do not have access to physical hardware. When a virtual machine is created, it is assigned a newly created child partition and a set of virtual devices that do not have direct access to the physical hardware. Instead, I/O requests from the virtual machine are routed through the parent partition to the physical adapters on the system.

The **indirect I/O model** used by Hyper-V allows virtual machines to be independent of the specific types of hardware devices used on the physical server. Because the drivers for these specific hardware devices of the physical computer run in the Windows Server 2008 R2 parent partition, only Microsoft drivers are installed in the hypervisor. This driver isolation improves the security footprint of the Microsoft hypervisor. The architecture allows Hyper-V to leverage the broad support available in Windows Server 2008 R2.

Operating systems installed within child partitions are commonly referred to as guest operating systems. The virtual devices that a virtual machine exposes to a guest operating system can be assigned to one of two broad categories. **Emulated virtual devices** are a software implementation of a typical PCI device. To the guest operating system, an emulated device appears as a physical PCI device. The second category of devices, **synthetic virtual devices**, only function with Hyper-V and are also implemented in software. The devices are based on architecture that is unique to Hyper-V, and they use a high-performance channel called the VMBus as the VSP-VSC communication mechanism between the different partitions:

- *Virtualization Service Provider (VSP)*—This component runs in the parent partition and directly communicates with the hardware drivers. VSP makes sure that the other virtual machines running on the same host can access the hardware successfully. VSP also ensures that hardware access and sharing by multiple virtual machines is secure. For example, VSP is responsible for sharing a common storage device across multiple virtual machines.

- *Virtualization Service Client (VSC)*—VSC runs in the child partitions and presents the virtual device to each child partition. Each VSC has a corresponding VSP in the parent partition. In other words, VSP and VSC exist as pairs. For example, a storage device would have a VSP/VSC pair.

- *VMBus*—This point-to-point memory bus is used for communication between VSP and VSC.

Using synthetic devices creates less processor overhead than using emulated devices.

In general, implementations in virtual environments that reduce overhead and improve guest operating system performance are called **enlightenments** by Microsoft. The synthetic device model is an example of device enlightenment. Enlightenments within a guest operating system's kernel allow the OS to know it is running in a virtual environment. This knowledge changes the operating system's behavior and reduces the amount of overhead traditionally associated with running an OS. The operating systems used in this textbook have enlightenments for Hyper-V.

The drivers for synthetic devices are provided by Microsoft as part of its Integration Services for Hyper-V. **Integration Services** are available for all supported guest operating systems and are installed after the guest operating systems are installed.

Integration Services are meant to provide better integration between child and parent partitions. Along with providing drivers for synthetic devices, Integration Services provide additional enhancements such as mouse integration, time synchronization, and the ability to shut down the guest operating system from the management console.

Hyper-V Manager is the management console from which you operate Hyper-V. You use Hyper-V Manager to create, start, stop, delete, and configure all your virtual machines, and to set the default locations for storing your virtual hard disks and virtual machine configuration files.

Hyper-V Manager is located under Administrative Tools, which is available in the Programs section of the Start menu. When you open Hyper-V Manager, the window shown in Figure 1-15 appears. Take a moment to become familiar with this window; you use it to configure and operate your virtual machines.

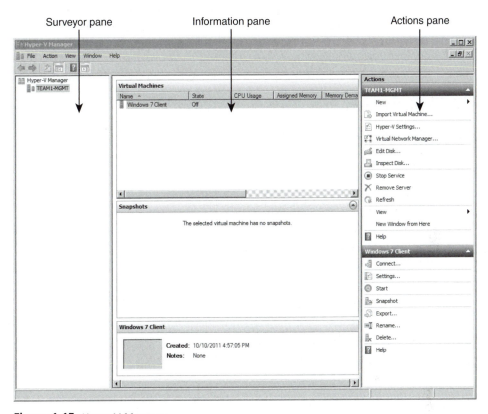

Figure 1-15 Hyper-V Manager

Source: Hyper-V Manager/Windows Server 2008 R2 SP1

The Hyper-V Manager window has three panes: Surveyor, Information, and Actions. Use the **Surveyor pane** on the left to select the host server. The middle pane is the **Information pane,** which provides information about the host computer. After you select a host server, the Information pane lists the virtual machines on the host computer. After you select a virtual machine, the Information pane lists any snapshots that have been made of it as well as an image of the virtual machine and information about it.

The Snapshots area in the middle of the window lists images of a virtual machine taken at particular points in time. You can return to these points at any stage. You will learn more about snapshots in Chapter 3.

The **Actions pane** shows the available actions for the host computer and selected virtual machine. For instance, if you select the host level and a virtual machine, available actions for both will be shown. The top half of the Actions pane lists actions that are available for the host computer. The bottom half of the Actions pane lists actions that are available for the selected virtual machine. You can see the same actions by right-clicking the item in the Information pane or Surveyor pane.

The **New Virtual Machine Wizard** provides a simple and flexible way to create a virtual machine. The wizard is available from Hyper-V Manager when you click New under the host name in the Actions pane and then click Virtual Machine. Within the wizard, you enter a name and other information about the virtual machine, assign memory to it, add a network adapter, and indicate the location of the installation files. You will create a virtual machine and install Windows 7 Enterprise in Activity 1-6.

Activity 1-5: Installing Hyper-V

Time Required: 30 minutes

Objective: Install the Hyper-V hypervisor role.

Description: In this activity, you will install the Hyper-V hypervisor role, which will enable you to run virtual machines. The third team member should lead during Steps 1 through 9 as the other team members watch and assist. The first team member should complete Steps 10 through 11.

1. If necessary, switch the KVM switch to port 1.
2. If necessary, log on to your MGMT server with a username of *Team1***Administrator**, substituting your team name for *Team1*. Enter a password of **P@ssw0rd**.
3. Click the **Roles** entry in the right pane, and then click **Add Roles**. To add the Hyper-V role, click **Server Roles**, click the **Hyper-V** check box, and then click **Next**.
4. Click the **Hyper-V Overview** link, read the overview, and then click **Next**.
5. Click the check box next to the network adapter entry, click **Next**, and then click **Install**.
6. Wait for the Restart Pending message, click **Close**, and then click **Yes**.
7. Wait for the computer to configure Windows features and restart.
8. Wait for the computer to complete the updates needed to install the Hyper-V hypervisor.
9. Review the results. If you do not see a message indicating that the installation succeeded, contact your instructor. Click **Close**.
10. To add the Hyper-V Manager icon to the desktop, click **Start**, point to **Administrative Tools**, right-click **Hyper-V Manager**, point to **Send to**, and then click **Desktop (create shortcut)**.
11. Remain logged on for the next lab activity.

You will learn more about Hyper-V Manager in Chapter 2.

Activity 1-6: Installing Windows 7 Enterprise

Time Required: 30 minutes

Objective: Install a guest operating system.

Description: In this activity, you will install Windows 7 Enterprise to verify that Hyper-V has been installed properly. In addition, you will learn to use the New Virtual Machine Wizard. The second team member should lead during Steps 1 through 10 as the other team members watch and assist. The third team member should complete Steps 11 through 27. The first team member should complete Steps 28 through 31.

1. If necessary, switch the KVM switch to port 1.

2. If necessary, log on to your MGMT server with a username of *Team1\Administrator*, substituting your team name for *Team1*. Enter a password of **P@ssw0rd**.

3. To start Hyper-V Manager, double-click the **Hyper-V Manager** icon on the desktop.

4. To start the New Virtual Machine Wizard, click the name of your management server, click **New** in the Actions pane, and then click **Virtual Machine**.

5. To name the new virtual machine, click **Specify Name and Location**, enter **Windows 7 Client** over the text "New Virtual Machine," and then click **Next**.

6. To assign memory for the new virtual machine, enter **768** over the 512, and then click **Next**.

7. To add a network adapter, click the **Connection** arrow, click the local area connection, and then click **Next**.

8. To accept the default name for the virtual hard disk, click **Next**.

9. To connect the DVD drive to the virtual machine, click **Install an Operating System from a boot CD/DVD-ROM**, and then click **Next**.

10. Review the description and then click **Finish**.

11. Insert the Windows 7 Enterprise DVD.

12. If the Autoplay window appears, close it.

13. To start the Windows 7 client, click **Start** in the Actions pane.

14. To connect to the Windows 7 client, click **Connect** in the Actions pane.

15. To focus on the Windows 7 client, click in the Windows 7 client window.

16. When the regional settings window appears, verify the selections for language, time, currency, and keyboard. Make corrections as needed, and then click **Next**.

17. Click the **Install now** link.

18. When the license terms appear, check **I accept the license terms**, and then click **Next**.

19. Click the **Custom (advanced)** icon, and then click **Next**.

20. Wait for Windows to copy and expand files, install features and updates, and restart the computer to complete the installation.

21. Wait while Windows prepares to start for the first time and then prepares the computer for use.

22. Remove the Windows 7 Enterprise DVD.

23. When the Set Up Windows window appears, enter **LocalAdmin** in the Type a user name text box. Next, enter *TEAM1-WIN7* in the Type a computer name text box, substituting your team name for *TEAM1*. When you finish, click **Next**.

24. Enter **P@ssw0rd** in the Type a password text box, re-enter the password in the next text box, enter **It's a Microsoft password** in the Type a password hint text box, and then click **Next**.

25. To delay the installation of updates, click **Ask me later**.

26. To set the time zone, click the **Set time zone** link. If necessary, click the **Change time zone** button and click the appropriate time zone. If necessary, change the time. When you finish, click **Next**.

27. Wait for Windows to complete the configuration. When the Set Network Location window appears, click **Work** and then click **Close**.

28. To shut down the Windows 7 client virtual machine, click the **Action** menu in the Virtual Machine Connection window, click **Shut Down**, and then click the **Shut Down** button.

29. Wait for the Windows 7 client to shut down and for the virtual machine to be turned off.

30. To shut down the host computer, click **Start**, click the arrow next to **Log off**, click **Shut down**, click the Option arrow, click **Operating System: Reconfiguration (Planned)**, and then click **OK**.

31. Wait for the host computer to shut down.

Chapter Summary

- Cloud computing is the use of multiple server computers on a digital network that work together as if they were one computer. Cloud computing differs from the traditional client/server model by providing applications from a server that are executed and managed by a client's Web browser.

- Virtualization uses software to simulate a physical computing environment and uses virtual hardware on which you can install a number of OSs and interact with them. With virtualization technology, you can run a range of OSs on top of an OS.

- Virtualization requires specific hardware for the host computers to function properly. X86 virtualization (Intel VT-x or AMD-V) allows multiple operating systems to simultaneously share processor resources safely and efficiently.

- The amount of memory required for effective processing is determined by the number of virtual machines that will run concurrently. For example, Windows Server 2008 R2 requires at least 512 MB of RAM; 1 GB is suggested.

- The number of network adapter cards you need is determined by the minimum number of networks required for the creation of private clouds.

- The Internet Small Computer System Interface (iSCSI) is an IP-based storage networking standard for linking host computers to data storage facilities.

- Several operating systems must be installed to support the lab activities in this textbook. Windows Server 2008 R2 SP1 Enterprise Edition will be installed on each of the three servers. On the management server, you will install Hyper-V, AD DS, DNS, and Windows Server Failover Clustering.

Key Terms

Actions pane   In Hyper-V Manager, the pane where host and virtual machine actions are initiated.

Active Directory Domain Services (AD DS)   A directory service from Microsoft that is part of the modern Windows Server family of operating systems, including Windows Server 2008.

child partition   In virtualization, the resident partition for a virtual machine.

client/server model   A network architecture in which each computer or process on the network is either a *client* or a *server*. Clients rely on servers for resources, such as files, devices, and even processing power.

cloud computing   A model that relies on sharing computing resources rather than having local servers or personal devices handle applications.

clustering   Connecting two or more computers so that they behave (or appear to behave) like a single computer.

domain   A group of computers and devices on a network that are administered as a unit with rights and permissions.

domain controller   A server that responds to security authentication requests in the Windows Server domain.

Domain Name Service (DNS)   Microsoft terminology for the Domain Name System, an Internet service that translates a host name into an IP address.

dual-core processor   A CPU that includes two complete execution cores per physical processor.

Dynamic Host Configuration Protocol (DHCP)   An Internet protocol and service used to assign IP addresses dynamically to devices on a network.

emulated virtual device   A device within an emulated hardware system that is emulated by software.

enlightenments   A Microsoft term for implementations that reduce overhead and improve guest operating systems in virtual environments.

failover   The capability to switch to a redundant or standby server when the active server fails.

forest   A Microsoft term for a collection of domain trees that share a common schema and have implicit trust relationships.

Group Policy   A set of rules that defines the settings and allowed actions for users and computers.

guests   In virtualization, an operating system being run as a virtual machine.

hexa-core processor   A CPU that includes six complete execution cores per physical processor.

host   In virtualization, the physical computer that supports the virtualization software.

Hyper-V   A hypervisor-based Windows Server virtualization platform included as a role in Windows Server 2008.

hypervisor   A software program that manages multiple operating systems on a single computer system.

indirect I/O model   A model that allows virtual machines to be independent of specific types of hardware devices used on the physical server.

Information pane In Hyper-V Manager, the pane where information is provided for virtual machines and snapshots.

Infrastructure as a Service (IaaS) A cloud computing service in which the service provider pays for servers, network equipment, storage, and backups. Customers pay only for the computing service, and they can build their own applications on the cloud.

Integration Services Support for components that require a secure interface between a parent partition and child partition, such as heartbeat, shutdown, and time synchronization.

Internet Small Computer System Interface (iSCSI) A TCP/IP-based protocol for establishing and managing connections between IP-based storage devices, hosts, and clients.

load balancing The even distribution of processing across a computer network so that no single computer is overwhelmed.

logical unit number (LUN) A unique identifier used to designate a unit of computer storage.

logon authentication The process of identifying a user, typically based on a username and password.

Network Address Translation (NAT) An Internet standard that enables a LAN to use one set of IP addresses for internal traffic and a second set of addresses for external traffic.

network-attached storage (NAS) A network appliance that is dedicated to file sharing.

New Virtual Machine Wizard In Hyper-V Manager, the wizard that helps users create a virtual machine.

organizational unit (OU) In Active Directory, the container that holds user and computer names and permits organization at the domain level.

parent partition The virtual machine that contains the Windows operating system after the Hyper-V role is added.

Platform as a Service (PaaS) A cloud computing service in which consumers create or acquire applications using programming languages and tools on a provider's cloud.

private cloud A cloud computing platform implemented within the corporate firewall of a private organization under the control of the IT department.

quad-core processor A CPU that includes four complete execution cores per physical processor.

rapid provisioning The addition of virtual machines to meet increased demands for processing online requests.

redundancy Duplication of server elements that provides alternatives in case of failure.

Redundant Array Independent Disk (RAID) An array of two or more disk drives that work together to improve fault tolerance and performance.

role-based security A system of controlling user access to resources based on the user's role.

self-service user role A role that grants users permission to create, operate, manage, store, and connect to their own virtual machines through the self-service portal of the System Center Virtual Machine Manager.

shared disk access The ability of a computer to access a device or information remotely from another computer.

Software as a Service (SaaS) A service that allows consumers to use a provider's applications running on a cloud infrastructure.

standard hardware system environment   A consistent set of hardware provided by the virtualization program.

storage area network (SAN)   A high-speed subnetwork of shared storage devices.

storage virtualization   A technology that treats storage as a single entity irrespective of the location of available physical media.

Surveyor pane   In Hyper-V Manager, the pane that permits the selection of a host server.

synthetic virtual devices   Virtual devices implemented in software that function only with Hyper-V.

System Center Virtual Machine Manager   A role that enables centralized management of a virtual IT infrastructure.

system image   A copy of a system that contains the operating system and related files, installed applications, and configuration preferences.

thin provisioning   The automated process of allocating the appropriate amount of server space at the appropriate time.

virtual LAN (VLAN)   A network of computers that appear to be connected to a single, logical network segment, even though they may be located on different segments of a LAN.

virtualization   The process of using software to simulate a physical environment and using virtual hardware on which you can install a number of operating systems (OSs) and interact with them.

Virtualization Service Client (VSC)   A component that redirects device requests to VSPs in the parent partition via the VMBus. The process is transparent to the guest OS.

Virtualization Service Provider (VSP)   A component that connects to the VMBus and handles device access requests from child partitions.

VMBus   A logical channel that enables communication between partitions in a Hyper-V environment.

Windows Server Failover Clustering   Software designed to allow servers to work together as a computer cluster, which provides failover and increased availability of applications.

Review Questions

1. _____ provides applications from a server that are executed and managed by the client's Web browser.

   a. Application software

   b. Cloud computing

   c. A client/server system

   d. A local area network

2. A private cloud is designed to remove which of the following objections to using public clouds? (Choose all correct answers.)

   a. control of corporate data

   b. security

   c. regulatory compliance

   d. inability to scale

3. _____ uses hardware and software to simulate a physical environment.

   a. A guest computer

   b. A host computer

   c. Virtualization technology

   d. A storage area network

4. The hypervisor is so named because it is _____.

   a. equal to a supervisory program

   b. inferior to a supervisory program

   c. one level higher than a supervisory program

   d. a replacement for a supervisory program

5. _____ permits virtual machines to be added to a system to meet demands for increased capacity.

   a. A storage area network

   b. The hypervisor

   c. Storage virtualization

   d. Rapid provisioning

6. The primary purpose of _____ is to store computer files that can be accessed by client computers.

   a. rapid provisioning

   b. a storage area network

   c. shared disk access

   d. thin provisioning

7. _____ is file-level data storage connected to a computer network to provide data access to clients.

   a. Network-attached storage

   b. A storage area network

   c. Shared disk access

   d. Thin provisioning

8. Two or more hard drives can be combined to form _____.

   a. network-attached storage

   b. a storage area network

   c. shared disk access

   d. Redundant Array Independent Disk (RAID) arrays

9. A logical unit number provides a connection between a server and _____.

    a. network-attached storage

    b. a storage area network

    c. shared disk access

    d. RAID

10. Thin provisioning _____.

    a. removes the access restrictions to a SAN

    b. permits the overallocation of disk space

    c. uses RAID

    d. permits shared disk access

11. _____ is connecting two or more computers to make them work as a unified system.

    a. Redundancy

    b. Failover

    c. Load balancing

    d. Clustering

12. Role-based security _____.

    a. requires DNS to locate roles

    b. is configured from the Server Manager

    c. provides finer control over virtual machines

    d. requires clustered computers

13. With _____, the service provider pays for servers, network equipment, storage, and backups.

    a. Infrastructure as a Service (IaaS)

    b. Platform as a Service (PaaS)

    c. Software as a Service (SaaS)

    d. Clouds as a Service (CaaS)

14. With _____, customers pay to use the service provider's software, particularly application software.

    a. Infrastructure as a Service (IaaS)

    b. Platform as a Service (PaaS)

    c. Software as a Service (SaaS)

    d. Clouds as a Service (CaaS)

15. With _____, the service provider offers business solutions for users.

    a. Infrastructure as a Service (IaaS)

    b. Platform as a Service (PaaS)

    c. Software as a Service (SaaS)

    d. Clouds as a Service (CaaS)

16. Hardware virtualization requires _____. (Choose all correct answers.)

    a. Intel Virt

    b. Intel VT-x

    c. AMD-V

    d. Hardware virtualization is not available.

17. _____ provides for block-mode data transfers over Ethernet with TCP packets.

    a. Shared disk access (SAD)

    b. Network-attached storage (NAS)

    c. Internet Small Computer System Interface (iSCSI)

    d. Block-level access (BLA)

18. Block-level data transfers are used by _____. (Choose all correct answers.)

    a. Shared disk access (SAD)

    b. Network-attached storage (NAS)

    c. Internet Small Computer System Interface (iSCSI)

    d. hard disk drives

19. Install _____ to manage virtual machines on cluster servers.

    a. Hypervisor Manager

    b. System Center Virtual Machine Manager

    c. Domain Name Service

    d. Active Directory Domain Services

20. _____ provides a central location for configuration information, authentication requests, and information about network objects.

    a. Hypervisor Manager

    b. System Center Virtual Machine Manager

    c. Domain Name Service

    d. Active Directory Domain Services

Case Projects

Case 1-1: Using Private Clouds—Hardware Requirements

Your boss has been reading about private cloud technology. She has asked you to write a summary report that describes the hardware components required to set up a private cloud and test the technology. Because your boss is technically savvy, your report must provide technical details.

Case 1-2: Using Private Clouds—Software Requirements

After seeing the hardware requirements, your boss requests a list of required software for the private cloud. Develop the list.

Case 1-3: Reasons for Using Private Clouds

You have been asked to deliver a brief presentation at your company's next TechShare meeting. Prepare a one-page summary that lists the advantages of private clouds over more conventional methods of providing computing services.

Case 1-4: Role-Based Security

Your boss continues to be interested in setting up a test site for a private cloud, but she is concerned about how you will control the creation of virtual machines. Prepare a position paper that outlines your solution.

chapter 2

Creating and Managing Virtual Machines

After reading this chapter and completing the exercises, you will be able to:

- Operate the Hyper-V Manager
- Create virtual hard disks
- Create virtual network switches
- Create and configure virtual machines
- Operate virtual machines

In Chapter 1, you created a Windows 7 virtual machine using the New Virtual Machine Wizard, and you installed Windows 7. In this chapter, you will learn the finer points of working with virtual machines. A virtual machine works like a physical computer. The Hyper-V hypervisor presents a virtualized environment that the guest operating system perceives to be a physical computer. Within this environment, virtual hard disks work like hard disks, and virtual network switches work like network adapters.

Hyper-V Manager provides a user interface for the Hyper-V virtualization environment. You can create and configure virtual machines with virtualized hardware components and operate virtual machines. This chapter explains how to be productive in the virtualization environment.

Virtualization provides the foundation for building an Infrastructure as a Service (IaaS) model of a private cloud. In successive chapters, you will add needed components to complete a working private cloud. You will gain the skills needed to scale up the private cloud to meet the requirements of larger IT organizations.

Operating Hyper-V Manager

To open Hyper-V Manager, click Start, point to Administrative Tools, and then click Hyper-V Manager. You can also open the program by double-clicking the Hyper-V Manager icon that you placed on the desktop in Activity 1-5.

The Hyper-V Manager window is shown in Figure 2-1.

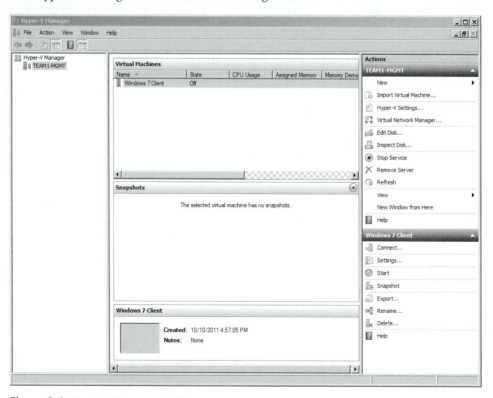

Figure 2-1 Hyper-V Manager window

Source: Hyper-V Manager/Windows Server 2008 R2 SP1

The window is arranged logically, but its design does not help you learn to use virtualization. The following overview summarizes the actions you can perform from the Actions pane when Hyper-V is running on the host computer:

- *New*—You can create a virtual machine, hard disk, or floppy disk. These procedures are covered later in this chapter.

- *Import Virtual Machine*—Add an existing virtual machine to be managed by Hyper-V Manager. See Chapter 3 for details.

- *Hyper-V Settings*—Update or change settings that affect all virtual machines, as explained later in this section.

- *Virtual Network Manager*—Create and remove virtual networks. These procedures are covered later in this chapter in the section on creating virtual network switches.

- *Edit Disk*—Modify virtual hard disks. This procedure is covered later in this chapter in the section on creating virtual hard disks.

- *Inspect Disk*—Obtain information about an existing Hyper-V virtual hard disk, such as its current size, maximum size, image file location, and disk type. For details, see the section on creating virtual hard disks.

- *Stop Service*—Stop the Virtual Machine Management service. You might want to stop the service when troubleshooting the Hyper-V management interface.

- *Remove Server*—Drop the existing Hyper-V host computer prior to adding another host computer.

- *Refresh*—Refresh the Hyper-V Manager window.

- *View*—Customize the Hyper-V view by showing or hiding items.

- *New Window from Here*—Set the focus of the Hyper-V Manager to the current host computer.

- *Help*—Get assistance for using Hyper-V.

You can modify the Hyper-V settings to specify where files are stored and control interactions such as keyboard combinations and logon credentials. There are two categories of Hyper-V settings:

- *Server settings*—Specify the default location of virtual hard disks and virtual machines. You can change the location of these files to make it easier to navigate to a virtual machine's settings.

- *User settings*—Customize interactions with **Virtual Machine Connection**, which provides access to the desktop of a running virtual machine. Settings for the Virtual Machine Connection tool include the mouse release key and Windows key combinations. When working with the various wizards, you can choose to display or hide messages and optional wizard pages.

To change settings, click Hyper-V Settings in the Actions pane (see Figure 2-1). In the navigation pane that appears, click the setting that you want to configure. After making the changes, click OK to save them and close the window, or click Apply to save the changes and configure other settings.

You can change the following Hyper-V settings on the host server, as shown in Figure 2-2:

- *Virtual Hard Disks*—By default, these settings are saved in the C:\Users\Public\Documents\ Hyper-V\Virtual Hard Disks folder. If you have another physical drive that has more available free space, you may want to create a folder on that drive and store the virtual hard drives in an alternate location.

- *Virtual Machines*—By default, the virtual machine configuration settings files are stored in C:\ProgramData\Microsoft\Windows\Hyper-V, which is a hidden folder.

- *Non-Uniform Memory Access (NUMA) Spanning*—By default, this spanning is enabled. **Non-Uniform Memory Access (NUMA)** is a memory design used in computers that have multiple processors. When each processor has dedicated memory, memory access time depends on the memory location relative to a given processor. Using the default setting, the hypervisor finds the best fit based on the resources that the virtual machine needs.

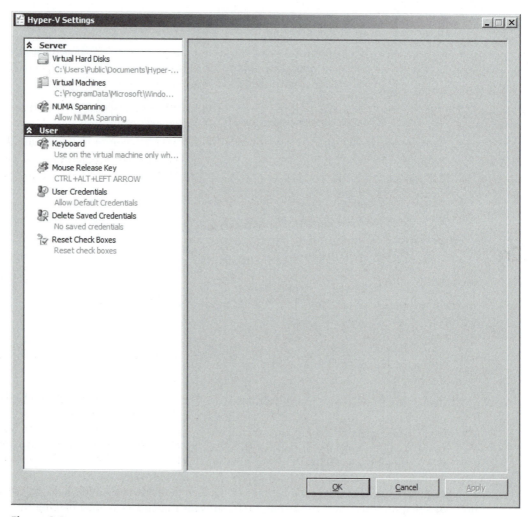

Figure 2-2 Hyper-V settings

Source: Hyper-V Manager/Windows Server 2008 R2 SP1

Figure 2-2 also shows user settings that you can modify in Hyper-V:

- *Keyboard*—You can indicate the action to take when a Windows key combination such as Alt+Tab is pressed while running a connection to a virtual machine. The default setting is to use the key combination only when the virtual machine is displayed in full-screen mode. You can also use the key combination on the physical computer (the host computer) or on the virtual machine (the guest computer).

- *Mouse Release Key*—Specify the key combination that releases the mouse pointer when running a connection to a virtual machine. Use this key combination to free the mouse pointer when installing an enlightened operating system or running an unenlightened operating system. The default key combination is Ctrl+Alt+left arrow.

The key combination that releases the mouse in Hyper-V may be the same one you use to rotate the screen. If so, you can use Ctrl+Alt+Shift+left arrow to trigger the mouse release without having to change the configuration.

- *User Credentials*—By default, you use the credentials that you entered to log on to the host computer. For security reasons, you may want to be prompted for an alternate user ID and password when a connection is made to a virtual machine.

- *Delete Saved Credentials*—Delete the user credentials that were used to connect to a running virtual machine. Use this option if you are not prompted for credentials after receiving an Access Denied error message when you try to connect to a virtual machine.

- *Reset Check Boxes*—Clear all check boxes that you selected when you chose to skip windows while working with wizards in Hyper-V. The undisplayed messages and hidden pages then will appear.

Creating Virtual Disks

A virtual hard disk can have the same contents as a physical hard disk drive, such as disk partitions and a file system. It is typically used as the hard disk of a virtual machine.

Types of Virtual Disks

Three types of virtual hard disks are supported. You define the type you want when creating the virtual disk:

- *Dynamically expanding*—The virtual hard disk file grows as data is stored to the disk. When you create a dynamically expanding virtual hard disk, you specify a maximum file size that limits how large the virtual disk can become. For example, if you create a 1-GB dynamically expanding virtual hard disk, the initial size of the virtual hard disk file will be about 3 MB. As a virtual machine uses the virtual hard disk, the size of the virtual hard disk file grows to accommodate the new data. The size of a dynamically expanding disk only grows; it does not shrink, even when you delete data. You may be able to reduce the size of a dynamically expanding disk by compacting it.

- *Fixed size*—The virtual hard disk file uses the full amount of space specified during creation.

- *Differencing*—The virtual hard disk file exists as a child disk in a parent/child relationship with an existing virtual hard disk. You can identify the parent file by looking for it with the Inspect Disk tool. The child file used as the differencing virtual hard disk stores all state changes to a virtual hard disk in a separate file. This allows you to isolate changes to a virtual machine and keep a virtual hard disk in an unchanged state. You do not specify a size for a differencing disk, which can be considered a special type of dynamically expanding disk. Differencing disks can grow as large as the parent disks to which they are associated.

 For production environments, a fixed-size virtual hard disk is recommended because it performs better than dynamically expanding and differencing disks.

When the operating system running in the virtual machine will benefit from direct access to the physical disk, a **passthrough disk** is often required. A passthrough disk is a physical disk mapped directly to a virtual machine. To the parent partition on the host computer, the disk is in an offline state. I/O requests from the virtual machine are passed through the parent partition to the disk. The parent partition no longer manages the disk, and additional CPU cycles are provided for virtual machine processing. When mapped to a passthrough disk, the guest operating system has direct access to the raw blocks of the physical storage device.

Creating a Virtual Disk

To begin creating a virtual hard disk file, click New in the Actions pane of Hyper-V Manager, and then click Hard Disk. The New Virtual Hard Disk Wizard appears, as shown in Figure 2-3. To review information about the types of available virtual hard disks, click the More about virtual hard disks link.

From the Choose Disk Type window, you can select the disk type from the three choices shown in Figure 2-4. When you finish, click Next.

From the window shown in Figure 2-5, you specify the name and location for the virtual hard disk file. Be sure to enter a descriptive name. For example, the first hard disk for the Windows 7 client virtual machine could be named *Windows 7 Client.vhd*. The second hard drive for the virtual machine could be called *Windows 7 Client Second Drive.vhd*. If you want to store the virtual hard disk file in an existing folder, click the Browse button and navigate to the desired folder.

If you chose a fixed-size or dynamically expanding virtual disk, you need to enter only a maximum size for the disk in the next window, as shown in Figure 2-6. Hyper-V also allows you to use this window to duplicate the contents of a physical drive on a new virtual hard disk. Consider the following requirements before migrating the physical disk's contents to a virtual hard disk:

- You can copy and convert only a physical disk, not a volume or a partition.
- You can migrate only a data disk; you cannot migrate an operating system disk.

If you chose the differencing type of virtual disk, you must select an existing fixed-size disk or dynamically expanding disk for the parent disk. Next, you join the child disk in the

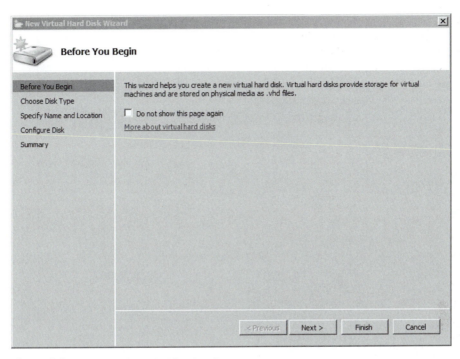

Figure 2-3 New Virtual Hard Disk Wizard

Source: Hyper-V Manager/Windows Server 2008 R2 SP1

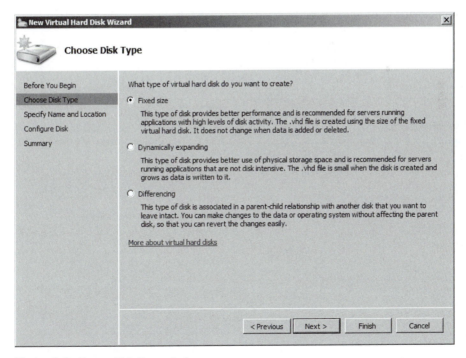

Figure 2-4 Choose Disk Type window

Source: Hyper-V Manager/Windows Server 2008 R2 SP1

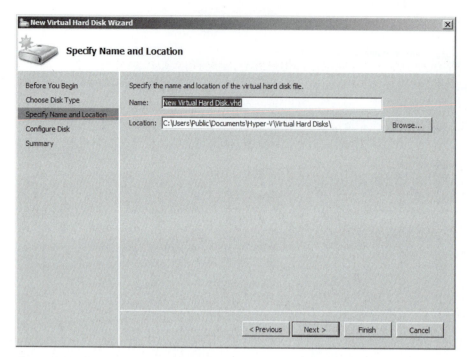

Figure 2-5 Specifying a name and location for the virtual hard disk file

Source: Hyper-V Manager/Windows Server 2008 R2 SP1

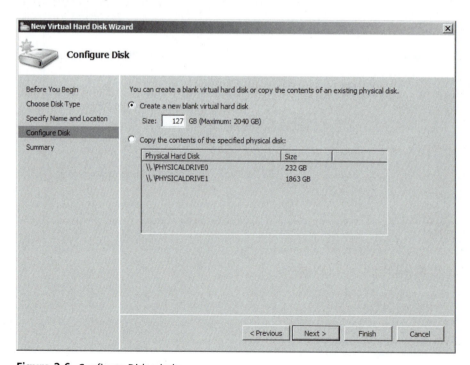

Figure 2-6 Configure Disk window

Source: Hyper-V Manager/Windows Server 2008 R2 SP1

parent/child relationship, as shown in Figure 2-7. Click the Browse button and select the parent .vhd file.

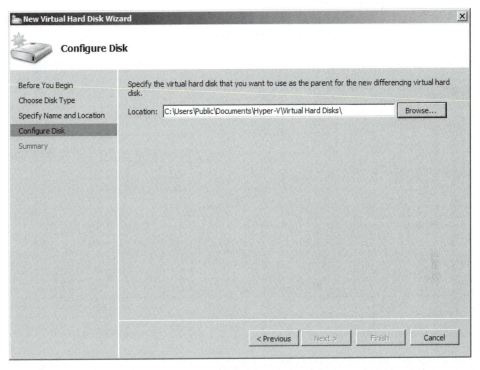

Figure 2-7 Configuring a child disk in a parent/child relationship

Source: Hyper-V Manager/Windows Server 2008 R2 SP1

From the Configure Disk window, you then have two choices:

- Click Next to proceed to the Summary window shown in Figure 2-8, where you can review the summary information, and then click Finish to create the .vhd file.
- Click Finish, skip the Summary window, and then create the .vhd file.

You can cancel your work on the new virtual hard disk at any time by clicking a Cancel button in the wizard.

If you create a virtual hard disk file and then decide to remove it later, you can safely delete the file as long as it is not attached to a virtual machine.

Editing a Virtual Disk

To start the Edit Virtual Hard Disk Wizard, click Edit Disk in the Actions pane of Hyper-V Manager. Click Next to skip the introductory window shown in Figure 2-9.

From the Locate Virtual Hard Disk window (see Figure 2-10), click Browse to navigate to the desired .vhd file, click Open, and then click Next.

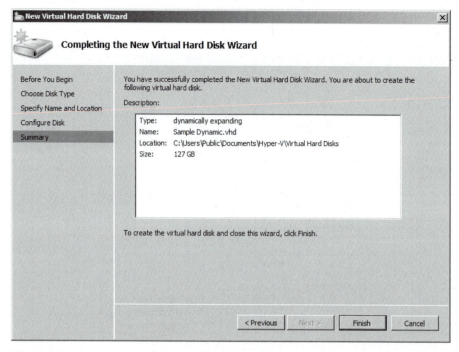

Figure 2-8 Summary information for virtual hard disk

Source: Hyper-V Manager/Windows Server 2008 R2 SP1

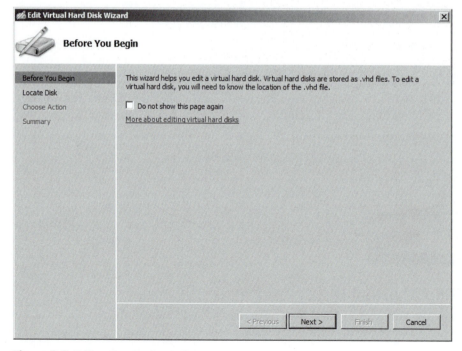

Figure 2-9 Before You Begin window

Source: Hyper-V Manager/Windows Server 2008 R2 SP1

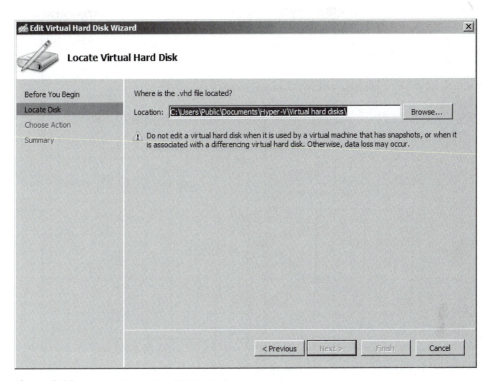

Figure 2-10 Locate Virtual Hard Disk window

Source: Hyper-V Manager/Windows Server 2008 R2 SP1

The next window (see Figure 2-11) shows options for the selected virtual hard disk:

- *Compact*—This option applies to dynamically expanding and differencing virtual hard disks with the New Technology File System (NTFS). Choose this option to reduce the size of the .vhd file by removing the blank space left behind when data is deleted from the virtual hard disk.

- *Convert*—Choose this option to convert a dynamically expanding virtual hard disk to a fixed-size virtual hard disk or vice versa.

- *Expand*—This option increases the storage capacity of a dynamically expanding or fixed-size virtual hard disk.

- *Merge*—This option applies only to differencing disks; it is not shown in Figure 2-11. You can use this option to combine the changes stored in a differencing disk with the contents of the parent disk. You can apply the changes to the parent disk or you can copy the contents of the parent disk and child (differencing) disk to a new virtual hard disk, which keeps both source disks intact.

Inspecting a Virtual Hard Disk

To see information about a virtual hard disk, click Inspect Disk in the Actions pane. In the window that appears, select the virtual hard disk you want to inspect, and then click Open. Hyper-V provides information similar to that shown in Figure 2-12.

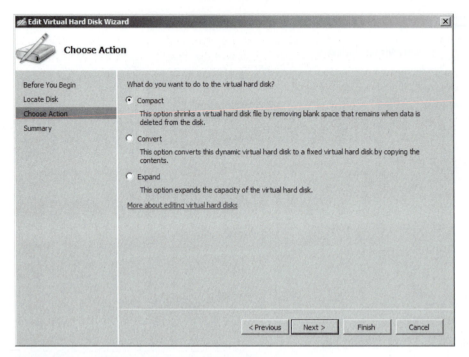

Figure 2-11 Options for selected virtual hard disk

Source: Hyper-V Manager/Windows Server 2008 R2 SP1

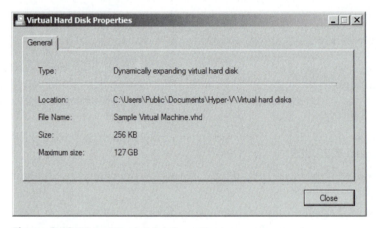

Figure 2-12 Virtual hard disk information

Source: Hyper-V Manager/Windows Server 2008 R2 SP1

Creating Virtual Networks

A **virtual network switch** works like a physical network switch, except that the switch is implemented in software. For this reason, a virtual network is sometimes referred to as a virtual network switch. Switch ports are added or removed automatically as virtual machines are connected to or disconnected from a virtual network.

Virtual Network Switches

When Windows Server 2008 is installed on a system with two network adapters, Figure 2-13 shows what the Network Connections window looks like. To open this window, click the network icon in the taskbar's system tray, click Open Network and Sharing Center, and click Change adapter setting. In the figure, the first local area connection is disabled on the host computer.

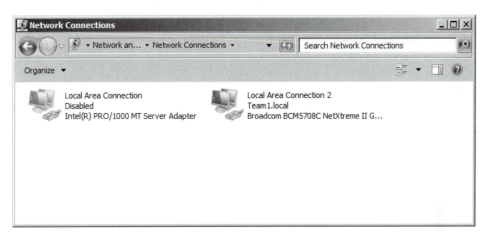

Figure 2-13 Network connections

Source: Hyper-V Manager/Windows Server 2008 R2 SP1

Figure 2-14 shows how your host computer is operating before the Hyper-V role is installed. The network adapter is attached directly to the physical network.

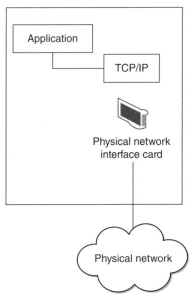

Figure 2-14 Network adapter attached directly

When Windows Server 2008 is installed on a system with two network adapters, Figure 2-15 shows what the Network Connections window looks like after the Hyper-V role is installed. Local Area Connection 2 is now the virtual network switch with only the Microsoft Virtual Network Switch Protocol enabled. The new Local Area Connection 3 has the IP configuration of the previous Local Area Connection 2. The Local Area Connection is disabled on the host computer.

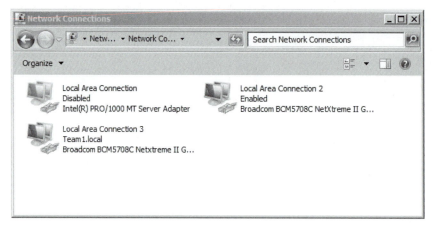

Figure 2-15 Network connections after Hyper-V role is installed

Source: Windows Server 2008 R2 SP1

Figure 2-16 shows how your system is operating after the Hyper-V role is installed. As you can see, the parent partition (host operating system) is now using a virtual network adapter

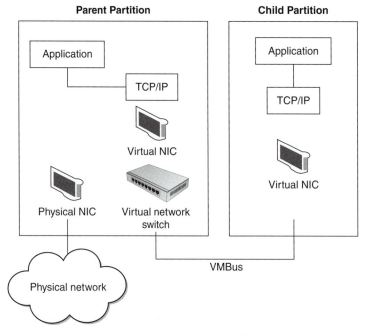

Figure 2-16 Network communications through virtual switch

to connect to the physical network. The virtual machine is using the VMBus to access the virtual network switch.

Figure 2-17 shows the network connections on the parent for the original network adapter, which now has nothing bound to it except the Microsoft Virtual Network Switch Protocol. Figure 2-18 shows properties for a new virtual network adapter, which now has all of the standard protocols and services bound to it instead of the original network adapter.

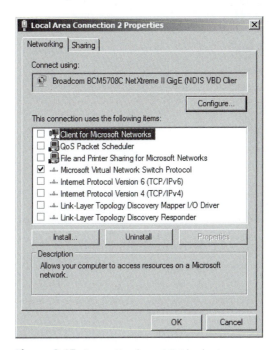

Figure 2-17 Properties for original adapter

Source: Windows Server 2008 R2 SP1

Types of Virtual Networks

Virtual Network Manager is available from Hyper-V Manager, and it offers three types of virtual networks that you can use for guest virtual machines and the host computer:

- *External virtual networks*—This type of network provides virtual machines with access to a physical network to communicate with externally located servers and clients. External virtual networks also allow virtual machines on the same host computer to communicate with each other.

- *Internal virtual networks*—This type of network allows communication between virtual machines on the same host computer and between virtual machines and the host computer. You would use an internal virtual network to build a test environment.

- *Private virtual networks*—This type of network allows communication only among virtual machines on the same host computer; the network is isolated from the host computer and from external servers and clients. A private virtual network is useful when you need to create an isolated networking environment, such as a test domain.

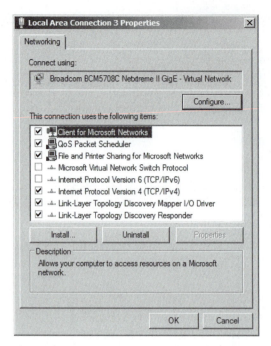

Figure 2-18 Properties for new network adapter

Source: Windows Server 2008 R2 SP1

Creating a Virtual Network

To open Virtual Network Manager, click Virtual Network Manager in the Actions pane of Hyper-V Manager. Figure 2-19 shows the Virtual Network Manager window.

To create a virtual network, click the type of network you want, and then click the Add button. Figure 2-20 shows the New Virtual Network window that appears. Enter the name of the virtual network switch in the Name text box over the existing text "New Virtual Network," and then click OK. If you decide to remove a virtual network switch later, click the name of the switch in the Virtual Networks pane, click Remove, and then click Apply or OK. You will learn to create internal virtual networks in Activity 2-7.

A virtual machine can be configured to use a static or dynamic Media Access Control (MAC) address. When the Hyper-V role is installed on the host computer, a pool of available addresses is created. As needed, Hyper-V assigns dynamic MAC addresses to virtual machines.

If you are working with more than one host computer running Hyper-V on the same subnet, and the virtual machines use dynamic addresses, the MAC address pools might be duplicates of each other. This duplication causes networking conflicts. You can use Virtual Network Manager on each host computer that runs Hyper-V to define different ranges of MAC

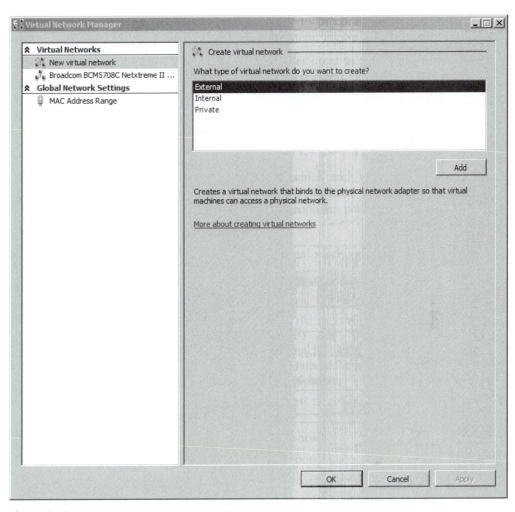

Figure 2-19 Virtual Network Manager window

Source: Hyper-V Manager/Windows Server 2008 R2 SP1

addresses and avoid the problem of duplicate MAC addresses. See Figure 2-21 for an example of specifying a MAC address range; to see this window, click MAC Address Range in the Virtual Networks pane.

When you modify the range of available MAC addresses, existing virtual machines that are configured with a dynamic MAC address are not updated. To correct this problem, you must remove and then re-add the virtual network adapter of the existing machine to receive a new dynamic MAC address.

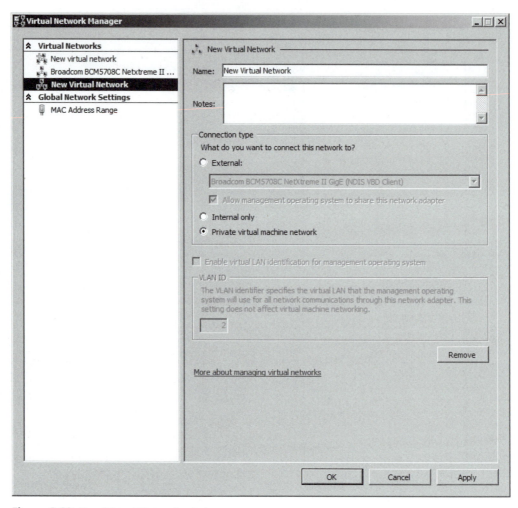

Figure 2-20 New Virtual Network window

Source: Hyper-V Manager/Windows Server 2008 R2 SP1

Creating and Configuring Virtual Machines

In this section, you will learn to create virtual machines with the New Virtual Machine Wizard and you will learn to configure existing virtual machines.

Using the New Virtual Machine Wizard

The New Virtual Machine Wizard provides a simple and flexible way to create a virtual machine. You used this wizard to create a Windows 7 virtual machine in Activity 1-6. To open the wizard, click New in the Actions pane of Hyper-V Manager, and then click Virtual Machine. The initial window of the wizard appears, as shown in Figure 2-22.

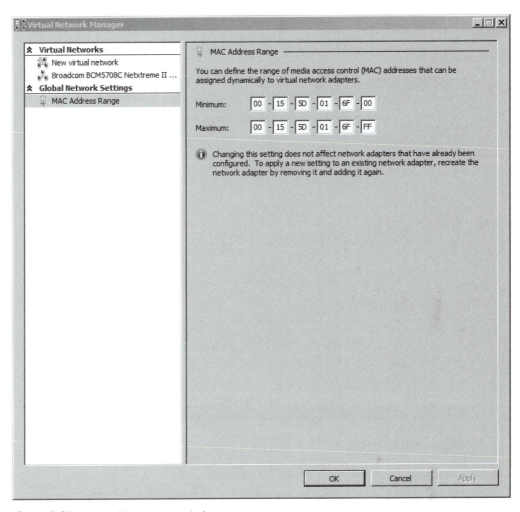

Figure 2-21 MAC Address Range window

Source: Hyper-V Manager/Windows Server 2008 R2 SP1

Click Next to proceed to the Specify Name and Location window, as shown in Figure 2-23. Enter the name of the virtual machine in the Name text box over the existing text "New Virtual Machine." Enter a descriptive name to make it easier to locate and work with the virtual machine later. To store the virtual machine in a folder other than the default location, click the "Store the virtual machine in a different location" check box, click the Browse button, and navigate to the folder you want.

Click Next to proceed to the Assign Memory window, which is shown in Figure 2-24. A virtual machine needs enough memory to run the anticipated workload. However, each virtual machine consumes memory only when it is running or paused. You can install Windows Server 2008 and Windows 7 with a minimum of 512 MB, but the performance of the virtual machine will improve with additional memory. The memory setting is a compromise between a larger memory allocation and the total number of virtual machines running on the Hyper-V server.

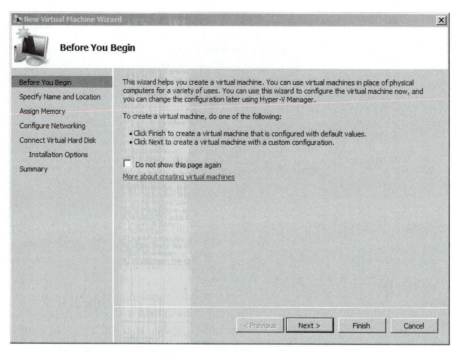

Figure 2-22 New Virtual Machine Wizard

Source: Hyper-V Manager/Windows Server 2008 R2 SP1

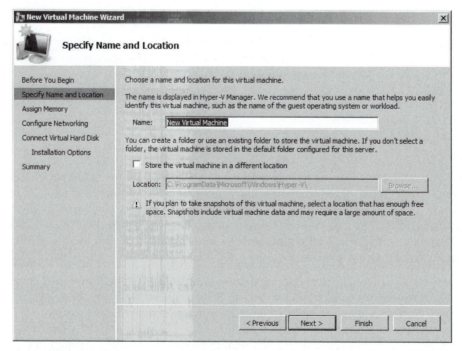

Figure 2-23 Specify Name and Location window

Source: Hyper-V Manager/Windows Server 2008 R2 SP1

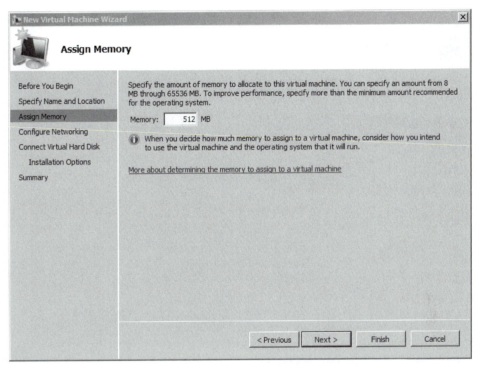

Figure 2-24 Assign Memory window

Source: Hyper-V Manager/Windows Server 2008 R2 SP1

You can change the memory allocation for any virtual machine that is not running or paused. The installation of an operating system is particularly memory intensive, so you might assign a larger memory value during the installation (perhaps 2 GB). After the installation completes, you could then shut down the virtual machine and reduce the memory allocation to a lower value, such as 768 MB.

Click Next to advance to the Configure Networking window shown in Figure 2-25. To see the available connections, click the Connection arrow. Providing a virtual machine with networking capabilities requires the same two basic components that a physical computer requires: a network adapter and an available network. When you create a virtual machine, it is automatically configured with one network adapter. If one or more virtual network switches are available on the host computer running Hyper-V, you can connect the network adapter to one of those networks when you create the virtual machine. Additional network adapters can be added later.

The next window, as shown in Figure 2-26, allows you to add the first hard disk to the virtual machine. The default option is to open the New Virtual Hard Disk Wizard, which you learned to use earlier in this chapter. The default virtual hard disk will use the same name as the virtual machine, and will have a .vhd extension.

You also have the option of connecting to an existing virtual hard disk, which is useful if you need to attach a copy of a previous .vhd file for a virtual machine. The final option allows you to connect the virtual hard disk after the virtual machine is created. You will learn how to do this later in the section on configuring virtual machines.

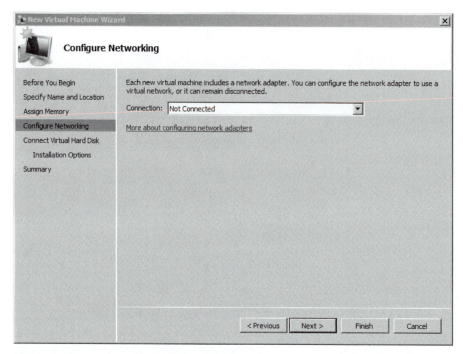

Figure 2-25 Configure Networking window

Source: Hyper-V Manager/Windows Server 2008 R2 SP1

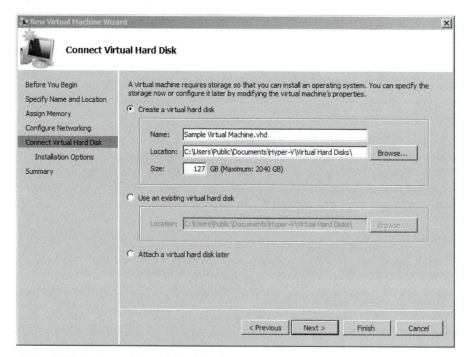

Figure 2-26 Connect Virtual Hard Disk window

Source: Hyper-V Manager/Windows Server 2008 R2 SP1

To advance to the Installation Options window, click Next. Figure 2-27 shows the options for installing the operating system files.

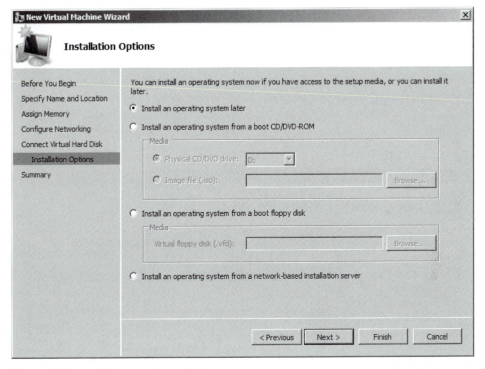

Figure 2-27 Installation Options window

Source: Hyper-V Manager/Windows Server 2008 R2 SP1

You install and run guest operating systems in virtual machines. Before you can install the guest operating system, however, you must specify the location of the installation media using one of the following four options:

- *Install an operating system later*—The installation files will be available later.

- *Install an operating system from a boot CD/DVD-ROM*—Use this option if you have burned the installation files from the .iso file to a CD/DVD-ROM or if you have copied the .iso file to a hard drive on the host computer.

- *Install an operating system from a boot floppy disk*—Install the guest operating system from a floppy disk image (.vfd file).

- *Install an operating system from a network-based installation server*—The installation files will be accessed from a server.

In a classroom setting, the most likely scenario is to use installation files that your instructor has downloaded to a file server. Your school can purchase a subscription to the Microsoft Software Development Network Academic Alliance (MSDN AA). When you have the .iso file, you have two choices:

- Create a physical DVD-ROM by burning it from the .iso file. Microsoft provides a utility called DVDBURN that accomplishes this task. The DVDBURN utility is in the Windows Server 2003 Resource Kit.

- Copy the .iso files to the hard disk of the host computer. The installation takes less time when the files are accessed from the hard drive rather than the DVD-ROM drive.

If you want to perform a network-based installation, you must configure the virtual machine to use a legacy network adapter and connect to an external virtual network. You can perform these tasks after the virtual machine has been created.

The last window in the wizard (see Figure 2-28) displays summary information about the new virtual machine. If you see something wrong, click Previous to return to a previous window of the wizard and fix the problem. Otherwise, click Finish to create the virtual machine.

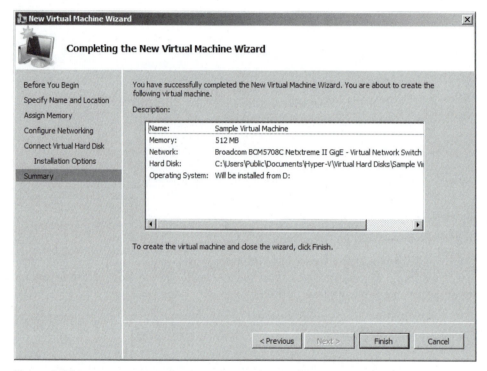

Figure 2-28 Summary information for new virtual machine

Source: Hyper-V Manager/Windows Server 2008 R2 SP1

Configuring Virtual Machines

The virtual machine settings allow you to adjust the configuration of a virtual machine after you have created it. From Hyper-V Manager, click a virtual machine in the Virtual Machines pane, and then click Settings in the Actions pane for the virtual machine. Figure 2-29 shows the settings for a selected virtual machine. The machine has one hard drive, which was created to store the operating system and is attached to the first Integrated Drive Electronics (IDE) controller. The DVD drive is attached to the second IDE controller.

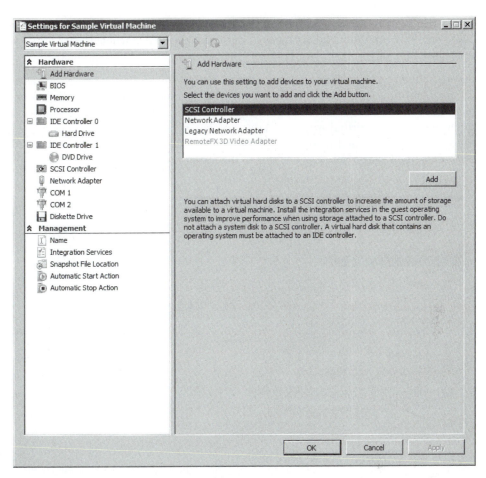

Figure 2-29 Settings for a sample virtual machine

Source: Hyper-V Manager/Windows Server 2008 R2 SP1

Adding Hardware Devices
From the initial configuration window shown in Figure 2-29, you can add the following hardware devices to a virtual machine:

- *SCSI controller*—Attach additional virtual hard disks for data storage. (An operating system cannot be started from a SCSI device.) The SCSI controller uses the VMBus for faster I/O transfers.

- *Network adapter*—Add another network adapter to an existing virtual network switch (synthetic device).

- *Legacy network adapter*—Add a network adapter to perform a network-based installation of the guest operating system. Some older operating systems, such as Windows Vista, require these adapters.

- ***RemoteFX 3D video adapter***—Add a rich graphics experience in a guest operating system. This option requires that you run the Add-WindowsFeature RDS-RemoteFX PowerShell script.

BIOS Settings Just like your host computer system, a virtual machine has a Basic Input Output System (BIOS). Although the range of options for a virtual machine is considerably narrower than those for a physical computer's BIOS, you can change the virtual machine BIOS settings.

Figure 2-30 shows the BIOS settings, which appear when you click BIOS in the Hardware list. You can turn on the Num Lock feature when the virtual machine starts by checking the Num Lock check box. You can use the Num Lock feature to activate the numeric keyboard when you start the virtual machine. You can change the boot order by clicking a device in the Startup order list and then using the up and down arrows. For a network-based installation, move the Legacy Network adapter to the top of the boot order.

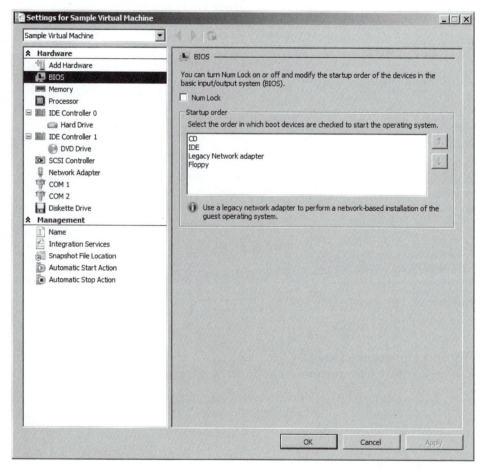

Figure 2-30 BIOS settings

Source: Hyper-V Manager/Windows Server 2008 R2 SP1

Memory Settings Virtual machines use the memory of the host computer on which Hyper-V is running. You can specify the amount of memory allocated to a virtual machine by clicking Memory in the Hardware list. Figure 2-31 shows the options for memory management. To specify static memory, enter the amount of memory you need in the RAM text box.

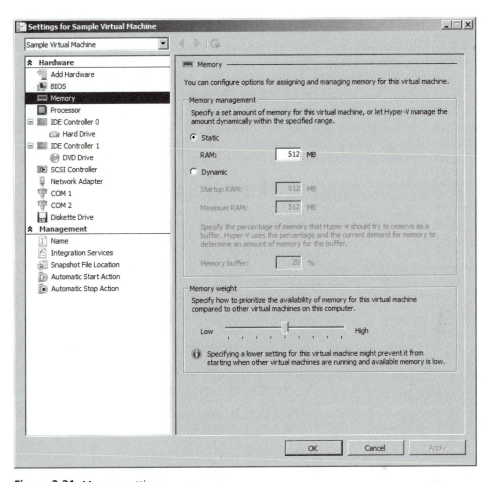

Figure 2-31 Memory settings

Source: Hyper-V Manager/Windows Server 2008 R2 SP1

Hyper-V manages dynamic memory using the following settings:

- *Startup RAM*—Specify the amount of memory needed to start the virtual machine. Consider this value carefully. The startup RAM must be adequate so that the guest operating system will start, but to allow additional virtual machines to run, it should be set as low as possible.

- *Maximum RAM*—Specify the maximum amount of memory that the virtual machine can use. This value can range from the Startup RAM value up to 64 GB. However, the maximum memory cannot exceed the amount of memory supported by the guest operating system. For example, Windows Server 2008 R2 Standard Edition has a limit of 32 GB.

- *Memory buffer*—Specify the amount of memory that Hyper-V tries to assign to the virtual machine compared with the memory needed by the virtual machine. Enter the Memory buffer value as a percentage.

- *Memory weight*—Provide Hyper-V with a way to rank and distribute memory among virtual machines when insufficient physical memory is available for them on the host computer.

You will learn to optimize memory in Chapter 3.

Logical Processor Settings   Hyper-V lets you control the number of individual "cores," or **logical processors**, that are assigned to a virtual machine. A quad processor has four cores, or four logical processors. If Intel **Hyper-Threading** is available, a quad-core processor can support up to eight logical processors. (Hyper-Threading makes each processing core appear to have two processors.) If you attempt to exceed the limit of logical processors on the host computer, the virtual machine will not start. The enlightened operating systems used in this textbook can have one to four logical processors. Figure 2-32 shows the window in which you can set the number of logical processors; to access this window, click Processor in the Hardware list.

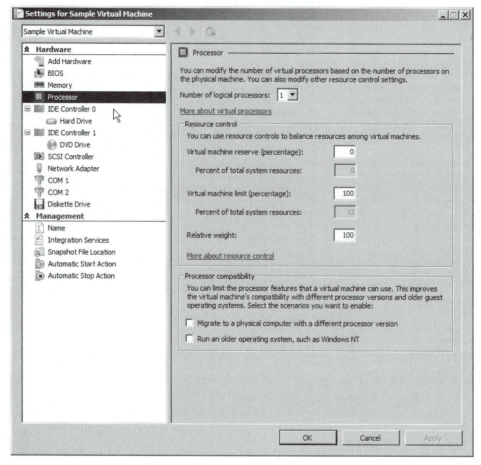

Figure 2-32 Processor settings

Source: Hyper-V Manager/Windows Server 2008 R2 SP1

You have several options for controlling how Hyper-V allocates logical processors to virtual machines:

- *Virtual machine reserve*—Specify the percentage of processing resources to reserve for the virtual machine. This setting guarantees that the percentage you specify will be available to the virtual machine. This setting can also affect how many virtual machines you can run at one time.

- *Virtual machine limit*—Specify the maximum percentage of processing resources that the virtual machine can use. This setting is applied regardless of whether other virtual machines are running.

- *Relative weight*—Provide Hyper-V with a way to rank and distribute logical processors to the selected virtual machine when more than one is running and the virtual machines compete for resources.

- *Processor compatibility*—This setting refers to the ability to "live migrate" virtual machines between different processor types. The feature is beyond the scope of this textbook.

You will learn to optimize logical processors in Chapter 3.

Hard Disk Controller Settings   Virtual machines have two IDE controllers and two IDE devices per controller, just like physical computers. However, up to 64 hard drives can be connected to a SCSI controller. The most typical configuration is to place the virtual hard disk for the guest operating system on IDE Controller 0 and a DVD drive on IDE Controller 1, as shown in Figure 2-33.

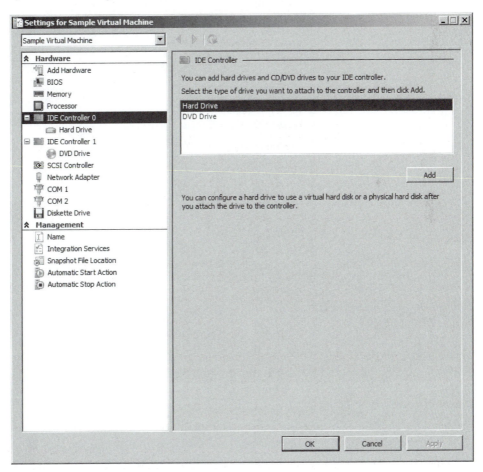

Figure 2-33 IDE controllers with devices

Source: Hyper-V Manager/Windows Server 2008 R2 SP1

You can add hard drives or DVD drives by clicking the IDE controller in the Hardware list, clicking Hard Drive or DVD Drive, and then clicking the Add button. Select the appropriate IDE controller and location by clicking the appropriate arrow buttons. The window shown in Figure 2-34 appears. If you click the New, Edit, or Inspect button, the New Virtual Hard Disk Wizard appears. If you need to link to an existing virtual hard disk, use the Browse button to navigate to the .vhd file.

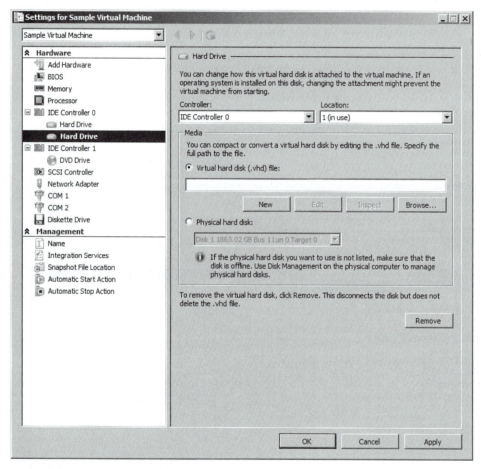

Figure 2-34 Hard drive settings

Source: Hyper-V Manager/Windows Server 2008 R2 SP1

To connect a physical disk to a virtual machine as a passthrough disk, click the Physical hard disk option button and then click the Physical hard disk arrow if necessary. The physical disk must be offline on the host computer, which you can verify using the Disk Management tool on the host computer.

To remove a virtual or physical hard disk, click the hard drive in the Hardware list and then click Remove. Remember that removing a hard disk does not delete the files from the host computer. You must delete the .vhd files using Windows Explorer.

The SCSI Controller functions are similar to the IDE Controller functions described earlier in this section. For SCSI support, Hyper-V uses a SCSI controller that is not emulated.

Instead, the synthetic SCSI controller uses the VMBus, which is much faster and requires less CPU overhead than an emulated IDE controller. An IDE controller must be used for the guest operating system. For data drives, SCSI is a better alternative.

Network Adapter Settings In order to connect a virtual machine to a virtual network, you need to have a virtual network adapter connected to the virtual machine. A single virtual machine can use multiple virtual network adapters, although each of these adapters can be connected to only one virtual network switch.

To change settings for a virtual network adapter, click Network Adapter in the Hardware list, as shown in Figure 2-35. You can modify the following settings in the window that appears:

- *Network*—Each virtual network switch can be connected as a single network connection.

- *MAC address*—The MAC address makes each network adapter unique. The role of the MAC address is beyond the scope of this textbook.

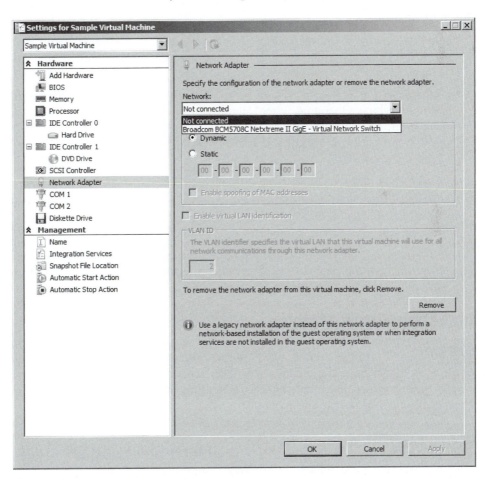

Figure 2-35 Network adapter settings

Source: Hyper-V Manager/Windows Server 2008 R2 SP1

The IEEE 802.1Q standard for **VLAN tagging** was created to allow you to use a network connection to transmit multiple streams of isolated network traffic. For example, two virtual machines cannot see each other's packets after configuration. However, if a router is used between the VLANs, the packets will be visible to both virtual machines. You will learn more about VLAN tagging in Chapter 6.

Communication Ports Microsoft does not support connections from virtual machines to physical COM ports. Microsoft does support piping between virtual machines, but the topic is beyond the scope of this textbook.

Diskette Drives Each virtual machine has a single virtual floppy diskette drive; there is no access to a physical diskette drive. Therefore, you must use virtual floppy disks (VFDs), which can be created with the Virtual Disk Wizard. To start the wizard, click New and then click Floppy Disk in Hyper-V Manager.

Management You have a number of options for managing your virtual machines, as shown in Figure 2-35:

- *Name*—Change the name of the virtual machine. This option is useful if you need to change a virtual machine name to avoid confusion with similar machine names.
- *Integration Services*—Limit one or more of the five Integration Services for the selected virtual machine: Operating system shutdown, Time synchronization, Data exchange, Heartbeat, and Backup (volume snapshot). All of the enlightened operating systems used in this textbook are capable of using each of the services.
- *Snapshot File Location*—Change the location of snapshots from their default location of C:\ProgramData\Microsoft\Windows\Hyper-V.
- *Automatic Start Action*—Change the option for restarting the virtual machine when the host computer starts. The default selection is "Automatically start if it was running when the service stopped."
- *Automatic Stop Action*—Change the option for stopping the virtual machine when the host computer stops. The default selection is "Save the virtual machine state."

Operating Virtual Machines

Operating a virtual machine is like operating a physical computer. You can start them, shut them down, and turn their power off. However, because they are virtual machines, you can perform additional tasks depending on whether the machine is off, running, or paused. To interact with a virtual machine, connect to it using the Virtual Machine Connection tool. The tool is described later in this section.

Virtual Machine Actions Table 2-1 describes the actions you can perform on a virtual machine that is not running.

Action	Description
Connect	Connect to a virtual machine to install the guest operating system or interact with it.
Settings	Review and update virtual machine settings.
Start	Turn on and boot a virtual machine.
Snapshot	Save a virtual machine's state, data, and configuration at a given point in time. For more details, see Chapter 3.
Export	Prepare the virtual machine's files for importing to another host computer later. For more details, see Chapter 3.
Rename	Change the name of the virtual machine.
Delete	Delete the virtual machine configuration. (Note that .vhd files will remain.)
Help	Obtain help for using Hyper-V.

Table 2-1 Actions you can perform when a virtual machine is off

© Cengage Learning 2014

Table 2-2 describes the actions you can perform on a virtual machine that is running or paused.

Action	Description
Connect	Connect to a virtual machine to install the guest operating system or interact with it.
Settings	Review the virtual machine settings.
Turn Off	Allow a "noncontrolled power-off" of a virtual machine, which is equivalent to pulling the power plug on a physical computer.
Shut Down	Allow a controlled power-off of a virtual machine, which requires Integration Services support.
Save	Stop virtual machine processing and save the memory and processor state to a file.
Pause	Suspend virtual machine processing.
Resume	Restart virtual machine processing after pausing it.
Reset	Allow a noncontrolled restart of a virtual machine, which is equivalent to pushing the reset button on a physical computer.
Snapshot	Save a virtual machine's state, data, and configuration at a given point in time. For more details, see Chapter 3.
Rename	Change the name of the virtual machine.
Help	Obtain help for using Hyper-V.

Table 2-2 Actions you can perform when a virtual machine is running or paused

© Cengage Learning 2014

Connecting to a Virtual Machine Use the Virtual Machine Connection tool to connect to a virtual machine and then install the guest operating system or interact with it. You can use Virtual Machine Connection to perform the following tasks:

- Connect to the video output of a virtual machine.
- Control the state of a virtual machine.
- Modify the settings of a virtual machine.

To connect to a virtual machine, right-click the virtual machine name in the Virtual Machines pane of Hyper-V Manager, and then click Connect. The Virtual Machine Connection window appears with the desktop of the running guest operating system. If the virtual machine is not currently running, you will see the black screen and message shown in Figure 2-36. To start the virtual machine, click the Action menu and then click Start.

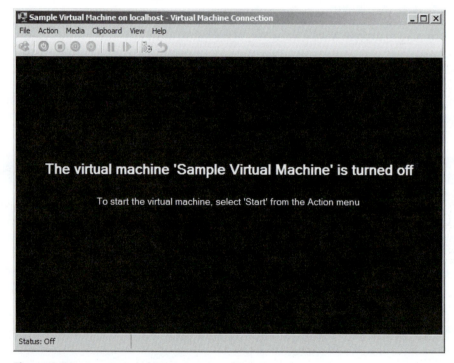

Figure 2-36 Virtual Machine Connection window

Source: Hyper-V Manager/Windows Server 2008 R2 SP1

You may find the following tips to be helpful when using Virtual Machine Connection:

- Until a guest operating system is installed, press the mouse release key combination, and then move the mouse pointer outside the virtual machine window. The default release key combination is Ctrl+Alt+left arrow.
- You can move the mouse pointer easily between the operating systems running on the host computer and the virtual machine. If the mouse pointer appears as a small dot when you connect to a running virtual machine, click anywhere in the virtual machine window.

- You cannot press Ctrl+Alt+Delete on the keyboard to send the key combination to a virtual machine, because it will interrupt the host computer. Use the menu command instead; from the Action menu, click Ctrl+Alt+Delete. You can also press Ctrl+Alt+End.
- You can switch from a window view to a full-screen view by selecting Full Screen Mode from the View menu of Hyper-V Manager. To switch back to window mode, press Ctrl+Alt+Break.

The Virtual Machine Connection window contains a menu bar with the following options:

- *File*—Access the settings for the connected virtual machine. If you select Exit to close the Virtual Machine Connection session, the virtual machine will continue to run in the background.
- *Action*—Send the Ctrl+Alt+Del sequence to the guest operating system. Other actions in the menu allow you to start, shut down, save, pause, and reset the virtual machine, take a snapshot of it, and revert to a previous state of the virtual machine. If the virtual machine is not currently running, most of these options will be disabled (grayed out).
- *Media*—Connect an .iso image file to a CD/DVD drive assigned to the virtual machine. You can also capture CD/DVD drives on the host computer for use by the virtual machine, eject currently mounted media, and specify a .vfd image to be connected to the virtual machine as a floppy disk.
- *Clipboard*—Paste text from the clipboard of the parent partition into the guest operating system. You can also take a screen shot of the current image of the virtual machine, which is placed into the clipboard of the parent partition.
- *View*—If you switch the view to full-screen mode, a small toolbar appears at the top of the screen. If you click the pushpin, the toolbar disappears. Move the mouse pointer to the top of the screen to make the toolbar reappear. To verify the remote connection, click the lock. To return to the normal window view, press Ctrl+Alt+Break. To hide the Virtual Machine Connection toolbar, you can also click the Toolbar option on the View menu.

Installing a Guest Operating System In Activity 1-6, you installed Windows 7 as a guest operating system, which is the operating system you run in a virtual machine. The procedure for installing a guest operating system in a virtual machine is similar to installing an operating system on a physical computer. Here is a brief list of the steps:

1. Configure the virtual machine with a virtual hard disk, virtual network, and installation media, as described earlier in this chapter.
2. Connect to the virtual machine with the Virtual Machine Connection tool.
3. From the Action menu in the Virtual Machine Connection window, click Start to start the virtual machine.
4. If necessary, press any key to boot from the CD or DVD.
5. The operating system installation starts, searches the startup devices, and loads the installation package.
6. Proceed through the installation.

You will install Windows Server 2008 R2 SP1 in Activity 2-2.

Activity 2-1: Cabling the Two Cluster Servers

Time Required: 10 minutes

Objective: Cable the two servers that will form the cluster servers (CLSTR1 and CLSTR2).

Description: In this activity, your team will prepare each of the two cluster servers (CLSTR1 and CLSTR2) for software installation in Activity 2-2. Pay attention to the steps to make future activities easier.

Table 2-3 provides the team member assignments for this activity.

Team Member	Steps	Host Computer		Team Member	Steps	Host Computer
1	1-4	CLSTR1		2	5-10	CLSTR2

Table 2-3 Team member assignments for Activity 2-1

© Cengage Learning 2014

Do not place network cables in the servers or switches until you are instructed to do so in each activity.

1. Locate the CLSTR1 server.
2. Cable the KVM switch to the CLSTR1 server using port 2.
3. Connect a blue cable between the top RJ45 connector on the CLSTR1 server and port 2 of a 5-port network switch.

You are adding the CLSTR1 and CLSTR2 servers to the management network, which your team started in Chapter 1.

4. Connect a power cable between the CLSTR1 server and the power strip.
5. Locate the CLSTR2 server.
6. Cable the KVM switch to the CLSTR2 server using port 3.
7. Connect a blue cable between the top RJ45 connector on the CLSTR2 server and port 3 of the 5-port switch used in Step 3.
8. Connect a power cable between the CLSTR2 server and the power strip.
9. If necessary, connect a blue cable between the classroom router and port 5 of the 5-port switch used in Step 3. You might have performed this step in Chapter 1.
10. If necessary, connect a cable between the wide area network (WAN) port of the classroom router and the school infrastructure. You might have performed this step in Chapter 1.

 If you are building this network at home to practice building a private cloud, use your home router as the classroom router.

Activity 2-2: Installing the Operating System on the Cluster Servers

Time Required: 60 minutes

Objective: Install Windows Server 2008 R2 SP1.

Description: In this activity, your team will install Windows Server 2008 on each of the two cluster servers (CLSTR1 and CLSTR2). Pay attention to the sequence of steps to make future activities easier.

Table 2-4 provides the team member assignments for this activity.

Team Member	Steps	Host Computer	Team Member	Steps	Host Computer
1	1-15	CLSTR1	2	41, 1-15	CLSTR2
2	16-25		3	16-25	
3	26-33		1	26-33	
1	34-40		2	34-40	

Table 2-4 Team member assignments for Activity 2-2

© Cengage Learning 2014

1. Locate the CLSTR1 server that you cabled in Activity 2-1.

2. Turn on the CLSTR1 server.

3. Switch the KVM switch to port 2.

4. Insert the Windows Server 2008 R2 SP1 DVD and press the **Reset** button.

5. When prompted to press any key to boot from the CD or DVD, press the **Spacebar**.

6. If the Windows Boot Manager appears, press **Enter**.

7. Wait for Windows to load files.

8. When the regional settings window appears, verify the selections for language, time, currency, and keyboard. Make corrections as needed, and then click **Next**.

9. Click the **Install now** link.

10. To indicate which version to install, click **Windows Server 2008 R2 Enterprise (Full Installation)**, and then click **Next**.

11. When the license terms window appears, check **I accept the license terms**, and then click **Next**.

12. Click the **Custom (advanced)** icon.

If a previous partition exists for Disk 0, click Drive options (advanced), click Delete, and then click OK.

13. Click **Disk 0 Unallocated Space** and then click **Next.**

14. Wait for Windows to copy and expand files, install features and updates, and restart the computer to complete the installation.

15. Wait while Windows prepares to start for the first time and then prepares the computer for use.

16. Remove the Windows Server 2008 R2 SP1 DVD.

17. When prompted that the user password must be changed before logging on for the first time, click **OK.** Enter **P@ssw0rd** in the New password text box, press **Tab,** enter **P@ssw0rd** in the Confirm password text box, press **Enter,** and then click **OK.**

When the Set Network Location window appears, click Work and then click Close.

18. To set the time zone, click the **Set time zone** link. If necessary, click the **Change time zone** button, click the appropriate time zone, click **OK,** click the **Change date and time** button, change the time, and then click **OK** twice.

19. To determine the IP configuration for your CLSTR1 computer, locate the team number assigned by your instructor in Table 2-5. This row contains the IP configuration.

It is very important that you use the correct IP addresses for your classroom network. Ask your instructor if an alternative IP addressing scheme will be used in your classroom.

Team#	IP Address	Subnet Mask	Default Gateway	DNS Server Address
1	192.168.0.112	255.255.255.0	192.168.0.1	192.168.0.111
2	192.168.0.122	255.255.255.0	192.168.0.1	192.168.0.121
3	192.168.0.132	255.255.255.0	192.168.0.1	192.168.0.131
4	192.168.0.142	255.255.255.0	192.168.0.1	192.168.0.141
5	192.168.0.152	255.255.255.0	192.168.0.1	192.168.0.151
6	192.168.0.162	255.255.255.0	192.168.0.1	192.168.0.161

Table 2-5 IP configurations for CLSTR1 server

© Cengage Learning 2014

20. To view the local area connections, click **Configure networking**. To disable the local area connection(s) that are currently not being used, right-click the message that a local area connection's network cable is unplugged. Then click **Disable**.

21. Repeat Step 20 for any remaining local area connection(s) that display the same message.

22. To enter the IP configuration, right-click the active local area connection. Click **Properties**, clear the **Internet Protocol Version 6 (TCP/IPv6)** check box, click **Internet Protocol Version 4 (TCP/IPv4)**, and then click **Properties**. Click **Use the following IP Address**, enter the IP address you identified in Step 19 in the IP address text box, and then press **Tab** twice; the subnet mask will appear in the Subnet mask text box. Next, enter the default gateway you identified in Step 19, press **Tab** twice, and enter the preferred DNS server address from Step 19. Click **OK**, click **Close**, right-click the active local area connection, click **Rename**, enter **Management**, and then press **Enter**. Close the Network Connections window.

23. To determine the computer name for your CLSTR1 computer, locate the team number assigned by your instructor in Table 2-6. This row contains the computer name.

 It is very important that you use the correct computer names. Failure to do so will make future lab activities difficult!

Team #	Cluster Server Name
1	TEAM1-CLSTR1
2	TEAM2-CLSTR1
3	TEAM3-CLSTR1
4	TEAM4-CLSTR1
5	TEAM5-CLSTR1
6	TEAM6-CLSTR1

Table 2-6 Computer names for CLSTR1 server

© Cengage Learning 2014

24. To enter the computer name, click **Provide computer name and domain**, click the **Change** button, and enter the computer name you located in the previous step in the Computer name text box. Click **OK** twice, click **Close**, and then click the **Restart Now** button.

25. Wait for the CLSTR1 computer to restart.

26. Press **Ctrl+Alt+Delete** and log on to your CLSTR1 server with a username of **Administrator** and a password of **P@ssw0rd**.

27. To set the screen resolution, right-click the desktop, click **Screen resolution**, click the **Resolution** arrow, and click **1280 x 1024** or a higher resolution of your choice. Click **Apply**, review the resolution, click **Keep changes**, and then click **OK**.

28. To place the Computer icon on the desktop, click **Start**, right-click **Computer**, and then click **Show on Desktop**.

29. To rename the Computer icon with the computer name, right-click the **Computer** icon, click **Rename**, and enter the computer name you determined in Step 23 for your CLSTR1 computer. Press **Enter** when you finish.

30. To display the Initial Configuration Tasks window, click the **Initial Configuration Tasks** icon on the taskbar. This icon depicts a server with a wrench.

31. To switch to the Server Manager window, click **Do not show this window at logon**, and then close the window.

32. If your school uses volume keys, click **Activate Windows**, ask your instructor to enter the product key, and press **Enter**. If your school does not use volume keys, click **Activate Windows**, enter the product key provided by your instructor, and press **Enter**. When you finish, click **Close**.

33. Wait for Windows to be activated.

 If Windows is not activated, contact your instructor.

34. If the Server Manager window is not displayed, click the **Server Manager** icon on the taskbar. This icon depicts a gray server with a toolbox.

35. Verify that the full computer name is the one you determined in Step 23.

36. If necessary, click **Change System Properties**, click **Change**, enter the correct computer name in the Computer name text box, click **OK** twice, click **Close**, and then click the **Restart Now** button. Wait for the CLSTR1 computer to restart. Press **Ctrl+Alt+Delete** and log on to your CLSTR1 server with a username of **Administrator** and a password of **P@ssw0rd**.

37. To verify that the IP configuration is correct, click **View Network Connections**, right-click the enabled local area connection, click **Status**, and then click **Details**. Match the IP configuration to the proper settings in Table 2-5. Click **Close** twice, and then close the Network Connections window.

38. If necessary, click **View Network Connections**, right-click the enabled local area connection, click **Properties**, and re-enter the IP configuration. If you need help, see Step 22 of this activity.

39. To change the password expiration date for the Administrator account, click **Start**, point to **Administrative Tools**, click **Computer Management**, and expand **Local Users and Groups**. Double-click **Users**, right-click **Administrator**, click **Properties**, click the **User cannot change password** check box, click the **Password never expires** check box, click **OK**, and then close the Computer Management window.

40. Remain logged on for future lab activities.

41. Repeat Steps 1 through 40 for the CLSTR2 server using the appropriate IP configuration in Table 2-7 and the appropriate computer name in Table 2-8.

Team#	IP Address	Subnet Mask	Default Gateway	DNS Server Address
1	192.168.0.113	255.255.255.0	192.168.0.1	192.168.0.111
2	192.168.0.123	255.255.255.0	192.168.0.1	192.168.0.121
3	192.168.0.133	255.255.255.0	192.168.0.1	192.168.0.131
4	192.168.0.143	255.255.255.0	192.168.0.1	192.168.0.141
5	192.168.0.153	255.255.255.0	192.168.0.1	192.168.0.151
6	192.168.0.163	255.255.255.0	192.168.0.1	192.168.0.161

Table 2-7 IP configurations for CLSTR2 server

© Cengage Learning 2014

Team#	Cluster Server Name
1	TEAM1-CLSTR2
2	TEAM2-CLSTR2
3	TEAM3-CLSTR2
4	TEAM4-CLSTR2
5	TEAM5-CLSTR2
6	TEAM6-CLSTR2

Table 2-8 Computer names for CLSTR2 server

© Cengage Learning 2014

Appendix B provides setup instructions for the private VM network. If you are using devices other than the Netgear FVS318G firewall and the Netgear GS105E switch, contact your instructor for the necessary configuration steps. Do not proceed without setting up the firewall and switch for the private virtual network.

Activity 2-3: Joining Cluster Servers to the Domain

Time Required: 15 minutes

Objective: Join the cluster servers to the local domain.

Description: In this activity, your team will join the two cluster servers (CLSTR1 and CLSTR2) to the local domain. Active Directory Domain Services manages the network resources for the three host computers.

Table 2-9 provides the team member assignments for this activity.

Team Member	Steps	Host Computer		Team Member	Steps	Host Computer
1	1-9	CLSTR1		2	10, 1-9	CLSTR2

Table 2-9 Team member assignments for Activity 2-3

© Cengage Learning 2014

1. Switch the KVM switch to port 1.

2. If necessary, press **Ctrl+Alt+Delete** and log on to your MGMT server with a username of **Team1\Administrator**, substituting your team name for *Team1*. Enter a password of **P@ssw0rd**.

3. Switch the KVM switch to port 2.

4. If necessary, press **Ctrl+Alt+Delete** and log on to your CLSTR1 server with a username of **Administrator** and a password of **P@ssw0rd**.

5. To verify that the IP configuration is correct, click **Start**, click **Command Prompt**, enter **ipconfig/all**, press **Enter**, and scroll backward to find "Ethernet adapter Management." Verify that the DNS server IP address is 192.168.0.111 (or the IP address of your MGMT server), and then close the Command Prompt window.

6. To join the domain, click **Start**, right-click your computer name (TEAM1-CLSTR1, for example), and click **Properties**. Click **Change settings**, click **Change**, click the **Domain** option button, and enter *Team1***.local**, substituting your team name for *Team1*. Click **OK**, and then log on with a username of *Team1***\Administrator**, substituting your team name for *Team1*. Enter a password of **P@ssw0rd**.

7. Wait for the message that welcomes you to the domain. The domain name should match the name you entered in the previous step.

8. Click **OK** twice, click **Close**, and then click **Restart Now**.

9. Wait for the computer to restart.

10. Repeat Steps 1 through 9 for the CLSTR2 server, which is on KVM switch port 3.

Activity 2-4: Installing Hyper-V

Time Required: 45 minutes

Objective: Install the Hyper-V hypervisor role.

Description: In this activity, your team will install the Hyper-V hypervisor role, which will enable you to run virtual machines on the future cluster servers (CLSTR1 and CLSTR2).

Table 2-10 provides the team member assignments for this activity.

Team Member	Steps	Host Computer		Team Member	Steps	Host Computer
1	1-12	CLSTR1		2	13, 1-12	CLSTR2

Table 2-10 Team member assignments for Activity 2-4

© Cengage Learning 2014

1. If necessary, switch the KVM switch to port 2.

2. If necessary, log on to your CLSTR1 server with a username of *Team1***Administrator**, substituting your team name for *Team1*. Enter a password of **P@ssw0rd**.

3. From the Server Manager window, click **Roles** and then click **Add Roles**.

4. To add the Hyper-V role, click **Server Roles**, click the **Hyper-V** check box, and then click **Next**.

5. Click the **Hyper-V Overview** link, read the overview, close the overview window, and then click **Next**.

6. Click the check box associated with the **Private VM**, click **Next**, and then click **Install**.

7. Wait for the Restart Pending message, click **Close**, and then click **Yes**.

8. Wait for the computer to configure Windows features and restart.

9. Wait for the computer to complete the updates needed to install the Hyper-V hypervisor.

10. Review the results. If you do not see a message indicating that the installation succeeded, contact your instructor. Click **Close**.

11. To add the Hyper-V Manager icon to the desktop, click **Start**, point to **Administrative Tools**, right-click **Hyper-V Manager**, point to **Send to**, and then click **Desktop (create shortcut)**.

12. Remain logged on for future lab activities.

13. Repeat Steps 1 through 12 for the CLSTR2 server, which is on KVM switch port 3.

Activity 2-5: Copying the Windows Server 2008 .iso File

Time Required: 15 minutes

Objective: Place a copy of the Windows Server 2008 R2 SP1 .iso file on each server.

Description: In this activity, your team will place a copy of the Windows Server 2008 R2 SP1 .iso file on the MGMT server. Next, your team will copy this file from the MGMT server to the future cluster servers (CLSTR1 and CLSTR2). Installing the .iso file to the hard drive will reduce the amount of time needed to install Windows Server 2008 in virtual machines. Table 2-11 provides the team member assignments for this activity.

Team Member	Steps	Host Computer		Team Member	Steps	Host Computer
3	1-9	MGMT		2	18, 10-17	CLSTR2
1	10-17	CLSTR1				

Table 2-11 Team member assignments for Activity 2-5

© *Cengage Learning 2014*

1. If necessary, switch the KVM switch to port 1.

2. If necessary, log on to your MGMT server with a username of *Team1***Administrator**, substituting your team name for *Team1*. Enter a password of **P@ssw0rd**.

3. To create a folder for .iso files, double-click the *Team1*-MGMT icon on the desktop, substituting your team name for *Team1*. Double-click **Local Disk (C:)**, click the **New folder** menu, enter **ISOFiles** over the text "New Folder," and then press **Enter**.

4. Right-click the **ISOFiles** folder, click **Share with**, click **Specific people**, click **Share**, and then click **Done**.

Your instructor will provide the location of the server that contains the Windows Server 2008 R2 SP1 .iso file. Substitute your classroom name for the servername and sharename in Step 5.

5. To locate the file, click **Start**, enter ***servername**sharename*, and then press **Enter**.

6. When the Explorer window appears for the server, right-click the filename for Windows Server 2008 R2 with SP1, and then click **Copy**.

7. Return to the window you used in Step 3.

8. Right-click **ISOFiles**, and then click **Paste**.

9. Wait for the file to be copied.

10. Switch the KVM switch to port 2.

11. To create a folder for .iso files, double-click the **CLSTR1** icon on the desktop, double-click **Local Disk (C:)**, click the **New folder** menu, enter **ISOFiles** over the text "New Folder," and then press **Enter**.

12. To locate the file, click **Start** and then enter ***Team1*-MGMT\\ISOFiles**, substituting your team name for *Team1*. Press **Enter**.

13. When the Explorer window appears for the server, right-click the filename for Windows Server 2008 R2 with SP1, and then click **Copy**.

14. Return to the window you used in Step 11.

15. Right-click **ISOFiles** and then click **Paste**.

16. Wait for the file to be copied.

17. Close the open windows and remain logged on for future activities.

18. Complete Steps 10 through 17 for CLSTR2, which is on port 3.

Activity 2-6: Creating a Windows Server 2008 Virtual Machine to Test RAID

Time Required: 45 minutes

Objective: Create a virtual machine that supports RAID 5.

Description: In this activity, your team will create a new virtual machine with three SCSI virtual hard drives and install Windows Server 2008 R2 SP1. Next, your team will configure the three SCSI hard drives as RAID 5.

For extra practice, you will repeat the steps on the CLSTR2 host computer. Table 2-12 provides the team member assignments for this activity.

Team Member	Steps	Host Computer	Team Member	Steps	Host Computer
1	1-16	CLSTR1	2	36, 1-16	CLSTR2
2	17-25		3	17-25	
3	26-35		1	26-35	

Table 2-12 **Team member assignments for Activity 2-6**

© Cengage Learning 2014

1. If necessary, switch the KVM switch to port 2.

2. If necessary, log on to your CLSTR1 server with a username of *Team1*\Administrator, substituting your team name for *Team1*. Enter a password of **P@ssw0rd**.

3. If necessary, double-click the Hyper-V Manager icon on the desktop.

4. To create a hard disk for RAID, click *Team1*-Clstr1 server in the left pane, substituting your team name for *Team1*. Click **New** in the Actions pane, click **Hard Disk**, click **Next**, and click the **Dynamically expanding** option button. Click **Next**, enter **First Disk for RAID** over the text "New Virtual Hard Disk," click **Next**, and enter 1 in the Size text box. Click **Next**, review the summary information, and click **Previous** if necessary to return to previous windows of the wizard and correct any mistakes. Click **Finish** when you are done.

5. Repeat Step 4 to create another disk named **Second Disk for RAID**.

6. Repeat Step 4 to create another disk named **Third Disk for RAID**.

7. To create the virtual machine, click **New** in the Actions pane, click **Virtual Machine**, and click **Next**. Enter **Server 2008 to test RAID**, click **Next**, enter **1024** in the Memory text box, and click **Next**. Click the **Connection** arrow, click **Private VM – Virtual Network**, click **Next**, review the virtual disk to be created, and click **Next**. Click **Install an operating system from a boot CD/DVD-ROM**, click **Image file (.iso)**, and then click **Browse**. Double-click **Local Disk (C:)**, double-click **ISOFiles**, click the Windows Server 2008 R2 SP1 filename, click **Open**, and click **Next**. Review the summary information, click **Previous** if necessary to return to previous windows and correct any mistakes, and then click **Finish**.

8. Wait for the virtual machine and virtual hard disk to be created. The progress bars close to indicate that the machine and hard disk have been created.

9. To connect to the virtual machine, right-click **Server 2008 to test RAID**, click **Connect**, click the **Action** menu in the Virtual Machine Connection window, and then click **Start**.

10. When the regional settings window appears, verify the selections for language, time, currency, and keyboard. Make corrections as needed, and then click **Next**.

11. Click the **Install now** link.

12. To indicate which version to install, click **Windows Server 2008 R2 Standard (Full Installation)**, and then click **Next**.

13. When the license terms window appears, check **I accept the license terms**, and then click **Next**.

14. Click the **Custom (advanced)** icon.

15. Click **Disk 0 Unallocated Space,** and then click **Next.**

16. Wait for Windows to copy and expand files, install features and updates, and restart the computer to complete the installation.

17. Wait while Windows prepares to start for the first time and then prepares the computer for use.

18. When prompted that the user password must be changed before logging on for the first time, click **OK.** Enter **P@ssw0rd** in the New password text box, press **Tab,** enter **P@ssw0rd** in the Confirm password text box, press **Enter,** and then click **OK.**

When the Set Network Location window appears, click Work and then click Close.

19. To set the time zone, click the **Set time zone** link. If necessary, click the **Change time zone** button, click the appropriate time zone, click **OK,** click the **Change date and time** button, change the time, and then click **OK** twice.

20. Click the **Action** menu in the Virtual Machine Connection window, click **Shut Down,** and then click the **Shut Down** button.

21. Wait for the virtual machine to shut down, and then minimize the Virtual Machine Connection window.

22. To view the virtual machine settings, right-click **Server 2008 to test RAID,** click **Settings,** and click **SCSI Controller** in the Surveyor pane. Click **Add,** click **Browse,** click **First Disk for RAID,** click **Open,** and then click **Apply.**

23. To add the next hard drive, click **SCSI Controller** in the Surveyor pane, click **Add,** click **Browse,** click **Second Disk for RAID,** click **Open,** and then click **Apply.**

24. To add the last hard drive, click **SCSI Controller** in the Surveyor pane, click **Add,** click **Browse,** click **Third Disk for RAID,** click **Open,** and then click **Apply.**

25. Click **DVD Drive,** click the **None** button under Media, and then click **OK.**

26. To connect to the virtual machine, right-click **Server 2008 to test RAID,** click **Connect,** click the **Action** menu in the Virtual Machine Connection window, and then click **Start.**

Pressing the Ctrl+Alt+Delete keys will interrupt the host computer. To interrupt the virtual machine, press Ctrl+Alt+End or click the Action menu and then click Ctrl+Alt+Delete.

27. To log on to the virtual machine, click the **Action** menu, click **Ctrl+Alt+Delete,** enter **P@ssw0rd,** and then press **Enter.**

28. To access the Disk Management tool, click **Start,** point to **Administrative Tools,** and click **Computer Management.** In the left pane under Storage, click **Disk Management.**

29. To initialize all the disks, click **OK.**

30. Scroll through the drive pane until Disk 1, Disk 2, and Disk 3 are displayed.

31. Right-click the **Disk 1** button, click **New RAID-5 Volume**, and click **Next**. Click **Disk 2**, click **Add**, click **Disk 3**, and click **Add**. Click **Next** three times, click **Finish**, and then click **Yes**.

32. Wait for the three disks to be converted into dynamic disks, for the RAID volume to be added, and for the volumes to be formatted.

33. Right-click **New Volume** in the Drives pane, click **Properties**, enter **RAID 5** over the text "New Volume," and then click **OK**.

34. If Internet access is not available, as indicated by an error on the Network icon in the taskbar's system tray, click the **Network** icon, and then click **Open Network and Sharing Center**. Click **Change adapter settings**, right-click **Private VM – Virtual Network**, and click **Properties**. Clear the **Internet Protocol Version 6 (TCP/IPv6)** check box, click **OK**, and then click **Diagnose this connection**.

35. When the diagnostics are complete, click **Close** and then close the Network Connections window.

36. Repeat Steps 1 through 35 for CLSTR2, which is on KVM switch port 3.

Activity 2-7: Creating and Testing an Internal Network

Time Required: 45 minutes

Objective: Create an internal network and test communications between the two virtual machines.

Description: In this activity, your team will create an internal network on the CLSTR1 host computer. Next, your team will create two virtual machines (Source and Destination) and test connectivity between them over the internal network.

Table 2-13 provides the team member assignments for this activity. Team members start on the CLSTR1 server and configure the Source virtual machine. Next, the Destination virtual machine will be configured. As with previous activities, the steps will be repeated on the CLSTR2 server. In the final step, the MGMT server is shut down.

Team Member	Steps	Server		Team Member	Steps	Server
1	1-5	CLSTR1		2	26, 1-5	CLSTR2
2	6-17			3	6-17	
3	18, 4-17			1	18, 4-17	
1	19-20			2	19-20	
2	21-25			3	21-25	
				1	27, 24-25	MGMT

Table 2-13 Team member assignments for Activity 2-7

© Cengage Learning 2014

1. If necessary, switch the KVM switch to port 2.

2. If necessary, log on to your CLSTR1 server with a username of *Team1\Administrator*, substituting your team name for *Team1*. Enter a password of **P@ssw0rd**.

3. To create the internal network, open Hyper-V Manager. In the Actions pane, click **Virtual Network Manager**, click **Internal**, click **Add**, enter **Test Network** over the text "New Virtual Network," and then click **OK**.

4. To create the first virtual machine, click **New** in the Actions pane, click **Virtual Machine**, and click **Next**. Enter **Source**, click **Next**, enter **1024** in the Memory text box, and click **Next**. Click the **Connection** arrow, click **Test Network**, and click **Next**. Review the virtual disk to be created, click **Next**, click **Install an operating system from a boot CD/DVD-ROM**, click **Image file (.iso)**, and click **Browse**. Double-click **Local Disk (C:)**, double-click **ISOFiles**, click **Windows Server 2008 R2 SP1**, click **Open**, and click **Next**. Review the summary information and click **Previous** if necessary to return to previous windows and correct any mistakes. Click **Finish** when you are done.

5. Wait for the virtual machine and virtual hard disk to be created.

6. To connect to the virtual machine, right-click **Source**, click **Connect**, click the **Action** menu in the Virtual Machine Connection window, and then click **Start**.

7. When the regional settings window appears, verify the selections for language, time, currency, and keyboard. Make corrections as needed, and then click **Next**.

8. Click the **Install now** link.

9. To indicate which version to install, click **Windows Server 2008 R2 Standard (Full Installation)**, and then click **Next**.

10. When the license terms window appears, check **I accept the license terms**, and then click **Next**.

11. Click the **Custom (advanced)** icon.

12. Click **Disk 0 Unallocated Space**, and then click **Next**.

13. Wait for Windows to copy and expand files, install features and updates, and restart the computer to complete the installation.

14. Wait while Windows prepares to start for the first time and then prepares the computer for use.

15. When prompted that the user password must be changed before logging on for the first time, click **OK**. Enter **P@ssw0rd** in the New password text box, press **Tab**, enter **P@ssw0rd** in the Confirm password text box, press **Enter**, and then click **OK**.

 When the Set Network Location window appears, click Work and then click Close.

16. To set the time zone, click the **Set time zone** link. If necessary, click the **Change time zone** button, click the appropriate time zone, click **OK**, click the **Change date and time** button, change the time, and then click **OK** twice.

17. To enter the IP configuration, click **Configure Networking**, right-click the local area connection, and click **Properties**. Clear the **Internet Protocol Version 6 (TCP/IPv6)** check box, click **Internet Protocol Version 4 (TCP/IPv4)**, and click **Properties**. Click **Use the following IP Address**, enter **192.168.30.141** in the IP address text box, and press **Tab** twice; the subnet mask will appear in the Subnet mask text box. Enter **192.168.30.1** in the Default gateway text box, click **OK**, click **Close**, and then close the Network Connections window.

18. Repeat Steps 4 through 17 for the Destination virtual machine, but enter an IP address of 192.168.30.142.

19. Return to the Destination virtual machine.

20. To set the firewall rule to permit inbound ICMP packets, click **Start,** point to **Administrative Tools,** and click **Windows Firewall with Advanced Security.** Click **Inbound Rules,** then scroll and right-click **File and Printer Sharing (Echo Request – ICMPv4-IN),** which is the first entry for File and Printer Sharing. Click **Enable Rule,** and then close the window.

21. Return to the Source virtual machine.

22. To test the connection, click **Start,** click **Command Prompt,** enter **ping 192.168.30.142,** and then press **Enter.**

If you do not receive a reply from the Destination virtual machine, contact your instructor.

23. To shut down the running virtual machines, click the **Action** menu in the Virtual Machine Connection window, click **Shut Down,** and then click the **Shut Down** button for each virtual machine.

24. To shut down the host computer, click **Start,** click the arrow next to **Log off,** click **Shut down,** click the **Option** arrow, click **Operating System: Reconfiguration (Planned),** and then click **OK.**

25. Wait for the host computer to shut down.

26. Repeat Steps 1 through 25 for CLSTR2, which is on KVM switch port 3.

27. Switch to the MGMT computer and repeat Steps 24 and 25.

Chapter Summary

- Hyper-V Manager provides a user interface for the Hyper-V virtualization environment. You can use Hyper-V Manager to create and configure virtual machines with virtualized hardware components.

- You can use the New Virtual Hard Disk Wizard to create a virtual hard disk. A virtual hard disk can have the same contents as a physical hard disk drive, such as disk partitions and a file system, which in turn can contain files and folders.

- You create virtual networks with the New Virtual Network window. A virtual network works like a physical network switch, except that the switch is implemented in software.

- After you have created a basic virtual machine, you can update its settings.

- Using the Virtual Machine Connection tool, you can turn on a virtual machine and boot it, log off and power down a virtual machine, stop processing and save the memory and processor status, review machine settings, and install a guest operating system.

Key Terms

differencing   A parent/child pair of disks in which the parent disk is read-only and changes are written to the child disk.

dynamically expanding   A disk that can grow from a minimum size to store additional data until the maximum size is reached.

external virtual network   A virtual network that permits virtual machines to access each other while accessing the host computer and external clients and servers.

fixed size   A disk that is allocated at the maximum size.

Hyper-Threading   An Intel proprietary technology used to improve parallelization of computations (performing multiple tasks at once).

internal virtual network   A virtual network that permits virtual machines to access each other while accessing the host computer; external clients and servers are not accessed.

logical processor   A CPU that presents itself as multiple logical CPUs to the operating system so that it will schedule threads on all logical CPUs simultaneously as though they were independent processors.

maximum RAM   In dynamic memory, the upper limit of RAM that the virtual machine is allowed to use.

memory buffer   In dynamic memory, the amount of extra memory reserved for the guest in addition to the committed memory that the guest virtual machine requests from Hyper-V.

memory weight   In dynamic memory, the importance of a virtual machine in terms of actual RAM allocation relative to other virtual machines.

mouse release key   A key combination that releases the mouse from a virtual machine's console window.

Non-Uniform Memory Access (NUMA)   A computer memory design used with multiprocessors in which the memory access time depends on the memory location relative to a processor.

passthrough disk   A disk that allows a virtual machine to access storage mapped directly to it without requiring the volume to be configured on the host computer.

private virtual network   A virtual network that permits virtual machines to access each other, but not to access external clients and servers or the host computer.

processor compatibility   The ability to migrate virtual machines between Intel and AMD processors.

relative weight   A Hyper-V setting that specifies how logical processors are allocated to a virtual machine when more than one virtual machine is running and the virtual machines compete for resources.

RemoteFX 3D video adapter   A device to a virtual machine that provides a Windows Display Driver Model (WDDM) driver with support for DirectX 9.0c.

SCSI controller   An interface that connects to SCSI devices. Hyper-V uses the VMBus, which is much faster and requires less CPU overhead than an IDE controller.

startup RAM   The amount of RAM that Hyper-V always gives to a virtual machine.

Virtual Machine Connection   A tool that supports access to a virtual machine's desktop or console.

virtual machine limit   A Hyper-V setting that prevents a virtual machine from consuming an excessive amount of the available host's CPU resources.

virtual machine reserve   A Hyper-V setting that reserves a percentage of the host machine's overall CPU resources for the selected virtual machine.

Virtual Network Manager   A tool in Hyper-V Manager that offers three types of virtual networks you can use for guest virtual machines and the host computer.

virtual network switch   A software component of virtualization software. Virtual machines are connected to a virtual switch to allow communication between the machines.

VLAN tagging   A method of creating independent logical networks. A unique number called the VLAN ID identifies each VLAN.

Review Questions

1. By default, virtual hard disks are stored in which of the following folders?

   a.   C:\Users\Documents\Hyper-V\Virtual Hard Disks

   b.   C:\Users\Public\Documents\Virtual Hard Disks

   c.   C:\Users\Public\Documents\Hyper-V\Virtual Hard Disks

   d.   C:\Public\Documents\Hyper-V\Virtual Hard Disks

2. The default setting for the mouse release key is _____.

   a.   Ctrl+Alt+Delete

   b.   Ctrl+Alt+right arrow

   c.   Ctrl+Alt+left arrow

   d.   Alt+R

3. For dynamically expanding virtual hard disks, the file _____. (Choose all correct answers.)

   a.   has an initial size of about 3 MB

   b.   is created with the New Virtual Hard Disk Wizard

   c.   can be automatically shrunk by the hypervisor

   d.   cannot be larger than the maximum size specified during creation

4. For differencing virtual hard disks, the file(s) _____. (Choose all correct answers.)

   a.   exists as a child in a parent/child relationship

   b.   exists as a parent in a parent/child relationship

   c.   contains both the parent and child in the same .vhd file

   d.   have a parent/child relationship that can be determined with the Inspect Disk tool

5. A _____ disk is a physical disk mapped directly to the virtual machine.

   a.   fixed

   b.   differencing

   c.   passthrough

   d.   dynamically expanding

6. Using the Edit Virtual Hard Disk Wizard, you can _____. (Choose all correct answers.)

    a.   edit the contents of the .vhd file

    b.   convert the .vhd file from a differencing disk to a fixed disk

    c.   reduce the size of a dynamically expanding .vhd file

    d.   increase the storage capacity of a dynamically expanding hard disk

7. When you add the Hyper-V role, you can choose a physical network to _____.

    a.   modify the local area connection by adding the Microsoft Virtual Network Switch to the existing protocols

    b.   convert to a virtual network switch

    c.   add to the parent partition

    d.   isolate a virtual network switch for security

8. Using _____, you can allow virtual machines to access the servers on the classroom network.

    a.   private virtual networks

    b.   physical networks

    c.   external virtual networks

    d.   internal virtual networks

9. To ensure the best security for virtual machines, you would use _____.

    a.   private virtual networks

    b.   physical networks

    c.   external virtual networks

    d.   internal virtual networks

10. To configure a virtual machine, you would probably need to _____. (Choose all correct answers.)

    a.   assign memory

    b.   specify the name and location

    c.   add a virtual network switch

    d.   specify the virtual machine connection to use

11. To install the Windows Server 2008 operating system, you must supply the installation files by _____. (Choose all correct answers.)

    a.   providing a .vfd file

    b.   booting a DVD-ROM

    c.   specifying the location of the .iso file on the host computer's hard disk

    d.   accessing the files from a network-based server

12. When configuring virtual machines, you can add which of the following hardware? (Choose all correct answers.)

    a.   SCSI controller

    b.   legacy network adapter

    c.   RemoteFX 3D video adapter

    d.   network adapter

13. For dynamic memory, the _____ should be as low as possible to allow for memory optimization.

    a.   startup RAM

    b.   maximum RAM

    c.   memory buffer

    d.   static

14. An Intel quad-core processor with Hyper-Threading would support _____ logical processors.

    a.   2

    b.   4

    c.   6

    d.   8

15. When running Hyper-V, SCSI controllers _____. (Choose all correct answers.)

    a.   permit up to four controllers

    b.   can be used to boot operating systems

    c.   support up to 256 virtual hard drives

    d.   should be used with virtual hard drives for data storage

16. _____ allows you to transmit multiple independent streams of network traffic over a network connection.

    a.   Traffic isolation

    b.   Independency

    c.   VLAN tagging

    d.   VLAN streaming

17. When a virtual machine is off, you can _____. (Choose all correct answers.)

    a.   connect to a virtual machine

    b.   start the virtual machine

    c.   shut down the virtual machine

    d.   modify the virtual machine settings

18. When a virtual machine is on, you can _____. (Choose all correct answers.)

    a. connect to a virtual machine

    b. start the virtual machine

    c. shut down the virtual machine

    d. modify the virtual machine settings

19. To log on to the operating system of a virtual machine, _____. (Choose all correct answers.)

    a. press Ctrl+Alt+End

    b. press Ctrl+Alt+Delete

    c. click Start from the Action menu

    d. click Ctrl+Alt+Delete from the Action menu

20. From the Virtual Machine Connection window, you can _____. (Choose all correct answers.)

    a. shut down a virtual machine

    b. eject the currently mounted media

    c. paste text from the clipboard of the host computer

    d. take a snapshot of the current screen image

Case Projects

CASE PROJECTS

Case 2-1: Using Virtual Hard Disks

One of your co-workers suggested in the weekly staff meeting that considerable time could be saved if the new virtual machines used differencing disks. A parent disk could be preconfigured for the base installation, and child disks could be created for each new virtual machine. This suggestion appears to be technically sound, but could there be other issues with the design? Write a one-page report that explains the issues that might be involved.

Case 2-2: Using Virtual Network Switches

You are trying to determine which type of virtual network switch to use with your Hyper-V server. The program development team will use the server to compile and test a new application they are developing. Your boss has asked you to evaluate the three types of virtual networks for their ability to meet the stated requirements. Write a one-page evaluation.

Case 2-3: Configuring Virtual Machines

You will make a presentation at the next TechShare meeting on configuring virtual machines. Your group is familiar with the New Virtual Machine Wizard. However, the group members are not sure how to configure a virtual machine after it has been created. Prepare a handout for your presentation that your co-workers could use to configure a virtual machine.

chapter 3

Configuring the Hyper-V Environment

After reading this chapter and completing the exercises, you will be able to:

- Optimize the Hyper-V server
- Monitor the performance of the Hyper-V environment
- Use snapshots in a test environment
- Export and import virtual machines
- Secure Hyper-V

You learned about Hyper-V in the first two chapters. This chapter contains the remaining information you need to use the Hyper-V environment effectively. First, you will learn to set dynamic memory and logical processors to optimize the running virtual machines. Using **Performance Monitor,** you can monitor the operation of the host computer and the running virtual machines. In a test environment, **snapshots** record the state of a virtual machine and permit the return to a previous state. To move the files for a virtual machine to a new host computer, use the export/import process. Finally, you will learn the criteria for securing the Hyper-V environment.

In this chapter, you will finish building the foundation for Hyper-V virtualization that is required to implement a private cloud. In succeeding chapters, you will learn to manage multiple host computers, put storage in place to store virtual machines, cluster the host servers to provide redundancy, and implement three strategies for users to access the virtual machines.

Optimizing the Hyper-V Server

This section explains how to optimize the Hyper-V server. The goal of optimization is to enable a server to perform more work given the constraints of the operating system and its roles. Optimization might be considered a balancing act between available resources, such as memory or processors, and the demand for these resources. Microsoft has provided several best practices for the Hyper-V environment, which are summarized at the end of this section.

Memory Optimization

When you attempt to optimize the Hyper-V host computer to support a private cloud, memory is the most significant resource. Hyper-V optimizes memory by using the techniques of dynamic memory.

Figure 3-1 shows the dynamic memory model. The startup memory specifies the amount of memory required to start the virtual machine. As the machine runs, additional RAM is requested above the initial amount provided at startup. The goal of dynamic memory is to calculate and provide the **target memory.** Hyper-V adds and removes memory in order to reach the target. The memory buffer allows you to specify the percentage of additional memory a virtual machine should be assigned as Hyper-V adjusts memory between virtual machines. This value is set to 20% by default, but you can adjust the value by changing the memory buffer percentage. The committed memory is the current amount that Hyper-V has allocated.

Some applications running in virtual machines will take as much memory as they can. For these applications, a low memory buffer setting will keep the virtual machine under control. For applications that request memory and release it quickly, assigning a high percentage will allow the program to run efficiently. Of course, maximum RAM specifies the maximum amount of memory that the virtual machine is allowed to use.

Memory pressure is another way to determine the amount of memory needed by a virtual machine. Hyper-V calculates memory pressure as the ratio of how much memory the virtual machine "wants" to how much memory it has. For example, the default buffer value of 20% means that additional memory of up to 20% of committed memory can be

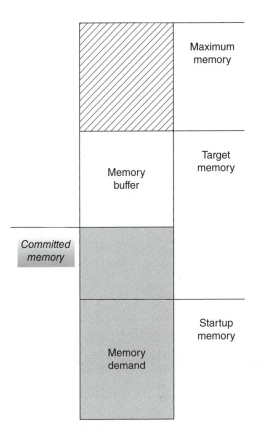

Figure 3-1 Dynamic memory model

© Cengage Learning 2014

allocated to the virtual machine. The guest operating system typically uses this additional memory for its system file cache to boost I/O performance of the operating system and applications.

The guest operating system running in the child partition communicates memory status to the parent partition though a Virtual Service Provider/Virtual Service Client (VSP/VSC) pair over the VMBus. This information is used by the **memory balancer** running in the parent partition to add or remove memory from the guest operating system.

Memory is also balanced between running virtual machines. When there is available physical memory, all virtual machines get the target amount. However, if there is not enough memory to go around, you need to consider memory weight, which is illustrated in Figure 3-2. The **memory weight** provides a scheme to determine which virtual machine is allocated the limited memory next. Hyper-V sets aside memory in the root reserve for the hypervisor and operating system in the parent partition. For the three virtual machines represented in the figure, the relative memory weight is configured as low (100), medium (200), and high (300). You can set the memory weight from 1 to 10,000; the default setting is 100. The virtual machine that has the highest memory weight gets the memory first.

The operating systems used in this textbook support dynamic memory. Table 3-1 shows the requirements for dynamic memory and supported guest operating systems.

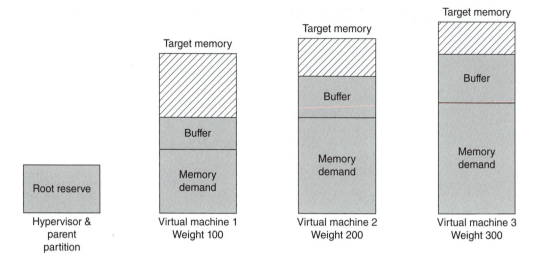

Figure 3-2 Dynamic memory weight

© *Cengage Learning 2014*

Requirements for Parent Partition	Child Operating Systems that Support Dynamic Memory
Windows Server 2008 R2 SP1, Microsoft Hyper-V Server 2008 R2 SP1	Windows Server 2003, 2008, & 2008 R2, Enterprise and Datacenter editions only; 32-bit & 64-bit versions
	Windows Vista and Windows 7, Enterprise and Ultimate editions only; 32-bit & 64-bit versions

Table 3-1 Operating systems with dynamic memory support

© *Cengage Learning 2014*

Microsoft recommends that you assign 512 MB of memory to the operating systems used in this textbook. Therefore, set the startup RAM at 512 MB. You can determine the remaining memory settings by performing the following steps:

1. Prepare the virtual machine to respond to dynamic memory.

2. Identify the memory consumption of a virtual machine.

3. Configure the dynamic memory settings.

4. Evaluate and compare performance measurements.

To prepare the virtual machine to support dynamic memory, you need to install a new driver in the guest operating system. Windows Server 2008 R2 SP1 and Windows 7 require an upgrade to Integration Services. When the virtual machine is running, you can update Integration Services by clicking the Action menu in the Virtual Machine Connection window, and then clicking Insert Integration Services Setup Disk. When the Autoplay window appears, click Install Hyper-V Integration Services, and click OK. Wait for the installation to complete, and then click Yes. Wait for the configuration to change and for the system to restart.

To establish the memory values, first identify the startup RAM, or static RAM. Right-click the virtual machine name in the Information pane of Hyper-V Manager, click Settings, click

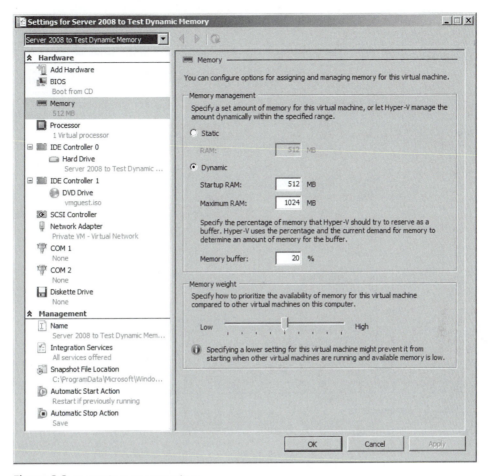

Figure 3-3 Dynamic memory settings

Source: Microsoft Windows Hyper-V Manager, Windows Server 2008 R2 SP1

Memory, and review the static RAM. Next, you configure dynamic memory. Click the Dynamic option button, enter 1024 or another value in the Maximum RAM text box, and then click OK. These settings are shown in Figure 3-3.

After setting the memory, you can connect and start the virtual machine. Log on and then return to the Information pane of Hyper-V Manager, where you will see the memory usage (see Figure 3-4).

The columns of interest in the Information pane are Assigned Memory, Memory Demand, and Memory Status. **Assigned memory** is the amount of memory that Hyper-V has determined the virtual machine currently needs. **Memory demand** is the amount of memory currently needed by the virtual machine, not including the requested memory buffer. If the assigned memory is less than the memory demand, then the virtual machine is probably paging to the hard disk. The **Memory Status** column shows "OK," "Low," or "Warning." A status of "OK" means that Hyper-V can meet the memory demand and at least 80% of the buffer value. A status of "Low" means that Hyper-V can meet the memory demand but cannot provide at least 80% of the required buffer value. A status of "Warning" means that Hyper-V cannot meet the memory demand for the virtual machine.

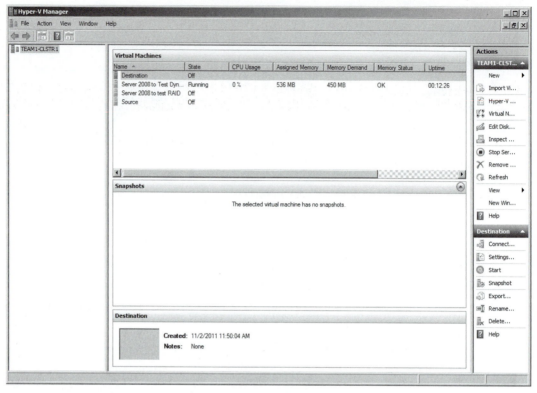

Figure 3-4 Memory status

Source: Microsoft Windows Hyper-V Manager, Windows Server 2008 R2 SP1

The last step is to monitor these values for a virtual machine over time. If you are dissatisfied with the memory configuration, Microsoft recommends that you try the following:

- Try increasing the size of the memory buffer for the virtual machine. This extra memory might help to improve performance of I/O-intensive applications and services by providing for a larger file cache.

- Try increasing the size of the startup RAM for the virtual machine. Because an application might assign fixed amounts of memory based on available memory, it might perform better with higher startup RAM values.

You will learn about performance monitoring in the next section.

Activity 3-1: Testing Dynamic Memory Optimization

Time Required: 45 minutes

Objective: Create a virtual machine to view various dynamic memory settings.

Description: In this activity, your team will create a new virtual machine and install the Enterprise version of Windows Server 2008 R2 SP1. Next, your team will prepare the operating system to support the configuration of dynamic memory. Your team will download and install the HeavyLoad stress program, which produces a load on the virtual machine. The HeavyLoad program will be configured to make memory allocation requests. Over a period of time, your team will monitor dynamic memory status in Hyper-V Manager. Table 3-2 provides the team member assignments for this activity.

Team Member	Steps	Host Computer		Team Member	Steps	Host Computer
1	1-22	CLSTR1		2	36, 2-22	CLSTR2
2	23-26			3	23-26	
3	27-35			1	27-35	

Table 3-2 Team member assignments for Activity 3-1

© Cengage Learning 2014

1. Start the MGMT server.

2. Start the CLSTR1 server.

3. Switch the KVM switch to port 2.

4. Log on to your CLSTR1 server with a username of **Team1\Administrator**, substituting your team name for *Team1*. Enter a password of **P@ssw0rd**.

5. To open Hyper-V Manager, double-click the **Hyper-V Manager** icon and click *TEAM1-CLSTR*, substituting your team name for *TEAM1*.

6. To create the virtual machine, click **New**, click **Virtual Machine**, and click **Next**. Enter **Server 2008 to Test Dynamic Memory**, click **Next**, enter **1024** in the Memory text box, and click **Next**. Click the **Connection** arrow, click **Private VM – Virtual Network**, click **Next**, review the virtual disk to be created, and click **Next**. Click **Install an operating system from a boot CD/DVD-ROM**, click **Image file (.iso)**, and click **Browse**. Double-click **Local Disk (C:)**, double-click **ISOFiles**, click **Windows Server 2008 R2 SP1**, click **Open**, and click **Next**. Review the summary information and click **Previous** if necessary to return to previous windows and correct any mistakes. Click **Finish** when you are done.

7. Wait for the virtual machine and virtual hard disk to be created.

8. To connect to the virtual machine, right-click **Server 2008 to Test Dynamic Memory**, click **Connect**, click the **Action** menu in the Virtual Machine Connection window, and then click **Start**.

9. When the regional settings window appears, verify the selections for language, time, currency, and keyboard. Make corrections as needed, and then click **Next**.

10. Click the **Install now** link.

11. To indicate which version to install, click **Windows Server 2008 R2 Enterprise (Full Installation)**, and then click **Next**.

12. When the license terms appear, check **I accept the license terms**, and then click **Next**.

13. Click the **Custom (advanced)** icon.

14. Click **Disk 0 Unallocated Space**, and then click **Next**.

15. Wait for Windows to copy and expand files, install features and updates, and restart the computer to complete the installation.

16. Wait while Windows prepares to start for the first time and then prepares the computer for use.

17. When prompted that the user password must be changed before logging on the first time, click **OK**. Enter **P@ssw0rd** in the New password text box, press **Tab**, enter **P@ssw0rd** in the Confirm password text box, press **Enter**, and then click **OK**.

When the Set Network Location window appears, click Work and then click Close.

18. To set the time zone, click the **Set time zone** link. If necessary, click the **Change time zone** button, click the appropriate time zone, click the **Change date and time** button, change the time, and then click **OK** twice.

19. To enter the IP configuration, click **Configure networking**, right-click **Local Area Connection**, click **Properties**, clear the **Internet Protocol Version 6 (TCP/IPv6)** check box, and then click **OK**.

20. To reset the IP configuration, right-click **Local Area Connection**, click **Diagnose**, and then click **Close**. Close the Network Connections window.

Contact your instructor if the IP connection is not reset and the local area connection is not enabled.

21. To shut down the guest operating system, click the **Action** menu, click **Shut Down**, and then click **Shut Down**.

22. To configure dynamic memory, right-click **Server 2008 to Test Dynamic Memory**, click **Settings**, click **Memory**, click **Dynamic**, enter **1024** for the Maximum RAM, and then click **OK**.

23. To restart the virtual machine, click the **Action** menu, and then click **Start**.

24. To log on to your virtual machine, click the **Action** menu, click **Ctrl+Alt+Delete**, enter **P@ssw0rd**, and press **Enter**.

25. To update Integration Services, click the **Action** menu, and then click **Insert Integration Services Setup Disk**. When the Autoplay window appears, click **Install Hyper-V Integration Services**, and then click **OK**. Wait for the installation to complete, and then click **Yes**.

26. Wait for the configuration change to complete and restart.

27. To log on to your virtual machine, click the **Action** menu, click **Ctrl+Alt+Delete**, and then enter a username of **Administrator** and a password of **P@ssw0rd**.

28. To switch to the Server Manager window, check **Do not show this window at logon**, and then close the Initial Configuration Tasks window.

29. To configure Internet Explorer to access Internet Web sites, click **Configure IE ESC**, click the **Administrators Off** option button, and then click **OK**.

30. To set up Internet Explorer 8 for first-time use, click **Start** and then click **Internet Explorer**. Click **Next**, click **No, don't turn on**, click **Next**, click **Use express settings**, and then click **Finish**.

> You can ignore the caution message that Internet Explorer Enhanced Security Configuration is not enabled.

31. To install and run the HeavyLoad program enter **heavy load download** in the Bing search box, and click **HeavyLoad – Free Stress Test Tool for Your PC**. Click the **Download** button, click **Download**, click the yellow message bar, click **Download File**, click **Run** twice, click **OK** to accept the language setting, and click **Next**. Click **I accept the agreement**, click **Next** three times, and then click **Finish**.

> Your instructor may have already downloaded this program for you in advance. Ask the instructor to verify the location of this program.

32. To configure HeavyLoad for memory testing, click **Test Options**, and then click **Allocate memory**.

33. To see the reported memory usage, return to the Hyper-V Manager window and view the Assigned Memory, Memory Demand, and Memory Status columns for at least 5 minutes.

34. Close Internet Explorer and the HeavyLoad window.

35. Remain logged on to the virtual machine for future activities.

36. Repeat Steps 2 through 35 for the CLSTR2 server on KVM switch port 3.

Processor Optimization

You can use Hyper-V to control the number of logical processors that a virtual machine may acquire from the pool of available processor cores on the host computer. If you have an Intel processor that supports Hyper-Threading, the number of cores is doubled. Note the message that appears at the top of the Processor settings window shown in Figure 3-5: "You can modify the number of *virtual* processors … on the physical machine." (You will use this window in Activity 3-2.)

Next, you are prompted to enter the number of *logical* processors. To clarify the difference between these apparently contradictory terms, a virtual processor is seen on the host computer as a single thread that can be scheduled for execution on any logical processor in the host computer.

You can assign a number of settings to optimize the processors for a machine. The first setting, the virtual machine reserve, is the percentage of total processor usage for the selected virtual machine. To help you determine the reserve, consider a series of hypothetical situations in which your host computer has a quad-core processor. Therefore, you have four logical processors. To make the math easier, you can also assume that each virtual machine has four virtual processors assigned.

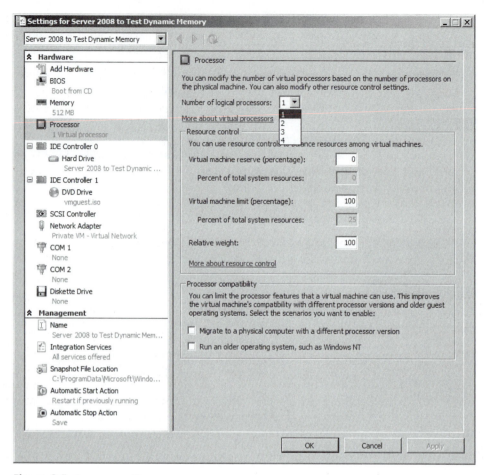

Figure 3-5 Processor settings

Source: Microsoft Windows Hyper-V Manager, Windows Server 2008 R2 SP1

Suppose that you set each virtual machine reserve to 20%, which is 20% of each core. This setting creates several scenarios:

1. You start five virtual machines, but 5 × 20% = 100%. Therefore, a sixth machine would not start because the processors would be "maxed out." Instead, you would receive an error message indicating that the sixth virtual machine could not be initialized.

2. If the first five virtual machines are idle (5 × 0% = 0%), you could start one of them and use 100% of the machine reserve because there would be no resource contention from the other four machines. Hyper-V can always use resources from an idle virtual machine, as long as the reserve total for running virtual machines does not exceed 100%.

3. You could choose not to use the features of the virtual machine reserve by retaining the default setting of 0%, which means the reserve is disabled. With the reserve disabled, you can still start additional virtual machines as long as their reserve is set to 0%.

When entering the virtual machine reserve, you are provided the percentage of total system resources for the particular resource control. This setting is a percentage of a virtual machine processor's time measured by how many processors are assigned to the virtual machine. For example, for a quad-processor host computer that you assign two logical processors and a virtual machine reserve of 20%, you will see 10% as the Percent of total system resources. In other words, 2 logical processors / 4 physical processors * 20% = 10%.

You also can set the virtual machine limit when optimizing the processors for a machine. A virtual machine is not allowed to use more than the specified percentage of its virtual processors. You would use the limit setting for a virtual machine running a poorly written application that is known to use as many processor cycles as it can. Entering the virtual machine limit ensures that the application does not use all of the processor's resources. As with the virtual machine reserve, when you enter the virtual machine limit, you are provided the percentage of total system resources for the particular resource control.

The next optimization setting, relative weight, permits a virtual machine to be favored over other virtual machines. If two virtual machines are contending for constrained processor resources, the machine with the higher relative weight gets the resources. The relative weight is a number between 1 and 10,000; the default weight is 100.

What happens if you attempt to use the three processor settings at the same time? The virtual machine reserve will define the lower limit of the processor resource, the virtual machine limit will define the upper boundary, and the relative weight will affect how the processor is handled between these two limits. However, you typically will not use all three settings at the same time.

One more processor value, **CPU usage**, is useful to know, but it is shown with the memory statistics explained in the previous section (refer back to Figure 3-4). The percentage value displayed for a virtual machine in the CPU Usage column is a complicated calculation from the three processor sources: virtual machine activity in the child partition, support from the parent partition, and the hypervisor activity relative to the virtual machine.

Activity 3-2: Testing Logical Processor Optimization

Time Required: 15 minutes

Objective: View logical processor settings.

Description: In this activity, your team will run the HeavyLoad program and observe the CPU usage for one logical processor. Next, your team will shut down the virtual machine, add a second logical processor, and observe the changes in CPU usage.

Table 3-3 provides the team member assignments for this activity.

1. If necessary, switch the KVM switch to port 2.

2. If necessary, log on to your CLSTR1 server with a username of *Team1*\Administrator, substituting your team name for *Team1*. Enter a password of **P@ssw0rd**.

Team Member	Steps	Host Computer		Team Member	Steps	Host Computer
1	1-7	CLSTR1		3	12, 1-7	CLSTR2
2	8-11			1	8-11	

Table 3-3 Team member assignments for Activity 3-2

3. If necessary, connect to the Server 2008 virtual machine that tests dynamic memory. Right-click **Server 2008 to Test Dynamic Memory**, click **Connect**, click the **Action** menu in the Virtual Machine Connection window, and then click **Start**.

4. If necessary, log on to your virtual machine. Click the **Action** menu, click **Ctrl+Alt+Delete**, enter **P@ssw0rd**, and press **Enter**.

5. If necessary, click **Start**, and then click **HeavyLoad**.

6. To view the CPU usage, maximize the Hyper-V Manager window, and then click **Server 2008 to Test Dynamic Memory**.

7. To shut down the guest operating system, click the **Action** menu, click **Shut Down**, and then click **Shut Down**.

8. To configure logical processors, right-click **Server 2008 to Test Dynamic Memory**, click **Settings**, click **Processor**, click the **Number of logical processors** arrow, click **2**, and then click **OK**.

9. To start the virtual machine, click **Server 2008 to Test Dynamic Memory** in the Virtual Machine Connection window, click the **Action** menu, and then click **Start**.

10. To view the CPU usage, maximize the Hyper-V Manager window, and then click **Server 2008 to Test Dynamic Memory**.

11. Remain logged on to the virtual machine for future activities.

12. Repeat Steps 1 through 11 for CLSTR2, which is on KVM switch port 3.

Hyper-V Best Practices

Microsoft suggests a number of best practices for the Hyper-V environment:

- Enable Hyper-Threading on Intel processors that support this technology. Hyper-Threading provides two threads for each processor core, which results in additional computing power. The net effect is a doubling of the logical processors for each core.

- Dedicate the host computer to run Hyper-V. Do not run additional roles on the host.

- Manage the physical hard disk effectively. The local disk (C:) should only contain the operating system and Hyper-V. Place the virtual machine configuration, virtual hard disks, and data for applications on other physical drives. Where available, use storage area networks (SANs) for this data.

- Use multiple network adapters on the host computer. Dedicate one adapter to Hyper-V Server management. Binding virtual networks to this management adapter might diminish your ability to manage the Hyper-V hosts. If all virtual machines share a single network adapter to access each other, monitor latency and throughput to ensure that the adapter is not being overwhelmed. Consider using two redundant adapters for access to SAN storage; with this method, even if the server hardware failed, a virtual machine could be accessed readily on the SAN and restarted on another server running Hyper-V.

- Use virtual network adapters (synthetic) instead of legacy network adapters (emulated).

- Use SCSI controllers rather than IDE controllers to attach virtual hard disks for data. SCSI controllers deploy synthetic devices, which use the VMBus.

- Implement storage options that are based on virtual machine roles and application work-load. The best solution is to use passthrough disks, which can be located on local hard disks or accessed from SANs. However, when you use physical storage, you lose the benefits of virtual hard disks, such as portability between hosts, snapshots, and thin provisioning.

- Snapshots are not recommended for a production environment.

- To avoid contention on the host at automatic startup, use a time delay. The setting for the **Automatic start delay** is in the virtual machine's Settings window under Automatic Start Action. Set increasing amounts of time to allow one virtual machine time to start before the next one starts.

- Avoid saving the state before shutdown—let the virtual machine shut down exactly like a physical computer. This is particularly important for domain controllers, where replication may be nullified.

You should use these best practices to maximize the performance of virtual machines that support a private cloud.

Monitoring Performance of the Hyper-V Server

Performance is the major goal for system administrators when supporting private clouds. The previous section explained how to configure the two most important performance elements: memory and processors. In this section, you will learn to use Performance Monitor to measure memory, processors, and two additional components: networks and disks.

Monitoring performance in a Hyper-V environment requires different strategies than when using servers running a single operating system. Consider the differences between two performance charts in Task Manager. Figure 3-6 shows a processor with 100% CPU usage on a virtual machine with one virtual processor. The Task Manager chart in Figure 3-7 shows 4%

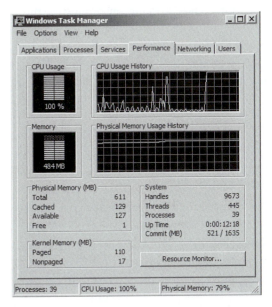

Figure 3-6 Task Manager for a virtual machine

Source: Microsoft Windows Hyper-V Manager, Windows Server 2008 R2 SP1

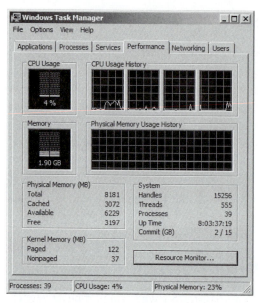

Figure 3-7 Task Manager for a host computer

Source: Microsoft Windows Hyper-V Manager, Windows Server 2008 R2 SP1

CPU usage for a host computer with four logical processors. As you can see, changes in performance monitoring will be needed.

Performance Monitor is a visualization tool for viewing performance data. To access the tool, click the Start button, point to Administrative Tools, and then click Performance Monitor. Figure 3-8 shows a graph of % Processor Time for a virtual machine. The % Processor Time graph measures how much time the processor spends working on productive threads versus how often it is busy servicing requests. If this counter's value continually exceeds 85 percent, you might need to allocate more logical processors.

By using the performance monitoring tools in Windows Server 2008, you can acquire important information about the health of your virtual machines. In general, acceptable performance is a subjective judgment that can vary significantly between virtual machines. To use the tools efficiently, you need to know how data is collected, what types of data are collected, and how to use the data to keep your system performing at its best.

Routine performance monitoring starts with establishing a default set of counters to track. You can use these counters to establish a **performance baseline**—the level of performance you can reliably expect during typical usage and workloads.

A **bottleneck** is anything that slows down a virtual machine's performance. Using a systematic approach to investigate bottlenecks is important in determining the correct solution.

To add a counter in Performance Monitor, click the green Add button on the toolbar above the graph. The Add Counters window appears, as shown in Figure 3-9.

The window contains options for the following items. You should set these options in the sequence shown:

- *Computers*—Use the controls at the top of the window to specify the source virtual machine of the item you select as the performance object. You can select the local

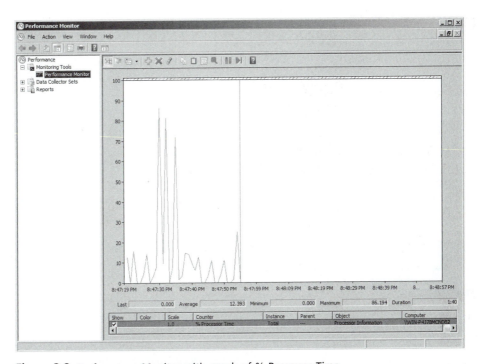

Figure 3-8 Performance Monitor with graph of % Processor Time

Source: Microsoft Windows Performance Monitor, Windows Server 2008 R2 SP1

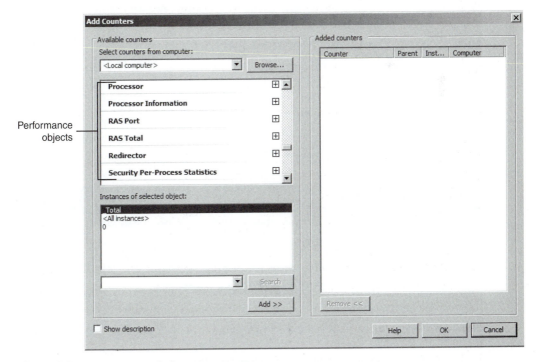

Figure 3-9 Add Counters window

Source: Microsoft Windows Performance Monitor, Windows Server 2008 R2 SP1

computer or another computer on your network by entering the computer name or IP address in the appropriate text box.

- *Performance objects*—From this list, select the area of the virtual machine that you want to monitor. You can select from a number of Hyper-V objects. Expand the performance object and view its counters.

- *Counters*—Select all counters or particular counters for the performance object you choose for monitoring; the counters depend on the performance object you select.

- *Instances*—Select all instances or the specific instance to measure when multiple objects of the same type exist on a single system. For example, if you select the Processor performance object, the instances list displays all the active processors on the specified virtual machine. If you have multiple logical processors, you may see *Total, 0, 1, 2, 3* in the list.

To view a description of each counter during the selection steps, click the Show description check box.

When you complete your selection for a counter, click the Add button. Your choice appears in the right pane. If you change your mind about a counter, click the Remove button. After you add the last counter, click OK. Ironically, the more performance counters you include simultaneously, the greater the adverse impact they can have on system performance itself! Therefore, you should only include counters that provide meaningful information when troubleshooting performance.

Monitoring Dynamic Memory Performance

Hyper-V provides new performance objects for monitoring how it allocates dynamic memory to virtual machines: the Hyper-V Dynamic Memory Balancer and the Hyper-V Dynamic Memory VM. You can locate these objects easily in Performance Monitor's list of performance objects because both have a prefix of Hyper-V.

Table 3-4 lists the counters for monitoring the performance of the Dynamic Balancer, which measures all of the virtual machines as a group.

Performance Counter	Description
Added Memory	The cumulative amount of memory added to virtual machines
Available Memory	The amount of memory left on the NUMA node
Average Pressure	The average memory pressure on the balancer's NUMA node
Memory Add Operations	The total number of add operations
Memory Remove Operations	The total number of remove operations
Removed Memory	The cumulative amount of memory removed from virtual machines

Table 3-4 Dynamic Balancer counters in Performance Monitor

Performance Counter	Description
Added Memory	The cumulative amount of memory added to the virtual machine
Average Pressure	The average pressure in the virtual machine
Current Pressure	The current pressure in the virtual machine
Guest Visible Physical Memory	The amount of memory visible in the virtual machine
Maximum Pressure	The maximum pressure band in the virtual machine
Memory Add Operations	The total number of add operations for the virtual machine
Memory Remove Operations	The total number of remove operations for the virtual machine
Minimum Pressure	The minimum pressure band in the virtual machine
Physical Memory	The current amount of memory in the virtual machine
Removed Memory	The cumulative amount of memory removed from the virtual machine

Table 3-5 Dynamic memory virtual machine counters in Performance Monitor

© Cengage Learning 2014

Table 3-5 lists the counters for monitoring the performance of dynamic memory for individual virtual machines. When you add a counter, you select the virtual machine instances to display in a graph. Recall that memory pressure is a means of determining the amount of memory needed by a virtual machine.

Activity 3-3: Monitoring Memory Performance

Time Required: 15 minutes

Objective: View counters that measure memory performance.

Description: In this activity, your team configures Performance Monitor on the host computer to measure several key counters related to memory performance. You also run the HeavyLoad program and observe the memory usage.

Table 3-6 provides the team member assignments for this activity.

1. If necessary, switch the KVM switch to port 2.

2. If necessary, log on to your CLSTR1 server with a username of *Team1\Administrator*, substituting your team name for *Team1*. Enter a password of **P@ssw0rd**.

Team Member	Steps	Host Computer		Team Member	Steps	Host Computer
1	1-8	CLSTR1		3	18, 1-8	CLSTR2
2	9-12			1	9-12	
3	13-17			2	13-17	

Table 3-6 Team member assignments for Activity 3-3

© Cengage Learning 2014

3. If necessary, connect to the Server 2008 virtual machine that tests dynamic memory. Right-click **Server 2008 to Test Dynamic Memory**, click **Connect**, click the **Action** menu in the Virtual Machine Connection window, and then click **Start**.

4. If necessary, log on to your virtual machine. Click the **Action** menu, click **Ctrl+Alt+Delete**, enter **P@ssw0rd**, and press **Enter**.

5. If necessary, click **Start**, and then click **HeavyLoad**.

6. To open Performance Monitor on the host computer, click **Start**, point to **Administrative Tools**, and then click **Performance Monitor**.

7. To show the default chart, which graphs % Processor Time, click **Performance Monitor**.

8. To remove the % Processor Time counter, click the **Delete** button on the toolbar. The Delete button contains a red X.

9. To add a counter for the memory balancer, click the **Add** button, which contains a green plus sign. Scroll through the list of performance objects, expand **Hyper-V Dynamic Memory Balancer**, click **Added Memory**, and then click **Add**.

10. To view the counters for the Hyper-V Dynamic Memory VM, scroll through the list of performance objects and expand **Hyper-V Dynamic Memory VM**.

11. To add counters for the Hyper-V Dynamic Memory VM, click **Average Pressure**. Under the instances of the selected counter, click **Server 2008 to Test Dynamic Memory**, and then click **Add**.

12. Repeat Step 11 for **Current Pressure** and **Guest Visible Physical Memory**, and then click **OK**.

13. To scale the Added Memory counter, right-click the Added Memory counter below the graph, observe the line color, and then click **Scale Selected Counters**.

14. To see the scaled value, point to the line color you observed in Step 13.

15. Repeat Steps 13 and 14 for the remaining counters.

16. Observe the changes on the graph for five minutes.

 To see the statistics for a counter, click the counter at the bottom of the graph.

17. Remain logged on to the virtual machine for future activities.

18. Complete Steps 1 through 17 on CLSTR2 on KVM switch port 3.

Monitoring Hypervisor Logical Processor Performance

Table 3-7 lists the counters for monitoring the performance of the hypervisor logical processors in Performance Monitor. When you add a counter, you select the hypervisor logical processor instances to display in a graph.

Counter	Description
%Guest Run Time	The percentage of time spent by the processor in guest code
%Hypervisor Run Time	The percentage of time spent by the processor in hypervisor code
%Idle Time	The percentage of time spent by the processor in an idle state
%Total Run Time	The percentage of time spent by the processor in guest and hypervisor code
Context Switches/sec	The rate of virtual processor context switches on the processor
Hardware Interrupts/sec	The rate of hardware interrupts on the processor (excluding hypervisor interrupts)
Total Interrupts/sec	The rate of hardware and hypervisor interrupts

Table 3-7 Hypervisor logical processor counters

© Cengage Learning 2014

Activity 3-4: Monitoring Logical Processor Performance

Time Required: 15 minutes

Objective: View the results of monitoring counters for logical processors.

Description: In this activity, your team configures Performance Monitor on the host computer to measure several key counters related to logical processor performance. You also run the HeavyLoad program and observe the logical processor usage.

Table 3-8 provides the team member assignments for this activity.

1. If necessary, switch the KVM switch to port 2.

2. If necessary, log on to your CLSTR1 server with a username of *Team1\Administrator*, substituting your team name for *Team1*. Enter a password of **P@ssw0rd**.

3. If necessary, connect to the Server 2008 virtual machine that tests dynamic memory. Right-click **Server 2008 to Test Dynamic Memory**, click **Connect**, click the **Action** menu in the Virtual Machine Connection window, and then click **Start**.

4. If necessary, log on to your virtual machine. Click the **Action** menu, click **Ctrl+Alt+Delete**, enter **P@ssw0rd**, and press **Enter**.

5. If necessary, click **Start**, and then click **HeavyLoad**.

Team Member	Steps	Host Computer		Team Member	Steps	Host Computer
1	1-8	CLSTR1		3	17, 1-8	CLSTR2
2	9-12			1	9-12	
3	13-16			2	13-16	

Table 3-8 Team member assignments for Activity 3-4

© Cengage Learning 2014

6. If necessary, open Performance Monitor on the host computer. Click **Start**, point to **Administrative Tools**, and then click **Performance Monitor**.

7. If necessary, show the default chart of % Processor Time by clicking **Performance Monitor**.

8. To clear the graph, click the **Delete** button on the toolbar until all of the counters are removed. The Delete button contains a red X.

9. Click the Add button that contains a green plus sign. To view the counters for the Hyper-V hypervisor logical processors, scroll through the list of performance objects and expand **Hyper-V Hypervisor Logical Processor**.

10. To add counters for the Hyper-V hypervisor logical processors, click **%Guest Run Time**, and then click **Add**.

11. Repeat Step 10 for **%Hypervisor Run Time, %Idle Time,** and **%Total Run Time,** and then click **OK**.

12. To scale the %Guest Run Time counter, right-click the **%Guest Run Time** counter below the graph, observe the line color, and then click **Scale Selected Counters**.

13. To see the scaled value, point to the line color you observed in Step 12.

14. Repeat Steps 12 and 13 for the remaining counters.

15. Observe the changes on the graph for five minutes.

To see the statistics for a counter, click the counter at the bottom of the graph.

16. Remain logged on to the virtual machine for future activities.

17. Repeat Steps 1 through 16 on CLSTR2, which is on KVM switch port 3.

Monitoring Virtual Network Adapter Performance

Hyper-V supports two types of network adapters: Hyper-V virtual network adapters, which are high-performance synthetic drivers, and Hyper-V legacy network adapters, which are low-performance emulated drivers. Performance Monitor provides counters for both of these adapters. Consider selecting the Bytes Received/sec and Bytes Sent/sec counters for these two adapters; each counter provides a measure of network traffic through the network adapter. In both cases, measurements are made across virtual networks that are created and bound to physical adapters in Hyper-V's Virtual Network Manager. If multiple virtual machines are running, the counter results may be aggregated across multiple virtual machines.

Activity 3-5: Monitoring Virtual Network Performance

Time Required: 15 minutes

Objective: View the results of monitoring counters for the virtual network.

Description: In this activity, your team configures Performance Monitor on the host computer to measure several key counters related to virtual network performance. You will also run the ping command from the source virtual machine to the destination virtual machine and observe the virtual network usage.

Team Member	Steps	Host Computer	Team Member	Steps	Host Computer
3	1-5	CLSTR1	1	18, 1-5	CLSTR2
1	6-8		2	6-8	
2	9-17		3	9-17	

Table 3-9 **Team member assignments for Activity 3-5**

© *Cengage Learning 2014*

Table 3-9 provides the team member assignments for this activity.

1. If necessary, switch the KVM switch to port 2.

2. If necessary, log on to your CLSTR1 server with a username of *Team1***Administrator**, substituting your team name for *Team1*. Enter a password of **P@ssw0rd**.

3. If necessary, open Performance Monitor on the host computer. Click **Start**, point to **Administrative Tools**, and then click **Performance Monitor**.

4. If necessary, show the default chart of % Processor Time by clicking **Performance Monitor**.

5. To clear the graph, click the **Delete** button on the toolbar until all of the counters are removed. The Delete button contains a red X.

6. Click the Add button that contains a green plus sign to open the Add Counters window. To view the counters for the Hyper-V virtual network, scroll through the list of performance objects and expand **Hyper-V Virtual Network Adapter**.

7. To add counters for the Hyper-V Virtual Network Adapter, click **Bytes Received/sec.** Under Instances of the selected object, click **Test Network**, and then click **Add**.

NOTE

The instance of the Test Network adapter has a **Globally Unique Identifier (GUID)** attached. A GUID is a 32-character hexadecimal string.

8. Repeat Step 7 for **Bytes Sent/sec** and then click **OK**.

9. Return to the Hyper-V Manager window.

10. To connect to the Destination virtual machine, right-click **Destination**, click **Connect**, click the **Action** menu in the Virtual Machine Connection window, and then click **Start**.

11. To connect to the Source virtual machine, right-click **Source**, click **Connect**, click the **Action** menu in the Virtual Machine Connection window, and then click **Start**. Click the **Action** menu, click **Ctrl+Alt+Delete**, enter **P@ssw0rd**, and press **Enter**.

12. To test the connection from the Source virtual machine, click **Start**, click **Command Prompt**, enter **ping 192.168.30.142 -n 500**, and then press **Enter**. The switch value "-n 500" provides 500 echo requests to the Destination virtual machine.

13. Return to Performance Monitor and observe the changes on the graph for five minutes.

14. To scale the Bytes Received counter, right-click the **Bytes Received/sec** counter below the graph, observe the line color, and then click **Scale Selected Counters**.

15. To see the scaled value, point to the line color you observed in Step 14.

16. Repeat Steps 14 and 15 for the **Bytes Sent/sec** counter.

To see the statistics for a counter, click the counter at the bottom of the graph.

17. Remain logged on to the virtual machines for future activities.

18. Repeat Steps 1 through 17 on CLSTR2, which is on KVM switch port 3.

Monitoring Virtual Hard Disk Performance

Hyper-V provides four counters to monitor the performance of hard disks attached to the Hyper-V virtual IDE controller. For read access, you can select the Read Bytes/sec and Read Sectors/sec counters. For write access, you can select the Write Bytes/sec and Written Sectors/sec counters. The size of the sector is 512 bytes. To monitor the SCSI controller's performance, use the Hyper-V Virtual Storage Device performance object with the Read Bytes/sec and Write Bytes/sec counters.

Activity 3-6: Monitoring Virtual Disk Controller Performance

Time Required: 15 minutes

Objective: View the results of monitoring counters for the virtual IDE controller.

Description: In this activity, your team configures Performance Monitor on the host computer to measure several key counters related to virtual IDE performance. You will also run the HeavyLoad program and observe the logical processor usage.

Table 3-10 provides the team member assignments for this activity.

1. If necessary, switch the KVM switch to port 2.

2. If necessary, log on to your CLSTR1 server with a username of *Team1\Administrator*, substituting your team name for *Team1*. Enter a password of **P@ssw0rd**.

3. If necessary, connect to the Server 2008 virtual machine that tests dynamic memory. Right-click **Server 2008 to Test Dynamic Memory**, click **Connect**, click the **Action** menu in the Virtual Machine Connection window, and then click **Start**. Click the **Action** menu, click **Ctrl+Alt+Delete**, and enter **P@ssw0rd**.

4. If necessary, click **Start**, and then click **HeavyLoad**.

5. To activate disk activity, click **Test Options** and then click **Write Temp File**.

Team Member	Steps	Host Computer		Team Member	Steps	Host Computer
2	1-7	CLSTR1		1	17, 1-7	CLSTR2
3	8-16			2	8-16	

Table 3-10 Team member assignments for Activity 3-6

© Cengage Learning 2014

6. If necessary, open Performance Monitor on the host computer. Click **Start**, point to **Administrative Tools**, and then click **Performance Monitor**.

7. If necessary, show the default chart of % Processor Time by clicking **Performance Monitor**.

8. To clear the graph, click the **Delete** button on the toolbar until all of the counters are removed. The Delete button contains a red X.

9. Click the Add button that contains a green plus sign to open the Add Counters window. To view the counters for the Hyper-V virtual IDE controller, scroll through the list of performance objects and expand **Hyper-V Virtual IDE Controller**.

10. To add counters for the Hyper-V virtual IDE controller, click **Read Bytes/sec**. Below the instances of the selected object, select **Server 2008 to Test Dynamic Memory**, and then click **Add**.

11. Repeat Step 10 for **Write Bytes/sec**, and then click **OK**.

12. To scale the Read Bytes/sec counter, right-click the **Read Bytes/sec** counter below the graph, observe the line color, and then click **Scale Selected Counters**.

13. To see the scaled value, point to the line color you observed in Step 12.

14. Repeat Steps 12 and 13 for the Write Bytes/sec counter.

15. Observe the changes on the graph for five minutes.

To see the statistics for a counter, click the counter at the bottom of the graph.

16. Remain logged on to the virtual machine for future activities.

17. Repeat Steps 1 through 16 on CLSTR2, which is on KVM switch port 3.

Using Snapshots in a Test Environment

To capture the beauty of a scene on a vacation trip, you might take a snapshot with a digital camera. When you create a snapshot in Hyper-V, you are taking a picture of a virtual machine at a point in time. The snapshot captures the state, data, and hardware configuration of a running virtual machine. A snapshot is composed of a configuration file, saved state files, and differencing disks (**.avhd files**). To take a snapshot, right-click the name of the virtual machine in Hyper-V Manager, and click Snapshot from the menu. The green arrow and Now marker indicate the current running virtual machine in the Snapshots pane (see Figure 3-10).

Snapshots provide a fast and easy way to return or "revert" the virtual machine to a previous state, which is particularly useful in a development environment. After taking a snapshot, you could make a change to a program and test the change. If the change did not work as intended, you could revert the virtual machine to the previous state and try a different program change.

When you create a snapshot, Hyper-V stops writing data to the original virtual hard drive file and begins writing data to a differencing disk. Snapshot data files are stored as .avhd files. Note that taking multiple snapshots can quickly consume significant hard disk space on your host computer. By default, snapshots are labeled using the virtual machine name concatenated with the creation timestamp. If you want to rename the snapshot, right-click it and then click Rename.

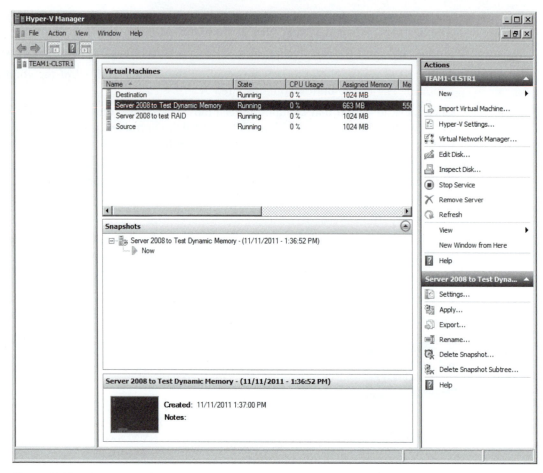

Figure 3-10   Taking a snapshot of a virtual machine

Source: Microsoft Windows Hyper-V Manager, Windows Server 2008 R2 SP1

If you revert a machine to its previous state, you go back to using the original virtual hard drive, which has not been used since the snapshot was created. To revert a virtual machine, right-click its name in Hyper-V Manager, and click Revert. Hyper-V stops the virtual machine and restarts the virtual machine at the state of the previous snapshot. The revert process can only return to the previous machine state.

Note that when you revert a machine, any configuration changes you made to the running virtual machine since taking the snapshot are discarded. None of the snapshots are altered during the revert operation. The Revert feature can be thought of as a single-level undo feature. After you have reverted a machine, using the Revert option again will continue to return the virtual machine to the configuration and state of the last snapshot taken.

Using the Apply Feature

If you have taken multiple snapshots and you want to skip several snapshots in the resulting hierarchy to return to a particular state, use the Apply feature. Figure 3-11 shows a tree

Figure 3-11 Snapshot tree

Source: Microsoft Windows Hyper-V Manager, Windows Server 2008 R2 SP1

structure that represents the hierarchy for a virtual machine with multiple snapshots. The root node of the tree is the first snapshot that was created. Under the root node, a child named Now represents the running version of the virtual machine.

You can return to a snapshot that is more than one level up from the running virtual machine. Simply right-click the desired snapshot, and then click Apply, as shown in Figure 3-12.

Before using the Apply feature, you must decide whether to take a snapshot of the running virtual machine or to apply the selected snapshot without saving the current state. As with the Revert option, if you do not take a snapshot prior to using the Apply option, the state of the running virtual machine will be lost. After you stop the virtual machine, the active .avhd file is deleted and a new one is created. The name of the new .avhd file is updated in the virtual machine configuration file, and the virtual machine is restarted (see Figure 3-13). You can also see that the Now marker has moved under the second snapshot to indicate that the running virtual machine is based on this snapshot.

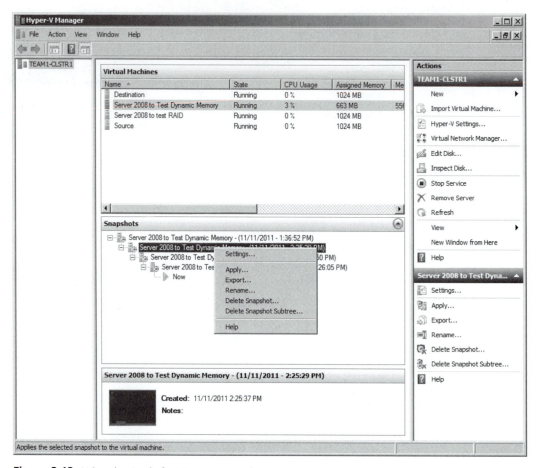

Figure 3-12   Using the Apply feature on a snapshot

Source: Microsoft Windows Hyper-V Manager, Windows Server 2008 R2 SP1

Deleting Snapshots

When you finish testing, you should delete the snapshots you created. You can delete many nested snapshots at the same time by right-clicking one and clicking Delete Snapshot Subtree. All that remains is the original virtual machine. To delete a single snapshot, right-click it and select Delete Snapshot.

Deleting a snapshot is much more complicated than deleting a file. Recall that a snapshot is composed of a configuration file, saved state files, and differencing disks (.avhd files). When you delete a snapshot, Hyper-V deletes the snapshot configuration file and saved state files immediately, and the snapshot entry is removed from the Information pane.

However, the .avhd files are still on the host computer's hard disk. Your ability to delete the .avhd files depends on the location of the snapshots in the tree and whether the virtual machine is running or off. To illustrate the situation, Figure 3-14 shows a snapshot tree.

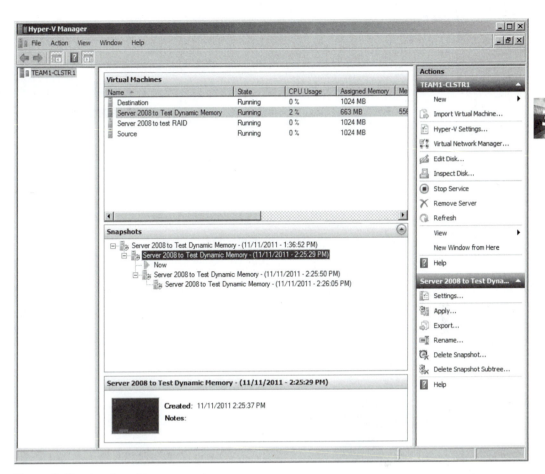

Figure 3-13 Virtual machine restarted

Source: Microsoft Windows Hyper-V Manager, Windows Server 2008 R2 SP1

Snapshot 4 has no other snapshots that depend on it, so Hyper-V can delete the snapshot immediately and remove the .avhd file. Once Snapshot 4 has been deleted, you can delete Snapshot 3 and its .avhd file immediately.

Consider another scenario: Snapshot 1 and Snapshot 2 with the running virtual machine. Both snapshots have other snapshots, Snapshot 3 and Snapshot 4, that depend on them. When these are deleted, Hyper-V will merge the .avhd files into the chain. However, this merging process can occur only when the virtual machine is not running; otherwise, the .avhd files will remain on the host computer's hard disk. If a number of snapshots exist in the tree, merging the differencing files will be time consuming.

The .avhd files are in the same folder as the virtual hard disks: C:\Users\Public\Public Documents\Hyper-V\Virtual hard disks. The .avhd filenames include the name of the virtual machine's virtual hard disk file with a concatenated GUID. When these files are gone, the merge is complete.

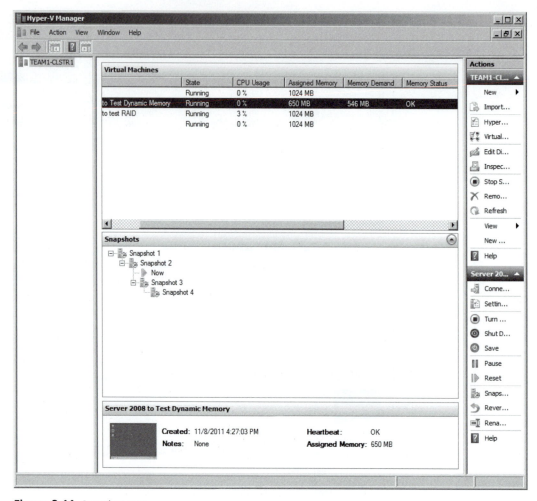

Figure 3-14 Snapshot tree

Source: Microsoft Windows Hyper-V Manager, Windows Server 2008 R2 SP1

Activity 3-7: Working with Snapshots

Time Required: 45 minutes

Objective: Practice working with snapshots.

Description: In this activity, your team will work with several snapshots and observe the creation of the .avhd files. Next, your team will revert to a previous snapshot and use the Apply feature with it. Finally, your team will delete snapshots and learn about snapshot dependency.

Table 3-11 provides the team member assignments for this activity.

1. If necessary, switch the KVM switch to port 2.

2. If necessary, log on to your CLSTR1 server with a username of *Team1\Administrator*, substituting your team name for *Team1*. Enter a password of **P@ssw0rd**.

Team Member	Steps	Host Computer		Team Member	Steps	Host Computer
1	1-6	CLSTR1		3	27, 1-6	CLSTR2
2	7-9			1	7-9	
3	10-19			2	10-19	
1	20-26			3	20-26	

Table 3-11   **Team member assignments for Activity 3-7**

© Cengage Learning 2014

3. If necessary, connect to the Source virtual machine. Right-click **Source**, click **Connect**, click the **Action** menu in the Virtual Machine Connection window, and then click **Start**. Click the **Action** menu, click **Ctrl+Alt+Delete**, enter a password of **P@ssw0rd**, and press **Enter**.

4. To take the initial snapshot, return to the Hyper-V Manager window, right-click **Source**, and then click **Snapshot**. Observe that a snapshot was taken and that the running virtual machine is called Now.

5. To rename the snapshot, right-click it, click **Rename**, enter **Snapshot 1**, and then press **Enter**.

6. Repeat Steps 4 and 5 to create **Snapshot 2**, **Snapshot 3**, **Snapshot 4**, and **Snapshot 5**.

7. To view the .avhd files, double-click **CLSTR1** on the desktop, double-click **Local Disk (C:)**, and navigate to C:\Users\Public\Public Documents\Hyper-V\Virtual hard disks. Observe that five .avhd files are associated with the Source virtual machine. Minimize this window.

8. To revert the current running machine, right-click **Source**, and then click **Revert** twice.

9. Wait for the virtual machine to stop and restart.

10. To return to a previous machine state, right-click **Snapshot 3**, and then click **Apply** twice.

11. Wait for the virtual machine to stop and restart. Because you did not choose the Take Snapshot and Apply option, the machine's current state is lost.

12. To take an additional snapshot, right-click **Source** and then click **Snapshot**. Observe that a snapshot was taken subordinate to Snapshot 4.

13. To rename the snapshot, right-click it, click **Rename**, enter **Snapshot 6**, and then press **Enter**.

14. Maximize the Virtual hard disks window by clicking the yellow folder on the taskbar. Observe that six .avhd files are associated with the Source virtual machine. Minimize this window.

15. To take an additional snapshot, return to Snapshot 3, right-click it, click **Apply**, and then click **Take Snapshot and Apply**. When the snapshot is saved, it is added below Snapshot 6.

16. To rename the snapshot, right-click it, click **Rename**, enter **Snapshot 7**, and then press **Enter**.

17. Maximize the Virtual hard disks window by clicking the yellow folder on the taskbar. Observe that seven .avhd files are associated with the Source virtual machine. Minimize this window.

18. To delete the last snapshot, right-click **Snapshot 7**, click **Delete Snapshot**, and then click **Delete**. The .avhd file has no subordinates, so it will be deleted immediately by Hyper-V.

19. Maximize the Virtual hard disks window by clicking the yellow folder on the taskbar. Observe that six .avhd files are now associated with the Source virtual machine. Minimize this window.

20. To delete the fourth snapshot, right-click **Snapshot 4**, click **Delete Snapshot**, and then click **Delete**. The .avhd file has subordinates, so it will not be deleted immediately by Hyper-V.

21. Maximize the Virtual hard disks window by clicking the yellow folder on the taskbar. Observe that six .avhd files are still associated with the Source virtual machine. Minimize this window.

22. To shut down the virtual machine, right-click **Source** and then click **Shut Down** twice.

23. To observe the merge operation, maximize the Virtual hard disks window by clicking the yellow folder on the taskbar. Observe that five .avhd files are now associated with the Source virtual machine. Minimize this window.

24. To delete the fifth snapshot, right-click **Snapshot 5**, click **Delete Snapshot**, and then click **Delete**. The .avhd file has no subordinates, so it will be deleted immediately by Hyper-V.

25. To delete the entire snapshot tree, right-click **Snapshot 1**, click **Delete Snapshot Subtree**, and then click **Delete**.

26. To observe the merge operation, maximize the Virtual hard disks window by clicking the yellow folder on the taskbar. Observe that the .avhd files associated with the Source virtual machine will be deleted. Minimize this window.

27. For extra practice, complete Steps 1 through 26 on CLSTR2 on KVM switch port 3.

Exporting and Importing Virtual Machines

To balance the workload across multiple host computers, you may need to move a virtual machine. Rather than just moving the files between the host computers, however, you should use an export/import procedure. You can easily locate the virtual hard disks for exporting, but Hyper-V places the configuration file in a hidden folder and then names the file for the virtual machine using a GUID.

The export procedure creates a folder for the necessary files and places the files in the folder, which can then be copied to the target host computer. The export procedure will create a file called config.xml in the folder to direct the import operation.

To export a virtual machine, first shut it down, then right-click the virtual machine entry in the Information pane of Hyper-V Manager and click Export. Figure 3-15 shows the Export

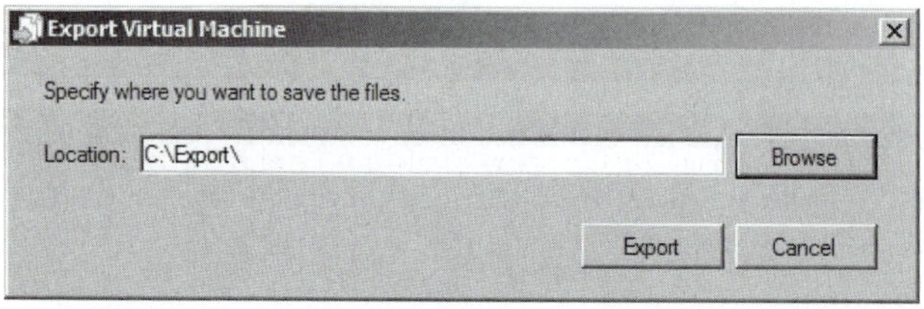

Figure 3-15 Export Virtual Machine window

Source: Microsoft Windows Hyper-V Manager, Windows Server 2008 R2 SP1

Virtual Machine window that appears. You are prompted to provide the folder for the export files. A subfolder that contains the name of the virtual machine is created automatically.

The export procedure does not remove the virtual machine from Hyper-V Manager. To delete the original virtual machine, right-click it and click Delete. This deletion does not remove the virtual hard disks associated with the deleted virtual machine. To remove these virtual hard disks, you must navigate to the folder where they are stored. By default, the virtual hard disks are stored in C:\Users\Public\Public Documents\Hyper-V\Virtual hard disks.

Before importing the virtual machine to the new host computer, you need to share the folder created by the export procedure. On the new host computer, connect to the shared folder on the first host computer by entering a string like \\TEAM1-CLSTR\ in the Start search text box. When you double-click the Export folder, Windows Explorer displays the contents of the shared folder. Copy the contents of the folder created by the export procedure to the new host computer. On the new host computer, click Import and browse to the location where the folder was copied, as shown in Figure 3-16. You can choose to keep the existing GUID or to create a new GUID. Also, you can duplicate the files so that you can import them again to create a second virtual machine.

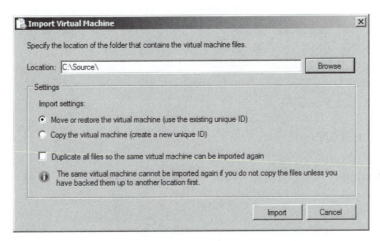

Figure 3-16 Import Virtual Machine window

Source: Microsoft Windows Hyper-V Manager, Windows Server 2008 R2 SP1

Activity 3-8: Exporting and Importing Virtual Machines

Time Required: 20 minutes

Objective: Practice exporting and importing a virtual machine.

Description: In this activity, your team will prepare a virtual machine for export. After copying the files to another host computer, you will import the virtual machine.

Table 3-12 provides the team member assignments for this activity.

1. If necessary, switch the KVM switch to port 2.

2. If necessary, log on to your CLSTR1 server with a username of *Team1\Administrator*, substituting your team name for *Team1*. Enter a password of **P@ssw0rd**.

Team Member	Steps	Virtual Machine		Team Member	Steps	Virtual Machine
1	1-6	Destination		3	16, 1-6	Source
2	7-12			1	7-12	
3	13-15			2	13-15	
				3	17-21	

Table 3-12 Team member assignments for Activity 3-8

© Cengage Learning 2014

3. Return to the Hyper-V Manager window. If the Destination virtual machine is running, right-click **Destination**, and then click **Shut Down** twice.

4. To remove the CD/DVD-ROM, right-click **Destination**, click **Settings**, click **DVD Drive**, click **None**, and click **OK**.

5. To create an Export folder, double-click **CLSTR1** on the desktop, double-click **Local Disk (C:)**, click **New Folder**, enter **Export** over the text "New Folder," and then press **Enter**.

6. To share this folder, right-click **Export**, click **Share with**, click **Specific people**, click **Share**, and then click **Done**. Close the Local Disk (C:) window.

7. To export the Destination virtual machine, right-click **Destination**, click **Export**, click **Browse**, double-click **Local Disk (C:)**, click **Export**, click **Select Folder**, and then click **Export**.

8. Switch the KVM switch to port 3.

9. If necessary, log on to your CLSTR2 server with a username of *Team1\Administrator*, substituting your team name for *Team1*. Enter a password of **P@ssw0rd**.

10. To open Windows Explorer and view the exported files, click **Start**, and then enter ***TEAM1*-CLSTR1** in the Start search box, substituting your team number for *TEAM1*. When you finish, press **Enter**.

11. To copy the files for the virtual machine, right-click the **Export** folder, click **Copy**, click **CLSTR2**, right-click **Local Disk (C:)**, and then click **Paste**.

12. Wait for the copy to be completed, and close the CLSTR2 window.

13. Return to the Hyper-V Manager window. To import the virtual machine, click **Import Virtual Machine**, click **Browse**, double-click **Local Disk (C:)**, double-click **Export**, click **Destination**, click **Select Folder**, click **Copy the virtual machine (Create a new unique ID)**, and then click **Import**.

14. To test the virtual machine, right-click the second Destination virtual machine, click **Connect**, click the **Action** menu in the Virtual Machine Connection window, and then click **Start**.

15. To shut down the Destination virtual machine, right-click **Destination**, and then click **Shut Down** twice.

16. For extra practice, repeat Steps 1 through 15 using the Source virtual machine.

17. To shut down the running virtual machines, click the **Action** menu in the Virtual Machine Connection window, click **Shut Down**, and then click the **Shut Down** button for each virtual machine.

18. To shut down the host computer, click **Start**, click the arrow next to **Log off**, click **Shut down**, click the **Option** arrow, click **Operating System: Reconfiguration (Planned)**, and then click **OK**.

19. Wait for the host computer to shut down.

20. Repeat Steps 17 through 19 for CLSTR1, which is on KVM switch port 2.

21. Return to the MGMT computer and repeat Steps 17 through 19.

Securing Hyper-V

Microsoft designed the Hyper-V hypervisor as a small microkernel that prohibits third-party code from running within the hypervisor. Because unknown security vulnerabilities in the hypervisor could compromise the security of the operating systems running in the parent and child partitions, Microsoft carefully reviewed and tested the Hyper-V source code to minimize the risks. In addition, the hypervisor was designed with minimal configuration requirements to reduce its attack surface.

After you install Hyper-V, you need to ensure that all appropriate security updates are installed. You can do this by choosing the Configuring Updates option for the parent partition in the Server Manager window and then clicking Install updates automatically. To configure Windows Update, click the Start menu, click Control Panel, and click System and Security. Click Windows Update, check for updates, and change the update settings. The default setting is to install updates automatically every day at 3:00 a.m. You can then view the update history.

Configuration files for each virtual machine are stored in a hidden, secured folder. The virtual machine configuration files stored in this directory are relatively small, and the default storage location should be acceptable. You should not attempt to edit these configuration files.

By default, new virtual hard disk files are stored in the C:\Users\Public\Public Documents\ Hyper-V\Virtual hard disks folder. You can change the location of these files if you want. If you specify a different storage location, assign permissions as indicated in Table 3-13.

Names	Permissions	Apply to
Administrators		
System	Full control	This folder, subfolders, and files
Creator, Owner	Full control	Subfolders and files only
Interactive Service Batch	Create files/write data Create folders/append data Delete Delete subfolders and files Read attributes Read extended attributes Read permissions Write attributes Write extended attributes	This folder, subfolders, and files

Table 3-13   Security permissions for virtual hard disks

The same security measures you would apply to a physical computer should be applied to virtual machines. For example, each guest operating system needs its own firewall and appropriate antivirus software for the environment.

You should give each virtual machine access only to the passthrough hard disks, virtual hard disks, and removable storage devices that it needs. Do not give the machine access to any other devices. If a virtual machine requires access to a resource like a CD/DVD drive only when you are installing software, remove the virtual drive from the virtual machine setting.

Remove the virtual hard disk files for decommissioned virtual machines. Not only will this free up storage space, it will eliminate opportunities for future abuse. In other words, removing the files ensures that they will not be added to Hyper-V Manager and run by an unauthorized user.

Deploy your virtual machines so that all of them share a similar level of trust on a given host computer, and then configure the computer to be at least as secure as the most secure virtual machine. Virtual machines such as Web servers require different security precautions than servers to which access is tightly controlled or limited to a small number of users.

You should enable auditing for sensitive virtual hard disks and configuration files. Carefully review the security logs to identify problem areas that require further research.

Time synchronization can be important in some auditing scenarios. The system time of virtual machines can drift out of sync with the host computer if they are under constant heavy load. For time synchronization to work properly, you need to update Hyper-V Integration Services on each virtual machine. You learned to install Integration Services in Activity 3-1.

You will learn more about securing the Hyper-V virtualization environment in the next chapter.

Chapter Summary

- It is important to keep the Hyper-V environment running efficiently. Hyper-V provides methods to optimize the use of two key resources: computer memory and logical processors. In addition, Microsoft has provided a number of best practices to make the best use of this environment.

- Performance of the Hyper-V environment is a major goal for a system administrator. Microsoft provides the Performance Monitor tool to help you measure and fine-tune the performance of key resources, such as memory, processors, networks, and disks.

- When you create a snapshot of a virtual machine in a development or test environment, you are taking a picture of a virtual machine at a point in time. A snapshot is composed of a configuration file, saved state files, and differencing disks (.avhd files). You can return to a previous snapshot of a virtual machine's state by using the snapshot tree in Hyper-V Manager.

- Microsoft provides an export/import process to move virtual machine files and configuration files from one host computer to another.

- Microsoft developed the hypervisor to provide a secure environment for running guest operating systems. To ensure that the Hyper-V environment remains secure, apply Microsoft security updates to stay ahead of security vulnerabilities. Assign permissions to disk resources to minimize unwanted access, and remove unneeded virtual hard disks.

Key Terms

.avhd files   Files used by Hyper-V to save snapshot images.

assigned memory   In Hyper-V, the amount of memory provided to a virtual machine.

automatic start delay   In Hyper-V, the number of seconds that the automatic start of a virtual machine is delayed when the host computer is started.

bottleneck   A situation in which performance is limited by a single resource.

CPU usage   In Hyper-V, the reported percentage of CPU resources allocated to a virtual machine.

globally unique identifier (GUID)   A unique reference number represented by a 32-character hexadecimal string.

memory balancer   In Hyper-V, the process that allocates a memory resource to multiple running virtual machines.

memory demand   In Hyper-V, the reported memory requested by the virtual machine.

memory pressure   In Hyper-V, the ratio of how much memory a virtual machine has to how much it wants.

memory status   In Hyper-V, a field that indicates the memory condition of a running virtual machine.

memory weight   In Hyper-V, a scheme to determine which virtual machine is next in line to receive the allocated amount of limited memory.

performance baseline   The level of performance you can reliably expect during typical usage and workloads; future performance is measured against the baseline.

Performance Monitor   A Microsoft tool that reports data for internal counters used by the Windows operating system. Counter data is often shown in the form of a graph.

snapshot   In Hyper-V, an image of a virtual machine at a particular point in time.

target memory   A calculation by Hyper-V that indicates the ideal amount of memory for a running virtual machine.

Review Questions

1. The _____ specifies the amount of memory required when a virtual machine starts.

   a. released memory

   b. startup memory

   c. target memory

   d. memory pressure

2. The goal of dynamic memory is to calculate the _____ .

    a.   released memory

    b.   startup memory

    c.   target memory

    d.   memory pressure

3. _____ is another way to calculate the amount of memory needed by a virtual machine.

    a.   Released memory

    b.   Startup memory

    c.   Target memory

    d.   Memory pressure

4. The memory balancer _____ . (Choose all correct answers.)

    a.   uses information from the guest operating system

    b.   balances memory between running virtual machines

    c.   removes memory from running virtual machines

    d.   uses the memory weight when memory is not available to determine the priority for memory allocation

5. The _____ column in the Information pane of Hyper-V Manager shows the amount of memory the virtual machine needs.

    a.   Memory Pressure

    b.   Assigned Memory

    c.   Target Memory

    d.   Released Memory

6. The Memory Status column in the Information pane can contain which of the following states? (Choose all correct answers.)

    a.   OK

    b.   Low

    c.   Error

    d.   Warning

7. A _____ is a thread that can be scheduled on any logical processor on the host computer.

    a.   hyper-processor

    b.   hyper-thread

    c.   guest processor

    d.   virtual processor

8. The virtual machine limit _____ .

   a. specifies the number of virtual processors assigned to a virtual machine

   b. restricts the percentage of processors used in a Hyper-V environment

   c. specifies the percentage of a processor to assign to a virtual machine

   d. restricts the number of processors in a Hyper-V environment

9. The relative weight _____ . (Choose all correct answers.)

   a. permits one virtual machine to be favored over another

   b. is a number between 1 and 10,000

   c. has a default setting of 5,000

   d. allows a virtual machine to gain memory

10. The CPU Usage values displayed in the Information pane are calculated from _____ . (Choose all correct answers.)

    a. virtual machine activity in the child partition

    b. virtual machine support from the parent partition

    c. hypervisor activity for the virtual machine

    d. hypervisor activity support for the parent partition

11. The _____ is the level of performance you can reliably expect during typical workloads.

12. A/n _____ slows down a virtual machine's performance.

13. Which of the following sequences do you use to specify settings in the Add Counters window?

    a. computers, performance objects, counters, and instances

    b. performance objects, counters, and instances

    c. performance objects, computers, counters, and instances

    d. computers, counters, and instances

14. Which of the following counters is used to monitor the performance of the Hyper-V Dynamic Memory Balancer? (Choose all correct answers.)

    a. Added Memory

    b. Removed Memory

    c. Memory Pressure

    d. Available Memory

15. Hyper-V supports which of the following types of network adapters? (Choose all correct answers.)

    a. Hyper-V virtual network adapters with emulated drivers

    b. Hyper-V virtual network adapters with synthetic drivers

    c. Hyper-V legacy network adapters with emulated drivers

    d. Hyper-V legacy network adapters with synthetic drivers

16. Which of the following counters is used to monitor the performance of the Hyper-V virtual IDE controller? (Choose all correct answers.)

    a. Read Bytes/sec

    b. Read Tracks/sec

    c. Write Bytes/sec

    d. Written Sectors/sec

17. When a snapshot is taken, Hyper-V captures a _____ . (Choose all correct answers.)

    a. configuration file

    b. registry file

    c. saved state file

    d. differencing disk

18. To return to a previous snapshot of a running virtual machine in the snapshot tree, you use the _____ option.

    a. previous

    b. return

    c. revert

    d. reverse

19. _____ is a step required to export a virtual machine. (Choose all correct answers.)

    a. Starting the virtual machine

    b. Stopping the virtual machine

    c. Sharing the export folder

    d. Providing a folder for the export

20. An option for importing a virtual machine is to _____ . (Choose all correct answers.)

    a. move or restore the virtual machine

    b. copy the virtual machine

    c. create a new GUID

    d. duplicate the files so the same virtual machine can be imported again

Case Projects

CASE PROJECTS

Case 3-1: Using Dynamic Memory

Your boss has been reading about dynamic memory and has asked you to write a nontechnical paper explaining how it can be optimized. In your paper, you should compare dynamic memory to a physical object.

Case 3-2: Using Integration Services

While viewing the Information pane in Hyper-V Manager, you see only the Assigned Memory values for the running Windows Server 2008 virtual machine. What will you do to correct the problem?

Case 3-3: Using Processors

You overhear two classmates discussing virtual and logical processors in the hallway outside your classroom. Your classmates know that the final exam will include a question about the differences between the two processors, and they turn to you for an answer. What will you tell them?

Case 3-4: Taking Snapshots

Your boss has asked you to make a presentation on snapshots at the next TechShare meeting. Create a one-page handout for your presentation.

chapter 4

Installing and Using Virtual Machine Manager

After reading this chapter and completing the exercises, you will be able to:

- Describe Virtual Machine Manager components
- Describe Virtual Machine Manager architecture
- Identify requirements for Virtual Machine Manager
- Install and configure a Virtual Machine Manager server
- Work with the Virtual Machine Manager administrator console

In this chapter, you will identify the hardware and software requirements for Virtual Machine Manager (VMM) R2 SP1, a Microsoft product that manages a series of host computers and virtual machines from a central console. From this point forward, the term *VMM* corresponds to Virtual Machine Manager 2008 R2 SP1. Next, you will build on your knowledge of Hyper-V to install and configure VMM. Finally, you will learn how VMM extends Hyper-V to manage a group of host computers and their virtual machines.

VMM provides the capability to manage virtualization components for an Infrastructure as a Service (IaaS) model of a private cloud. In successive chapters, you will add needed components to complete a working private cloud. VMM must be purchased from Microsoft, but the product helps you take a big step toward fulfilling the requirements for a working private cloud. You will gain the skills needed to scale up the private cloud to meet the needs of larger IT organizations.

Describing Virtual Machine Manager Components

VMM provides a comprehensive solution for managing Microsoft operating systems in a virtualization environment. VMM scales to manage hundreds of host computers running thousands of virtual machines. Figure 4-1 shows a typical implementation of the server roles for VMM. At the center of the figure, the VMM server functions as the controller of the virtual

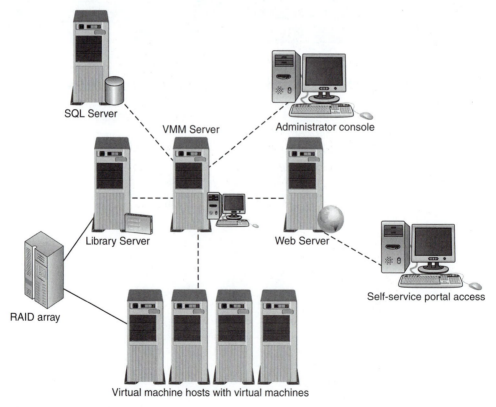

SQL Server

VMM Server

Administrator console

Library Server

Web Server

RAID array

Self-service portal access

Virtual machine hosts with virtual machines

Figure 4-1 Typical VMM implementation

© *Cengage Learning 2014*

management environment. Access to the VMM servers is through the VMM administrator console.

The VMM server provides a number of services, including management of the host computers. To perform these management tasks, such as creating virtual machines, jobs are created by VMM in Windows PowerShell and then run. **PowerShell** is a Microsoft scripting language that interfaces with the operating system to perform most management tasks.

Microsoft SQL Server provides the database to store various configurations. The library server manages the virtual hard disks, which are typically stored on a storage area network (SAN) for access by the host computers and virtual machines. Microsoft Internet Information Server (IIS) supports a VMM self-service portal that provides Web access to the VMM environment; from the Internet Explorer Web browser, users can create and manage their virtual machines in a controlled environment. The VMM self-service portal provides access to the virtual machines supporting the private cloud. Of course, the virtual machine hosts provide virtualization to run the guest operating systems. You will learn more about these components later in this section.

The consolidated VMM implementation used in this textbook is shown in Figure 4-2. Other than the hosts for the virtual machines, the various server roles have been consolidated on

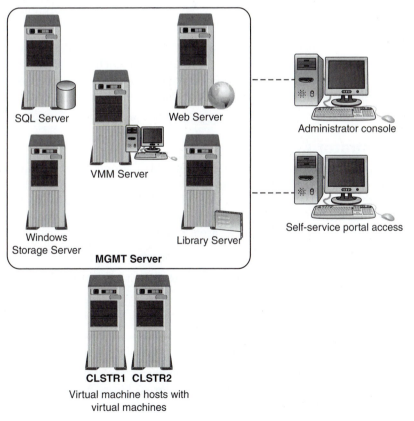

Figure 4-2 Consolidated VMM implementation

the management (MGMT) server. Windows Storage Server, a Microsoft implementation for iSCSI-based SAN storage, replaces the RAID device. The two host computers (CLSTR1 and CLSTR2) continue to provide the virtualization services to run the virtual machines. You will build this configuration as you work through this chapter and succeeding chapters, and you will finish the configuration with the component installations in Chapter 6.

VMM Server and VMM Database

The VMM server component is crucial to the VMM environment, and it should be the first component installed. Within the VMM server is the VMM engine, which connects to the VMM database. The VMM database stores all of the configuration and management information that VMM requires. The VMM engine performs three major tasks:

- It handles requests for information and updates to the VMM database. For example, when the VMM console needs information, the VMM engine contacts the VMM database for the data.

- It communicates and executes commands with the VMM agents on the host computers. Such commands include requesting that a VMM agent start a virtual machine on a host computer.

- It coordinates the execution of VMM jobs. Every operation in the VMM environment is handled by a VMM job. In addition, the VMM engine monitors jobs and reports their progress, and informs you whether the jobs succeed or fail.

The VMM database is a Microsoft SQL database. When you install the VMM server in Activity 4-2, you will use SQL Server 2005 Express Edition SP3. The VMM setup procedure will define the **database schema**, which specifies the database fields and attributes. Because the VMM engine interacts with the Microsoft SQL database, you will not need to interact with the database directly.

VMM Administrator Console

Use the VMM administrator console to manage the VMM environment (see Figure 4-3). The console resembles Hyper-V Manager and has three panes. The pane on the left side of the window contains three sections that let you control the information shown in the console. Depending on the management view you select at the bottom of this pane, the entire console window changes. The VMM administrator console has five management views:

- *Hosts view*—Use this view to manage the host computers that run the virtual machines.

- *Virtual Machines view*—Use this view to manage and change the settings for individual virtual machines.

- *Library view*—This view lists the resources for building virtual machines.

- *Jobs view*—This view lists the status of the current running jobs and the history of past jobs.

- *Administration view*—This view includes the administrative components of VMM. For example, it shows graphs for four summary categories: Hosts, Virtual Machines, Recent Jobs, and Library Resources.

If you select the Hosts view, the pane on the left side of the console contains Host Groups and Filters sections in addition to the management views. Because all of the hypervisors are

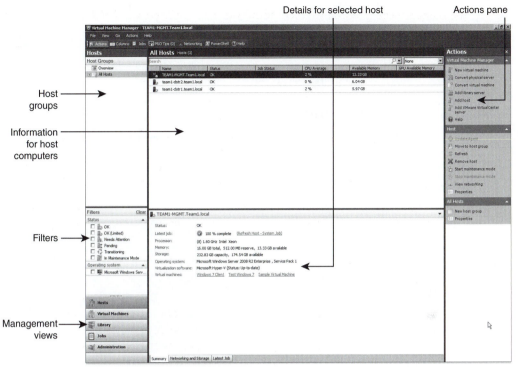

Figure 4-3 Hosts view of administrator console

Source: Microsoft Virtual Machine Manager 2008 R2 SP1, Windows Server 2008 R2 SP1

Hyper-V, you can select All Hosts as the host group. In the Filters section, you can limit the number of hosts to view. Filters are useful if you are managing a large number of hosts and you want to limit the number shown to meet a particular criterion, such as Needs Attention.

Note that the filters change depending on the view you choose. For example, if you choose the Jobs view, the filters allow you to display particular jobs created by the VMM engine.

If you have selected the Hosts view, the middle section of the console displays information about host computers. The top half of the section shows the Hyper-V hosts that are being managed by VMM. The bottom half of the section displays detailed information about the selected host computer.

As with the other two panes, the Actions pane on the right side of the console changes depending on the view you select. If you have selected the Hosts view, you can use the Virtual Machine Manager options to perform global tasks, such as adding host computers. Use the Host section to work with individual host computers and view the network connections to a particular host computer. The All Hosts section deals with host groups and permits you to segment a large number of host computers, which would be useful if you needed to create geographical groups.

Figure 4-4 shows how the administrator console looks when you select a running virtual machine in the Virtual Machines view. The basic layout of this management view is similar

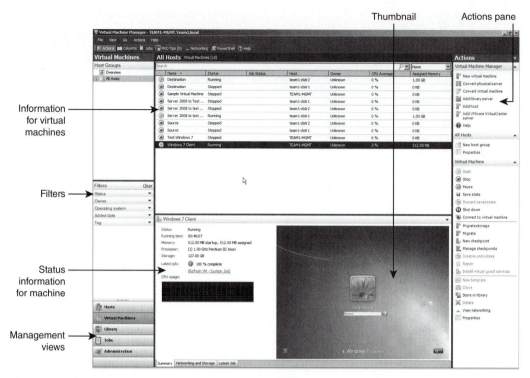

Figure 4-4 Virtual Machines view of administrator console

Source: Microsoft Virtual Machine Manager 2008 R2 SP1, Windows Server 2008 R2 SP1/Windows 7 Enterprise

to that of the Hosts view. The status information for the selected virtual machine includes a graph of CPU usage. By double-clicking the thumbnail of the virtual machine, you can open a connection to it. The bottom section of the Actions pane contains virtual machine options that are very similar to those in Hyper-V Manager.

The Library view is shown in Figure 4-5. This view follows the familiar layout of the other views. You will learn to use this view in the next chapter to deploy virtual machines in the cloud.

Use the Jobs view (see Figure 4-6) to see the status of jobs created by the VMM engine to perform various management tasks. You learn how to use this view in the next chapter.

Figure 4-7 shows the Administration view, which includes graphs for four summary categories: Hosts, Virtual Machines, Recent Jobs, and Library Resources. You will learn to use this view in Chapter 9.

Windows PowerShell Interface

Before the VMM engine can perform management tasks, such as the addition of host computers, jobs must be created in Windows PowerShell and run to perform these tasks. Microsoft describes PowerShell as a task-based command-line shell and scripting language designed especially for system administration. Because PowerShell is built on the **.NET Framework**, a

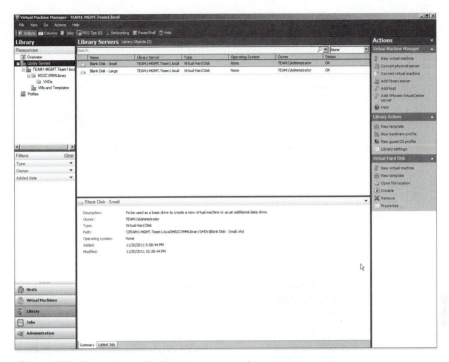

Figure 4-5 Library view of administrator console

Source: Microsoft Virtual Machine Manager 2008 R2 SP1, Windows Server 2008 R2 SP1

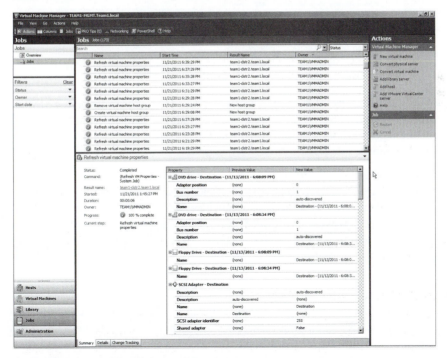

Figure 4-6 Jobs view of administrator console

Source: Microsoft Virtual Machine Manager 2008 R2 SP1, Windows Server 2008 R2 SP1

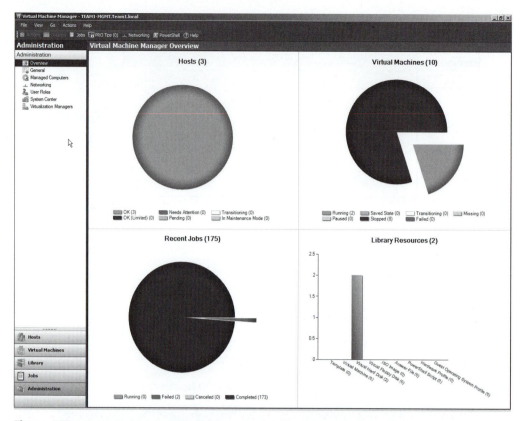

Figure 4-7 Administration view of administrator console

Source: Microsoft Virtual Machine Manager 2008 R2 SP1, Windows Server 2008 R2 SP1

library of software that provides access to operating system functionality, VMM has access to the required Windows Server 2008 resources to manage the VMM environment. To perform these management tasks, PowerShell provides a wide range of **cmdlets**, small scripting commands that can be invoked in PowerShell scripts.

The VMM wizards allow you to display these generated scripts by clicking the View Script button on any wizard summary page. For example, Figure 4-8 shows the generated script to add a new virtual machine. Although you can view a script to see how VMM performs a task, you do not need to write PowerShell scripts. In Chapter 10, you will learn to extend PowerShell scripts to automate tasks. For example, you will extend a script that creates one virtual machine to create multiple virtual machines.

VMM Agents

VMM communicates with the VMM agents installed on the host computers, and it provides an automatic method for deploying remote agents. When host computers are added to the VMM environment from the VMM administrator console, a job is run to deploy the agents to the selected host computers. The only requirement is that the host computer be a member of the same Active Directory domain with the appropriate user credentials.

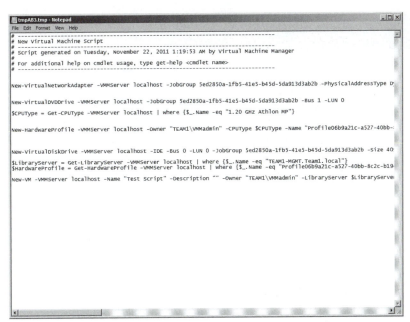

Figure 4-8 PowerShell script to add a new virtual machine

Source: Microsoft Notepad, Windows Server 2008 R2 SP1

VMM Library

The VMM library is the central location for the building blocks necessary to construct virtual machines. Rapid provisioning takes advantage of the VMM library to deploy virtual machines in the private cloud. A hardware profile, software profile, and stored image are combined to construct a new virtual machine in a matter of minutes; the same operation might take several hours using conventional operating system installations. The library can be used to store all file-based resources, including virtual hard disks, ISO images, operating system and hardware profiles, and PowerShell scripts.

VMM Self-Service Portal

The VMM self-service portal provides Web access to the VMM environment. From the Internet Explorer Web browser, users can create and manage their virtual machines in the private cloud in a controlled environment. You can create self-service roles from the VMM administrator console to control this access. Figure 4-9 shows the Virtual Machine Permissions window; you can use it to select permissions to tailor a self-service role for a remote user. You will learn more about the self-service portal in Chapter 6.

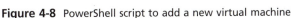

VMM Architecture

In this section, you will learn about the communications protocols and port assignments used by VMM system components. This information is useful when you need to troubleshoot problems in the VMM environment. Figure 4-10 shows the communications protocols used between the various VMM system components.

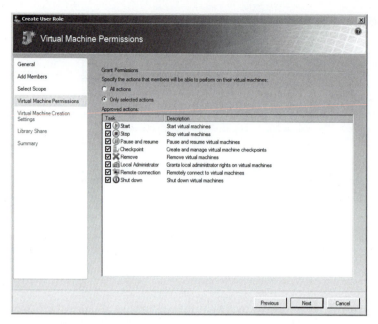

Figure 4-9　Self-service Virtual Machine Permissions window

Source: Microsoft Virtual Machine Manager 2008 R2 SP1, Windows Server 2008 R2 SP1

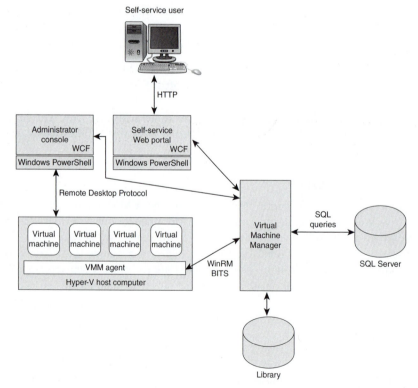

Figure 4-10　VMM communications between components

© Cengage Learning 2014

VMM Protocols

VMM combines a number of Microsoft communications protocols and Internet protocols to communicate between components. The central hub of these communications is the VMM server. The following list summarizes VMM communications and the protocols used:

- VMM communicates with VMM agents on the host computers using **Windows Remote Management (WinRM)**, the Microsoft implementation of the **WS-Management protocol**, which is a public standard for remotely exchanging management data between computers. VMM always initiates this communication by polling for information or sending commands.

- VMM uses the **Background Intelligent Transfer Service (BITS)** for transferring data files between server roles. BITS maximizes the transfer of files between machines using idle network bandwidth.

- For communications between the VMM server, administrator console, and PowerShell cmdlets, VMM uses the **Windows Communication Foundation (WCF)**. Microsoft describes the WCF as a part of the .NET Framework for rapidly building Internet applications, such as online sales and order tracking, customer relations management, and health management.

- VMM uses the **Remote Desktop Protocol (RDP)** to connect to a virtual machine and provide a console session to the user. The RDP was developed by Microsoft to provide a GUI from a connected remote computer.

- For private cloud users, VMM uses the **HyperText Transfer Protocol (HTTP)**, an Internet protocol for the transmission and formatting of Web pages. For secured Web pages, VMM uses **HyperText Transfer Protocol Secure (HTTPS)**, which is the secure version of HTTP.

Table 4-1 shows the communication ports required by VMM. As you run the setup procedure to install VMM, the required ports are opened in the Windows firewall. The default communication ports will work.

VMM Components	Network Port	Protocol
VMM server	80	HTTP, WinRM
	443	BITS
	8100	WCF
SQL Server	1433	Remote SQL
	1434	SQL Browser
Windows host	80	HTTP, WinRM
	443	BITS
	3389	RDP
Hyper-V host	2179	RDP port listener
Self-service portal	80	HTTP
	443	HTTPS

Table 4-1 Default network ports used by VMM

Identifying Requirements for Virtual Machine Manager

VMM is Microsoft's suite of management tools for the virtualized environment of Hyper-V host computers. This section outlines the hardware and software that is required to implement the VMM environment.

Requirements for VMM Server

You can install VMM on a single computer; this minimal configuration can serve up to 10 host computers. For heavier workloads, Microsoft recommends that the server roles be distributed on dedicated computers.

Table 4-2 contains information that you could use to plan for the installation of the VMM server role on up to 150 host computers.

Table 4-3 lists the software that must be installed prior to installing the VMM server. You will accomplish these tasks in Activity 4-1.

The VMM administrator console is normally installed on the VMM server or any accessible computer running the Windows Server 2008 Standard or Enterprise edition. However, you could install the console on a desktop computer that is running Windows 7 Enterprise.

Requirements for VMM Database Server

VMM uses a Microsoft SQL Server database to store data for the managed virtual machines, host computers, jobs, and other related data. This data is the basis for the information that you view in the VMM administrator console. You have a number of choices when selecting the location of this SQL server. For example, you can select an existing local or remote supported version, or you can allow the VMM setup procedure to install SQL Server 2005 Express Edition SP3. For this version of SQL Server 2005, the database is limited to 4 GB, but the version can support up to 150 host computers.

Number of Host Computers	Hardware Component	Minimum	Recommended
Up to 10 hosts	Processor	Dual-core 2 GHz (x64)	Quad-core 2 GHz (x64) or greater
	RAM	4 GB	6 GB
	Hard disk space	100 GB	200 GB
11 to 20 hosts	Processor	Dual-core 2.4 GHz (x64)	Quad-core 2.4 GHz (x64) or greater
	RAM	4 GB	8 GB
	Hard disk space	100 GB	200 GB
21 to 150 hosts	Processor	Dual-core 2.8 GHz (x64)	Quad-core 2.8 GHz (x64) or greater
	RAM	4 GB	8 GB
	Hard disk space	100 GB	200 GB

Table 4-2 Minimum and recommended hardware requirements for VMM server

Software Requirements	Installed Component	How Installed
Operating system	Windows Server 2008 R2 SP1	OS installation
Windows PowerShell 2.0	Windows Server 2008 R2 SP1	OS installation
Windows Remote Management (WinRM)	Windows Server 2008 R2 SP1	OS installation
Microsoft .NET Framework 3.0 SP1	Windows Server 2008 R2 SP1	OS installation
Windows Automated Installation Kit (WAIK) 1.1	VMM	VMM 2008 R2 installations
Windows Server Internet Information Services (IIS)	Windows Server 2008 R2 SP1	You must install with required role services
Microsoft SQL Server	VMM	VMM 2008 R2 installs Microsoft SQL Server Express

Table 4-3 Software requirements for VMM server

© *Cengage Learning 2014*

Requirements for VMM Library Server

If a VMM object is not stored in the SQL database, it is stored on the VMM library server. You can expect to find a wide range of files stored on this server:

- *Virtual machine templates*—Standardized hardware and software settings, including an installed OS that can be used to provision virtual machines in the private cloud

- *Virtual hard disk*—Virtualized hard disk with a file system

- *Virtual floppy disk*—Virtualized floppy disk with a file system

- *PowerShell scripts*—Programs written to use the PowerShell cmdlets to perform tasks with the Windows Server 2008 operating system

- *Hardware profiles*—Hardware settings that will be used by a virtual machine

- *Guest operating system profiles*—Operating system settings to ensure constant configurations for virtual machines

- *Stored virtual machines*—Virtual machines that have been removed from the hard disks of host computers and stored in the library

When you install VMM, the setup procedure automatically adds the management computer as the default library server with a default library share of "MSSCVMMLibrary." Because you cannot delete or rename it, be careful when specifying the location and name for the default library share. After you complete the setup procedure, you can add more library shares. To support the large number of files needed by the private cloud environment, you will add iSCSI storage as a library share. You will install Windows Storage Server to provide the iSCSI storage in Chapter 8.

Requirements for VMM Self-Service Portal

The VMM self-service portal requires a Web server with Windows Server IIS. This is available as a role service from Windows Server 2008 R2 SP1. You will add the Web Server IIS role and then install the following server role services:

- *IIS 6 Metabase Compatibility*—This service supports the IIS repository so that you can run applications and scripts written in earlier versions of IIS.

- *IIS 6 WMI Compatibility*—This service provides **Windows Management Instrumentation (WMI)** scripting interfaces to run scripts that manage and automate tasks. WMI allows operating system information to be shared with management software.

- *Static Content*—With this service, IIS can publish static HTML pages and image files.

- *Default Document*—IIS is provided a default file to use when users do not specify a file in a URL.

- *Directory Browsing*—Users see the contents of a directory on your IIS server.

- *HTTP Errors*—Error messages are returned to users' browsers when IIS detects an error.

- *ASP.NET*—This service provides a programming environment for building Web sites and Web applications.

- *.NET Extensibility*—Programmers can use this service to write Web applications with extended functionality.

- *ISAPI Extensions*—This service provides support for programmers to develop dynamic Web content.

- *ISAPI Filters*—A link is provided between incoming requests and the programs developed to support the requests.

In Chapter 6, you will work with the self-service Web portal to access virtual machines running in the private cloud.

Requirements for PowerShell CLI

The PowerShell command-line interface (CLI) is implemented as a support component for scripting on computers running Windows Server 2008. The administrator console and self-service portal are built using PowerShell components. The VMM PowerShell CLI component is installed as the administrator console is installed.

Requirements for VMM Virtual Machine Hosts

The Hyper-V virtualization environment used in this textbook, Windows Server 2008 R2 SP1, is fully supported by VMM. Support also exists for other virtualization environments, such as Microsoft Virtual Server 2005 and VMware ESXi Server, but these environments are beyond the scope of this textbook.

When you install the VMM server, you specify which ports will be used for communication between the VMM server components. As you are installing VMM on a computer using the Windows firewall, the setup procedure automatically configures these firewall port exceptions.

Network Requirements for VMM

As virtual machines run, the virtual hard disk files can grow from 4 GB to as large as 15 GB, depending on the operating system, applications, and services. For this reason, Microsoft recommends network connections of 1 gigabit (Gb). In addition, a SAN device is needed to store the virtual hard disk files in the private cloud. You will implement SAN storage in Chapter 8.

The computer you select to run VMM must be a member of a domain in Active Directory Domain Services. Microsoft recommends using a domain controller that is at the Windows

Server 2008 domain functional level. The domain controller you installed in Chapter 2 meets this functional level.

Installing and Configuring a Virtual Machine Manager Server

In this section, you will first prepare to install VMM. Next, you will scan the management server with the VMM Configuration Analyzer, a tool that informs you of potential hardware and software problems that could affect the installation and operation of VMM. Next, you will deploy the VMM server with the necessary software support. The last task is to install the VMM administrator console so that you can communicate with VMM.

Using the VMM Configuration Analyzer

Microsoft provides a VMM Configuration Analyzer to verify that the computer you choose to become the VMM server is compliant. Before running the VMM Configuration Analyzer, you must install the Microsoft Baseline Configuration Analyzer (MBCA), which analyzes a computer to determine if it is properly configured to run the VMM server. Figure 4-11 shows a scan run by the VMM Configuration Analyzer. Because the management server will

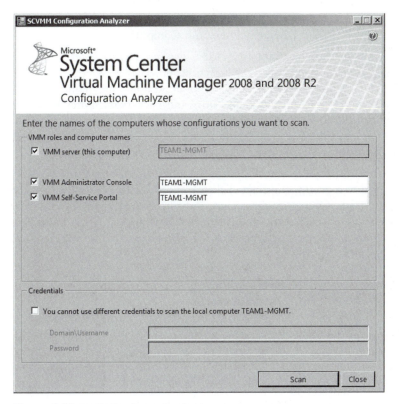

Figure 4-11 VMM Configuration Analyzer

Source: Microsoft Virtual Machine Manager 2008 R2 SP1, Windows Server 2008 R2 SP1

run each of the three VMM roles, leave the check boxes checked. To start the scan, click Scan. After a few minutes, a report will be displayed in Internet Explorer. A common error is to forget to install Windows IIS or a role service. If you do, you must rerun the scan. When you see a message that no configuration issues were found, the management server is ready to install VMM.

Activity 4-1: Verifying the Management Computer

Time Required: 30 minutes

Objective: Verify that the management server is ready to install VMM.

Description: In this activity, your team takes care of several issues prior to analyzing the management computer. You will create a user account to administer VMM and install Windows IIS. Next, you will install the Microsoft Baseline Configuration Analyzer, which is required by the VMM Configuration Analyzer. Finally, you will install and run the VMM Configuration Analyzer.

Table 4-4 provides the team member assignments for this activity.

1. Switch the KVM switch to port 1.

2. Log on to your MGMT server with a username of *Team1\Administrator*, substituting your team name for *Team1*. Enter a password of **P@ssw0rd**.

3. To open Active Directory Users and Computers, click **Start**, point to **Administrative Tools**, and then click **Active Directory Users and Computers**.

4. To create an administrator account for VMM, expand *Team1.local*, substituting your team name for *Team1*. Click **Users**, click **Action**, point to **New**, and click **User**. Enter **VMM** in the First name text box, enter **Admin** in the Last name text box, enter **VMMAdmin** in the User logon name text box, and click **Next**. Enter **P@ssw0rd** in the Password text box, and enter **P@ssw0rd** in the Confirm password text box. Clear the **User must change password at next logon** check box, check **User cannot change password**, check **Password never expires**, click **Next**, and then click **Finish**.

5. To place the VMMAdmin account in the proper administrator groups, right-click **VMM Admin**, click **Add to a group**, and then click **Advanced**. Click **Find Now**, scroll and click **Administrators**, click **OK**, and then click **Advanced**. Click **Find Now**, scroll and click **Domain Admins**, click **OK**, and then click **Advanced**. Click **Find Now**, scroll and click **Enterprise Admins**, and then click **OK** three times. Close the Active Directory Users and Computers window.

Team Member	Steps	Host Computer
1	1–3	MGMT
2	4	
3	5–9	
1	10–16	

Table 4-4   Team member assignments for Activity 4-1

6. To install Windows Internet Information Services, click the **Server Manager** icon, expand **Roles**, click **Add Roles**, and click **Server Roles**. Click **Application Server**, click **Add Required Features**, click **Web Server (IIS)**, and click **Next** twice. Click **Web Server (IIS) Support**, click **Add Required Role Services**, click **Role Services** under Web Server (IIS), scroll and click **IIS 6 Management Compatibility**, click **Next**, and then click **Install**.

 You can ignore the Windows Update warning message.

7. Wait for the installation to be completed, and then click **Close**.

8. To configure Internet Explorer to access Internet Web sites, click Server Manager (**TEAM1-MGMT**), substituting your team name for *TEAM1*. Click **Configure IE ESC**, click the **Administrators Off** option button, and then click **OK**.

9. To set up Internet Explorer 8 for first-time use, click **Start** and then click **Internet Explorer**. Click **Next**, click **No, don't turn on**, click **Next**, click **Use express settings**, and then click **Finish**.

 You can ignore the caution message that Internet Explorer Enhanced Security Configuration is not enabled.

10. Close the Internet Explorer window.

11. To download and install the Microsoft Baseline Configuration Analyzer, click **Start**, click **Internet Explorer**, enter **Download Microsoft Baseline Configuration Analyzer** in the search box, and press **Enter**. Click the **Microsoft Baseline Configuration Analyzer** link, click **Download** next to MBCASetup64.msi, click **Run** twice, and click **Next**. Click **I accept the terms in the License Agreement**, click **Next** three times, click **Install**, and then click **Finish**. Close the Internet Explorer and Notepad windows.

 The VMM Configuration Analyzer requires the first version of the MBCA. If you installed version 2, contact your instructor.

12. To download and install the VMM Configuration Analyzer, click **Start**, click **Internet Explorer**, enter **Download VMM Configuration Analyzer** in the search box, and press **Enter**. Click the first Microsoft link that downloads the VMM Configuration Analyzer. (Do not click the Microsoft Baseline Configuration Analyzer 2.0 link.) Scroll and click **Download**, click **Run** twice, and click **Next**. Click **I accept the terms of this agreement**, click **Next** twice, and click **Install**. Click **Finish**. Close the Internet windows.

13. To reset the port for the default Web page, click **Start**, point to **Administrative Tools**, and click **Internet Information Services (IIS) Manager**. Expand *TEAM1*-MGMT (*TEAM1*\Administrator), substituting your team name for *TEAM1*. Expand **Sites**, right-click **Default Web Site**, click **Edit Bindings**, and click the http entry. Click **Edit**, enter 8080 for the port, click **OK**, click **Close**, and then close the Internet Information Services (IIS) Manager window.

14. To run the VMM Configuration Analyzer, click **Start**, click **Configuration Analyzer**, and then click **Scan**.

 If you do not see a message that no configuration issues were found, contact your instructor.

15. Close Internet Explorer and the SCVMM Configuration Analyzer window. Minimize the Server Manager window.

16. Leave the MGMT computer logged on for additional activities.

Deploying the VMM Server

You must make a number of decisions before you install the VMM server. Most notably, you must decide what version of Microsoft SQL Server to use; SQL Server 2005 Express Edition SP3 meets the requirements. You also must decide where to store the files required by the virtual machines. The default library share will be sufficient until a second library share for the iSCSI storage is implemented in Chapter 8.

The VMM server is the cornerstone of the VMM environment. The installation wizard helps you install the server, as explained in Activity 4-2.

Activity 4-2: Installing the VMM Server

Time Required: 45 minutes

Objective: Install VMM R2 SP1.

Description: In this activity, your team installs the VMM server.

Table 4-5 provides the team member assignments for this activity.

1. If necessary, switch the KVM switch to port 1.

2. If necessary, log on to your MGMT server with a username of **Team1\Administrator**, substituting your team name for *Team1*. Enter a password of **P@ssw0rd**.

3. To start the installation, insert the VMM DVD, click **Run setup.exe**, and click **VMM Server**. Wait for the temporary files to be expanded and copied.

4. To accept the end-user license agreement (EULA), click **I accept the terms of this agreement**, and then click **Next**.

5. To avoid participation in the **Customer Experience Improvement Program (CEIP)**, which collects and sends data anonymously about the usage of the product, click **No, I am not willing to participate**, and then click **Next**.

Team Member	Steps	Host Computer
1	1–13	MGMT
2	14–16	

Table 4-5 Team member assignments for Activity 4-2

© Cengage Learning 2014

6. Enter **VMM Admin** as your username. You can also enter an organization name, but it is not required. Click **Next**.

7. Wait for the hardware and software prerequisites to be checked. These prerequisites were met when the VMM Configuration Analyzer scan was completed successfully in Activity 4-1. When the check is complete, click **Next**.

8. Review the default location for the program files, and then click **Next**.

9. The next window asks you which version and configuration of SQL Server to use. Click **Install SQL Server 2005 Express Edition SP3**, and then click **Next**.

10. To create the initial library share, click **Create a new library share**, and then click **Next**.

11. To specify the VMM service account, click **Other account**, and then enter *Team1* **VMMAdmin** for the username and domain, substituting your team name for *Team1*. You created the VMMAdmin account in Activity 4-1; you need to use it here for security reasons. Enter **P@ssw0rd** for the password, and then click **Next**.

12. Review the configuration settings. If necessary, click **Previous** to return to previous windows of the wizard and make changes. When you finish, click **Install**.

13. Wait for the installation to be completed.

If you do not see a message that the Virtual Machine Manager server installation was completed successfully, contact your instructor.

14. When prompted to check for the latest Virtual Machine Manager updates, leave the check box selected; you want to receive the latest updates. Click **Close**.

If you have the time, you can install the Windows updates. These updates may take one hour or more, depending on the distribution of the VMM software you are using.

15. The Windows Update window appears. If you have the time, click **Install updates**. Click **I accept the license terms**, and then click **Finish**.

16. Leave the MGMT computer logged on for additional activities.

Installing the VMM Administrator Console

The next task is to install a client to communicate with VMM. This short installation is similar to the VMM server installation.

Activity 4-3: Installing the VMM Console

Time Required: 20 minutes

Objective: Install the VMM administrator console.

Description: In this activity, your team installs and configures the VMM administrator console.

Table 4-6 provides the team member assignments for this activity.

Team Member	Steps	Host Computer
1	1–4	MGMT
2	5–11	
3	12–15	
1	16–21	

Table 4-6 Team member assignments for Activity 4-3

© Cengage Learning 2014

1. If necessary, switch the KVM switch to port 1.

2. If necessary, log on to your MGMT server with a username of *Team1*\Administrator, substituting your team name for *Team1*. Enter a password of **P@ssw0rd**.

3. Switch the KVM switch to port 2.

4. Log on to your CLSTR1 server with a username of *Team1*\Administrator, substituting your team name for *Team1*. Enter a password of **P@ssw0rd**.

5. Switch the KVM switch to port 3.

6. Log on to your CLSTR2 server with a username of *Team1*\Administrator, substituting your team name for *Team1*. Enter a password of **P@ssw0rd**.

7. Switch the KVM switch to port 1.

8. To start the installation, remove and insert the VMM DVD, click **Run setup.exe**, and click **VMM Administrator Console**. Wait for the temporary files to be copied.

9. To accept the EULA, click **I accept the terms of this agreement**, and then click **Next**.

10. Click **Next** four times and then click **Install**.

11. Wait for the installation to be completed.

12. Uncheck **Check for latest Virtual Machine Manager Updates**, and then click **Close**.

13. Click **Exit**. Remove the VMM DVD.

14. To open the VMM console, double-click **SCVMM Admin Console**, leave the **Make this server my default** option checked, and then click **Connect**.

15. To add the host computers, click **Add host** in the Actions pane, and then enter *TEAM1***Administrator** for the User name, substituting your team name for *TEAM1*. Enter **P@ssw0rd** for the Password, click **Next**, and click **Search**. When the Computer Search window appears, click **Search**.

16. Click the first search entry, and then click **Add**.

17. Click the second search entry, and then click **Add**.

18. Click the third search entry, click **Add**, and then click **OK**.

19. To run the job that adds the host computers, click **Next**, click **Yes**, click **Next** twice, and then click **Add Hosts**.

20. Wait for the jobs to be completed.

If any jobs show a status of Failed, contact your instructor.

21. Leave the three host computers logged on for additional activities.

Working with the VMM Administrator Console

In this section, you build on the skills that you developed while running virtual machines in the Hyper-V Manager environment. Hyper-V Manager and the administrator console both manage the Hyper-V environment, so they are very similar. For example, when you select a virtual machine from the administrator console, you see a thumbnail of the running virtual machine. You can connect to the virtual machine by double-clicking the thumbnail.

Working with the Hosts View

The Hosts view, as shown in Figure 4-12, shows the three host computers you added in Activity 4-3. VMM manages these host computers.

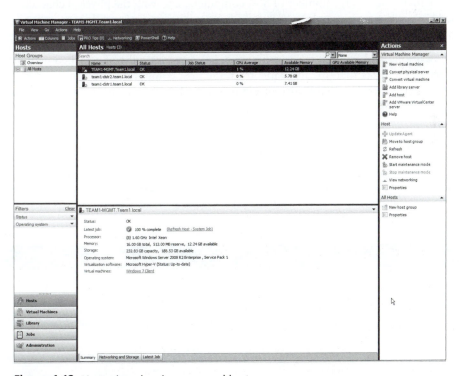

Figure 4-12 Hosts view showing managed hosts

Source: Microsoft Virtual Machine Manager 2008 R2 SP1, Windows Server 2008 R2 SP1

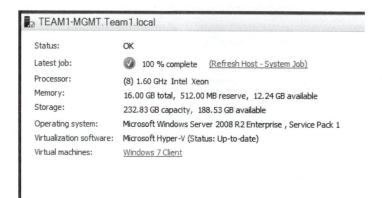

Figure 4-13 Summary details for selected host computer

Source: Microsoft Virtual Machine Manager 2008 R2 SP1, Windows Server 2008 R2 SP1

Figure 4-13 shows an example of the summary details pane, which displays status information and statistics for the selected host computer at the bottom of the Hosts view. A job runs automatically every 30 minutes to check the host computer's status. To refresh the status, click the Refresh Host – System Job link. A job will be run to contact the VMM agent on the host for the current status. Table 4-7 shows some of the status values that you might encounter.

If you are managing a large number of host computers, knowing the physical characteristics of a selected host computer is useful. For example, how much memory or disk space is available? The last line of the summary details pane lists the virtual machines assigned to the host computer.

The Networking and Storage tab (see Figure 4-14) provides a list of attached networks and a summary of the disks that are accessible from the host computer. You can use the disk information to verify that you have adequate disk space. To view this tab, click Networking and Storage at the bottom of the console window.

To check the status of the last job run, click the Latest Job tab at the bottom of the console window. Figure 4-15 shows status information that appears when you refresh a host.

If you need to manage a large number of host computers, you can use filters to display only the host computers that you need to use (see Figure 4-16). For example, to view host computers that need attention, click the Needs Attention check box. The filters are listed in the left pane of the console window.

Status Value	Description
OK	No issues exist with the host.
Needs Attention	A problem exists that requires corrective action.
In Maintenance Mode	You have placed the host computer in maintenance mode to apply updates or replace hardware.
Not Responding	The VMM server is unable to communicate with the VMM agent on the host computer.

Table 4-7 Examples of status values

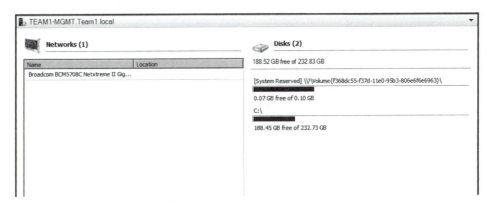

Figure 4-14 Networking and storage details for the selected host computer

Source: Microsoft Virtual Machine Manager 2008 R2 SP1, Windows Server 2008 R2 SP1

Figure 4-15 Job status information for the selected host computer

Source: Microsoft Virtual Machine Manager 2008 R2 SP1, Windows Server 2008 R2 SP1

Figure 4-16 Filters for host computers

Source: Microsoft Virtual Machine Manager 2008 R2 SP1, Windows Server 2008 R2 SP1

The Actions pane for the VMM console (see Figure 4-17) resembles the Actions pane in Hyper-V Manager. Table 4-8 shows some of the options that you might encounter.

The Host Properties window contains information about the selected host computer. Figure 4-18 shows information on the Summary tab. This tab presents less information than that shown in the summary details pane of the Hosts view.

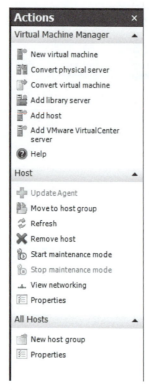

Figure 4-17 VMM Actions pane

Source: Microsoft Virtual Machine Manager 2008 R2 SP1, Windows Server 2008 R2 SP1

The Status tab, shown in Figure 4-19, is a good place to check on the health of communications between the VMM server and the VMM agents. Similar information is also available about Hyper-V virtualization on the host computer.

Action	Description
New virtual machine	Start the New Virtual Machine Wizard.
Convert physical server	Start the Physical to Virtual (P2V) Wizard.
Add library server	Add a new library server to store virtual machine building blocks.
Add host	Add a new host to be managed by VMM.
Remove host	Remove a host computer from the managed hosts.
Start maintenance mode	Indicate that a host server is unavailable to run virtual machines due to hardware or software maintenance.
View networking	Display a diagram that shows the network adapters and virtual switches with the connected virtual machines.
Properties	Display the Host Properties window, which is explained next.

Table 4-8 VMM Actions pane

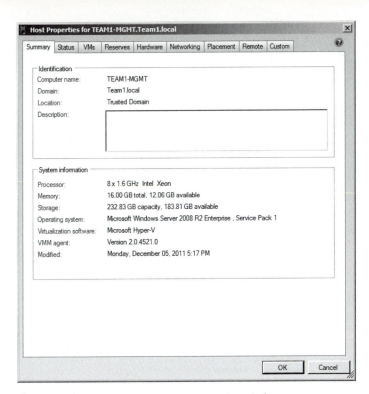

Figure 4-18 Summary tab of Host Properties window

Source: Microsoft Virtual Machine Manager 2008 R2 SP1, Windows Server 2008 R2 SP1

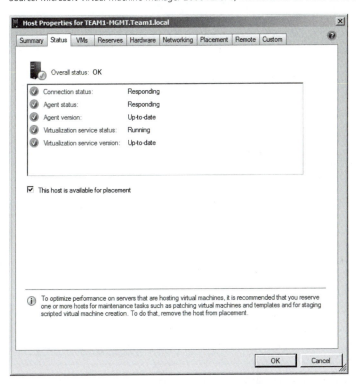

Figure 4-19 Status tab of Host Properties window

Source: Microsoft Virtual Machine Manager 2008 R2 SP1, Windows Server 2008 R2 SP1

To see summary information about the virtual machines placed on the host, click the VMs tab. Figure 4-20 shows the status of the Windows 7 Client virtual machine.

If you need to set aside resources for the version of Windows Server 2008 running in the parent partition, click the Reserves tab. From this tab, you can enter values for the reserves shown in Figure 4-21.

Of the remaining tabs, the Hardware tab provides a summary of the host machine's hardware. The Networking tab lists the virtual networks. To see the folder(s) that VMM uses for virtual machines, click the Placement tab. Click the Remote tab to view or change the port number that VMM uses to listen for remote connections. If you need to add a new property to a host, such as the city where the host computer resides, you can click the Custom tab.

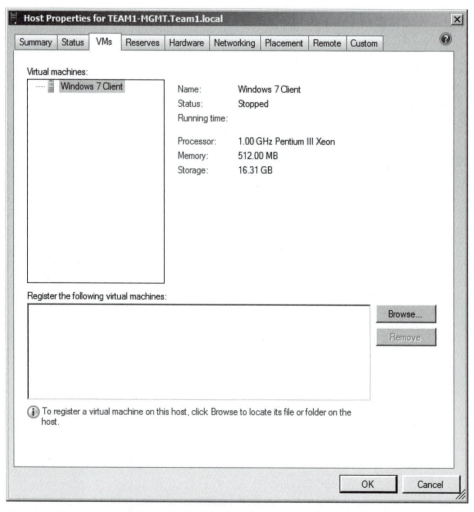

Figure 4-20 Virtual machine status shown in VMs tab of Host Properties window

Source: Microsoft Virtual Machine Manager 2008 R2 SP1, Windows Server 2008 R2 SP1

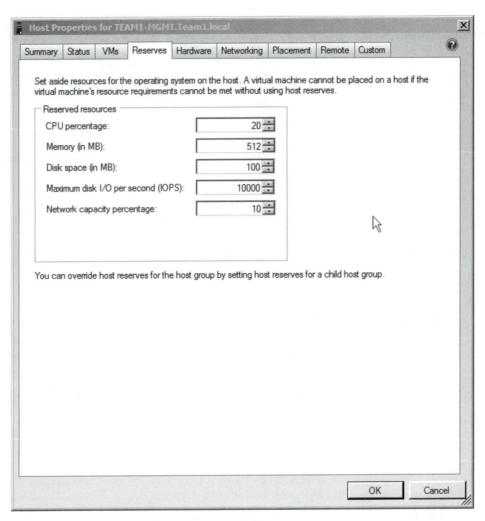

Figure 4-21 Reserves tab of Host Properties window

Source: Microsoft Virtual Machine Manager 2008 R2 SP1, Windows Server 2008 R2 SP1

Activity 4-4: Working with the Hosts View

Time Required: 15 minutes

Objective: Learn to use the major features of the VMM Hosts view.

Description: In this activity, your team works with the Hosts view of the VMM administrator console.

Table 4-9 provides the team member assignments for this activity.

1. If necessary, switch the KVM switch to port 1.

2. If necessary, log on to your MGMT server with a username of **Team1\Administrator**, substituting your team name for *Team1*. Enter a password of **P@ssw0rd**.

3. If necessary, switch the KVM switch to port 2.

Team Member	Steps	Host Computer	Team Member	Steps	Host Computer
1	1–13	CLSTR1	2	22, 3–13	CLSTR2
2	14–21		3	14–21	

Table 4-9   Team member assignments for Activity 4-4

© Cengage Learning 2014

4. If necessary, log on to your CLSTR1 server with a username of *Team1\Administrator*, substituting your team name for *Team1*. Enter a password of **P@ssw0rd**.

5. Switch the KVM switch to port 1.

6. If necessary, open the VMM console by double-clicking **SCVMM Admin Console**.

7. To select the host computer to manage, click the **Hosts** bar in the bottom-left corner of the console window, and then click *team1*-clstr1.*team1*.**local** in the list of computers, substituting your team name for *team1*.

8. To start a job to refresh the host properties, click **Refresh VM Properties – System Job** below the list of host computers.

9. Review the properties, and then click the **Hosts** bar.

10. To view the two networks and the disks on the host computer, click the **Networking and Storage** tab at the bottom of the console window.

11. To view the status of the job you started in Step 8, click the **Latest Job** tab at the bottom of the console window.

12. To view a diagram of the networks, click **View networking** in the Actions pane.

13. Review the network connections. Note that the Private VM Network is attached to the Server 2008 to Test Dynamic Memory virtual machine and the Server 2008 to Test RAID virtual machine. The Source and Destination virtual machines are attached to the internal network Test Network.

14. Close the Networking–Network Configuration window.

15. To view the host properties, click **Properties** in the Actions pane under Host.

16. Review the Summary tab in the Host Properties window. Verify that the amount of memory and storage is adequate to run virtual machines.

17. To check the status of the host computer, click the **Status** tab.

18. To see the status of the virtual machines placed on the host computer, click the **VMs** tab.

19. To list the hardware on the host computer, click the **Hardware** tab.

20. Close the Host Properties window.

21. Leave the host computer logged on for additional activities.

22. Repeat Steps 3 through 21 for CLSTR2, which is on port 3.

Working with the Virtual Machines View

The Virtual Machines view (see Figure 4-22) shows the virtual machines placed on the three host computers. To switch to this view from the Hosts view, click the Virtual Machines bar

Figure 4-22 Virtual Machines view

Source: Microsoft Virtual Machine Manager 2008 R2 SP1, Windows Server 2008 R2 SP1/Windows 7 Enterprise

in the bottom-left corner of the console window. Because All Hosts is selected in the left pane of the console window, all of the virtual machines are displayed. You could also expand All Hosts and select a particular host computer.

The filters in the left pane of the console window allow you to select criteria that control the display of virtual machines. Figure 4-23 shows the virtual machine filters you can select, and Table 4-10 describes the filters.

The columns in the All Hosts pane identify the contents of the listed virtual machines, as shown in Figure 4-22. You can click the column headings to sort the virtual machines in various ways. For example, to sort the virtual machines by hosts, click the Host column heading. Because the Windows 7 Client is the selected virtual machine in the figure, the bottom half of the All Hosts pane shows status information and a thumbnail for the client.

To access this client, double-click the thumbnail; the virtual machine appears in the Virtual Machine Viewer (see Figure 4-24). From this point, the virtual machine behaves like the Virtual Machine Connection tool in Hyper-V Manager. Click within the window to work with the virtual machine.

Note the Ctrl-Alt-Del and Full Screen options at the top of the Virtual Machine Viewer. When you click Full Screen, a small toolbar appears at the top of the screen. If you click the pushpin, the toolbar disappears. To make the toolbar reappear, click Full Screen twice.

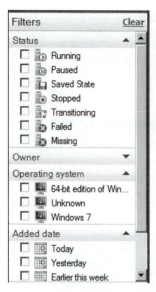

Figure 4-23 Virtual machine filters

Source: Microsoft Virtual Machine Manager 2008 R2 SP1, Windows Server 2008 R2 SP1

To verify the remote connection, click the lock. Use the window buttons to minimize, restore, or close the Virtual Machine Viewer window.

If you close the window, you terminate the connection to the virtual machine, although it continues to run. If you accidentally terminate the connection, you can return to the Virtual Machines view for the virtual machine and click the Connect to virtual machine option, or you can wait for the thumbnail to be re-established and double-click the thumbnail.

From the Actions pane in the Virtual Machines view, you will find familiar options such as Start, Stop, Pause, Shut down, and Connect to a virtual machine. The Actions pane also contains several options for **checkpoints**, which are very similar to the snapshots you learned about in Chapter 3. A checkpoint is an image of a virtual machine at a particular point in time. To create a checkpoint, click New checkpoint in the Actions pane.

Filter	Description
Running	The virtual machine is running.
Paused	The virtual machine is suspended and consuming memory resources.
Saved State	The virtual machine is suspended and memory is written to disk.
Stopped	The virtual machine is stopped and does not consume memory.
Transitioning	The job has the virtual machine under control.
Failed	The virtual machine failed to start.
Missing	The virtual machine has one or more missing components.

Table 4-10 Virtual machine status descriptions

© Cengage Learning 2014

Figure 4-24 Virtual Machine Viewer

Source: Microsoft Virtual Machine Manager 2008 R2 SP1, Windows Server 2008 R2 SP1/Windows 7 Enterprise

 See "Using Snapshots in a Test Environment" in Chapter 3 for additional information about snapshots.

As long as the host computer is running Hyper-V, there is one small difference between snapshots and checkpoints: When using checkpoints, you can add a comment to help identify them in the Description field, as shown in Figure 4-25. As with other tasks in VMM, a job is run to take the checkpoint. If you view a snapshot in Hyper-V Manager, you will not see the comment.

To see the checkpoints you have created, click Manage checkpoints in the Actions pane. Figure 4-26 shows a checkpoint on the Checkpoints tab of the Virtual Machine Properties window. Click the New button to create a new checkpoint in the current highlighted location. To remove a checkpoint, select it in the list and then click Remove. To restore a checkpoint, select it and then click Restore. To see additional information about a selected checkpoint, click the Properties button.

Figure 4-27 shows properties for a virtual machine. To view these properties, right-click a virtual machine and then click Properties from the menu that appears. You should be familiar

Figure 4-25 Creating a checkpoint with a comment

Source: Microsoft Virtual Machine Manager 2008 R2 SP1, Windows Server 2008 R2 SP1

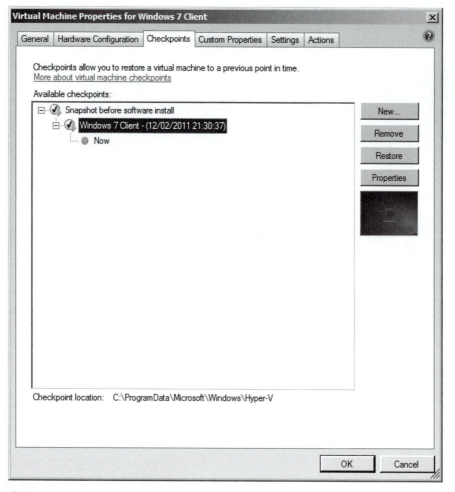

Figure 4-26 Checkpoint created

Source: Microsoft Virtual Machine Manager 2008 R2 SP1, Windows Server 2008 R2 SP1

Virtual Machine Properties for Windows 7 Client   [x]

| General | Hardware Configuration | Checkpoints | Custom Properties | Settings | Actions |

Name: Windows 7 Client

Description:

Computer name: TEAM1-WIN7

Owner: Select...

Cost center:

Tag: (none)

Type: Virtual Machine

Operating system: Windows 7

VM guest services: Detected

Added: Monday, November 21, 2011 1:32 PM

Modified: Friday, December 02, 2011 9:56 PM

Last refresh error: No Error

Last refresh time: Friday, December 02, 2011 10:00 PM

OK   Cancel

Figure 4-27 General tab of Virtual Machine Properties window

Source: Microsoft Virtual Machine Manager 2008 R2 SP1, Windows Server 2008 R2 SP1

with most of the information shown on the General tab, although one item requires further explanation. You can use the Owner text box to go to Active Directory and assign a username or security group to the virtual machine. You will learn about owners in Chapter 6.

The Hardware Configuration tab displays information about the virtual machine's hardware configuration, as shown in Figure 4-28. You should recognize most of this information from Hyper-V Manager, but note that VMM includes additional configuration settings.

When you scroll down the pane on the left, you will see three more Advanced options: Integration Services, Priority, and Availability. You can click a check box to activate each of the five Integration Services that are offered to the virtual machine: Operating system shutdown, Time synchronization, Data exchange, Heartbeat, and Backup by volume snapshot. By default, all five options are selected.

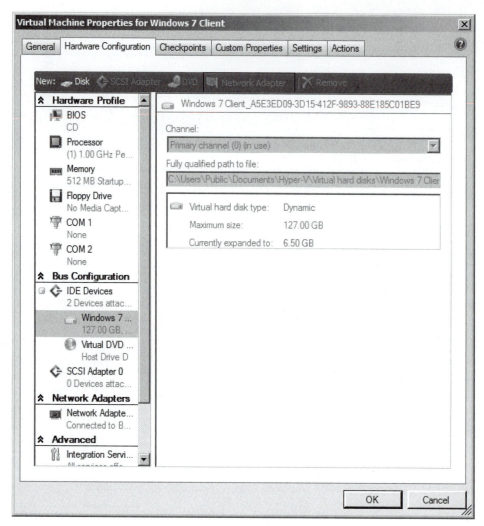

Figure 4-28 Hardware Configuration tab of Virtual Machine Properties window

Source: Microsoft Virtual Machine Manager 2008 R2 SP1, Windows Server 2008 R2 SP1

Use the Priority settings to specify the relative priority of memory or processor resources that are given to each virtual machine. When resource usage on a host computer is high, virtual machines with higher priority are allocated resources before virtual machines with lower priority. You can select a priority of High, Normal, or Low, or you can assign a custom priority. For memory resources, the lowest setting is 0 (low priority), the default value is 5,000 (normal priority), and the highest setting is 10,000 (high priority). For processor resources, the settings range from 0 to 10,000.

The Availability option allows you to place a virtual machine on a high-availability cluster. You will learn about this option in the next chapter.

If you need to add a new property, such as an application running on the virtual machine, you can click the Custom Properties tab and enter up to 10 properties. Use the Settings tab with the self-service portal to set a quota for the virtual machine. (See Chapter 6 for more information on quotas.) From the Actions tab, you can control what the virtual machine does when the Hyper-V server starts or stops. You also can set a delay so that the startup for virtual machines is staggered.

Activity 4-5: Modifying Virtual Machine Settings

Time Required: 15 minutes

Objective: Learn to modify the settings for an existing virtual machine.

Description: In this activity, your team works with the Virtual Machines view of the VMM administrator console. You modify the dynamic memory settings from the Hardware Configuration tab of the Virtual Machine Properties window. Also, you start and shut down the virtual machine from the Actions pane.

Table 4-11 provides the team member assignments for this activity.

1. If necessary, switch the KVM switch to port 1.

2. If necessary, log on to your MGMT server with a username of *Team1\Administrator*, substituting your team name for *Team1*. Enter a password of **P@ssw0rd**.

3. If necessary, open the VMM console by double-clicking **SCVMM Admin Console**.

4. To select the virtual machine, click the **Virtual Machines** bar in the bottom-left corner of the console window, and then click **Windows 7 Client**.

5. View the hardware settings for the virtual machine. In the Actions pane, scroll down if necessary, click **Properties** under Virtual Machines, and then click the **Hardware Configuration** tab.

6. To configure dynamic memory, click **Memory**, click **Dynamic**, enter **1024** over the number shown in the Maximum memory text box (65536), and then click **OK**.

7. Wait for the job to be completed.

8. To start the Windows 7 Client, click **Start** in the Actions pane.

9. Wait for the job to be completed, and then double-click the **Windows 7 Client** thumbnail in the **Summary** tab at the bottom of the window.

10. Log on with a username of **LocalAdmin** and a password of **P@ssw0rd**.

11. To shut down the virtual machine, return to the VMM window, click **Shut down** in the Actions pane, and then click **Yes**.

12. Wait for the job to be completed.

Team Member	Steps	Host Computer
3	1–7	MGMT
1	8–12	

Table 4-11 Team member assignments for Activity 4-5

Activity 4-6: Working with Checkpoints

Time Required: 15 minutes

Objective: Learn to take checkpoints.

Description: In this activity, your team creates and manages checkpoints.

Table 4-12 provides the team member assignments for this activity.

1. If necessary, switch the KVM switch to port 1.

2. If necessary, log on to your MGMT server with a username of *Team1\Administrator*, substituting your team name for *Team1*. Enter a password of **P@ssw0rd**.

3. If necessary, open the VMM console by double-clicking **SCVMM Admin Console**.

4. To select the virtual machine, click the **Virtual Machines** bar in the bottom-left corner of the console window, and then click **Windows 7 Client**.

5. To start the Windows 7 Client, click **Start** in the Actions pane.

6. Wait for the job to be completed, and then double-click the **Windows 7 Client** thumbnail.

7. Log on with a username of **LocalAdmin** and a password of **P@ssw0rd**. Position the window on the left side of the screen so that the Actions pane is visible.

8. To take the initial checkpoint, click **New checkpoint**. Enter **Before configuration** in the Description text box, and then click **Create**.

9. Wait for the job to be completed, and restore the Virtual Machine Viewer by clicking the blue server icon on the taskbar.

10. To change the desktop, right-click it, click **Personalize**, click **Change desktop icons**, check **Computer**, click **OK**, and close the open window.

11. To manage the checkpoints, click **Manage checkpoints** in the Actions pane of the console window.

12. To create an additional checkpoint, click **New**. Enter **After configuration** in the Description text box and then click **Create**.

13. To return to a previous checkpoint, click the second Windows 7 Client entry, click **Restore**, and then click **Yes**.

14. Wait for the job to be completed, click **OK**, and then double-click the **Windows 7 Client** thumbnail.

15. Verify that the Computer icon is no longer present.

Team Member	Steps	Host Computer
3	1–7	MGMT
1	8–12	
2	13–20	

Table 4-12   Team member assignments for Activity 4-6

© Cengage Learning 2014

16. To manage the checkpoints, click **Manage checkpoints** in the Actions pane of the console window.

17. To remove the last checkpoint, click the last Windows 7 Client entry, click **Remove**, and then click **Yes**.

18. Wait for the job to be completed, and then click **OK**.

19. To shut down the virtual machine, click **Shut down** in the Actions pane, and then click **Yes**.

20. Wait for the job to be completed.

Migrating Virtual Machine Files

VMM allows you to move the files of a virtual machine from one folder to another using the Migrate Virtual Machine Wizard. To start this wizard, go to the Virtual Machines view of the console window, click the desired virtual machine, and then click Migrate storage in the Actions pane. The Migrate storage option is similar to the Hyper-V export and import features you learned about in Chapter 3.

Figure 4-29 shows the Select Path window of the wizard after the new storage path is selected. Click the Browse button and navigate to the target folder.

After you review the settings, as shown in Figure 4-30, you can see the PowerShell script for the migration job by clicking View Script. Click Move to run the job.

Figure 4-31 shows the progress of the jobs. Note that PowerShell steps can run concurrently, which results in faster script completion.

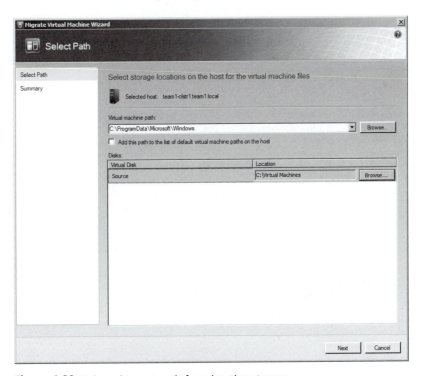

Figure 4-29 Selected target path for migrating storage

Source: Microsoft Virtual Machine Manager 2008 R2 SP1, Windows Server 2008 R2 SP1

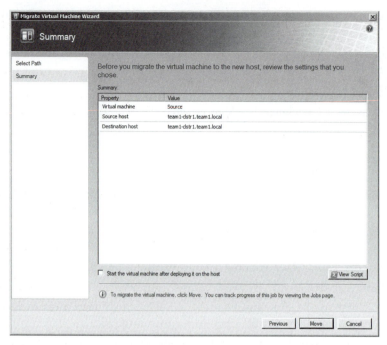

Figure 4-30 Summary information for migrating storage

Source: Microsoft Virtual Machine Manager 2008 R2 SP1, Windows Server 2008 R2 SP1

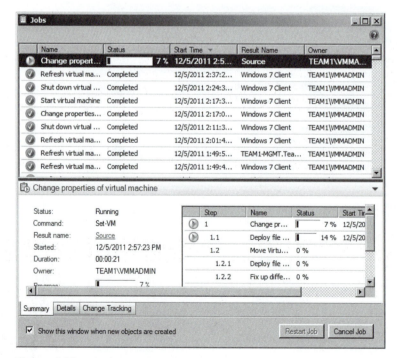

Figure 4-31 Jobs for migrating storage

Source: Microsoft Virtual Machine Manager 2008 R2 SP1, Windows Server 2008 R2 SP1

Activity 4-7: Migrating Storage for a Virtual Machine

Time Required: 15 minutes

Objective: Learn to migrate the storage for an existing virtual machine.

Description: In this activity, your team migrates the virtual hard disk for an existing virtual machine to a new location on the same host computer. You will use the Virtual Machines view of the VMM administrator console.

Table 4-13 provides the team member assignments for this activity.

1. If necessary, switch the KVM switch to port 1.
2. If necessary, log on to your MGMT server with a username of *Team1\Administrator*, substituting your team name for *Team1*. Enter a password of **P@ssw0rd**.
3. If necessary, switch the KVM switch to port 2.
4. If necessary, log on to your CLSTR1 server with a username of *Team1\Administrator*, substituting your team name for *Team1*. Enter a password of **P@ssw0rd**.
5. To open Windows Explorer and create a new folder, click **Start**, click **Computer**, double-click **Local Disk (C:)**, click **New Folder**, enter **Virtual Machines** over the text "New Folder," and then press **Enter**.
6. To share the Virtual Machines folder, right-click **Virtual Machines**, point to **Share with**, click **Specific people**, click **Share**, and then click **Done**.
7. Close the Windows Explorer window.
8. Switch the KVM switch to port 1.
9. If necessary, open the VMM console by double-clicking **SCVMM Admin Console**.
10. To select the virtual machine, click the **Virtual Machines** bar in the bottom-left corner of the console window, expand **All Hosts**, and click **Source** on the team1-clstr1 host computer.
11. To start the storage migration, click **Migrate storage** in the Actions pane. View the location of the virtual machine configuration files in the Virtual machine path field and the virtual hard disks under Disks.
12. To specify a new location for the virtual hard disk, click **Browse** next to the virtual disk named Source, scroll and click **Virtual Machines**, click **OK**, and then click **Next**.
13. To view the script, click **View Script**.
14. After viewing the script, close Notepad.

Team Member	Steps	Host Computer	Team Member	Steps	Host Computer
3	1–2	MGMT	1	25, 3–7	CLSTR2
1	3–7	CLSTR1	3	8–14	MGMT
2	8–14	MGMT	2	15–24	
3	15–24		1	26, 22–23	

Table 4-13 Team member assignments for Activity 4-7

15. To move the virtual machine, click **Move**.

16. View the progress of the jobs while waiting for them to be completed.

17. Close the Jobs window.

18. To start and connect to the virtual machine, click **Start** in the Actions pane, and double-click the **Source** thumbnail or click the reconnect link.

19. To log on, click the **Ctrl-Alt-Del** button, and log on with a password of **P@ssw0rd**.

20. To shut down the Source virtual machine, right-click it, click **Shut down**, and then click **Yes**.

21. Wait for the job to be completed.

22. Switch the KVM switch to port 2.

23. To shut down the host computer, click **Start**, click the arrow next to **Log off**, click **Shut down**, click the **Option** arrow, click **Operating System: Reconfiguration (Planned)**, and then click **OK**. If necessary, click **Yes**.

24. Wait for the host computer to shut down.

25. Complete Steps 3 through 24 for CLSTR2, which is on KVM switch port 3.

26. Return to the MGMT computer on KVM switch port 1, and repeat Steps 23 through 24 to shut down the MGMT server.

Chapter Summary

- Virtual Machine Manager (VMM) R2 SP1 is a Microsoft product that manages a series of host computers and virtual machines from a central console. The VMM server functions as the controller of the virtual management environment. Access to the VMM servers is through the VMM administrator console. The VMM server provides a number of services, including management of the host computers.

- VMM uses PowerShell, a Microsoft scripting language, to perform management tasks. Microsoft SQL Server provides the database to store various configurations. The library server manages the virtual hard disks, which are typically stored on a SAN for access by the host computers and virtual machines. Microsoft Internet Information Server (IIS) supports a VMM self-service portal that provides Web access to the VMM environment; from the Internet Explorer Web browser, users can create and manage their virtual machines in a controlled environment. Of course, the virtual machine hosts provide virtualization to run the guest operating systems.

- VMM combines a number of Microsoft communications protocols, such as Windows Remote Management, Background Intelligent Transfer Service, and Remote Desktop Protocol, with Internet protocols to communicate between components. The central hub of these communications is the VMM server.

- Prior to installing the VMM server, a check is made with the VMM Configuration Analyzer to ensure that the chosen computer is compliant. Considerations for installing the VMM server include choosing an SQL server and the location of the library files.

- The VMM administrator console manages the host computing environment. Its layout is similar to that of Hyper-V Manager. The virtual machines on the various host computers are managed with PowerShell scripts generated by VMM.

Key Terms

.NET Framework   A library of software that provides access to operating system functions.

Background Intelligent Transfer Service (BITS)   Microsoft communications software that maximizes the transfer of files between machines using idle network bandwidth.

checkpoint   An image of a virtual machine at a particular point in time. Checkpoints are very similar to snapshots, which you learned about in Chapter 3.

cmdlets   Small, task-oriented PowerShell commands.

Customer Experience Improvement Program (CEIP)   An optional Microsoft customer program that provides user data collected about the usage of a Microsoft product.

database schema   The structure of a database defined in the language of the database.

HyperText Transfer Protocol (HTTP)   A networking protocol for distributed, hypertext information systems.

HyperText Transfer Protocol Secure (HTTPS)   A secure version of HTTP.

PowerShell   A Microsoft scripting language used to provide system-oriented task management.

Remote Desktop Protocol (RDP)   A Microsoft communications protocol that provides a graphical console to a remote client.

Virtual Machine Manager (VMM) R2 SP1   A version of Microsoft's virtualization management software that is used in this textbook.

Windows Communication Foundation (WCF)   A Microsoft communications protocol that supports communication between services.

Windows Management Instrumentation (WMI)   An extension of the Microsoft driver model that provides access to operating system components.

Windows Remote Management (WinRM)   A Microsoft protocol that provides secure communication with remote clients.

WS-Management protocol   A public standard protocol for communication between devices.

Review Questions

1. _____ is a Microsoft scripting language that interfaces with the operating system to perform management tasks.

2. The VMM engine performs which of the following tasks? (Choose all correct answers.)

   a. connects to the VMM database

   b. handles updates for information and requests data from the SQL database

   c. communicates and executes commands with VMM agents on host computers

   d. coordinates the execution of VMM jobs

3. Microsoft specifies which of the following network requirements? (Choose all correct answers.)

   a.   1-gigabit network adapters for network transfers

   b.   A SAN device to store virtual hard disk files

   c.   A domain controller at the Windows Server 2008 domain level

   d.   15-GB virtual hard disk files

4. The VMM administrator console contains which of the following panes on the right side of the window?

   a.   Explorer

   b.   Surveyor

   c.   Information

   d.   Actions

5. The bottom-left corner of the VMM administrator console displays the _____.

   a.   hosts

   b.   management views

   c.   library

   d.   jobs

   e.   administration

6. The _____ view shows status information for the selected virtual machine.

7. VMM communicates with the _____ installed on host computers.

8. The VMM library contains _____. (Choose all correct answers.)

   a.   virtual hard disks

   b.   ISO images

   c.   operating system profiles

   d.   PowerShell scripts

9. VMM communicates with VMM agents on the host computers using the _____ protocol.

10. _____ maximizes the transfer of files using idle network bandwidth.

11. The _____ was developed by Microsoft to connect to a virtual machine and provide a graphical interface.

12. The _____ tool informs you of potential hardware and software problems that could affect the installation of VMM.

   a.   VMM administrator console

   b.   SQL database

   c.   VMM Configuration Analyzer

   d.   VMM Server

13. The _____ analyzes a computer to determine if it is properly configured to run the VMM server.

14. Examples of status values for host computers include _____ . (Choose all correct answers.)

    a. OK

    b. Needs Attention

    c. In Maintenance Mode

    d. Missing

    e. Not Responding

15. Options that you might encounter for the VMM hosts include _____ . (Choose all correct answers.)

    a. New virtual machine

    b. Add host

    c. Remove host

    d. View networking

    e. Properties

16. To sort the Name column in the Virtual Machines view, _____ .

    a. This cannot be done.

    b. click Sort in the Actions pane

    c. click Sort in the Surveyor pane

    d. click the Name column heading

17. When you examine virtual machines in the Virtual Machine Viewer, the options include _____ . (Choose all correct answers.)

    a. the File menu

    b. View

    c. Full Screen

    d. Ctrl-Alt-Del

18. After you click Manage checkpoints in the Virtual Machines view, which of the following actions are available? (Choose all correct answers.)

    a. Create a new checkpoint.

    b. Remove a checkpoint.

    c. Restore a checkpoint.

    d. Revert a checkpoint.

19. The Hardware Configuration tab in the Virtual Machine Properties window has a Priority section that includes which possible priorities? (Choose all correct answers.)

    a. High

    b. Medium

    c. Normal

    d. Low

20. The _____ is similar to the Hyper-V export and import features.

Case Projects

Case 4-1: Justifying the Cost of Virtual Machine Manager

You would like to recommend that your firm implement VMM. You know that your boss is cost conscious, so you decide to search the Web for a case study that will bolster your opportunity to discuss VMM. Select the best case study you can find, and summarize the findings in a one-page paper.

Case 4-2: Comparing Hyper-V Manager to the VMM Administrator Console

You have been asked to make a brief presentation at the next TechShare meeting. Prepare a handout that compares Hyper-V Manager and the VMM administrator console.

Case 4-3: Preparing to Install the VMM Server

You will install the management server for your VMM installation. You have installed the proper version of Windows Server 2008, joined an Active Directory domain, and installed the Hyper-V role. Now prepare a checklist prior to the VMM server installation.

chapter 5

Working with Virtual Machines

After reading this chapter and completing the exercises, you will be able to:

- Work with the VMM library
- Deploy a virtual machine
- Migrate and convert machines

In this chapter, you work with the VMM library, which is a prerequisite for rapidly provisioning virtual machines in private clouds to meet increased application demand. You create templates and virtual hard disks for the library, and then you deploy virtual machines to host computers. You also migrate, or move, virtual machines between host computers. Finally, you convert physical machines to virtual machines, which provides a method to move existing physical servers into the private cloud.

Working with the Library

VMM stores the building blocks for virtual machines in a common share called a library. Figure 5-1 shows the library resources for the default library share defined during the VMM setup. By reusing building blocks, you rapidly provision virtual machines in the private cloud. VMM stores the following building blocks in the library:

- *Hardware profiles*—Common settings used to define the hardware for a virtual machine, such as number of virtual processors, memory, virtual disks, and network adapters

- *Operating system profiles*—Settings for guest operating systems (OS), which apply to a new template or virtual machine created from a template

- *Templates*—Hardware and operating system settings used to create a new virtual machine

- *Virtual hard disks*—.vhd files that are not attached to a virtual machine; these files are used for future deployments of virtual machines

- *Virtual floppy disk*—.vfd files that are not attached to a virtual machine

- *ISO files*—Operating system installation files

- *Stored virtual machines*—Virtual machines imported from host computer storage

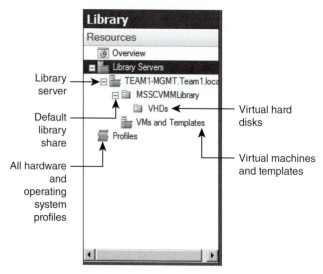

Figure 5-1 Library resources

Source: Microsoft Virtual Machine Manager 2008 R2 SP1, Windows Server 2008 R2 SP1

You create virtual hard disks and templates to store in the VMs and Templates folder. To see this folder icon and the Library pane shown in Figure 5-1, double-click SCVMM Admin Console on the desktop, and then click the Library bar in the lower-left corner of the console window. You can use Windows Explorer to paste files in the VMM library by right-clicking the library share in the Library pane and clicking Explore. You will not immediately see objects added to the library because VMM refreshes all library shares once every hour by default. If you need to work with objects before the library is updated, you can manually refresh an individual library share by right-clicking it in the Library pane and then clicking Refresh. You can add folders to the library by using the Explore option. However, they will not appear until they contain an object such as a virtual hard disk.

Hardware Profiles

Hardware profiles contain the most common settings for a virtual machine. To create a hardware profile, click New hardware profile in the Actions pane of the Library view. Create a name for the hardware profile that identifies the settings within the profile. Figure 5-2 shows one method of identifying the hardware profile; the name defines the components in abbreviated fashion.

The completed General tab is shown in Figure 5-3. After entering the profile name, add a descriptive paragraph that identifies the configured components.

To begin configuring the hardware components, click the Hardware Settings tab. Figure 5-4 shows that a 3.07 GHz Xeon processor is selected as the CPU type. Refer to Activity 5-1 to determine this setting. Your CPU type might be a bit different from the processor identified by Device Manager. For example, a 3.07 GHz Xeon processor works in place of a 3.1 GHz Xeon processor identified by Device Manager. You should avoid mixing Intel and AMD processors or processors of a different class, such as a Pentium 4 and Pentium D. The CPU types are one example of a resource used in **intelligent placement**, in which VMM indicates the best computer host to use for the deployed virtual machine.

The settings for dynamic memory are shown in Figure 5-5. To see these settings, click Memory in the Hardware Profile list. In this scenario, the basic assumptions are that the virtual machine starts with 512 MB of memory and grows to an upper limit of 1,024 MB. The memory buffer remains at the default setting of 20%. Notice that Network Adapter 1 is

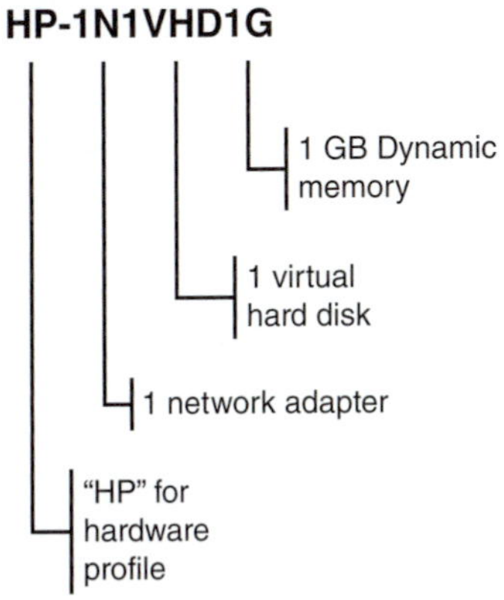

HP-1N1VHD1G

1 GB Dynamic
memory

1 virtual
hard disk

1 network adapter

"HP" for
hardware
profile

Figure 5-2 Creating a hardware profile name with indicated components

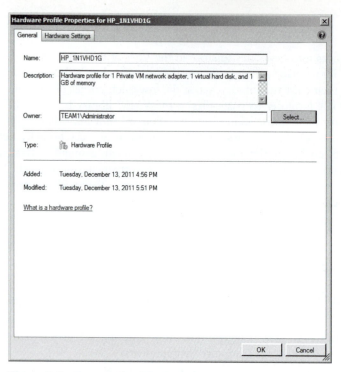

Figure 5-3 Completed hardware profile on the General tab

Source: Microsoft Virtual Machine Manager 2008 R2 SP1, Windows Server 2008 R2 SP1

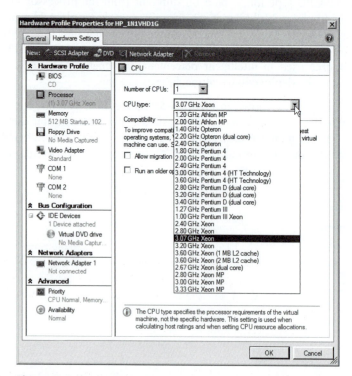

Figure 5-4 CPU type selected

Source: Microsoft Virtual Machine Manager 2008 R2 SP1, Windows Server 2008 R2 SP1

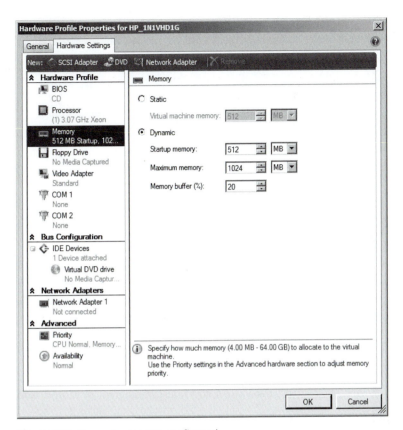

Figure 5-5 Dynamic memory configured

Source: Microsoft Virtual Machine Manager 2008 R2 SP1, Windows Server 2008 R2 SP1

shown as Not connected, which means that the network switch is attached when the host computer is determined during virtual machine deployment. After you click OK, the new hardware profile will appear when you click the Profiles folder.

Activity 5-1: Creating a Hardware Profile

Time Required: 15 minutes

Objective: Create a hardware profile.

Description: In this activity, your team creates a hardware profile named HP_1N1VHD1G with a network adapter, a virtual hard disk, and 1 gigabyte of memory. Because future deployments will be to the CLSTR1 and CLSTR2 servers, you will need to determine the processor type for both servers.

Table 5-1 provides the team member assignments for this activity.

1. Switch the KVM switch to port 1.

2. Turn on the power, and log on to your MGMT server with a username of **Team1\ Administrator**, substituting your team name for *Team1*. Enter a password of **P@ssw0rd**.

Team Member	Steps	Host Computer
1	1-3	MGMT
2	4-6	CLSTR1
3	7, 4-6	CLSTR2
1	8-15	MGMT

Table 5-1 Team member assignments for Activity 5-1

© Cengage Learning 2014

3. To open the Hosts view, double-click **SCVMM Admin Console** on the desktop, click the Hosts bar in the lower-left corner of the console window, and then expand **All Hosts**.

4. Switch the KVM switch to port 2.

5. Turn on the power, and log on to your CLSTR1 server with a username of *Team1\ Administrator*, substituting your team name for *Team1*. Enter a password of **P@ssw0rd**.

6. To determine the processor type, click **Start**, point to **Administrative Tools**, click **Computer Management**, click **Device Manager**, and expand **Processors**. Record the processor type on a piece of paper, and close the windows you opened in this step.

7. Repeat Steps 4 through 6 for the CLSTR2 server on KVM switch port 3.

If the processors are not the same for the CLSTR1 and CLSTR2 servers, contact your instructor. If you use different processors, you will not be able to complete the lab activities in Chapter 8.

8. Switch the KVM switch to port 1.

9. If necessary, open the Library view. Double-click **SCVMM Admin Console** on the desktop, and then click the **Library** bar in the lower-left corner of the console window.

10. To open the New hardware profile wizard, click **New hardware profile** in the Actions pane.

11. To name and describe the hardware profile, enter **HP_1N1VHD1G** in the Name text box, and enter **Hardware profile for 1 Private VM network adapter, 1 virtual hard disk, and 1GB of memory** in the Description text box.

12. To modify the hardware profile, click the **Hardware Settings** tab.

13. To change the processor, click **Processor**, and then scroll and click the CPU type from Step 6. If necessary, click the Number of CPUs text box and click **2**.

14. To set the dynamic memory, click **Memory**, click **Dynamic**, and enter **1024** over the number shown in the Maximum memory text box (65536).

15. After reviewing the entries, click **OK**.

Software Guest OS Profiles

By creating guest OS profiles, you ensure that operating systems are deployed consistently. Creating a guest OS profile is similar to creating a hardware profile. To create a guest OS profile, click New guest OS profile in the Actions pane of the Library view.

The Guest OS tab settings provide an opportunity to preconfigure the general settings you need for installing a Windows server operating system. Figure 5-6 shows the Identity Information settings.

When entering a name in the Computer name text box, you have three options:

1. You can randomly generate a computer name for each virtual machine and accept the default value, which is an asterisk (*). For the virtual machine to have an identifiable computer name, you must rename it after deployment. However, if you rename the virtual machine, you might create extraneous host name registrations in DNS. You should delete these extra registrations.
2. Enter a specific, complete computer name in which each virtual machine has the same name. If the virtual machines are connected to the same network, duplicate computer names are not permitted. To resolve this problem, you should rename the virtual machine after each one is deployed.

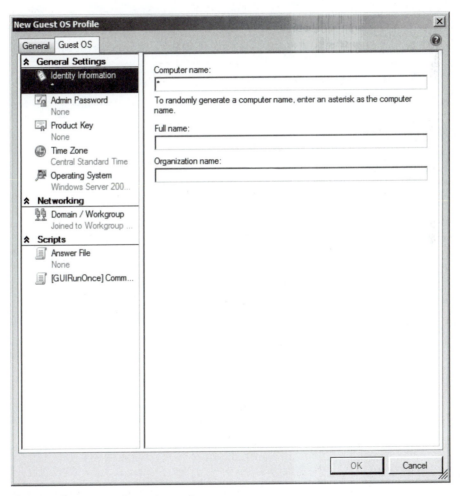

Figure 5-6 Identity Information settings

Source: Microsoft Virtual Machine Manager 2008 R2 SP1, Windows Server 2008 R2 SP1

3. Enter a partial name, such as the prefix *CloudSRV-*. If the virtual machines are connected to the same network, duplicate computer names are not permitted. Later, when you can complete the name for each computer (such as CloudSRV-01, CloudSRV-02, and so on), you can connect the virtual machines to the same network.

In the Full name text box, enter a role name or a user name. This name appears on the General tab of a computer's System Properties window under the Registered to settings.

In the Organization name text box, enter the name of the organization. This name is optional.

Next, click Admin Password under General Settings. Figure 5-7 shows the administrator's password set and confirmed. Recall that you are using P@ssw0rd in this textbook. In the workplace, you need to create passwords that are consistent with your organization's standards.

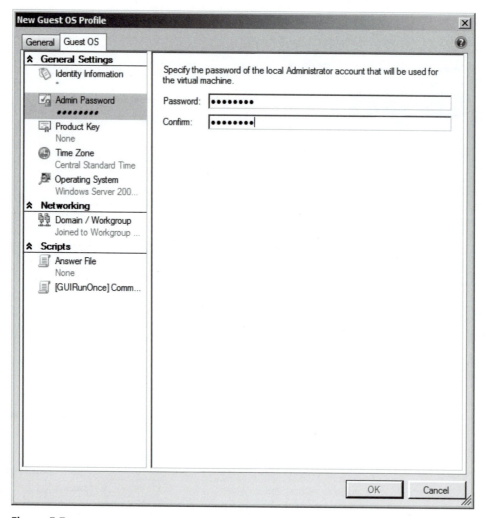

Figure 5-7 Password settings

Source: Microsoft Virtual Machine Manager 2008 R2 SP1, Windows Server 2008 R2 SP1

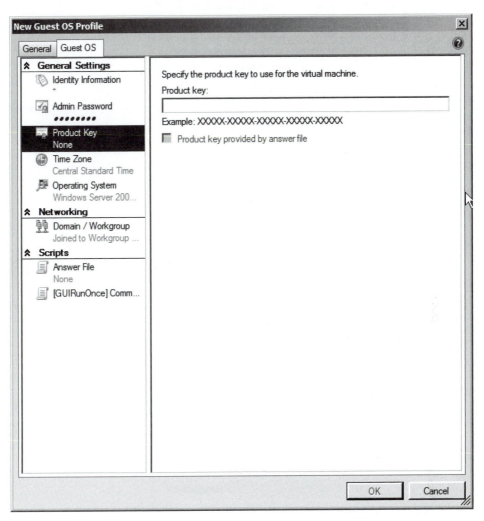

Figure 5-8 Entering a product key

Source: Microsoft Virtual Machine Manager 2008 R2 SP1, Windows Server 2008 R2 SP1

Click Product Key under General Settings to move to the next pane, and then enter the product key provided by Microsoft (see Figure 5-8). If your organization is using a **volume license,** which is needed when an organization purchases the contractual right to install the same operating system on multiple computers, enter the volume license key. This approach saves money because the organization needs only one copy of the installation media. If volume licensing is not needed, use the individual key from the installation software. When entering the product key, enter a dash between each set of five characters.

When you install a Windows operating system, you need to select the time zone where the virtual machine will reside. This selection ensures that the time offset from Greenwich Mean Time (GMT) will be correct. Figure 5-9 shows the time zone options.

Figure 5-10 shows the options for the guest OS, which is the Windows version that will run in the virtual machine.

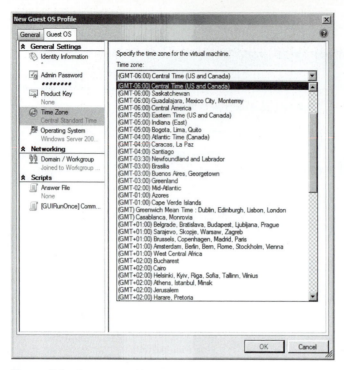

Figure 5-9 Time zone options

Source: Microsoft Virtual Machine Manager 2008 R2 SP1, Windows Server 2008 R2 SP1

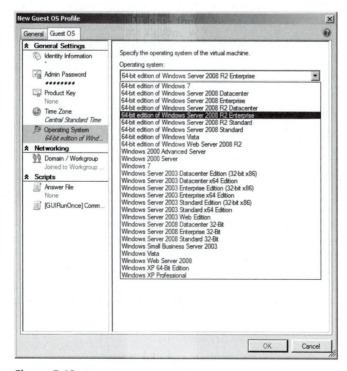

Figure 5-10 Operating system options

Source: Microsoft Virtual Machine Manager 2008 R2 SP1, Windows Server 2008 R2 SP1

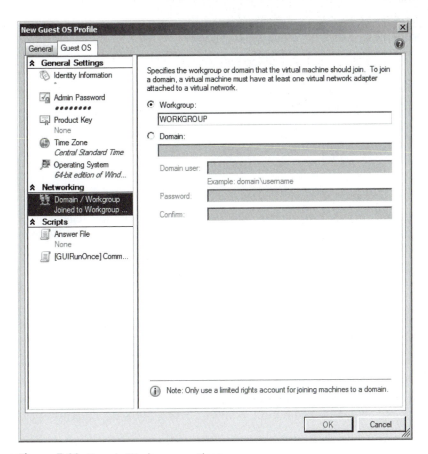

Figure 5-11 Domain/Workgroup options

Source: Microsoft Virtual Machine Manager 2008 R2 SP1, Windows Server 2008 R2 SP1

The Domain/Workgroup options, shown in Figure 5-11, permit you to enter a default workgroup or domain. If you need to deploy a number of virtual machines to the same Active Directory domain, enter the domain name and the user credentials.

The remaining options allow you to specify installation scripts and commands to be run the first time the virtual machine runs. These options are beyond the scope of this textbook.

Activity 5-2: Creating a Guest OS Profile

Time Required: 15 minutes

Objective: Create a software guest OS profile.

Description: In this activity, your team creates a software guest OS profile for the Windows Server 2008 R2 SP1 Enterprise Edition.

Table 5-2 provides the team member assignments for this activity.

1. Switch the KVM switch to port 1.

2. If necessary, log on to your MGMT server with a username of *Team1***Administrator**, substituting your team name for *Team1*. Enter a password of **P@ssw0rd**.

Team Member	Steps	Host Computer
2	1-8	MGMT
3	9-11	

Table 5-2 Team member assignments for Activity 5-2

© Cengage Learning 2014

3. If necessary, open the Library view. Double-click **SCVMM Admin Console** on the desktop, and then click the **Library** bar in the lower-left corner of the console window.

4. To open the New guest OS profile wizard, click **New guest OS profile** in the Actions pane.

5. To name the profile and enter the description, click the General tab, enter **SP_W2K8R2SP1ENT** for the name, and enter **Software profile for Windows Server 2008 R2 SP1 Enterprise** for the description.

6. To complete the identity information, click the Guest OS tab, click **Identity Information**, retain the * entered as the computer name, enter **Cloud Student** in the Full name text box, and enter your team name in the Organization name text box.

7. To enter a default administrator password, click **Admin Password**, enter **P@ssw0rd** in the Password text box, and enter **P@ssw0rd** in the Confirm text box.

8. To enter the time zone, click **Time Zone**, click the **Time zone** arrow, and then scroll and click the appropriate time zone.

9. To enter the guest OS that the virtual machine will run, click **Operating System**, and then scroll and click **64-bit edition of Windows Server 2008 R2 Enterprise**.

10. After reviewing the entries, click **OK**.

11. Remain logged on for future activities.

Creating VHDs and Templates

An easy way to create a virtual hard disk (VHD) or template is to start with an existing virtual hard disk. To start the process with the New Template Wizard, click New template under Library Actions in the Library view of the administrator console. Figure 5-12 shows the Select Source window, which lets you select the location of the existing virtual hard disk. This virtual hard disk could be stored in the library or on the host computer. To create this template, select the virtual hard disk from the host computer that was previously created using Hyper-V Manager.

The creation of the template destroys the source virtual machine. The message shown in Figure 5-13 is displayed; you must confirm that you want to continue. When you do, VMM will use the Microsoft **Sysprep** tool on the existing virtual hard disk to remove system-specific data from Windows. For example, during installation, a computer **Security ID (SID)** is created randomly as a unique 96-bit number. This SID is the prefix for the creation of user accounts. If the SID is not removed, you could have duplicate SIDs during deployment, which might allow access to unauthorized files.

The next window in the wizard lets you identify the template. Figure 5-14 shows the completed Template Identity window. The wizard enters the name of the virtual hard disk by default. You can keep this name or enter a new one. You should enter a description that reflects the software configuration of the virtual machine.

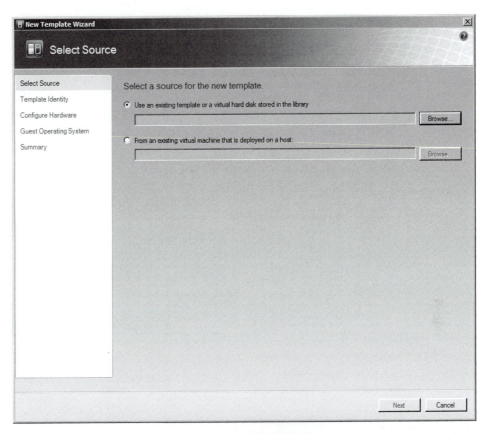

Figure 5-12 Select Source window of New Template Wizard

Source: Microsoft Virtual Machine Manager 2008 R2 SP1, Windows Server 2008 R2 SP1

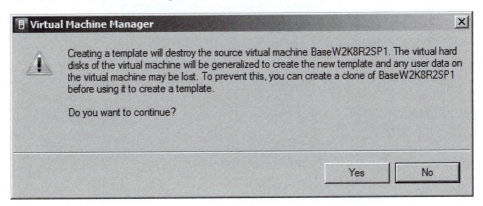

Figure 5-13 Warning message in New Template Wizard

Source: Microsoft Virtual Machine Manager 2008 R2 SP1, Windows Server 2008 R2 SP1

The next window in the wizard displays the hardware profile. You cannot change the hardware settings imported from the virtual machine, which means that you cannot import a hardware profile or create a new one. To see the available hardware profiles, click the Hardware profile arrow shown in Figure 5-15.

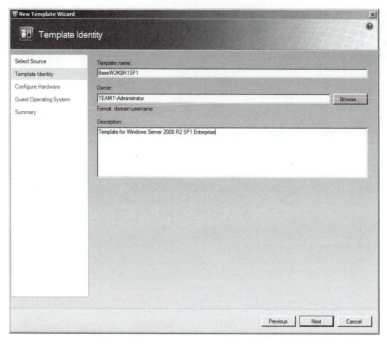

Figure 5-14 Template Identity window in New Template Wizard

Source: Microsoft Virtual Machine Manager 2008 R2 SP1, Windows Server 2008 R2 SP1

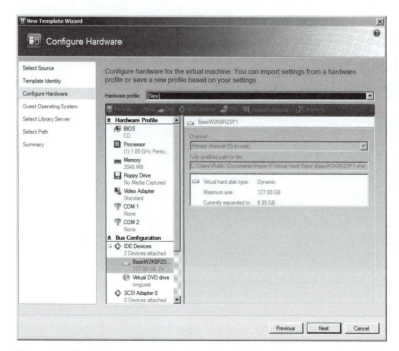

Figure 5-15 Hardware profile in New Template Wizard

Source: Microsoft Virtual Machine Manager 2008 R2 SP1, Windows Server 2008 R2 SP1

In the next window of the wizard, you can use the existing guest OS profile imported from the virtual machine or change the settings by importing a guest OS profile or creating a new profile. Figure 5-16 shows the selection options for a guest OS profile. The [Customization not required] option merits an explanation: When Linux is the guest OS, VMM cannot customize the virtual machine to run in the VMM environment, so you should select this option.

In the Select Library Server window, as shown in Figure 5-17, you indicate which library server should store the template. The template is stored on the MGMT server where the VMM library was created during VMM setup.

Next, you specify the folder for the template. VMM allows you to click Browse and then navigate to the folder, as shown in Figure 5-18. Expand the individual folders until you locate the one you want.

You reach a decision point next, as shown in Figure 5-19. You might want to return to a previous step by clicking Previous and correcting your entries. To reject the settings and start over, click Cancel. To see the PowerShell script, click View Script; VMM displays the script in Notepad. To wrap the PowerShell script lines and make them more readable, click Format and then click Word Wrap. The PowerShell script that creates the template is shown in Figure 5-20.

To create the template, click Create in the Summary window. VMM runs the PowerShell script to create the template. The Jobs window resembles Figure 5-21.

After the job is complete, you can review the steps to create the template. Locate and click the job in the Jobs information pane. To see the steps, click Details. Figure 5-22 shows these steps. The first major task (Step 1.1) is to use the Sysprep tool on the virtual machine. This task is performed in Steps 1.1.1 and 1.1.2. The next task (Step 1.2) is to store the template in the library and clean up the files that were left behind. This task is performed in Steps 1.2.1 through 1.2.7.

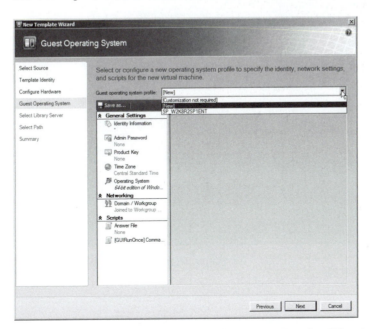

Figure 5-16 Guest Operating System window in New Template Wizard

Source: Microsoft Virtual Machine Manager 2008 R2 SP1, Windows Server 2008 R2 SP1

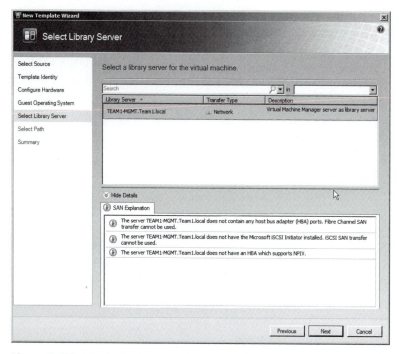

Figure 5-17 Selecting a library server in New Template Wizard

Source: Microsoft Virtual Machine Manager 2008 R2 SP1, Windows Server 2008 R2 SP1

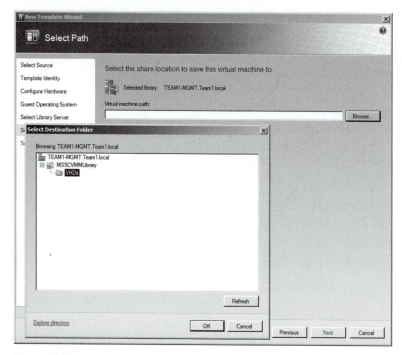

Figure 5-18 Selecting a destination folder in New Template Wizard

Source: Microsoft Virtual Machine Manager 2008 R2 SP1, Windows Server 2008 R2 SP1

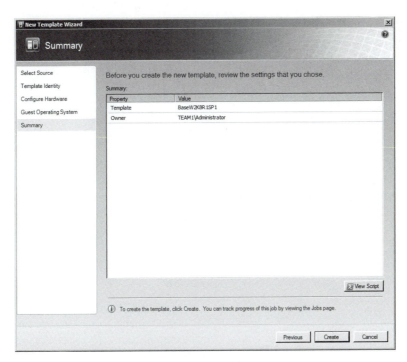

Figure 5-19 Summary window in New Template Wizard

Source: Microsoft Virtual Machine Manager 2008 R2 SP1, Windows Server 2008 R2 SP1

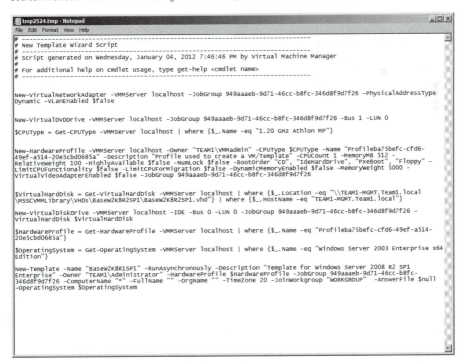

Figure 5-20 PowerShell script that creates the template

Source: Microsoft Notepad, Windows Server 2008 R2 SP1

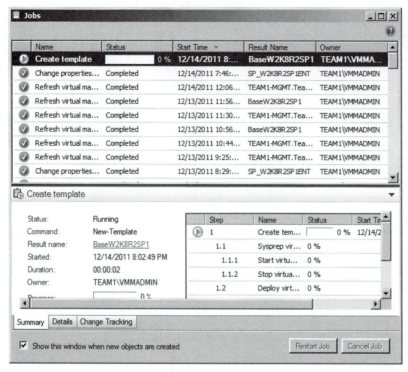

Figure 5-21 Jobs to create the template

Source: Microsoft Virtual Machine Manager 2008 R2 SP1, Windows Server 2008 R2 SP1

	Step	Name	Status	Start Time	End Time
✓	1	Create template	100 %	12/14/2011 8:02:49 PM	12/14/2011 8:20:30 PM
✓	1.1	Sysprep virtual machine	100 %	12/14/2011 8:02:49 PM	12/14/2011 8:07:32 PM
✓	1.1.1	Start virtual machine for sys...	100 %	12/14/2011 8:03:38 PM	12/14/2011 8:03:50 PM
✓	1.1.2	Stop virtual machine	100 %	12/14/2011 8:07:07 PM	12/14/2011 8:07:07 PM
✓	1.2	Store virtual machine from T...	100 %	12/14/2011 8:07:32 PM	12/14/2011 8:20:30 PM
✓	1.2.1	Run pre checks for transfer	100 %	12/14/2011 8:07:33 PM	12/14/2011 8:07:35 PM
✓	1.2.2	Change virtual machine status	100 %	12/14/2011 8:07:36 PM	12/14/2011 8:07:36 PM
✓	1.2.3	Deploy file (using LAN)	100 %	12/14/2011 8:07:36 PM	12/14/2011 8:07:36 PM
✓	1.2.4	Export Hyper-V virtual mach...	100 %	12/14/2011 8:07:36 PM	12/14/2011 8:07:38 PM
✓	1.2.5	Deploy file (using LAN)	100 %	12/14/2011 8:07:38 PM	12/14/2011 8:20:23 PM
✓	1.2.6	Remove virtual machine	100 %	12/14/2011 8:20:23 PM	12/14/2011 8:20:27 PM
✓	1.2.7	Fix up differencing disks	100 %	12/14/2011 8:20:29 PM	12/14/2011 8:20:29 PM

Figure 5-22 Steps taken to create a template

Source: Microsoft Virtual Machine Manager 2008 R2 SP1, Windows Server 2008 R2 SP1

Besides starting from a virtual hard disk file on the host, you have other options for creating a template: You can create it from a virtual hard disk file in the library and from an existing template in the library, as shown earlier in Figure 5-12. No matter which option you choose, you follow the steps in the New Template Wizard, as described earlier in this section. Table 5-3 shows the basic steps you take in the wizard when using any of the three methods to create a template. The three options all begin with the Select Source window and then vary depending on your choice.

Steps	Create from a VHD on Host Computer	Create from a VHD in Library	Create from a Template in Library
Select source	.vhd file on host	.vhd file in library	Template in library
Identify template	Yes	Yes	Yes
Hardware profile	Disabled	Existing or new	Disabled
Guest OS profile	Existing or new	Existing or new	Existing or new
Select library	Yes	Not needed	Not needed
Select path	Yes	Not needed	Not needed

Table 5-3 Wizard steps for creating templates

© Cengage Learning 2014

In this section, you learned to create a template from a virtual hard disk stored on the host computer, which is the first method summarized in Table 5-3. In the next two activities, you create the remaining template types. In Activity 5-3, you store a template in the library after creating a virtual machine from a blank virtual hard disk. In Activity 5-4, you create a new template from an existing template.

If you want to modify the created template, click the template name in the information pane of the Library view, and click Properties in the Actions pane under Template. For example, to change a hardware setting, click the Hardware Configuration tab. Figure 5-23 shows a

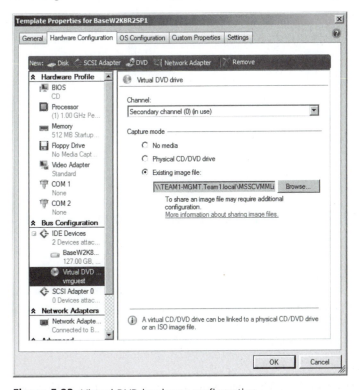

Figure 5-23 Virtual DVD hardware configuration

Source: Microsoft Virtual Machine Manager 2008 R2 SP1, Windows Server 2008 R2 SP1

virtual DVD that is no longer needed; for security reasons, it should be dropped from the profile. To make the deletion, click Virtual DVD and then click No media. When you have completed your review and made any changes, click OK.

To review the guest OS settings, click the OS Configuration tab. You can review and change each item. For example, Figure 5-24 shows the Identity Information settings. When you have completed your review and made any changes, click OK.

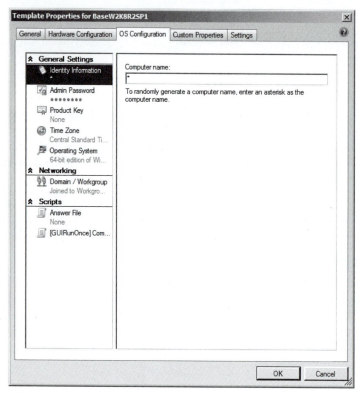

Figure 5-24 Identity Information settings

Source: Microsoft Virtual Machine Manager 2008 R2 SP1, Windows Server 2008 R2 SP1

Activity 5-3: Creating a Template from a Virtual Hard Disk

Time Required: 15 minutes

Objective: Create a template from an existing virtual hard disk in the library.

Description: In this activity, your team creates a template from a default virtual hard disk provided in the library by VMM. You configure the new template with the hardware and guest OS profiles. Table 5-4 provides the team member assignments for this activity.

1. If necessary, switch the KVM switch to port 1.

2. If necessary, log on to your MGMT server with a username of *Team1\Administrator*, substituting your team name for *Team1*. Enter a password of **P@ssw0rd**.

Team Member	Steps	Host Computer
1	1-8	MGMT
2	9-13	
3	14-18	

Table 5-4 Team member assignments for Activity 5-3

© Cengage Learning 2014

3. If necessary, open the VMM administrator console by double-clicking **SCVMM Admin Console** on the desktop.

4. To open the MSSCVMMLibrary with Windows Explorer and create a folder for .iso files, click the **Library** bar in the lower-left corner of the console window. Right-click **MSSCVMMLibrary**, click **Explore**, click **New folder**, enter **ISOFiles** over the text "New folder," and press **Enter**.

5. To locate and copy the Windows Server 2008 R2 SP1 .iso file, double-click *Team1*-**MGMT** on the desktop, substituting your team name for *Team1*. Double-click **Local Disk (C:)**, double-click **ISOFiles**, right-click the Windows Server 2008 R2 SP1 .iso file, and click **Copy**.

6. Return to the MSSCVMMLibrary window, right-click **MSSCVMMLibrary**, click **Explore**, double-click **ISOFiles**, click **Organize**, and click **Paste**.

7. Wait for the copy to be completed and close the Windows Explorer windows.

8. To refresh the library, right-click **MSSCVMMLibrary**, and click **Refresh**.

9. To open the New Template Wizard, click the **Library** bar in the lower-left corner of the console window, and click **New template** under Library Actions.

10. To locate the template, click **Browse**, expand the name column by dragging the right bar to the right, click **Blank Disk – Small** under Type: Virtual Hard Disk, click **OK**, and then click **Next**.

11. To identify the template, enter **InstallW2K8R2SP1ENT** in the Template name text box, enter **Template to install W2K8 R2 SP1 Enterprise** in the Description text box, and then click **Next**.

12. To change the hardware profile, click the **Hardware profile** list arrow, and then click **HP_1N1VHD1G**.

13. To link to the Windows 2008 R2 SP1 installation files, click **Virtual DVD Drive**, click **Existing image file**, click **Browse**, click the Windows Server 2008 R2 SP1 file, click **OK**, and then **Next**.

14. To change the guest operating system profile, click the **Guest operating system profile** arrow, click **SP_W2K8R2SP1ENT**, and then click **Next**.

15. To view the PowerShell script, click **View Script**, click **Format** in the Notepad window, click **Word Wrap**, examine the script, and close the Notepad window.

16. Review the Summary window, and then click **Previous** if necessary to return to a previous window and change a setting. When you are satisfied with the settings, click **Create**.

17. Verify that the job was completed successfully, and then close the Jobs window.

18. Remain logged on to the MGMT server.

Team Member	Steps	Host Computer
3	1-6	MGMT
1	7-8	
2	9-12	

Table 5-5 Team member assignments for Activity 5-4

© Cengage Learning 2014

Activity 5-4: Creating a Template from a Template

Time Required: 15 minutes

Objective: Create a template from an existing template.

Description: In this activity, your team creates a template from the template created in Activity 5-3. Table 5-5 provides the team member assignments for this activity.

1. If necessary, switch the KVM switch to port 1.

2. If necessary, log on to your MGMT server with a username of **Team1\Administrator**, substituting your team name for **Team1**. Enter a password of **P@ssw0rd**.

3. If necessary, open the VMM administrator console by double-clicking **SCVMM Admin Console** on the desktop.

4. To open the New Template Wizard, click the **Library** bar in the lower-left corner of the console window, and click **New template** under Library Actions.

5. To locate the existing template, click **Browse**, click **InstallW2K8R2SP1ENT** under Type: Template, click **OK**, and then click **Next**.

6. To identify the template, enter **InstallBaseCWS** in the Template name text box, enter **Install for Base Cloud Web Sales application** in the Description text box, and then click **Next**.

7. To change the hardware profile, click the **Hardware profile** arrow, click **HP_1N1VHD1G**, and then click **Next**.

8. To change the guest operating system profile, click the **Guest operating system profile** arrow, click **SP_W2K8R2SP1ENT**, and then click **Next**.

9. To view the PowerShell script, click **View Script**. If necessary, click **Format** in the Notepad window, click **Word Wrap**, examine the script, and close the Notepad window.

10. Review the Summary window, and then click **Previous** if necessary to return to a previous window and change a setting. When you are satisfied with the settings, click **Create**.

11. Verify that the job was completed successfully, and then close the Jobs window.

12. Remain logged on to the MGMT server.

Deploying Virtual Machines

With the VHDs and templates in the VMM library, deploying virtual machines is a simple yet repetitive task. In Activity 5-3, you created a template to install an operating system. In this section, you learn to build an image with an operating system and installed applications. These images provide a degree of standardization. In the Infrastructure as a Service (IaaS) model, a standard image is created for each application. As these applications need greater computing power in the private cloud, additional virtual machines are deployed.

To start the New Virtual Machine Wizard and deploy a virtual machine with an operating system and applications, click New virtual machine in the Actions pane of the Virtual Machines view. Figure 5-25 shows the Select Source window. To locate the template to serve as the basis for the deployed virtual machine, click Browse; the contents of the library are shown.

To see more information in the Description column, shrink the size of the Virtualization Platform column and expand the Description column, as shown in Figure 5-26. Because you are working from virtual hard disks, you pick from the Type: Virtual Hard Disk list. After making a selection, click OK and then click Next to go to the next window.

In the Virtual Machine Identity window, you enter a unique name for the new virtual machine and enter a description, as shown in Figure 5-27. You will learn about owners in Chapter 6. Click Next to advance to the next window.

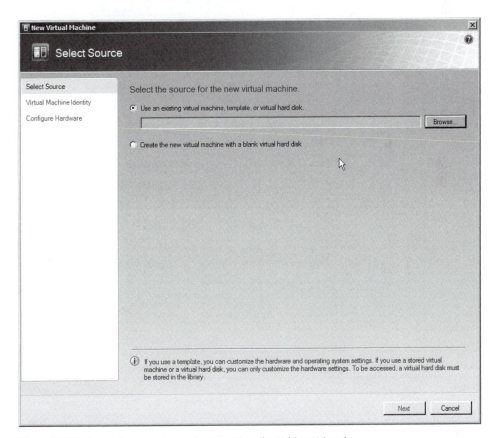

Figure 5-25 Select Source window in New Virtual Machine Wizard

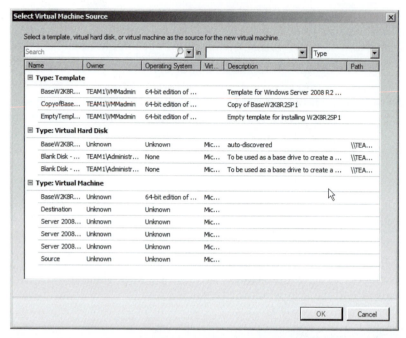

Figure 5-26 Select Virtual Machine Source window with Description column expanded

Source: Microsoft Virtual Machine Manager 2008 R2 SP1, Windows Server 2008 R2 SP1

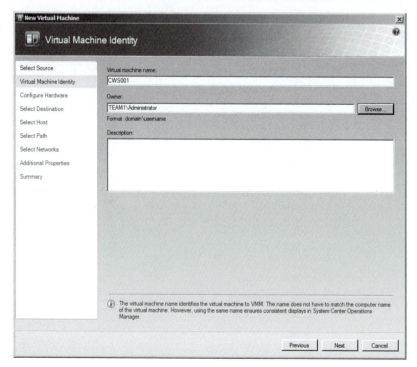

Figure 5-27 Virtual Machine Identity window in New Virtual Machine Wizard

Source: Microsoft Virtual Machine Manager 2008 R2 SP1, Windows Server 2008 R2 SP1

In the Configure Hardware window, you change the hardware profile to match the target host computer, which will be CLSTR1 or CLSTR2. Click the Hardware profile arrow and then click HP_1N1VHD1G, as shown in Figure 5-28. Click Next to advance to the next window.

In the Guest Operating System window, you can change the computer name to match the name of the virtual machine, which makes it easier to work with the host name in DNS (see Figure 5-29). Click Next to advance to the next window.

Because the target for this virtual machine is a host computer, the default option shown in Figure 5-30 is appropriate. Click Next to select the host for deployment.

Figure 5-31 shows a selected target host. Because TEAM1-MGMT.Team1.local is the management server, you would not deploy to it. Review the ratings for the two remaining servers; team1-clstr2.team1.local has a five-star rating, and the other server has a 4.5 rating.

The **star rating** system was developed by Microsoft to assist with the placement of virtual machines. VMM assigns host ratings that range from zero (not suitable) to five stars (highly suitable). The rating is based on the virtual machine's resource requirements, such as processor, memory, disk, and network I/O capacity. You will learn more about the star rating system in Chapter 6. Click Next to select the path for the selected host computer.

Figure 5-28 Hardware profile in New Virtual Machine Wizard

Source: Microsoft Virtual Machine Manager 2008 R2 SP1, Windows Server 2008 R2 SP1

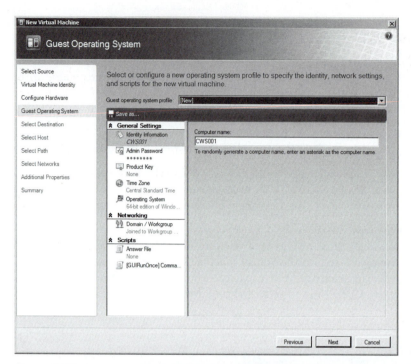

Figure 5-29 Guest operating system profile in New Virtual Machine Wizard

Source: Microsoft Virtual Machine Manager 2008 R2 SP1, Windows Server 2008 R2 SP1

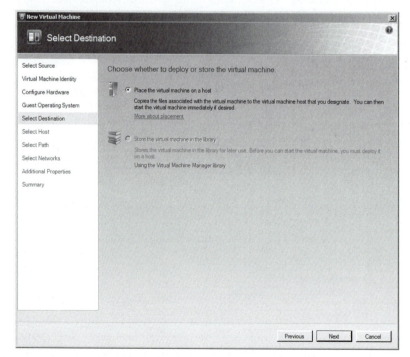

Figure 5-30 Select Destination window in New Virtual Machine Wizard

Source: Microsoft Virtual Machine Manager 2008 R2 SP1, Windows Server 2008 R2 SP1

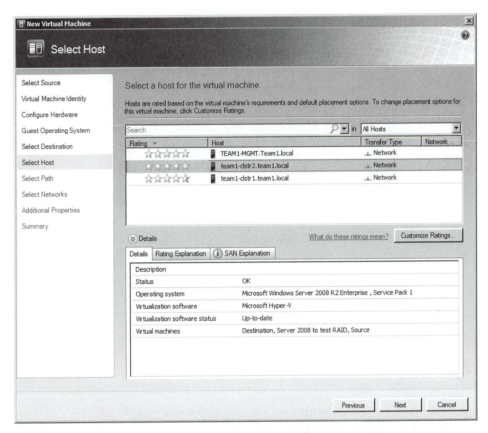

Figure 5-31 Select Host window in New Virtual Machine Wizard

Source: Microsoft Virtual Machine Manager 2008 R2 SP1, Windows Server 2008 R2 SP1

Virtual machines can be started only from a local hard disk on the host computer. The virtual machine path shown in Figure 5-32 meets this requirement. In Chapter 8, you will learn to use iSCSI storage for virtual machines in a private cloud. Click Next to advance to the next window.

The virtual machine requires at least one virtual network. Figure 5-33 shows the virtual network connected to the private VM network. To make this connection, click the Virtual Network arrow and make a choice. Click Next to advance to the next window.

The default settings in the Additional Properties window (see Figure 5-34) meet the needs of this virtual machine. When the physical server (host computer) starts, you have three choices: never automatically turn on the virtual machine, always automatically turn on the virtual machine, or automatically turn on the virtual machine when the physical server is stopped. If you choose to start the virtual machine, you can set a delay so that you can stagger the start of the virtual machines. (The delay option is disabled in Figure 5-34.) When the physical server stops, you have three choices: Save State, Turn off virtual machine, and Shut down guest OS. To go to the Summary window, click Next.

Figure 5-35 shows the Summary window of the wizard, where you can review the previous settings. You can return to a previous window if necessary by clicking Previous and making changes. Click Cancel to start over and enter new settings. Click Create to create the virtual machine and deploy it. View the jobs page to see the progress.

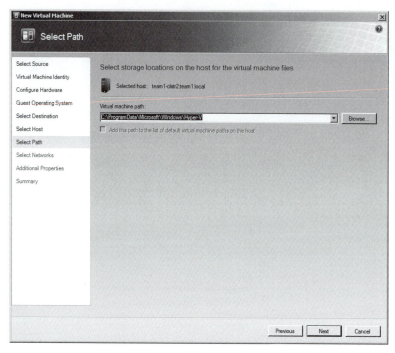

Figure 5-32 Select Path window in New Virtual Machine Wizard

Source: Microsoft Virtual Machine Manager 2008 R2 SP1, Windows Server 2008 R2 SP1

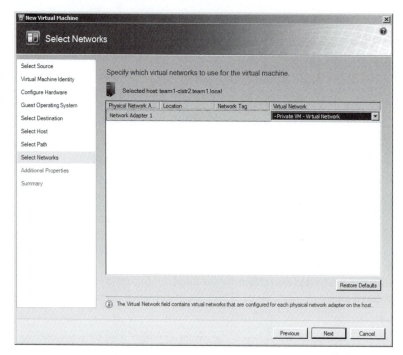

Figure 5-33 Select Networks window in New Virtual Machine Wizard

Source: Microsoft Virtual Machine Manager 2008 R2 SP1, Windows Server 2008 R2 SP1

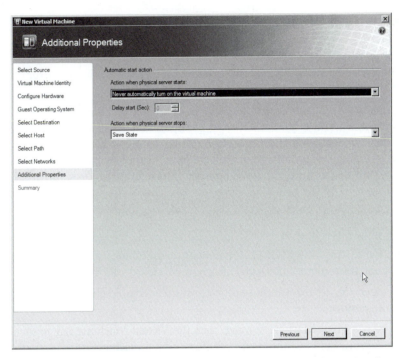

Figure 5-34 Additional Properties window in New Virtual Machine Wizard

Source: Microsoft Virtual Machine Manager 2008 R2 SP1, Windows Server 2008 R2 SP1

Figure 5-35 Summary window in New Virtual Machine Wizard

Source: Microsoft Virtual Machine Manager 2008 R2 SP1, Windows Server 2008 R2 SP1

Activity 5-5: Creating a Base Virtual Machine

Time Required: 60 minutes

Objective: Create a base virtual machine image with a blank virtual hard disk in the library.

Description: In this activity, your team creates a base virtual machine image with a blank virtual hard disk in the library. You install and configure a virtual machine to become the base for future deployments with the Enterprise version of Windows Server 2008 R2 SP1. You prepare the operating system to support the configuration of dynamic memory, configure Internet Explorer, and install and configure Internet Information Services (IIS) to support a future Web application. The last task is to store the base virtual machine in the library.

Table 5-6 provides the team member assignments for this activity.

1. Switch the KVM switch to port 1.

2. If necessary, log on to your MGMT server with a username of *Team1*\Administrator, substituting your team name for *Team1*. Enter a password of **P@ssw0rd**.

3. If necessary, open the VMM administrator console by double-clicking **SCVMM Admin Console** on the desktop.

4. To open the New Virtual Machine Wizard, click the **Virtual Machines** bar in the lower-left corner of the console window, and then click **New virtual machine** in the Actions pane.

5. In the Select Source window, click **Create the new virtual machine with a blank virtual hard disk.** Click **Next**.

6. To identify the virtual machine, enter **BaseCWS** in the Virtual machine name text box, enter **Install for Base Cloud Web Sales application** in the Description text box, and then click **Next**.

7. To change the hardware profile, click the **Hardware profile** arrow, click **HP_1N1VHD1G**, and then click **Next**.

8. To link to the Windows 2008 R2 SP1 installation files, click **Virtual DVD Drive**, click **Existing image file**, click **Browse**, click the Windows Server 2008 R2 SP1 file, click **OK**, and then click **Next**.

9. To place the virtual machine on a host, click **Next**.

10. To select the host, click the cluster host (CLSTR1 or CLSTR2) that has the best star rating, and click **Next**.

Team Member	Steps	Host Computer
1	1-16	MGMT
2	17-24	
3	25-33	
1	34-40	
2	41-50	

Table 5-6 Team member assignments for Activity 5-5

© Cengage Learning 2014

11. To accept the default virtual machine path, click **Next**.

12. To specify the network adapter, click the **Virtual Network** arrow, click **–Private VM – Virtual Network**, and then click **Next**.

13. To enter the guest OS that the virtual machine will run, click the **Specify the operating system you will install in the virtual machine** arrow, scroll and click **64-bit edition of Windows Server 2008 R2 Enterprise**, and then click **Next**.

14. To view the PowerShell script, click **View Script**, click **Format** in the Notepad window, click **Word Wrap**, examine the script, and close the Notepad window.

15. Review the Summary window, and then click **Previous** if necessary to return to a previous window and change a setting. When you are satisfied with the settings, click **Create**.

16. Wait for the virtual machine to be completed, and then close the Jobs window.

Ignore the message that Virtual Machine Manager cannot locate the boot or system volume.

17. To connect to the virtual machine, click **BaseCWS**, click **Start**, and then click **Connect to virtual machine**.

18. When the regional settings window appears, verify the selections for language, time, currency, and keyboard. Make corrections as needed, and then click **Next**.

19. Click the **Install now** link.

20. To indicate which version to install, click **Windows Server 2008 R2 Enterprise (Full Installation)**, and then click **Next**.

21. When the license terms appear, check **I accept the license terms**, and then click **Next**.

22. Click the **Custom (advanced)** icon.

23. Click **Disk 0 Unallocated Space**, and then click **Next**.

24. Wait for Windows to copy and expand files, install features and updates, and restart the computer to complete the installation.

25. Wait while Windows prepares to start for the first time and then prepares the computer for use.

26. When prompted that the user password must be changed before logging on the first time, click **OK**. Enter **P@ssw0rd** in the New password text box, press **Tab**, enter **P@ssw0rd** in the Confirm password text box, press **Enter**, and then click **OK**.

27. To set the time zone, click the **Set time zone** link. If necessary, click the **Change time zone** button, click the appropriate time zone, click the **Change date and time** button, change the time, and then click **OK** twice.

28. To enter the IP configuration, click **Configure networking**, right-click **Local Area Connection**, click **Properties**, clear the **Internet Protocol Version 6 (TCP/IPv6)** check box, and then click **OK**.

When the Set Network Location window appears, click Work and then click Close.

29. To reset the IP configuration, right-click **Local Area Connection**, click **Diagnose**, and then click **Close**. Close the Network Connections window.

Contact your instructor if the Diagnose option did not reset the IP connection and enable the local area connection.

30. To switch to the Server Manager window, check **Do not show this window at logon**, and then close the Initial Configuration Tasks window.

31. To configure Internet Explorer to access Internet Web sites, click **Configure IE ESC**, click the **Administrators Off** option button, and then click **OK**.

32. To set up Internet Explorer 8 for first-time use, click **Start**, and then click **Internet Explorer**. Click **Next**, click **No, don't turn on**, click **Next**, click **Use express settings**, and then click **Finish**.

You can ignore the caution message that Internet Explorer Enhanced Security Configuration is not enabled.

33. Close the Internet Explorer window.

34. To install Windows Internet Information Services, click **Roles**, click **Add Roles**, and click **Next**. Click **Application Server**, click **Add Required Features**, and click **Next** twice. Click **Web Server (IIS) Support**, click **Add Required Role Services**, click **Next** three times, and then click **Install**.

35. Wait for the installation to be completed, and then click **Close**.

36. To open Notepad and place a message on the default Web page, click **Start**, right-click **Notepad**, and click **Run as administrator**.

37. Enter the following lines:

```
<html>
<body>
<h1>Web Sales</h1>
Under Development
</body>
</html>
```

38. To save the file, click **File**, click **Save As**, click **Computer**, double-click **Local Disk (C:)**, double-click **inetpub**, and double-click **wwwroot**. Click the **Save as type** arrow, click **All Files**, enter **Default.htm** in the File name text box, and then click **Save**.

39. To test the default Web page, click **Start**, click **Internet Explorer**, enter **localhost** in the address bar, and press **Enter**.

If the Web page did not appear, return to Notepad, make the necessary corrections, and retest the Web page.

40. Close the Internet Explorer and Notepad windows.

41. To open the command prompt, click **Start**, right-click **Command Prompt**, and click **Run as administrator**.

42. To change the subdirectory to the location of the Sysprep tool, enter **cd \Windows\ System32\sysprep**, and then press **Enter**.

43. To open the Sysprep tool, enter **sysprep**, and press **Enter**.

44. Click the **Generalize** check box, click the **Shutdown Options** arrow, and click **Shutdown**. Click **OK**.

45. When the Sysprep tool is finished, close the Virtual Machine Viewer.

46. To store the virtual machine in the library, scroll and click **Store in library** in the Actions pane, click **Next**, click **Browse**, expand **MSSCVMMLibrary**, click **VHDs**, click **OK**, click **Next**, and then click **Store**.

47. Wait for the job to be completed, and then close the Jobs window.

48. To see the stored virtual machine, click the **Library** bar in the lower-left corner of the VMM administrator console window, click **MSSCVMMLibrary**, click **Refresh**, and click **VMs and Templates**.

49. To remove the installation DVD from the hardware profile, click **VMs and Templates**, right-click **BaseCWS**, click **Properties**, click the **Hardware Configuration** tab, click **Virtual DVD**, click **No Media**, and then click **OK**.

50. Remain logged on to the MGMT server.

Activity 5-6: Deploying Virtual Machines

Time Required: 75 minutes

Objective: Deploy a virtual machine with an operating system and applications.

Description: In this activity, your team deploys a virtual machine with an operating system. Your team uses the virtual machine image created in Activity 5-5.

Table 5-7 provides the team member assignments for this activity.

1. Switch the KVM switch to port 1.

2. If necessary, log on to your MGMT server with a username of *Team1*\Administrator, substituting your team name for *Team1*. Enter a password of **P@ssw0rd**.

Team Member	Steps	Host Computer
1	1-15	MGMT
2	16-31	
3	32, 4-31	
1	33, 4-31	
2	34, 4-31	
3	35, 4-31	
1	36, 4-31, 37	

Table 5-7 Team member assignments for Activity 5-6

3. If necessary, open the Library view. Double-click **SCVMM Admin Console** on the desktop, and click the **Virtual Machines** bar in the lower-left corner of the console window.

4. To start the New Virtual Machine Wizard, click **New virtual machine** under Virtual Machine Manager on the right side of the administrator console.

5. To select the base virtual machine, click **Browse**, click **BaseCWS** under Type: Virtual Machine, click **OK**, and then click **Next**.

6. To identify the virtual machine, enter **CWS001** in the Virtual machine name text box, enter **First virtual machine for cloud web sales application** in the Description text box, and click **Next**.

7. To select the hardware profile, click the Hardware profile arrow, click **HP_1N1VHD1G**, and then click **Next**.

8. To place the virtual machine on a host, click **Next**.

9. To select the host, click the cluster host (CLSTR1 or CLSTR2) that has the best star rating, and click **Next**.

10. To accept the default virtual machine path on the host computer, click **Next**.

11. To connect a network adapter, click the **Virtual Network** arrow, click **–Private VM – Virtual Network**, and then click **Next**.

12. To accept the default settings in the Additional Properties window, click **Next**.

13. To view the PowerShell script, click **View Script**. If necessary, click **Format** in the Notepad window, click **Word Wrap**, examine the script, and close the Notepad window.

14. Review the Summary window, and then click **Previous** if necessary to return to a previous window and change a setting. When you are satisfied with the settings, click **Create**.

15. Wait for the job to be completed, verify that it was successful, and then close the Jobs window.

 Ignore the message about virtualization guest services.

16. To start and connect to the virtual machine, click **CWS001**, click **Start** in the Actions pane, and then click **Connect to virtual machine**.

17. Wait for the virtual machine to complete the setup procedure and restart.

18. When the regional settings window appears, verify the selections for language, time, currency, and keyboard. Make corrections as needed, and then click **Next** twice.

19. When the license terms appear, check **I accept the license terms**, and then click **Start**.

20. When prompted that the user password must be changed before logging on the first time, click **OK**. Enter **P@ssw0rd** in the New password text box, press **Tab**, enter **P@ssw0rd** in the Confirm password text box, press **Enter**, and then click **OK**.

21. To enter the IP configuration, click **View Network Connections**, right-click **Local Area Connection**, click **Properties**, clear the **Internet Protocol Version 6 (TCP/IPv6)** check box, and then click **OK**.

When the Set Network Location window appears, click Work and then click Close.

22. If necessary, reset the IP configuration, right-click **Local Area Connection**, click **Diagnose**, and then click **Close**.

23. Close the Network Connections window.

24. To start Windows activation, click **Activate Windows**.

25. If your school is using volume license product keys, click **Product Key**, ask your instructor to enter the product key, and click **Next**. If your school is using product keys other than volume license keys, click **Product Key**, enter the product key provided by your instructor, and click **Next**.

26. Minimize the Server Manager window.

27. Wait for Windows activation to be completed, and then click **Close**.

28. Restore the Server Manager window.

29. To change the computer name, click **Change System Properties**, click **Change**, enter **CSW001** as the computer name, click **OK** twice, click **Close**, and then click **Restart Now**.

30. Wait for the virtual machine to restart.

31. Click **Ctrl-Alt-Del** on the menu bar. Enter **P@ssw0rd** as the password.

32. Repeat Steps 4 through 31 to create the CWS002 virtual machine.

33. Repeat Steps 4 through 31 to create the CWS003 virtual machine.

34. Repeat Steps 4 through 31 to create the CWS004 virtual machine.

35. Repeat Steps 4 through 31 to create the CWS005 virtual machine.

36. Repeat Steps 4 through 31 to create the CWS006 virtual machine.

37. Remain logged on to the MGMT server, and leave the virtual machines running.

Migrating and Converting Machines

Network Migration

To move the files for a virtual machine from one host computer to another, you perform a **network migration**. This procedure is similar to the export/import procedure in Hyper-V Manager, which you learned about in Chapter 3. To start the migration process, click the desired virtual machine, and then click Migrate in the Actions pane of the VMM administrator console. If the virtual machine is running, you see the message shown in Figure 5-36. If you click Yes, the virtual machine is saved prior to the migration. If the machine is not running, you will continue with the next step: selecting a target host.

To select a target host, as shown in Figure 5-37, you should note the number of stars in the Rating column, which indicates the most suitable host for the virtual machine. You should

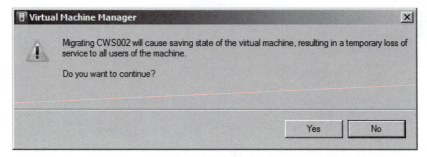

Figure 5-36 Virtual Machine Manager message

Source: Microsoft Virtual Machine Manager 2008 R2 SP1, Windows Server 2008 R2 SP1

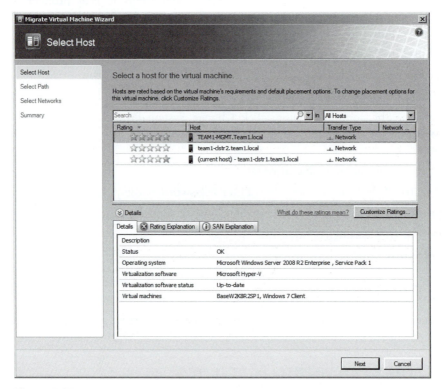

Figure 5-37 Selecting a target host

Source: Microsoft Virtual Machine Manager 2008 R2 SP1, Windows Server 2008 R2 SP1

select the CLSTR2 server, which has five stars; click team1-clstr2.team1.local, and then click Next.

Figure 5-38 shows the storage locations on the target host computer. In this window, VMM prompts you to enter the virtual machine path. To accept the default selection, click Next. Otherwise, click Browse and navigate to the desired path.

To select a network connection, as shown in Figure 5-39, click the Virtual Network arrow. Because all of the host computers may have different network connections, you must ensure that you select the correct one.

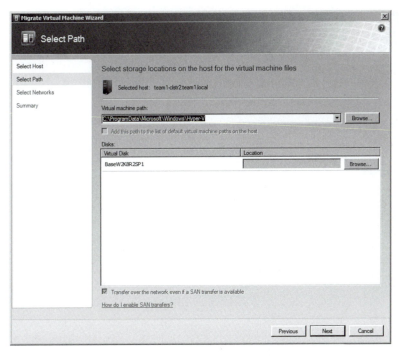

Figure 5-38 Storage location on target host computer

Source: Microsoft Virtual Machine Manager 2008 R2 SP1, Windows Server 2008 R2 SP1

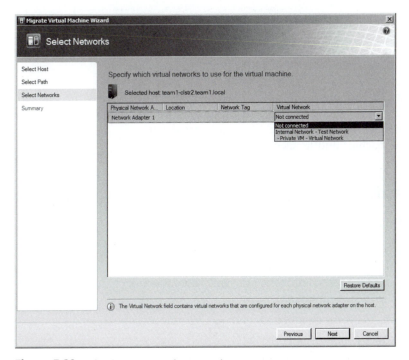

Figure 5-39 Selecting a network connection

Source: Microsoft Virtual Machine Manager 2008 R2 SP1, Windows Server 2008 R2 SP1

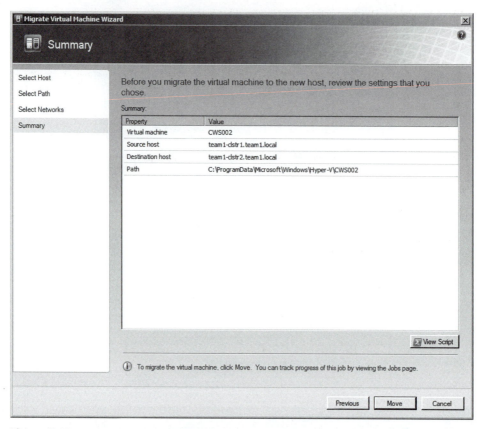

Figure 5-40 Migration Summary window

Source: Microsoft Virtual Machine Manager 2008 R2 SP1, Windows Server 2008 R2 SP1

Click Next to see the Summary window shown in Figure 5-40. Review the summary; if necessary, you can click Previous to return to a previous window and change a setting. If the summary information is correct, click Move to start the transfer. VMM will run a job to move the virtual machine and its files to the target host computer.

Activity 5-7: Migrating Virtual Machines

Time Required: 45 minutes

Objective: Migrate a virtual machine from one host computer to another.

Description: In this activity, your team migrates a running virtual machine from one host computer to a second host computer. You will shut down each running virtual machine and shut down the host computers.

Table 5-8 provides the team member assignments for this activity.

1. Switch the KVM switch to port 1.

2. If necessary, log on to your MGMT server with a username of *Team1***Administrator**, substituting your team name for *Team1*. Enter a password of **P@ssw0rd**.

Team Member	Steps	Host Computer
1	1-10	MGMT
2	11-12, 13	
3	14-16	
1	17, 14-16	CLSTR2
2	18, 14-16	MGMT

Table 5-8 Team member assignments for Activity 5-7

© Cengage Learning 2014

3. If necessary, open the Virtual Machines view. Double-click **SCVMM Admin Console** on the desktop, and then click the **Virtual Machines** bar in the lower-left corner of the console window.

4. To migrate a virtual machine, click **CWS001**, click **Migrate** in the Actions pane, and click **Yes**.

5. To select a target host, click the host computer (CLSTR1 or CLSTR2) that is not the current host, and then click **Next**.

6. To select the virtual disk to migrate, click **BaseCWS_disk-1** under Virtual Disk, and click **Next**.

7. To connect a network adapter, click the **Virtual Network** arrow, click **–Private VM – Virtual Network**, and then click **Next**.

8. To view the PowerShell script, click **View Script**. If necessary, click **Format** in the Notepad window, click **Word Wrap**, examine the script, and close the Notepad window.

9. Review the Summary window, and then click **Previous** if necessary to return to a previous window and change a setting. When you are satisfied with the settings, click **Move**.

10. Verify that the job was completed successfully, and close the Jobs window.

11. To shut down the virtual machines, right-click each virtual machine, click **Shut down**, and then click **Yes**.

12. Wait for the job to be completed.

13. Repeat Steps 11 and 12 for each running virtual machine.

14. Switch the KVM switch to port 2.

15. To shut down the host computer, click **Start**, click the arrow next to **Log off**, click **Shut down**, click the **Option** arrow, click **Operating System: Reconfiguration (Planned)**, and then click **OK**. If necessary, click **Yes**.

16. Wait for the host computer to shut down.

17. Complete Steps 14 through 16 for CLSTR2, which is on KVM switch port 3.

18. Complete Steps 14 through 16 for MGMT, which is on KVM switch port 1.

Physical to Virtual (P2V) Conversion

To move the operating systems and applications of existing physical computers to a private cloud, you perform a **Physical to Virtual (P2V) conversion**. This conversion permits the preservation of existing investments in operating systems and application development. To start the conversion process, click Convert physical server in the Actions pane of the VMM administrator console. The conversion wizard appears; the steps are similar to the steps taken to create a virtual machine. A VMM agent will be installed on the running virtual machine. The VMM agent completes a number of tasks, such as scanning the physical computer, returning the scanned information, providing a Volume Configuration page that permits volumes to be chosen for conversion, creating the virtual machine, and deploying the virtual machine to a host computer.

Moving an existing application and data to a private cloud is not as easy as it might seem. Not every application is suitable for migration to a private cloud. For example, most existing applications are not designed with the cloud in mind. Use caution when choosing physical computers and applications for conversion. Due to hardware limitations, the conversion of physical machines is beyond the scope of this textbook.

Virtual to Virtual (V2V) Conversion

When an organization has virtual machines running on hypervisors other than Hyper-V, such as VMware ESX, you perform a **Virtual to Virtual (V2V) conversion**. The source must have a VMware ESX virtual machine located in a VMM library or residing on a VMware ESX host managed by VMM. V2V converts the volume that contains the guest operating system to a .vhd file. V2V requires that the guest operating system be installed on a volume formatted as NTFS or FAT32. Due to software limitations, the conversion of virtual machines is beyond the scope of this textbook.

Chapter Summary

- Components of the VMM library include hardware profiles, guest OS profiles, .iso files, templates, and virtual machines.

- You can create templates and virtual hard disks for the library. Next, you can deploy virtual machines to host computers, which is a prerequisite for rapidly provisioning virtual machines in the private cloud.

- By migrating virtual machines, you can move them between host computers. VMM can convert physical machines to virtual machines, which provides a method to move existing physical servers into a private cloud.

Key Terms

intelligent placement   A Microsoft technique that identifies the best computer host to use for a deployed virtual machine.

network migration   A procedure to move virtual machines between host computers.

Physical to Virtual (P2V) conversion   A procedure to migrate an operating system and applications from a physical computer to a host computer as a virtual machine.

Security ID (SID)   A randomly generated, unique 96-bit number that serves as the prefix for user IDs and security groups.

star rating   A rating system developed by Microsoft to assist with the placement of virtual machines.

Sysprep   A Microsoft tool that removes system-specific data from installed Windows operating systems.

Virtual to Virtual (V2V) conversion   A procedure used to migrate an operating system and applications from a hypervisor, such as VMware ESX, to Microsoft Hyper-V.

volume license   A license needed when an organization purchases the contractual right to install the same operating system on multiple computers.

Review Questions

1. By using the building blocks in the library, you can _____ virtual machines in the cloud.

2. Which of the following are components in the library? (Choose all correct answers.)

   a.   Guest OS profiles

   b.   Language compilers

   c.   Virtual hard disks

   d.   Stored virtual machines

   e.   Templates

   f.   Operating system files

3. VMM refreshes the library every _____ minutes.

   a.   15

   b.   30

   c.   45

   d.   60

   e.   90

4. To start the hardware profile wizard, _____.

   a.   run the Start hardpro command from the command prompt

   b.   click New hardware profile in the Virtual Machines view

   c.   click New hardware profile in the Hosts view

   d.   click New hardware profile in the Library view

5. Which of the following components can you configure on the Hardware Settings tab? (Choose all correct answers.)

   a.   Processor

   b.   Memory

   c.   Floppy drive

   d.   Virtual DVD

    e.   Network adapter

    f.   CPU priority

    g.   Memory priority

6. To start the guest OS profile wizard, _____.

    a.   run the Start Guestpro command from the command prompt

    b.   click New guest OS profile in the Virtual Machines view

    c.   click New guest OS profile in the Hosts view

    d.   click New guest OS profile in the Library view

7. Which of the following can be used to specify a computer name? (Choose all correct answers.)

    a.   An asterisk

    b.   A complete computer name

    c.   A partial name

    d.   A user name concatenated to an organization name

8. A/n _____ is used when an organization has purchased operating system licenses in bulk.

9. _____ is a Microsoft tool that removes system-specific data from Windows.

10. A/n _____ is a 96-bit prefix for the creation of user accounts.

11. When _____ is the guest OS, VMM cannot customize the operating system.

12. To see the PowerShell script that VMM uses for tasks, _____.

    a.   double-click the PowerShell script in the generated scripts folder

    b.   click View Script in the Summary window

    c.   click Notepad in the Summary window

    d.   You cannot view PowerShell scripts.

13. Which of the following are common steps when using the New Template Wizard? (Choose all correct answers.)

    a.   Select source

    b.   Identify template

    c.   Hardware profile

    d.   Guest OS profile

    e.   Select library

    f.   Select path

14. When deploying virtual machines, what are the options from which you can choose? (Choose all correct answers.)

    a.   Template with an empty virtual hard disk

    b.   Virtual hard disk with operating system and applications

c. Hardware profile

d. Guest OS profile

15. To deploy a virtual machine with applications, you _____. (Choose all correct answers.)

a. click New template in the Library view

b. click New template in the Virtual Machines view

c. click New application in the Virtual Machines view

d. click New virtual machine in the Virtual Machines view

16. Microsoft created the _____ feature to assist with virtual machine placement.

17. In the Additional Properties settings, you can _____. (Choose all correct answers.)

a. never turn on the virtual machine automatically

b. always turn on the virtual machine automatically

c. automatically turn on the virtual machine when the physical server is stopped

d. automatically save the virtual machine when the physical server starts

18. To reset the IP connection and enable the local area connection, you _____.

a. click the Connect button

b. click the LAN button

c. click the Diagnose button

d. run the Connect command from the command prompt

19. To move virtual machine files between hosts, you perform a/n _____.

20. To convert the operating system on an existing physical server, you perform _____.

a. a Physical to Virtual (P2V) conversion

b. a Virtual to Virtual (V2V) conversion

c. a Physical to Physical (P2P) conversion

d. a Virtual to Physical (V2P) conversion

Case Projects

CASE PROJECTS

Case 5-1: Library Refresh Does Not Show Folder

You have created a new folder in the library and manually refreshed the library, but the folder is not visible. Research this problem on the Internet and prepare a one-page explanation to solve the problem.

Case 5-2: Steps for Deploying Virtual Machines

You have been asked to make a brief presentation at the next TechShare meeting. Prepare a handout that lists the steps to deploy a virtual machine.

Case 5-3: Converting Machines

Your boss has e-mailed you a question about converting existing Web servers to work in the private cloud. You are aware that the application was not built using current development technology. How will you respond? You can research this assignment on the Microsoft Web site and other Internet sites as needed. Prepare a one-page evaluation of this proposal both for business needs and technical issues.

chapter 6

Installing and Using the Self-Service Portal

After reading this chapter and completing the exercises, you will be able to:

- Install the self-service portal
- Configure user roles for the self-service portal
- Manage virtual machines with the self-service portal
- Use virtual LANs
- Troubleshoot the self-service portal

In previous chapters, you installed and managed virtual machines using either the Hyper-V Manager or Virtual Machine Manager. In this chapter, you learn to use the self-service portal, which provides a Web-based interface to virtual machines within an Infrastructure as a Service (IaaS) model of a private cloud. This key element of the private cloud includes standardized applications provided as a service, which enables business groups to request and manage capacity for their applications. Other benefits include increased business agility and significantly reduced provisioning. After installing the self-service portal, you will configure user roles to control access to the virtual machines running in the cloud. For security in the private cloud, you use a virtual local area network (VLAN) to control which virtual machines can access a network. You will also practice troubleshooting common problems that occur when installing, configuring, and using the self-service portal.

Installing the Self-Service Portal

Microsoft Internet Information Server supports a Virtual Machine Manager (VMM) self-service portal that provides Web access to the VMM environment. From the Internet Explorer Web browser, users can create and manage their virtual machines in a controlled environment. The VMM self-service portal provides access to virtual machines that support the private cloud. One prerequisite for using the self-service portal is Internet Information Services (IIS), which you installed in Chapter 4.

The self-service portal installation creates a Web site for your users to access the portal. To open the IIS console, click Start, point to Administrative Tools, and click Internet Information Services (IIS). To view the Web site created during the self-service portal installation, expand *TEAM1*-MGMT (*TEAM1*\administrator), substituting your team name for *TEAM1*. Next, expand Sites and select the Microsoft System Center Virtual Machine Manager 2008 R2 Self-Service Portal (x64). See Figure 6-1.

The installation of the self-service portal is similar to the VMM server installation that you completed in Chapter 4. You will install the self-service portal in Activity 6-1.

By default, communications to the self-service portal from a remote client are not encrypted; they use HTTP port 80. For more secure communications, you should switch to HTTPS port 443, which uses **Secure Sockets Layer (SSL)**. This protocol lets you make secure payments online with vendors such as PayPal.

When you use SSL, unauthorized parties are prohibited from viewing the contents of packets between the remote client and the self-service portal, including sensitive information such as passwords.

You should also use certificates to know the parties with whom you are communicating. To use certificates, you must add two services. With the **Active Directory Certificate Services Role**, you create a Web certificate for use by IIS. The **Certificate Authority Role service** manages certificates for host computers in the domain. You install these services in Activity 6-2.

Figure 6-2 shows the interaction between the IIS and the Certificate Authority Role service, which follows these steps:

1. From the Web server for the self-service portal Web site, you request a domain certificate from the certificate authority. It is placed in the Pending Requests folder for the certificate authority.

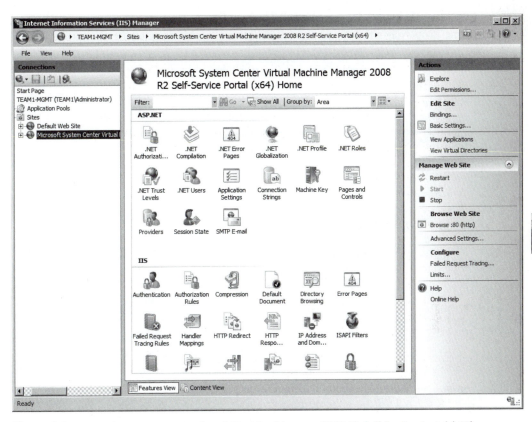

Figure 6-1 Microsoft System Center Virtual Machine Manager 2008 R2 Self-Service Portal (x64)

Source: Microsoft Virtual Machine Manager 2008 R2 SP1 and Internet Information Services 7, on Windows Server 2008 R2 SP1

2. From the certificate authority, review the request and issue the certificate. The certificate is placed in the Issued Certificates folder. Next, create a binary file for the certificate and store it in a common folder.

3. Open the binary file for the certificate, install the certificate, and bind it to the Web site for the self-service portal.

The rest of this section explains these three steps in more detail. For example, to request a certificate for your Web server, click *TEAM1*-MGMT (*TEAM1*\administrator), substituting your team name for *TEAM1*. Next, double-click Server Certificates and click Create Domain Certificate.

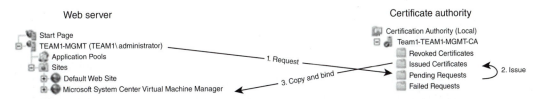

Figure 6-2 Requesting and receiving a certificate for IIS

Complete the certificate request by supplying the following information in the Distinguished Name Properties window, as shown in Figure 6-3. After reviewing the entries, click Next.

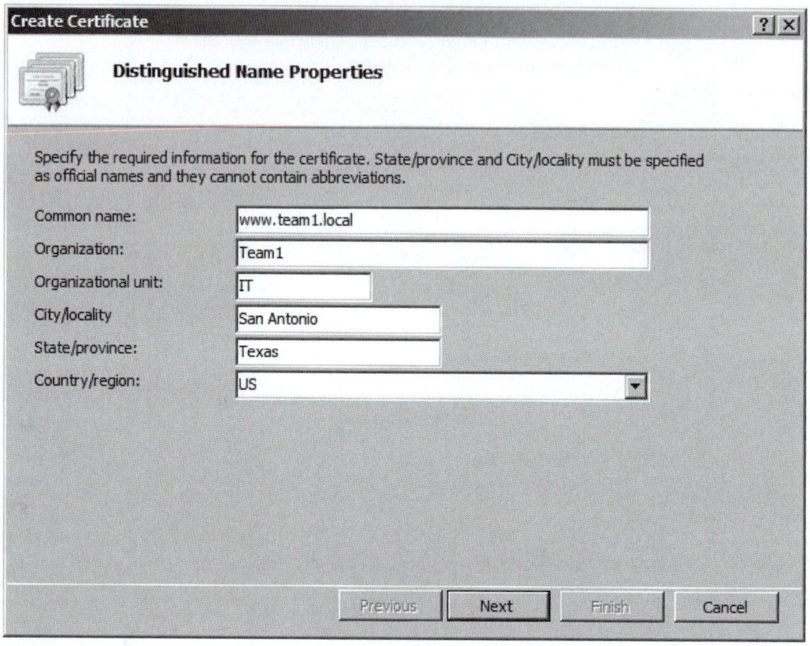

Figure 6-3 Completed certificate request for IIS Web server

Source: Microsoft Internet Information Services 7, Windows Server 2008 R2 SP1

- *Common name*—The computer name through which the certificate will be accessed (usually the fully qualified domain name of the self-service portal, such as www. Team1.local)
- *Organization*—The legally registered name of your organization
- *Organizational unit*—The name of your department within the organization (frequently this entry is IT)
- *City/locality*—Your organization's city
- *State/province*—Your organization's state
- *Country/region*—The U.S. or two-character country code

Figure 6-4 shows the completed Online Certification Authority window. *Team1-TEAM1-MGMT-CA* is the certification authority that was generated when the Certificate Authority Role service was added. *Team1*-MGMT is the server where the role service was added. Enter a name in the Friendly name text box so you can identify the certificate easily. After completing the two entries, click Finish. You will see a message that the certificate request was submitted to the online authority, but was not issued. Click Cancel.

The next step is to issue the certificate. To open the certification authority, click Start, point to Administrative Tools, and click Certification Authority. Expand *Team1-TEAM1-MGMT-CA*, substituting your team name for *Team1*. Figure 6-5 shows the certsrv certification authority where you work with certificates. To approve the request, click Pending Requests, right-click the request, point to All Tasks, and click Issue.

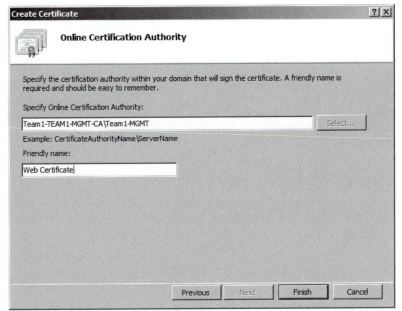

Figure 6-4 Completed entries to identify the certificate authority

Source: Microsoft Internet Information Services 7, Windows Server 2008 R2 SP1

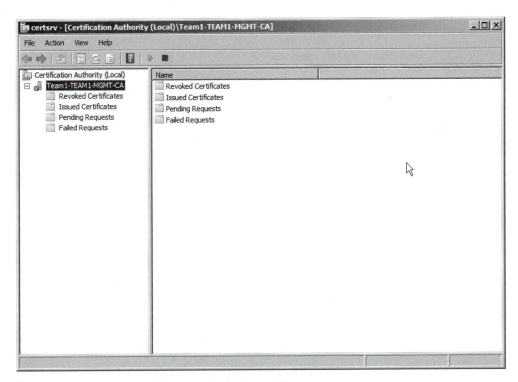

Figure 6-5 The certsrv certification authority for certificates

Source: Microsoft Certificate Authority, Windows Server 2008 R2 SP1

The last interaction between the IIS and the Certificate Authority Role service is to store the binary image of the certificate where the Web site can open it. (Refer back to Figure 6-2 if necessary.) To convert the certificate to a binary file, click Issued Certificates, right-click the certificate, point to All Tasks, and click Export Binary Data. Click Save binary data to a file, click Documents under Libraries, and click Save.

To complete the installation of the certificate, use the Web site for the self-service portal. Click Complete Certificate Request in the right pane, and then click the Browse button. Figure 6-6 shows the completed link between the certificate from the certificate authority and IIS.

When the Open window appears (see Figure 6-7), click the file extension arrow, click *.*, click the file saved by the certificate authority, and then click Open. The Complete Certificate Request window appears again. In the Friendly name text box, enter a name that you will recognize and remember later. You will use this name in the binding step. When you finish, click OK.

To start the binding process, click Microsoft System Center Virtual Machine Manager 2008 R2 Self-Service Portal (x64) in the left pane. (Refer back to Figure 6-1 if necessary.) To add the binding to use SSL, click Bindings in the right pane, and then click Add. Click the Type arrow, click HTTPS, and enter the IP address for your Web server. Click the SSL certificate arrow, click the friendly name you entered previously, click OK, and click Close. A completed bind is shown in Figure 6-8.

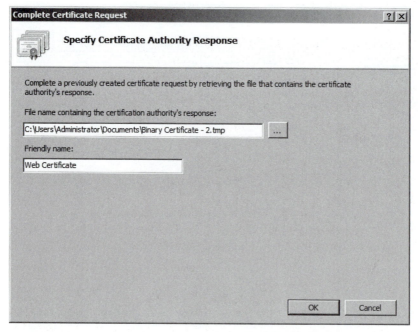

Figure 6-6 Linking the generated certificate to the friendly name

Source: Microsoft Internet Information Services 7, Windows Server 2008 R2 SP1

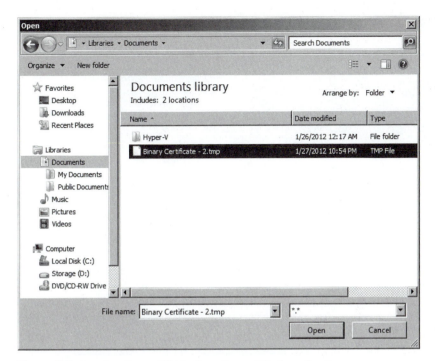

Figure 6-7 Opening the certificate from the certificate authority

Source: Microsoft Internet Information Services 7, Windows Server 2008 R2 SP1

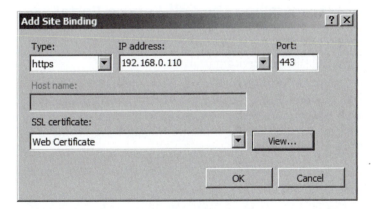

Figure 6-8 Completed Add Site Binding window

Source: Microsoft Internet Information Services 7, Windows Server 2008 R2 SP1

To test access to the self-service portal Web site, open Internet Explorer. Enter https://www.
team1.local, substituting your team name for *team1*, and press Enter. Figure 6-9 shows the
self-service portal logon window. You will request the certificate and bind it to the self-
service portal Web site in Activity 6-2.

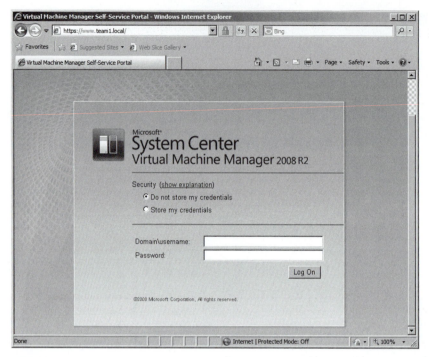

Figure 6-9 Self-service portal logon window

Source: Microsoft Virtual Machine Manager 2008 R2 SP1 and Internet Explorer 8, on Windows Server 2008 R2 SP1

Activity 6-1: Installing the Self-Service Portal

Time Required: 30 minutes

Objective: Install the self-service portal.

Description: In this activity, your team installs the self-service portal. You create a new host group to contain the host computers and then identify the two host computers. You assign an IP address for the Web server and create a host record in DNS for name resolution. You reorder the startup sequence for the Virtual Machine Manager Agent and the Windows Remote Management (WS-Management) services.

Table 6-1 provides the team member assignments for this activity.

1. Switch the KVM switch to port 1.

2. Turn the power on, and then log on to your MGMT server with a username of *Team1*
   Administrator, substituting your team name for *Team1*. Enter a password of **P@ssw0rd**.

3. Switch the KVM switch to port 2.

4. Turn the power on, and then log on to your CLSTR1 server with a username of *Team1*
   Administrator, substituting your team name for *Team1*. Enter a password of **P@ssw0rd**.

5. Switch the KVM switch to port 3.

6. Turn the power on, and then log on to your CLSTR2 server with a username of *Team1*
   Administrator, substituting your team name for *Team1*. Enter a password of **P@ssw0rd**.

7. Switch the KVM switch to port 1.

Team Member	Steps	Host Computer
1	1-11	MGMT, CLSTR1, CLSTR2
2	12-17	MGMT
3	18-23	
1	24-27	CLSTR1
2	28, 24-27, 29	CLSTR2

Table 6-1 Team member assignments for Activity 6-1

© Cengage Learning 2014

8. To open the Virtual Machine Manager, double-click the **SCVMM Admin Console** icon on the desktop.

9. To create a host group for the self-service portal, click **All Hosts**, click **New host group**, enter **Self Service** over the text "New host group," and press **Enter**.

10. To remove the cluster servers from the host group, expand **All Hosts**, and then click **team1-clstr1**, substituting your team name for *team1*. Click **Remove host** in the Actions pane, click **Yes**, enter **P@ssw0rd** as the password, and click **OK**. Next, click **team1-clstr2**, substituting your team name for *team1*. Click **Remove host**, click **Yes**, enter **P@ssw0rd** as the password, and click **OK**.

11. To add the host computers in the Self Service host group, click **Self Service**, click **Add host** in the Actions pane, enter **P@ssw0rd** as the password, and click **Next**. Click **Search** twice, hold down the **Shift** key, and then click both **team1-clstr1.*team1*.local** and **team1-clstr2.*team1*.local**, substituting your team name for team1. Click **Add**, click **OK**, click **Next**, click **Yes**, and click the **Add the selected new hosts to the following host group** arrow. Click **Self Service**, click **Next** twice, and then click **Add Hosts**. Wait for the job to be completed, and then close the Jobs window.

12. To start the installation, insert the VMM DVD, click **Run setup.exe**, and click **VMM Self-Service Portal**.

13. Wait for the temporary files to be expanded and copied.

14. To accept the end-user license agreement (EULA), click **I accept the terms of this agreement**, and then click **Next**.

15. Click **I don't want to use Microsoft Update**, and click **Next**, if necessary.

16. Wait for the prerequisites check to be completed. Click **Next** three times, and click **Install**.

 If you see error messages after the prerequisites check, contact your instructor.

17. Wait for the installation to be completed, clear the **Check for the latest Virtual Machine Manager updates** check box, click **Close**, and click **Exit**. Remove the VMM DVD.

18. To determine the IP·address for your Web server, locate the team number assigned by your instructor in Table 6-2. This row contains the IP address. Record the IP address.

Team#	IP Address
1	192.168.0.110
2	192.168.0.120
3	192.168.0.130
4	192.168.0.140
5	192.168.0.150
6	192.168.0.160

Table 6-2 IP address for Web server

© Cengage Learning 2014

19. To open the DNS console, click **Start,** point to **Administrative Tools,** and click **DNS.**

20. Expand *Team1*-**MGMT,** substituting your team name for *Team1.* Click **Forward Lookup Zones,** and then double-click *Team1*.**local.**

21. To add a host record with the IP address for the Web server, click the **Action** menu, click **New Host (A or AAAA),** enter **WWW** as the name, enter the IP address from Step 18, click **Add Host,** and click **OK.** Click **Done.**

22. Close the DNS console window.

23. To add the IP address for the Web server, click the **Network** icon on the taskbar, click **Open Network and Sharing Center,** and click **Change adapter settings.** Right-click **Local Area Connection,** click **Properties,** click **Internet Protocol Version 4 (TCP/IPv4),** and click **Properties.** Click **Advanced,** click **Add,** enter the IP address from Step 18, press **Tab,** click **Add,** click **OK** twice, and click **Close.**

 If you cannot find the correct network adapter, ask your instructor for help.

24. Switch the KVM switch to port 2.

25. To install the Windows Remote Management (WinRM) IIS extension, restore Server Manager, click **Features,** and click **Add Features.** Scroll and click **WinRM IIS Extension,** click **Add Required Role Services,** click **Next** three times, and click **Install.**

26. Wait for the installation to be completed, and then click **Close.** Close the Services window.

27. To reorder the service startup for the Virtual Machine Manager Agent and Windows Remote Management (WS-Management), click **Start,** point to **Administrative Tools,** and click **Services.** Scroll and right-click **Virtual Machine Manager Agent,** click **Properties,** click the **Startup type** arrow, click **Automatic (Delayed Start),** and click **OK.** Scroll and right-click **Windows Remote Management (WS-Management),** click **Properties,** click the **Startup type** arrow, click **Automatic,** and click **OK.**

28. Repeat Steps 24 through 27 for the CLSTR2 server, which is on switch port 3.

29. Leave the host computer logged on for additional lab activities.

Activity 6-2: Installing Certificates

Time Required: 20 minutes

Objective: Install certificates.

Description: In this activity, your team installs Active Directory Certificate Services and the Certificate Authority. You request and bind a certificate for the Web server to provide access to the self-service portal Web site using the HTTPS protocol.

Table 6-3 provides the team member assignments for this activity.

1. Switch the KVM switch to port 1.

2. If necessary, log on to your MGMT server with a username of *Team1*\Administrator, substituting your team name for *Team1*. Enter a password of **P@ssw0rd**.

3. Restore the Server Manager.

4. To install the certificate software, click **Roles**, click **Add Roles** in the right pane, click **Server Roles**, click **Active Directory Certificate Services**, click **Next** three times, click **Standalone**, and then click **Next**. Retain **RootCA**, and click **Next**. Retain **Create a new private key**, and click **Next**. Click **SHA512** to select the hash algorithm for signing certificates issued by this CA, and then click **Next**. Record the common name for this CA, click **Next** three times, and then click **Install**.

5. Wait for the installation to be completed, and then click **Close**.

6. To open the Internet Information Services (IIS) console, click **Start**, point to **Administrative Tools**, and click **Internet Information Services (IIS)**.

7. To view the server settings, click *TEAM1*-MGMT (*TEAM1*\administrator), substituting your team name for *TEAM1*.

8. To request a certificate, double-click **Server Certificates**, click **Create Domain Certificate**, and enter **www.***Team1*.**local** in the Common name text box, substituting your team name for *Team1*. Enter your team name as the organization, and enter **IT** as the organizational unit. Enter your city/locality, state/province, and country/region code, and then click **Next**.

9. Enter *Team1*-TEAM1-MGMT-CA*Team1*-MGMT in the Specify Online Certification Authority text box, substituting your team name for *Team1*. Enter **Web Certificate** in the Friendly name text box, and click **Finish**.

10. When informed that the certificate request was submitted to the online authority but was not issued, click **OK** and then click **Cancel**.

11. Minimize the Internet Information Services (IIS) Manager window.

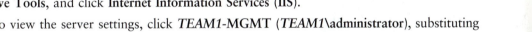

Team Member	Steps	Host Computer
1	1-11	MGMT
2	12-15	
3	16-20	

Table 6-3 Team member assignments for Activity 6-2

12. To open the certification authority, click **Start**, point to **Administrative Tools**, and click **Certification Authority**. Expand *Team1-TEAM1-MGMT-CA*, substituting your team name for *Team1*.

13. To approve the request, click **Pending Requests**, right-click the request, point to **All Tasks**, and click **Issue**.

14. To convert the certificate to a binary file, click **Issued Certificates**. Right-click the certificate, point to **All Tasks**, and click **Export Binary Data**. Click **Save binary data to a file**, click **OK**, click **Documents** under Libraries, and click **Save**. Close the certsrv window.

15. Restore the Internet Information Services (IIS) Manager window.

16. To install the certificate, click **Complete Certificate Request** in the right pane, click the **Browse** button, click the file extension arrow, click *.*, click **Binary Certificate – 2.tmp**, and click **Open**. Enter **Web Certificate** in the Friendly name text box, and click **OK**.

17. To view the Web site created during the self-service portal installation, expand **Sites**, and click **Microsoft System Center Virtual Machine Manager 2008 R2 Self-Service Portal (x64)**.

18. To add the binding to use SSL, click **Bindings** in the right pane, click **Add**, click the **Type** arrow, and click **HTTPS**. Enter the IP address for your Web server from Step 18 of Activity 6-1. Click the **SSL certificate** arrow, click **Web Certificate**, click **OK**, and click **Close**.

19. To open the default Web page created during the self-service portal installation, click **Start**, and then click **Internet Explorer**. Enter **https://www.*team1*.local** in the Address bar, substituting your team name for *team1*. When you finish, press **Enter**. Click **OK**, if necessary.

If you see any error messages in red, contact your instructor.

20. Leave the MGMT computer logged on for additional activities.

Activity 6-3: Creating a Template for Installation

Time Required: 60 minutes

Objective: Create a template from a virtual machine on a host computer.

Description: In this activity, your team creates a base virtual machine template from a deployed virtual machine. You install and configure a virtual machine to become the basis for future deployments with the Enterprise version of Windows Server 2008 R2 SP1. The last task is to store the base virtual machine in the library as a template.

Table 6-4 provides the team member assignments for this activity.

Team Member	Steps	Host Computer
1	1-16	MGMT
2	17-25	
3	26-29	
1	30-35	

Table 6-4   Team member assignments for Activity 6-3

© Cengage Learning 2014

1. Switch the KVM switch to port 1.

2. If necessary, log on to your MGMT server with a username of *Team1\Administrator*, substituting your team name for *Team1*. Enter a password of **P@ssw0rd**.

3. If necessary, open the VMM administrator console by double-clicking **SCVMM Admin Console** on the desktop.

4. To open the New Virtual Machine Wizard, click the **Virtual Machines** bar in the lower-left corner of the console window, and then click **New virtual machine** in the Actions pane.

5. In the Select Source window, click **Create the new virtual machine with a blank virtual hard disk**. Click **Next**.

6. To identify the virtual machine, enter **SSPPrep** in the Virtual machine name text box, enter **Install for Self Service Portal** in the Description text box, and then click **Next**.

7. To change the hardware profile, click the **Hardware profile** arrow, and click **HP_1N1VHD1G**.

8. To link to the Windows 2008 R2 SP1 installation files, click **Virtual DVD Drive**, click **Existing image file**, click **Browse**, click the Windows Server 2008 R2 SP1 file, click **OK**, and then click **Next**.

9. To place the virtual machine on a host, click **Next**.

10. To select the host, click the cluster host (clstr1 or clstr2) that has the best star rating, and click **Next**.

11. To accept the default virtual machine path, click **Next**.

12. To specify the network adapter, click the **Virtual Network** arrow, click **–Private VM – Virtual Network**, and then click **Next**.

13. To enter the guest OS that the virtual machine will run, click the **Specify the operating system you will install in the virtual machine** arrow, scroll and click **64-bit edition of Windows Server 2008 R2 Enterprise**, and then click **Next**.

14. To view the PowerShell script, click **View Script**, click **Format** in the Notepad window, click **Word Wrap**, examine the script, and close the Notepad window.

15. Review the Summary window, and then click **Previous** if necessary to return to a previous window and change a setting. When you are satisfied with the settings, click **Create**.

16. Wait for the virtual machine to be completed, and then close the Jobs window.

Ignore the message that Virtual Machine Manager cannot locate the boot or system volume.

17. To connect to the virtual machine, click **SSPPrep**, click **Start**, and then click **Connect to virtual machine**.

18. When the regional settings window appears, verify the selections for language, time, currency, and keyboard. Make corrections as needed, and then click **Next**.

19. Click the **Install now** link.

20. To indicate which version to install, click **Windows Server 2008 R2 Enterprise (Full Installation)**, and then click **Next**.

21. When the license terms appear, check **I accept the license terms**, and then click **Next**.

22. Click the **Custom (advanced)** icon.

23. Click **Disk 0 Unallocated Space**, and then click **Next**.

24. Wait for Windows to copy and expand files, install features and updates, and restart the computer to complete the installation.

25. Wait while Windows prepares to start for the first time and then prepares the computer for use.

26. When prompted that the user password must be changed before logging on the first time, click **OK**. Enter **P@ssw0rd** in the New password text box, press **Tab**, enter **P@ssw0rd** in the Confirm password text box, press **Enter**, and then click **OK**.

27. To set the time zone, click the **Set time zone** link. If necessary, click the **Change time zone** button, click the appropriate time zone, click the **Change date and time** button, change the time, and then click **OK** twice.

28. To enter the IP configuration, click **Configure networking**, right-click **Local Area Connection**, click **Properties**, clear the **Internet Protocol Version 6 (TCP/IPv6)** check box, and then click **OK**.

 If the Set Network Location window appears, click Work, and then click Close.

29. To reset the IP configuration, right-click **Local Area Connection**, click **Diagnose**, and then click **Close**. Close the Network Connections window.

 Contact your instructor if the Diagnose option did not reset the IP connection and enable the local area connection.

30. To switch to the Server Manager window, check **Do not show this window at logon**, and then close the Initial Configuration Tasks window.

31. To shut down the virtual machine, click **Start**. If necessary, click the **Log off** arrow, click **Shut down**, click the **Option** arrow, click **Operating System Reconfiguration (Planned)**, and click **OK**.

32. To remove the installation DVD, right-click **SSPPrep**, click **Properties**, click the **Hardware Configuration** tab, click **Virtual DVD**, and click **No media**. Click **OK**.

33. To create the template, click the **Library** bar in the lower-left corner of the console window, click **New template** in the right pane, click **From an existing virtual machine that is deployed on a host**, and click **Browse**. Click **SSPPrep**, click **OK**, and click **Next**. Click **Yes**. Enter **SSPDeploy** in the Template name text box, enter **Self Service template to deploy virtual machines** in the Description text box, and click **Next**. Review the hardware profile and click **Next**. Review the General settings and click **Next** twice. Click **Browse**, click **MSSCVMLibrary**, and click **OK**. Click **Next** and then click **Create**.

34. Wait for the template to be created, and close the Jobs window.

35. Remain logged on for future lab activities.

Configuring User Roles for the Self-Service Portal

The self-service portal is designed to help self-service users create and manage their own virtual machines. Rather than using the VMM administrator console, you access your virtual machines through a browser-based interface. Using role-based security, administrators define fine-grained control over the actions a user can perform when working with their virtual machines.

There are three types of users:

- VMM administrators control access with policies that designate capabilities.
- Delegated administrators manage a scoped environment. For example, a delegated administrator might control a geographical area such as Dallas. Within that scope, an administrator can control access with policies that further designate capabilities.
- Self-service users must use the self-service portal to access their virtual machines; within these virtual machines, they are listed as the owner in the system properties. Typically, self-service users have a quota that restricts the number of virtual machines they can run in the private cloud.

The user roles are defined using three components: Membership, Profile, and Scope. The following list briefly describes each component of the user role:

- *Membership*—This component specifies which users are part of a particular user role. Members can be individual Active Directory user accounts or security groups.
- *Profile*—This component specifies which actions are permitted, such as creating, starting, or shutting down a virtual machine. This component also specifies which user interface is accessible, such as the self-service portal or remote desktop, and specifies how the scope is defined.
- *Scope*—This component specifies the objects with which a user can interact.

Self-service portal roles are created and managed from the User Roles node in the Administration view of the VMM console, as shown in Figure 6-10.

To add a user role, click New user role in the right pane. Enter a name and description for the user role. Figure 6-11 shows the completed General tab for JDoe. When defining a user role, document the actions the user might take with particular virtual machines. Click Next to continue.

To add the John Doe user account for the user role, click Add, click Advanced, and enter J in the Name Starts with text box. Click Find Now, click John Doe, click OK twice, and click Next. Figure 6-12 shows John Doe added as a role member. You will create a user account in Activity 6-4. Click Next to specify the virtual machine scope.

In Activity 6-1, you created a host group called Self Service that contains the two host computers, CLSTR1 and CLSTR2, where virtual machines run. Figure 6-13 shows the virtual machine scope for Role_JDoe, which is the Self Service host group. Click Next to continue.

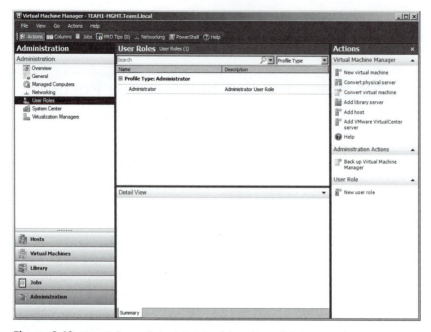

Figure 6-10 User Roles node in Administration view of VMM console

Source: Microsoft Virtual Machine Manager 2008 R2 SP1, Windows Server 2008 R2 SP1

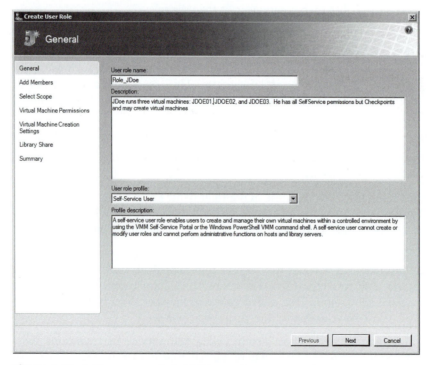

Figure 6-11 Adding a user role in VMM console

Source: Microsoft Virtual Machine Manager 2008 R2 SP1, Windows Server 2008 R2 SP1

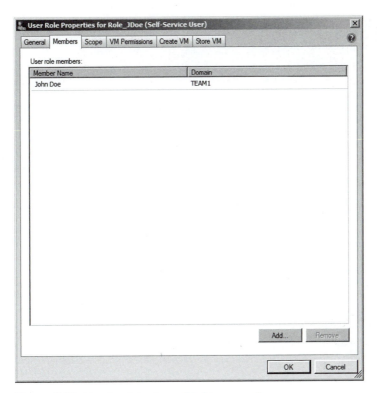

Figure 6-12 Member John Doe added to user role

Source: Microsoft Virtual Machine Manager 2008 R2 SP1, Windows Server 2008 R2 SP1

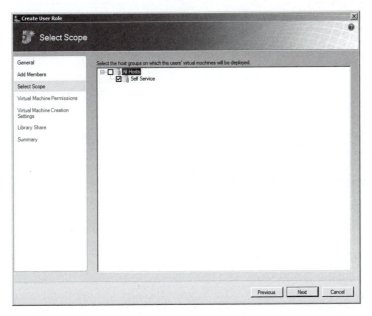

Figure 6-13 Virtual machine scope for Role_JDoe

Source: Microsoft Virtual Machine Manager 2008 R2 SP1, Windows Server 2008 R2 SP1

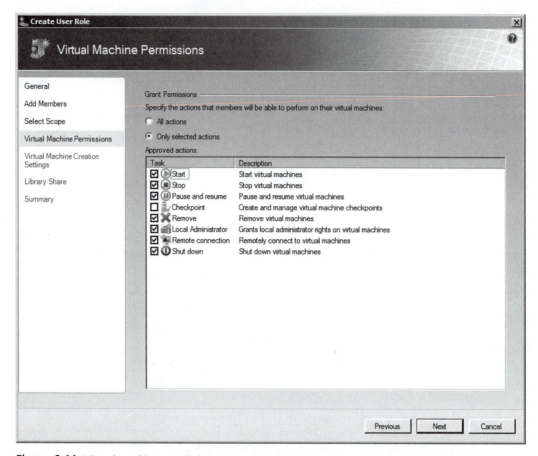

Figure 6-14 Virtual machine permissions

Source: Microsoft Virtual Machine Manager 2008 R2 SP1, Windows Server 2008 R2 SP1

Figure 6-14 shows the virtual machine permissions. John Doe has all permissions except Checkpoint. Restricting checkpoints reduces the hard disk space required for differencing disks.

You control the creation of virtual machines and the number of running virtual machines in the Virtual Machine Creation Settings window. The completed settings are shown in Figure 6-15. By checking the "Allow users to create new virtual machines" check box, you permit users to create virtual machines. Otherwise, users can run only the virtual machines you specify. To add templates, click Add, click the template in the library, and click OK.

Using quota points, you can control the number of virtual machines that the user can run simultaneously. You can assign up to 10 quota points for each virtual machine and more than 100 total quota points. To keep things simple, specify one quota point per virtual machine with a maximum of three quota points. Click Next to advance to the Library Share window.

In the Library Share window, you indicate the library servers with which the user can interact to build virtual machines. (See Figure 6-16.) By default, the user has read-only access to the templates and operating system files in the library. If you want the user to be able to store virtual machines in the library, check the box at the top of the window. You can reduce library maintenance by restricting access to read-only. Click Next to continue.

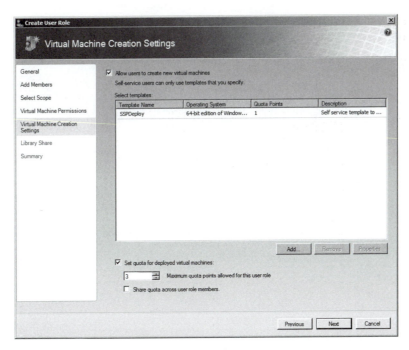

Figure 6-15 Virtual machine creation settings

Source: Microsoft Virtual Machine Manager 2008 R2 SP1, Windows Server 2008 R2 SP1

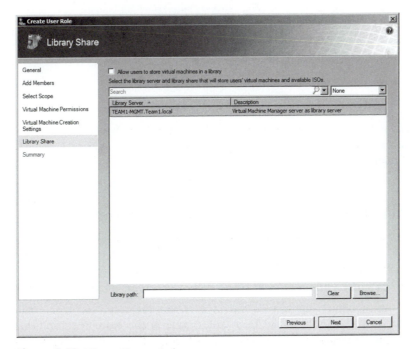

Figure 6-16 Library Share window

Source: Microsoft Virtual Machine Manager 2008 R2 SP1, Windows Server 2008 R2 SP1

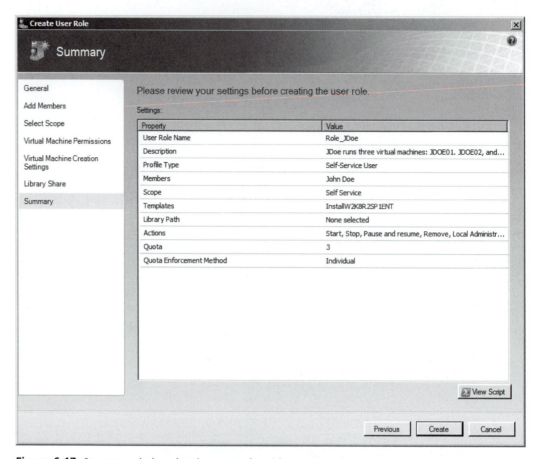

Figure 6-17 Summary window showing user role settings

Source: Microsoft Virtual Machine Manager 2008 R2 SP1, Windows Server 2008 R2 SP1

Figure 6-17 shows the Summary window. Review the settings, and then click Previous if necessary to return to a previous window and change a setting. When you are satisfied with the settings, click Create.

Activity 6-4: Configuring User Roles for the Self-Service Portal

Time Required: 15 minutes

Objective: Configure a user role for the self-service portal.

Description: In this activity, your team creates a user role for user John Doe. You create a user account for user Jdoe. Within the User Roles node in the Administration view of the VMM console, you configure access to virtual machines.

Table 6-5 provides the team member assignments for this activity.

Team Member	Steps	Host Computer
1	1-7	MGMT
2	8-16	

Table 6-5 Team member assignments for Activity 6-4

© Cengage Learning 2014

1. If necessary, switch the KVM switch to port 1.

2. If necessary, log on to your MGMT server with a username of *Team1*\Administrator, substituting your team name for *Team1*. Enter a password of **P@ssw0rd**.

3. To open the Active Directory Users and Computers console, click **Start**, point to **Administrative Tools**, and click **Active Directory Users and Computers**.

4. To create the John Doe user, expand *Team1*.local, substituting your team name for *Team1*. Click **Users**, click the **Action** menu, point to **New**, and click **User**.

5. Enter **John** in the First name text box, enter **Doe** in the Last name text box, enter **Jdoe** in the User logon name text box, and click **Next**.

6. Enter **P@ssw0rd** in the Password text box, enter **P@ssw0rd** in the Confirm password text box, clear the **User must change password at next logon** check box, click **User cannot change password**, and click **Password never expires**. Click **Next**, and then click **Finish**.

7. Close the Active Directory Users and Computers window.

8. If necessary, open the Virtual Machine Manager by double-clicking the **SCVMM Admin Console** icon on the desktop.

9. To add a user role for John Doe, click the **Administration** bar in the lower-left corner, click **User Roles** in the left pane, and click **New user role** in the right pane. Enter **Role_JDoe** as the user role name. In the Description text box, enter **Jdoe runs three virtual machines: JDOE01, JDOE02, and JDOE03. He has self-service permissions for all but Checkpoints and may create virtual machines.** When you finish, click **Next**.

10. To add a user account for the user role, click **Add**, click **Advanced**, and enter **J** in the Name Starts with text box. Click **Find Now**, click **John Doe**, and click **OK** twice. Click **Next**.

11. To indicate the host group, expand **All Hosts**, click **Self Service**, and click **Next**.

12. To specify the virtual machine permissions, click **Only selected actions**, clear the **Checkpoint** check boxes, and click **Next**.

13. To indicate which templates can be used, click **Allow users to create new virtual machines**, and click **Add**. Click **SSPDeploy**, click **OK**, click **Set quota for deployed virtual machines**, and enter **3** as the maximum quota points allowed for the user role. Click **Next**.

14. To prevent users from storing virtual machines in the library, leave the **Allow users to store virtual machines in the library** check box empty, and click **Next**.

15. Review the Summary window, and then click **Previous** if necessary to return to a previous window and change a setting. When you are satisfied with the settings, click **Create**.

16. Wait for the job to be completed, and then close the Jobs window.

Managing Virtual Machines with the Self-Service Portal

When managing virtual machines with the self-service portal, you can use many of the functions that you learned about in previous chapters. However, the user interface looks slightly different, as shown in Figure 6-18.

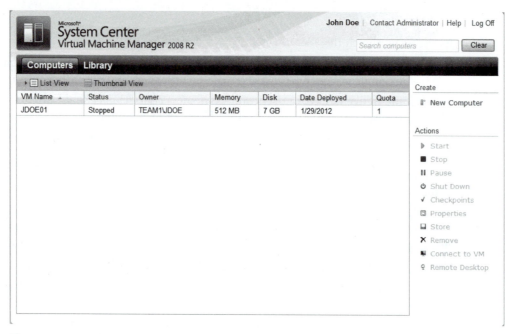

Figure 6-18 Virtual Machine Manager self-service portal

Source: Microsoft Virtual Machine Manager 2008 R2 SP1, Windows Server 2008 R2 SP1

To begin creating a new computer, click New Computer in the right pane. Figure 6-19 shows the completed entries that specify a new virtual machine. If you want the setup routine to generate a computer name automatically, leave the asterisk. Otherwise, enter a computer name. You must enter and confirm the password for the Administrator user account, and you must enter a product key in the correct format. Failure to enter any of the four preceding items results in a setup error. After entering the information for the virtual machine, click Create. The self-service portal displays a message that the virtual machine was created, which means the PowerShell script was created and a job was started. You will create three new virtual machines in Activity 6-6.

Earlier in this textbook, you used star ratings to determine the best host for a virtual machine. In the self-service portal, Microsoft's **intelligent placement** feature is used to automatically determine the best host computer on which to place a virtual machine. Various performance ratings for items such as CPUs, memory, and disks are collected from the virtual machine's hardware profile and the host computer where the virtual machine will potentially run. All of

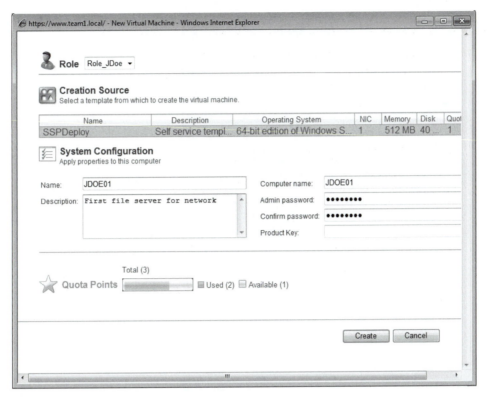

Figure 6-19 Entries for new computer

Source: Microsoft Virtual Machine Manager 2008 R2 SP1, Windows Server 2008 R2 SP1

this information is combined to generate a set of ratings for each host in the host group. To specify your placement preferences and access the Placement Settings window, click the Administration bar in the lower-left corner of the console window, click the General tab, click Placement Settings, and click Modify in the right pane. Slide the bars to adjust the settings, as shown in Figure 6-20.

Figure 6-21 shows the self-service portal window with three virtual machines created. To work with your virtual machines, use the options in the right pane.

To connect to a running virtual machine, click Connect to VM in the right pane. Figure 6-22 shows a connection. Each session is identified with a unique GUID, as shown at the top of the Remote Control Session window. If you want to work with multiple virtual machines, minimize and restore the Internet Explorer windows as needed. Note the Send Ctrl+Alt+Del button in the lower-left corner. If you lose a virtual machine session, the screen image disappears; click the Reconnect button to bring the session back.

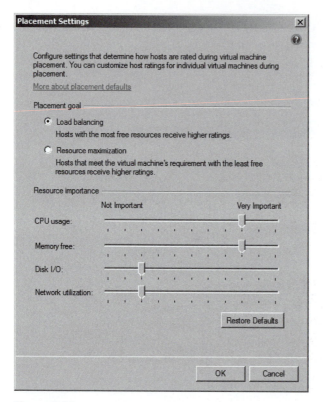

Figure 6-20 User preferences for virtual machines

Source: Microsoft Virtual Machine Manager 2008 R2 SP1, Windows Server 2008 R2 SP1

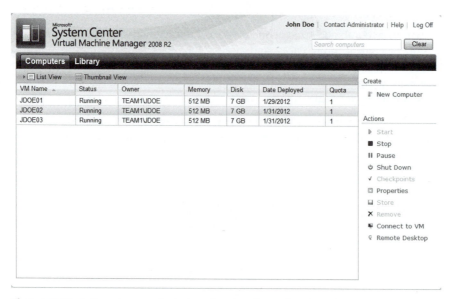

Figure 6-21 Self-service portal window showing three virtual machines running

Source: Microsoft Virtual Machine Manager 2008 R2 SP1, Windows Server 2008 R2 SP1

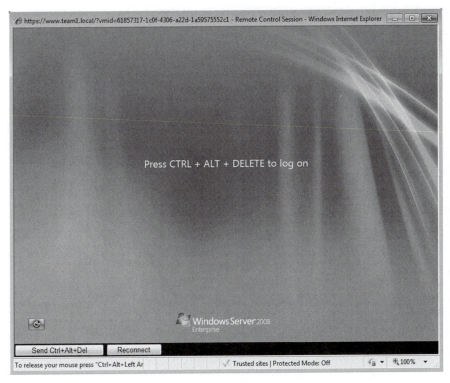

Figure 6-22 Remote Control Session window for virtual machine

Source: Microsoft Virtual Machine Manager 2008 R2 SP1 and Internet Explorer 8, on Windows Server 2008 R2 SP1

Activity 6-5: Configuring the Windows 7 Client to Access the Self-Service Portal

Time Required: 15 minutes

Objective: Configure the Windows 7 client to access the self-service portal.

Description: In this activity, your team configures the Windows 7 client to access the self-service portal. You installed the Windows 7 client in Chapter 1. You will also add a virtual network to the MGMT computer to enable access to the Management network. Then, you will configure Internet Explorer to access the self-service portal.

Table 6-6 provides the team member assignments for this activity.

Team Member	Steps	Host Computer
3	1-13	MGMT
1	14-17	
2	18-25	

Table 6-6 Team member assignments for Activity 6-5

© *Cengage Learning 2014*

1. If necessary, switch the KVM switch to port 1.

2. If necessary, log on to your MGMT server with a username of **Team1\Administrator**, substituting your team name for *Team1*. Enter a password of **P@ssw0rd**.

3. If necessary, open the Virtual Machine Manager by double-clicking the **SCVMM Admin Console** icon on the desktop.

4. To add an external virtual network that is connected to the existing Management network, click the **Hosts** bar in the lower-left corner, and then click **Team1-MGMT** in the left pane, substituting your team name for *Team1*. Click **Properties** in the right pane, click the **Networking** tab, click **Add** in the menu bar, and enter **Management Virtual** over the text "New Virtual Network #0." Click **Physical network adapter**, click **Add**, click the **Host network adapter** arrow, click the network adapter, click **OK** twice, and click **Yes**.

5. Wait for the job to be completed, and then close the Jobs window.

6. To rename the network adapter for the management switch, click the **Network** icon on the taskbar, click **Open Network and Sharing Center**, and click **Change adapter settings**. Right-click the physical adapter, which is identified with a vendor name, and then click **Rename**. Enter **Management Switch** and press **Enter**.

7. To add a network adapter to the Windows 7 client, click the **Virtual Machines** bar in the lower-left corner, right-click **Windows 7 Client**, and click **Properties**. Click the **Hardware Configuration** tab, click **Network Adapter** in the menu bar, click **Synthetic network adapter**, click **Connected to**, confirm that the text reads "Management Virtual or Local Area Connection - Virtual Network," and click **OK**.

If you cannot add a network adapter to the Windows 7 client, continue with Step 8.

8. To start the Windows 7 client, click the **Virtual Machines** bar, click **Windows 7 Client**, click **Start**, and click **Connect to virtual machine**.

9. Log on with a password of **P@ssw0rd**.

If the Set Network Location window appears, click Work network and click Close.

10. To determine the IP configuration for your Windows 7 client computer, locate the team number assigned by your instructor in Table 6-7. This row contains the IP configuration.

It is very important that you use the correct IP addresses for your classroom network. Ask your instructor if an alternative IP addressing scheme will be used in your classroom.

11. To enter the IP configuration, click the **Network** icon on the taskbar, click **Open Network and Sharing Center**, click **Change adapter settings**, and right-click the local area connection. Click **Properties**, clear the **Internet Protocol Version 6 (TCP/IPv6)** check box, click **Internet Protocol Version 4 (TCP/IPv4)**, and then click **Properties**. Click **Use**

Team#	IP Address	Subnet Mask	Default Gateway	DNS Server Address
1	192.168.0.116	255.255.255.0	192.168.0.1	192.168.0.111
2	192.168.0.126	255.255.255.0	192.168.0.1	192.168.0.121
3	192.168.0.136	255.255.255.0	192.168.0.1	192.168.0.131
4	192.168.0.146	255.255.255.0	192.168.0.1	192.168.0.141
5	192.168.0.156	255.255.255.0	192.168.0.1	192.168.0.151
6	192.168.0.166	255.255.255.0	192.168.0.1	192.168.0.161

Table 6-7 IP configurations for Windows 7 client

© Cengage Learning 2014

the following **IP Address**, enter the IP address you identified in Step 10 in the IP address text box, and then press **Tab** twice; the subnet mask will appear in the Subnet mask text box. Next, enter the default gateway you identified in Step 10, press **Tab** twice, and enter the preferred DNS server address from Step 10. Click **OK**, and then click **Close**. Close the Network Connections window.

12. To activate Windows, click **Start**, right-click **Computer**, click **Properties**, and then scroll and click **Change product key**. Enter the product key provided by your instructor, and click **Next**.

13. When the activation is complete, click **Close**. Close the Control Panel window.

14. To place the Windows 7 client on the domain, click **Start**, right-click **Computer**, and click **Properties**. Scroll and click **Change settings**, click **Change**, click **Domain**, and enter *Team1*.**local**, substituting your team name for *Team1*. When you finish, click **OK**.

15. Enter **Administrator** as the user name, enter **P@ssw0rd** as the password, and click **OK**.

16. When the welcome message appears, click **OK** twice. Click **Close**, and then click **Restart Now**.

17. Wait for the virtual machine to restart.

18. Click the **Action** menu, click **Send Ctrl+Alt+Delete**, and click **Switch User**. Click **Other User**, and then log on using **jdoe** as the user name and **P@ssw0rd** as the password.

19. To set up Internet Explorer, click the **Internet Explorer** icon on the taskbar, and click **Next**. Click **No, don't turn on**, click **Next**, click **Use express settings**, and click **Finish**.

20. If the AutoComplete Passwords window appears, click the **Don't offer to remember any more passwords** check box, and then click **No**.

21. To open the self-service portal, enter **https://www.team1.local** in the address bar, and press **Enter**.

22. To make the self-service portal the default Web site, close all Web sites but the Virtual Machine Manager self-service portal. Click **Tools**, click **Internet Options**, click **Use Current**, and click **OK**. Maximize the Internet Explorer window.

23. Log on to the self-service portal with a username of *team1*\jdoe, substituting your team name for *team1*. Enter a password of **P@ssw0rd**. Click the **Don't offer to remember any more passwords** check box, and click **No**.

24. To assign the self-service portal to trusted sites, click **Tools**, click **Internet Options**, and then click the **Security** tab. Click **Trusted Sites**, click **Sites**, click **Add**, click **Close**, and click **OK**.

25. Leave the virtual machine running for future lab activities. Leave the Windows 7 client running, and leave the self-service portal window open.

Activity 6-6: Working with Virtual Machines in the Self-Service Portal

Time Required: 90 minutes

Objective: Create and configure virtual machines for the self-service portal.

Description: In this activity, your team creates a virtual machine for JDoe. You install the ActiveX control to permit access to the running virtual machine. You configure the virtual machine, including the IP configuration. You repeat the creation and configuration steps for two additional virtual machines and test their connectivity.

Table 6-8 provides the team member assignments for this activity.

1. To create a virtual machine, click **New Computer** in the right pane, enter **JDOE01** as the name, enter **First file server for network** as the description, enter **P@ssw0rd** as the password, and enter **P@ssw0rd** in the Confirm password text box.

2. If your school uses volume keys, ask your instructor to enter the product key.

3. If your school does not use volume keys, enter the product key provided by your instructor.

Enter product keys in the following format: xxxxx-xxxxx-xxxxx-xxxxx-xxxxx.

4. To submit the PowerShell script, click **Create**.

5. When informed that the virtual machine was created successfully, click **OK**.

6. Wait for the files to be created completely.

It may take up to 30 minutes to complete the Background Intelligent Transfer Service (BITS) transfer and virtual machine customization.

Team Member	Steps	Host Computer
3	1-14	MGMT
1	15, 9-14	
2	16-19	
3	20, 16-19	
1	21, 16-19	
2	22-25	

Table 6-8   Team member assignments for Activity 6-6

7. To install the ActiveX control and view the running virtual machines, click the **Thumb-nail** view, click the yellow message under the Internet Explorer menu bar, and click **Install This Add-on for All Users on This Computer.** Log on by entering *Team1* **Administrator,** substituting your team name for *Team1.* Enter a password of **P@ssw0rd,** and then click **Yes.**

8. Wait for the transfer and customization to be completed and for the message status to appear as Stopped.

If the transfer or customization was not completed successfully, refer to the troubleshooting section later in this chapter.

9. To create the second virtual machine, click **New Computer** in the right pane, enter **JDOE02** as the name, enter **Second file server for network** as the description, enter **P@ssw0rd** as the password, and enter **P@ssw0rd** in the Confirm password text box.

10. If your school uses volume keys, ask your instructor to enter the product key.

11. If your school does not use volume keys, enter the product key provided by your instructor.

12. To submit the PowerShell script, click **Create.**

13. When you see the message that the virtual machine was created successfully, click **OK.**

14. Wait for the transfer and customization to be completed and for the message status to appear as Stopped.

15. Repeat Steps 9 through 14, but enter **JDOE03** as the name and **Third file server for network** as the description.

16. To start the JDOE01 virtual machine, click **JDOE01** under VM Name, click **Start,** and click **Connect to VM.**

17. To log on, click the **Send Ctrl+Alt+Del** button at the bottom of the window, enter **P@ssw0rd,** and press **Enter.**

18. Click **View Network Connections,** and right-click **Local Area Connection.** Click **Properties,** clear the **Internet Protocol Version 6 (TCP/IPv6)** check box, click **Internet Protocol Version 4 (TCP/IPv4),** and then click **Properties.** Click **Use the following IP Address,** enter **192.168.30.101** in the IP address text box, and then press **Tab** twice; the subnet mask will appear in the Subnet mask text box. Next, enter **192.168.30.1** as the default gateway, press **Tab** twice, and enter **192.168.30.1** for the preferred DNS server. Click **OK,** and click **Close.** Close the Network Connections window.

19. To open the inbound ICMP port, click **Start,** point to **Administrative Tools,** and click **Windows Firewall with Advanced Security.** Click **Inbound Rules,** scroll and right-click **File and Printer Sharing (Echo Request – ICMPv4-In),** and click **Enable Rule.** Close the Windows Firewall with Advanced Security window. Minimize the Virtual Machine Viewer window. Keep the Virtual Machine Manager window open.

20. Repeat Steps 16 through 19 for JDOE02 with an IP address of **192.168.30.102.**

21. Repeat Steps 16 through 19 for JDOE03 with an IP address of **192.168.30.103**.

22. To open a command prompt, click **Start,** and then click **Command Prompt.**

23. To test connectivity to JDOE01, enter **ping 192.168.30.101**, and press **Enter.**

24. To test connectivity to JDOE02, enter **ping 192.168.30.102**, and press **Enter.**

25. Leave the virtual machines running for future lab activities. Leave the Windows 7 client running and leave the self-service portal window open.

Using Virtual LANs

VMM supports virtual local area networks (VLANs) for virtual machines running on Hyper-V host computers. In Chapter 1, you were introduced to VLANs, which you can use to create independent logical networks within a physical network. VLANs are useful when a set of virtual machines requires an independent network for security purposes. You configure VLANs by assigning a numerical value called a **VLAN identifier** (**VLAN ID**) to the adapter for a virtual network on the virtual machine. To enable virtual machines to communicate correctly, you configure static IP addresses. The switch on the private VM network should be capable of working with VLAN tagging.

Activity 6-7: Working with Virtual LANs

Time Required: 25 minutes

Objective: Practice working with virtual LANs.

Description: In this activity, your team works with VLANs. You will reconfigure a virtual adapter to support VLANs and attach it to the virtual machines. You will also test connectivity over the VLAN.

Table 6-9 provides the team member assignments for this activity.

Team Member	Steps	Host Computer
3	1-5	CLSTR1
1	6, 1-5	CLSTR2
	7-11	MGMT
	12-13	CLSTR1
	14, 12-13	CLSTR2
	15-20	MGMT
	21-23	CLSTR1
	24, 21-23	CLSTR2
	25, 21-23	MGMT

Table 6-9 Team member assignments for Activity 6-7

© Cengage Learning 2014

Do not continue with Activity 6-7 until you complete Activity B-3 in Appendix B to configure the Netgear GS105E to support VLAN tagging. Check with your instructor if you need help configuring a switch other than the Netgear GS105E.

1. Switch the KVM switch to port 2.

2. If necessary, log on to your CLSTR1 server with a username of *Team1*\Administrator, substituting your team name for *Team1*. Enter a password of **P@ssw0rd**.

3. To start Hyper-V Manager, double-click the **Hyper-V Manager** icon on the desktop.

4. Click *Team1*-**CLSTR1**, substituting your team name for *Team1*.

5. Click **Virtual Network Manager** in the right pane. Click **Private VM – Virtual Network**, click the **Enable virtual LAN identification for management operating system** check box, and click **OK**.

6. Repeat Steps 1 through 5 for CLSTR2, which is on switch port 3.

7. Switch the KVM switch to port 1.

8. Return to the JDOE03 virtual machine.

9. To open a command prompt, click **Start**, and then click **Command Prompt**.

10. To test connectivity to JDOE01, enter ping **192.168.30.101**, and press **Enter**.

11. To test connectivity to JDOE02, enter ping **192.168.30.102**, and press **Enter**.

12. Switch the KVM switch to port 2.

13. Click **Virtual Network Manager** in the right pane. Click **Private VM – Virtual Network**, clear the **Enable virtual LAN identification for management operating system** check box, and click **OK**.

14. Repeat Steps 12 and 13 for CLSTR2, which is on switch port 3.

Do not continue with this activity until you complete Activity B-4 in Appendix B to configure the Netgear GS105E to remove VLAN tagging. Check with your instructor if you need help configuring a switch other than the Netgear GS105E.

15. Switch the KVM switch to port 1 to return to the self-service portal.

16. Return to the JDOE03 virtual machine, and minimize the Virtual Machine Viewer.

17. Click the JDOE01 virtual machine, click **Shut Down**, and click **OK**.

18. Wait for the virtual machine to display a status of Stopped.

19. Repeat Steps 17 and 18 for the JDOE02 and JDOE03 virtual machines.

20. To shut down the Windows 7 client, click **Start**, and then click **Shut down**.

21. Switch the KVM switch to port 2.

22. To shut down the host computer, click **Start**, click the arrow next to **Log off**, click **Shut down**, click the **Option** arrow, click **Operating System: Reconfiguration (Planned)**, and then click **OK**. If necessary, click **Yes**.

23. Wait for the host computer to shut down.

24. Complete Steps 21 through 23 for CLSTR2, which is on KVM switch port 3.

25. Complete Steps 21 through 23 for MGMT, which is on KVM switch port 1.

Troubleshooting the Self-Service Portal

This section identifies several problems that you might encounter when working with the self-service portal. Specific prescriptions are outlined for common errors. If these prescriptions do not resolve your problem, search the Internet for a possible solution. When searching, enter as much information about the error as possible.

Check Existing Host Computer Configurations

Use the Virtual Machine Manager Configuration Analyzer (VMMCA) as a diagnostic tool to evaluate important configuration settings for computers that are serving VMM roles or other VMM functions. The VMMCA performs the following tasks:

- Scans the hardware and software configurations
- Evaluates configurations of the host computers against a set of predefined rules
- Displays error messages and warnings for any configurations that are not optimal for the VMM role or for other VMM functions

To run the VMMCA, click Start, point to All Programs, click Virtual Machine Manager Configuration Analyzer, and click Configuration Analyzer. Click Scan to start the scan. Wait for the scan to complete. Disregard the two warning messages about hot fixes and reporting.

Check Process for Running Job

Figure 6-23 shows the progress for a running job. For example, to check the progress of a job that creates a new virtual machine, follow these steps:

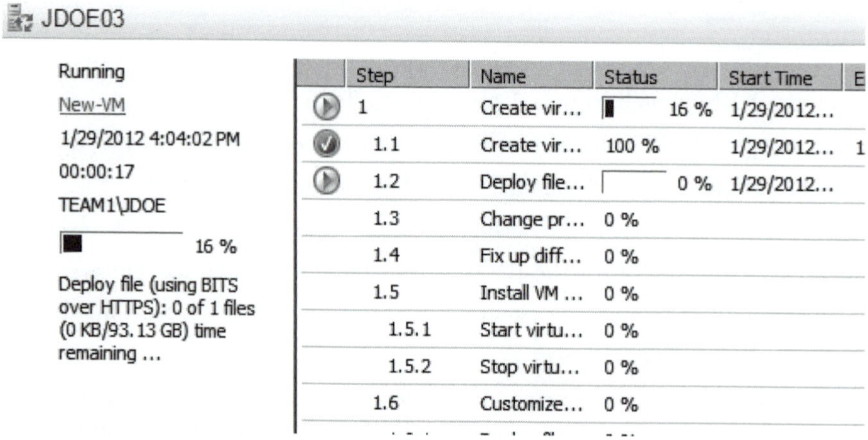

Figure 6-23 Progress for virtual machine creation

Source: Microsoft Virtual Machine Manager 2008 R2 SP1, Windows Server 2008 R2 SP1

1. Return to the Virtual Machine Manager console on the MGMT host computer.

2. Click the Hosts bar in the lower-left corner, click Self Service, and click the entry for the virtual machine.

3. Click the Latest Job tab.

Internal Error Message 2912

If you receive the internal error message shown in Figure 6-24, you must rebuild the extensible counters and all other performance counters. Follow these steps:

1. To determine which host computer failed, click the VM name with the Creation Failed message in the VMM self-service portal window. Click Properties, click the Latest Job tab, and examine the error message block to identify the failing host computer (CLSTR1 or CLSTR2). Click OK.

2. Switch to the host computer.

3. Click Start, right-click Command Prompt, and click Run as administrator.

4. Enter "cd\windows\system32," and then press Enter.

5. Enter "lodctr /R," and press Enter. Note that in this command, the "R" is uppercase. You should see a message that the performance counters were rebuilt.

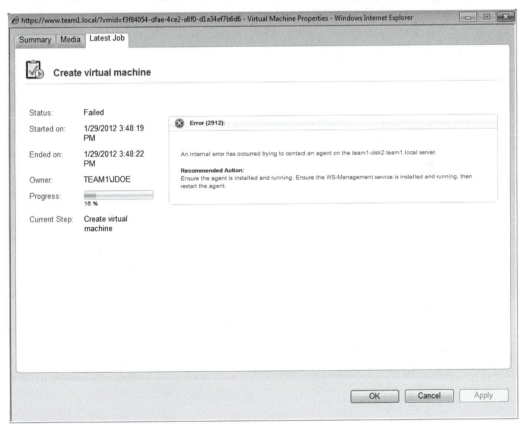

Figure 6-24 Internal error message

Source: Microsoft Virtual Machine Manager 2008 R2 SP1, Windows Server 2008 R2 SP1

6. Close the Command Prompt window.

7. To restart the host computer, click Start, click the Log off arrow, click Restart, click the Option arrow, click Operating System: Reconfiguration (Planned), and click OK.

Frozen BITS Transfer

This problem occurs because of a conflict between two protocols, BITS and HTTPS, that are trying to use the same port 443. (Refer back to Figure 6-23.) To fix this problem, move BITS to another port and open the Advanced Firewall inbound port on the host computers, as described in the following steps:

1. Switch the KVM switch to port 1.

2. To start the Registry Editor, click Start, right-click Command Prompt, click Run as administrator, enter "start regedit," and press Enter.

3. To change the key, expand HKEY_LOCAL_MACHINE, expand SOFTWARE, expand Microsoft, and scroll and expand Microsoft System Center Virtual Machine Manager Server. Click Settings, right-click BITSTcpPort, click Modify, click Decimal, enter 8500, and click OK. Close the Registry Editor window.

4. To open the new port, click Start, point to Administrative Tools, and click Windows Firewall with Advanced Security. Click Inbound Rules, click New Rule in the right pane, click Port, and click Next. Enter 8500, click Next, click Allow the connection, click Next twice, enter Open 8500 in the Name text box, and click Finish. Close the Windows Firewall with Advanced Security window.

5. Switch the KVM switch to port 2.

6. To open the new port, click Start, point to Administrative Tools, and click Windows Firewall with Advanced Security. Click Inbound Rules, click New Rule in the right pane, click Port, and click Next. Enter 8500, click Next, click Allow the connection, click Next twice, enter Open 8500 in the Name text box, and click Finish. Close the Windows Firewall with Advanced Security window.

7. To restart the management services, click Start, point to Administrative Tools, and click Services. Scroll and right-click Windows Remote Management (WS-Management), click Restart, and click Yes. Wait for the services to restart. Close the open windows.

8. Repeat Steps 5 through 7 for CLSTR2 on KVM switch port 3.

Excessive Time to Create the Virtual Machine

If a new virtual machine takes longer than 30 minutes to create, you might have a Windows setup problem. To resolve this problem, you need to connect to the virtual machine and view the setup process. You might have a missing product key, as shown in Figure 6-25, or an invalid entry in the answer file created by the self-service portal. To view the setup, complete these steps:

1. Return to the Virtual Machine Manager console on the MGMT host computer.

2. Click the Hosts bar in the lower-left corner, click Self Service, and click the entry for the virtual machine.

3. Click Connect to virtual machine.

4. Review the error and develop a plan to solve the problem.

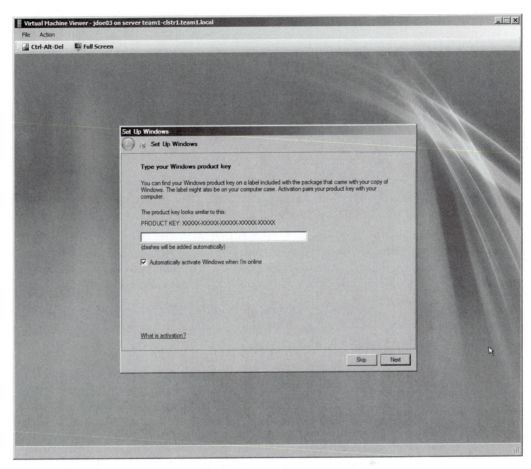

Figure 6-25 Missing product key during setup

Source: Microsoft Virtual Machine Manager 2008 R2 SP1, Windows Server 2008 R2 SP1

Excessive Time for BITS to Copy the Files

If BITS takes longer than 30 minutes to copy files, you might have a problem with the network adapter configuration. For example, some Ethernet adapter cards have incompatibilities with Hyper-V. To fix the problem, the Offload functions must be disabled on each network adapter. For example, you should disable the IPv4 Checksum Offload, Large Send Offload Version 2 (IPv4), Large Send Offload Version 2 (IPv6), TCP Checksum Offload (IPv4), TCP Checksum Offload (IPv6), UDP Checksum Offload (IPv4), and UDP Checksum Offload (IPv6). To verify that a problem exists, complete the following steps.

1. Return to the Virtual Machine Manager console on the MGMT host computer.

2. Click the Virtual Machines bar in the lower-left corner, expand Hosts, click the Self Service node, and click the entry for the virtual machine.

3. Click the Latest Job tab.

4. Review the error and develop a plan to solve the problem.

Next, you need to connect to each host computer (MGMT, CLSTR1, and CLSTR2) and remove the Offload settings for Management network adapters. To correct the problem, complete the following steps:

1. To open the local area connection on each host computer, right-click the Network icon on the taskbar, click Open Network and Sharing Center, and click Change Adapter Settings.

2. For each network adapter or switch on the Management network, right-click the local area connection, click Properties, click Configure, and click the Advanced tab. Click each of the offload items, click the Value arrow, and click Disabled. When you finish, click OK.

3. To start the Registry Editor, click Start, right-click Command Prompt, and click Run as administrator. Enter "start regedit," and then press Enter.

4. To change the key, expand HKEY_LOCAL_MACHINE, expand System, expand CurrentControlSet, scroll and expand Services, scroll and expand TCPIP, and expand Parameters. Right-click DisableTaskOffload, click Modify, click Decimal, enter 1, and click OK. Close the Registry Editor and Command Prompt windows.

Chapter Summary

- The self-service portal provides a Web-based interface to the virtual machines in the private cloud. You install the self-service portal to manage virtual machines.

- You configure user roles to control access to the virtual machines running in the private cloud.

- You can create templates to deploy virtual machines, and then create virtual machines from the self-service portal.

- You can use VLANs to control access to networks.

- Troubleshooting is sometimes necessary to solve common problems that occur while installing, configuring, and using the self-service portal.

Key Terms

Active Directory Certificate Services Role   A Microsoft feature that lets you create and manage certificates used in software security systems.

Certificate Authority Role service   A Microsoft feature that issues digital certificates.

intelligent placement   A Microsoft feature that places virtual machines on the most appropriate host computer.

Secure Sockets Layer (SSL)   A protocol that allows Web browsers to communicate across a network without allowing eavesdropping.

VLAN identifier (VLAN ID)   A number that identifies the VLAN to which the frame belongs.

Review Questions

1. _Vlans_ provide a Web-based interface to virtual machines in the private cloud.

2. Unencrypted communications between a Web browser and a Web site use the _____ protocol.

3. Encrypted communications between a Web browser and a Web site use the _SSL_ protocol.

4. To use certificates with a Web server, you install _____. (Choose all correct answers.)

   a. Active Directory Domain Services

   b. the Active Directory Certificate Services Role

   c. the Certificate Authority Role service

   d. Domain Name Services

5. What is the proper sequence when working with certificates?

   a. Create a binary file, request a domain certificate, issue the certificate, and bind the certificate to the Web site.

   b. Request a domain certificate, issue the certificate, create a binary file, install the certificate, and bind the certificate to the Web site.

   c. Request a domain certificate, create a binary file, install the certificate, issue the certificate, create a binary file, and bind the certificate to the Web site.

   d. Request a domain certificate, issue the certificate, and bind the certificate to the Web site.

6. Which of the following fields are required when requesting a certificate? (Choose all correct answers.)

   a. Common Name

   b. Organization

   c. Organizational unit

   d. Web administrator

   e. City/locality

   f. State/province

   g. Country/region

7. A/n _____ is used to identify the certificate for the binding step.

8. A/n _____ record is used to identify the Web server in DNS.

9. To begin creating a certificate, you open _____ in IIS.

10. Which of the following user types are available with user roles? (Choose all correct answers.)

    a. VMM administrators

    b. delegated administrators

    c. shadow

    d. self-service

    e. constrained

11. With _____ security, administrators define fine-grained control over the actions a user can perform when working with virtual machines in the self-service portal.

12. What are the components of the user role? (Choose all correct answers.)

    a. Membership

    b. User account

    c. Profile

    d. Scope

13. The _____ specifies the virtual machines with which a user can interact.

14. A/n _____ contains the host computers that will run the user's virtual machines in the self-service portal.

15. With _____, you control the number of virtual machines that a user can run in the self-service portal.

16. By default, the user has only _____ access to the templates and operating system files in the library.

    a. read/write

    b. read

    c. full control

    d. no

    e. write

17. When you are creating a new computer from the self-service portal window, which of the following items are required? (Choose all correct answers.)

    a. computer name

    b. product key

    c. password

    d. confirmation of password

    e. template name

18. _____ automatically determines the best host computer on which to place a virtual machine.

19. Prior to logging on to a virtual machine in the Remote Control Session window, you _____.

    a. press the Ctrl+Alt+Delete keys

    b. click Action and then click Ctrl-Alt-Del

    c. click the Send Ctrl+Alt+Del button

    d. click Ctrl-Alt-Del

20. To check the progress of a job submitted from the self-service portal, you _____. (Choose all correct answers.)

    a. return to the MGMT host computer

    b. click the Hosts bar

    c. right-click the entry for the virtual machine

    d. click the Latest Job tab

Case Projects

Case 6-1: Self-Service Portal Demonstration

You have installed the self-service portal for your organization, and you have been asked to demonstrate the self-service portal at the next TechShare meeting. Prepare a detailed outline for your presentation.

Case 6-2: Using User Roles

Your boss is concerned that the self-service portal might allow unrestricted placement of virtual machines on the host computers. Prepare a one-page policy statement on how to use the self-service portal.

Case 6-3: Problem with TCP Offload

BITS has taken longer than 30 minutes to copy files, and the operation is still not complete. You know that some network adapters do not work well with Hyper-V when you are using TCP Offload functions. On the Internet, research the network adapters that might cause this problem, and compare them with the network adapters you are using in your lab. Prepare a one-page report of your findings.

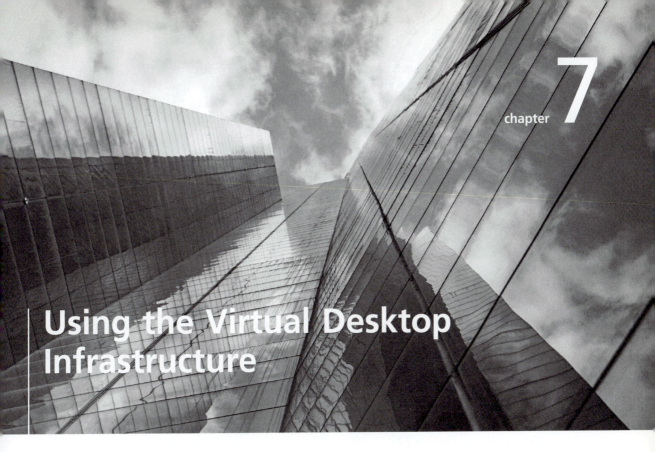

chapter 7

Using the Virtual Desktop Infrastructure

After reading this chapter and completing the exercises, you will be able to:

- Describe the remote Virtual Desktop Infrastructure (VDI)
- Install components for the VDI
- Configure personal virtual desktops
- Configure roaming profiles and folder redirection

In this chapter, you learn to use Virtual Desktop Infrastructure (VDI), which gives users the freedom to access their Windows desktops on a computer of their choice. By using VDI, users can work almost anywhere, whether they are inside or outside the organization's network. Also, it encourages organizations to implement "bring your own" device initiatives, which means that employees can use their own computer equipment both for personal reasons and work. The Remote Desktop role services implement VDI and give administrators a choice of using personal virtual desktops or pooled virtual desktops. Roaming profiles and folder redirection allow users' settings and data files to follow them when working with virtual desktops. The private cloud provides the resources for implementing VDI.

Describing Remote Virtual Desktop Infrastructure (VDI)

In Chapter 6, you learned to use the self-service portal to create, start, run, and stop virtual machines. While IT personnel feel comfortable with the self-service portal, many users benefit from an environment that is easier to use, such as VDI. VDI is an alternative delivery model that allows users to access secure and centrally managed desktops running within the private cloud. VDI appeals to organizations with a mobile workforce or knowledge workers with a need for flexible desktop access, including contractors, sales personnel, and office workers who require flexible locations or need to work from home.

Another benefit of VDI is the ability to reuse existing PCs. Microsoft encourages customers to repurpose existing PCs as **thin clients** by providing a smaller, more secure version of Windows 7.

VDI does not convert a user's physical computer to a virtual machine; instead, VDI provides standardized desktops as part of a strategy for organizations to reduce management costs. Its major benefit is centralizing the maintenance of operating systems and applications software.

VDI puts the user's desktop on a host computer running Hyper-V, rather than on a PC at someone's desk. Generally speaking, VDI offers two solutions:

- A personal desktop assigned to a user (**personal virtual desktops**)
- A pool of desktops available to a set of users on a temporary basis (**pooled virtual desktops**)

When you worked with the self-service portal in Chapter 6, you selected the virtual machine. With VDI, you can use a shortcut on the Start menu to the right host computer and make sure the virtual machine is ready for connection.

With the personal virtual desktop, the administrator determines how much control the user has over the desktop. On the other hand, users cannot alter a shared pool of virtual desktops. You configure Remote Desktop Services to discard changes and place the virtual machine in the state saved when you log off.

In terms of applications, the two types of desktops also have differences. On a personal virtual desktop, you can allow users to download and install applications. On pooled virtual desktops, it is difficult to support personalization because all desktops have the same applications and personal installations do not work.

Remote Desktop Role Services

Four services support the Remote Desktop (RD) role, as shown in Figure 7-1:

- RD connection broker, which manages connections to sessions
- RD session host server, which runs in redirection mode to route requests
- RD virtualization host, which integrates with Hyper-V
- RD Web access, which provides a Web site for access to virtual desktops from Web browsers

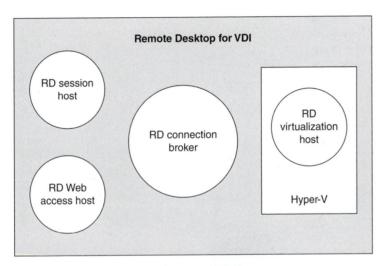

Figure 7-1 Four role services for Remote Desktop

© *Cengage Learning 2014*

Figure 7-2 shows the relationships among these four role services. Starting from the bottom, the user initiates a connection from the Web page or through the **RemoteApp and Desktop Connections** shortcut on the Start menu. The RD session host routes the request to the RD connection broker, which locates the virtual machine for the user with the help of the RD virtualization host. The user connects to the virtual machine with the provided IP address.

The main purpose of the **RD connection broker** is to arrange a user connection to an appropriate host computer. Brokering of the connection involves the following:

- Identifying the virtual machine for the user's personal desktop.
- Preparing the virtual machine for remote connections by communicating with the RD virtualization host (for example, waking the virtual machine from a saved state).
- Querying the IP address of the virtual machine by communicating with the RD virtualization host. This IP address is returned to the Remote Desktop session host, which is then returned to the requesting client.
- Monitoring user sessions in a virtual desktop pool scenario. A user with an existing session in a pool is redirected to the hosting virtual machine.

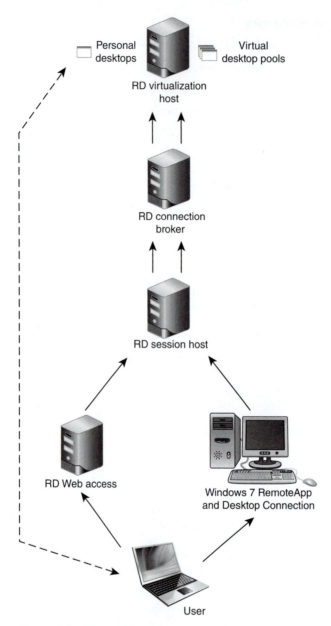

Figure 7-2 Relationships between four role services and clients

The purpose of the **RD session host** is to securely redirect a client connection to a virtual machine. When a user requests a virtual machine, the RD session host queries the RD connection broker, which in turn provisions a virtual machine for the user and returns its IP address to the RD session host. The RD session host will then redirect the client to connect to the virtual machine by using the IP address.

The **RD virtualization host** integrates with Hyper-V to provide virtual machines that can be used as personal virtual desktops or virtual desktop pools. An RD virtualization host has the following functions:

- Monitoring virtual machine guest sessions and reporting these sessions to the RD connection broker

- Preparing the virtual machine for a remote desktop connection when requested by the RD connection broker

RD Web access provides a user with an aggregated view of desktop connections via a Web browser. Using RD Web access, a user can view all available virtual desktops, including all personal virtual desktops and virtual desktop pools. VDI virtual machines are also accessible via the RemoteApp and Desktop Connections shortcut on the Start menu in Windows 7.

Discovering a Virtual Machine

The first step to using a virtual machine is discovering that it exists. To allow users to discover virtual machines (see Figure 7-3), you assign a personal desktop using the RD connection broker. Assignments for personal virtual machines are recorded in Active Directory as part of the user account. Also, you can create a virtual machine pool to be shared by multiple users.

When a user—call her Ann Little—navigates to the RemoteApp and Desktop Connections shortcut on the Start menu, she sees a folder with an icon representing the virtual machine. Clicking the icon for the virtual machine starts a transfer of user credentials to the RD connection broker. The RD connection broker contacts Active Directory, which returns the user resources. The personal virtual machine name is returned to Ann.

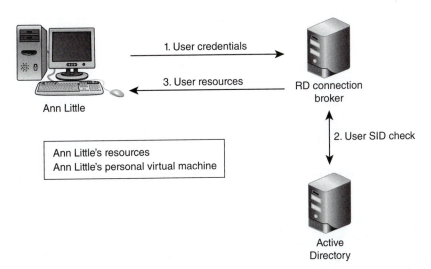

Figure 7-3 How virtual machine discovery works

Ann initiates the brokering phase by clicking the personal desktop icon. The brokering must give her access to her virtual machine. The RD connection broker uses the virtual machine plug-in to provide the IP address for the virtual machine. The final stage is **orchestration**, in which the virtual machine is made ready for connection (see Figure 7-4). Orchestration makes it possible to put a virtual machine to sleep, place the virtual machine in the saved state, and wake it up on demand. Saving the virtual machine to disk conserves valuable computer memory.

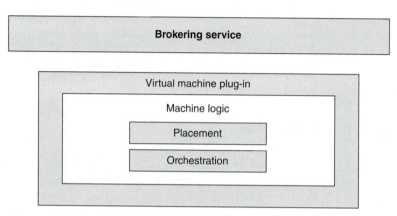

Figure 7-4 RD Connection engages virtual machine plug-in

© Cengage Learning 2014

Installing VDI Components

In this section, you install and configure the four Remote Desktop services that support VDI in the private cloud. These installations are described in more detail in Activities 7-1 and 7-2.

Installing the RD Connection Broker

You cannot add the RD connection broker to an operating system that is running any other Remote Desktop role service. One solution is to create a virtual machine specifically for the connection broker.

To add the RD connection broker host to the virtual machine, click Roles in the left pane of Server Manager, click Add Roles, and click Next. Click the Remote Desktop Services check box, and click Next. Click Role Services, click Next, click the Remote Desktop Connection Broker check box, click Next, and click Install.

Installing the RD Virtualization Host

You install the RD virtualization host from Server Manager. To start the installation, click Roles in the left pane of Server Manager, click Add Roles in the right pane, and then click Next. Click Remote Desktop Services in the next window of the Add Roles Wizard, as shown in Figure 7-5. Click Next to continue.

In the next window, click Role Services, as shown in Figure 7-6.

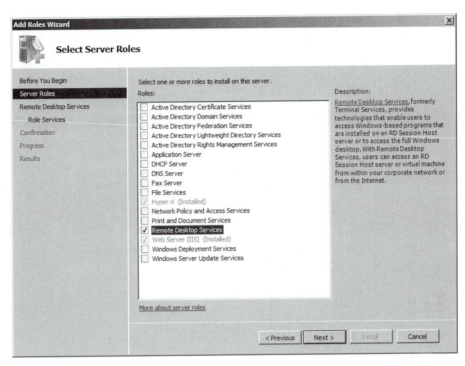

Figure 7-5 Remote Desktop Services selected in Select Server Roles window

Source: Microsoft Virtual Machine Manager 2008 R2 SP1, Windows Server 2008 R2 SP1

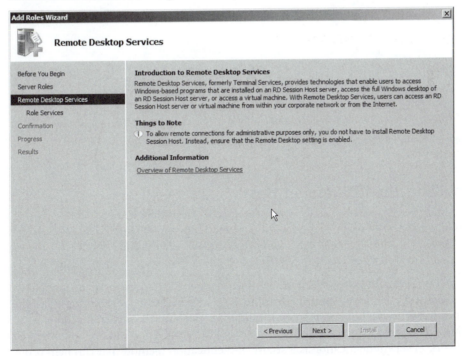

Figure 7-6 Remote Desktop Services window

Source: Microsoft Virtual Machine Manager 2008 R2 SP1, Windows Server 2008 R2 SP1

To complete the installation, click Remote Desktop Virtualization Host. Note that its check box becomes grayed out and the Core Services option is checked. (See Figure 7-7.) Click Next, and then click Install. When the installation is complete, the Server Manager window appears again.

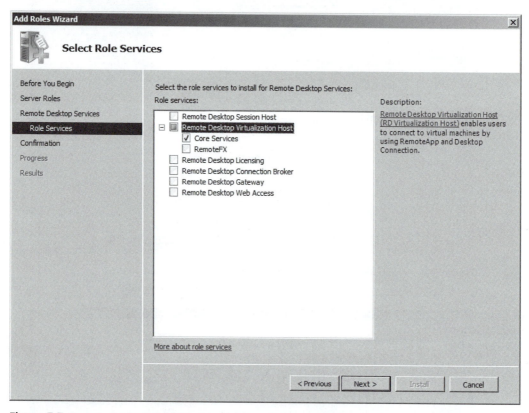

Figure 7-7 Remote Desktop virtualization with Core Services selected

Source: Microsoft Virtual Machine Manager 2008 R2 SP1, Windows Server 2008 R2 SP1

Installing the RD Session Host

To install the RD session host, you must specify an authentication method and a licensing option, and identify users in the security group. To begin, expand Roles, click Remote Desktop Services in the left pane, and then scroll and click Add Role Services in the right pane. Next, click the Remote Desktop Session Host check box, as shown in Figure 7-8.

Click Next twice and then specify the authentication method for user logons. Network Level Authentication enhances security for the RD session host by requiring that the user be authenticated to the host prior to establishing a session on the virtual machine. This authentication occurs before you establish a remote desktop connection and the logon screen appears. Network Level Authentication is a secure authentication method that can help protect remote computers from malicious users and malware. (See Figure 7-9.)

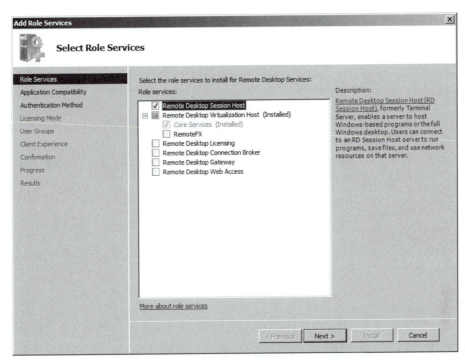

Figure 7-8   Remote Desktop Session Host selected

Source: Microsoft Virtual Machine Manager 2008 R2 SP1, Windows Server 2008 R2 SP1

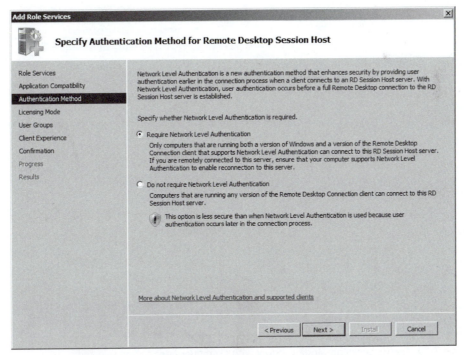

Figure 7-9   Network Level Authentication selected

Source: Microsoft Virtual Machine Manager 2008 R2 SP1, Windows Server 2008 R2 SP1

To access Remote Desktop, a license is required. RD licensing manages the Remote Desktop Services client access licenses (RDS CALs) that are required for each user to connect to a Remote Desktop session host. There are three licensing modes:

- *Configure later*—Delay the configuration of the RD licensing server for 120 days. This option is a common selection for organizations that are piloting Remote Desktop Services.

- *Per Device*—When a client computer connects to an RD session host for the first time, the client computer is issued a temporary license by default. When this connection is made the second time, if the RD licensing server is activated and enough RDS per-device CALs are available, the license server issues the client computer a permanent per-device license.

- *Per User*—This CAL gives one user the right to access an RD session host from an unlimited number of client computers.

The Configure later option is selected in Figure 7-10. Choosing this option is appropriate in this example because you are running a pilot of Remote Desktop Services. Click Next to continue.

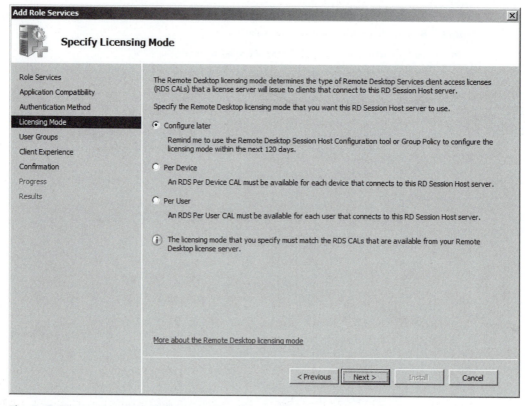

Figure 7-10 Specify Licensing Mode window with Configure later option selected

Source: Microsoft Virtual Machine Manager 2008 R2 SP1, Windows Server 2008 R2 SP1

Next, you need to add a security group to indicate which users have the security permissions to access the RD session host. To add a security group, you add user groups or user accounts from Active Directory, as explained in Activity 7-1. Figure 7-11 shows a security group added. Click Next to advance to the Configure Client Experience window.

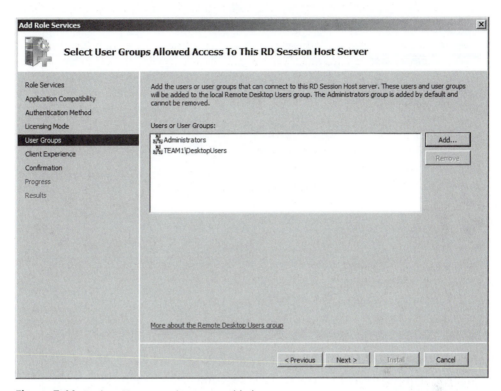

Figure 7-11 DesktopUsers security group added

Source: Microsoft Virtual Machine Manager 2008 R2 SP1, Windows Server 2008 R2 SP1

You can configure a Windows Server 2008 R2 SP1 server to provide a number of features that are available in Windows 7. When you select one or more of the features shown in Figure 7-12, the Desktop Experience feature is added to the RD session host to support Remote Desktop Services. However, note that performance might suffer if you add this feature.

Click Next, review the installation selections, and click Install. After the installation is complete, you will need to restart the server.

Installing RD Web Access

To install RD Web access, you must identify the server where you will install the default Web site and the link to the RD connection broker. To begin, click Remote Desktop Services in the left pane, and then scroll and click Add Role Services in the right pane. Next, click the Remote Desktop Web Access check box, as shown in Figure 7-13.

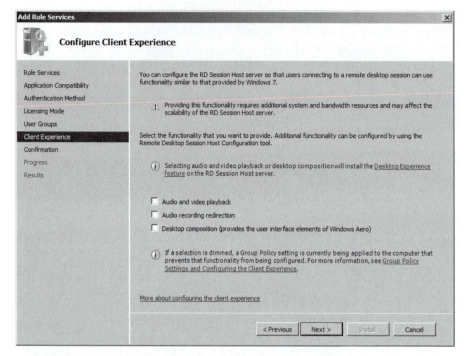

Figure 7-12 Configure Client Experience window

Source: Microsoft Virtual Machine Manager 2008 R2 SP1, Windows Server 2008 R2 SP1

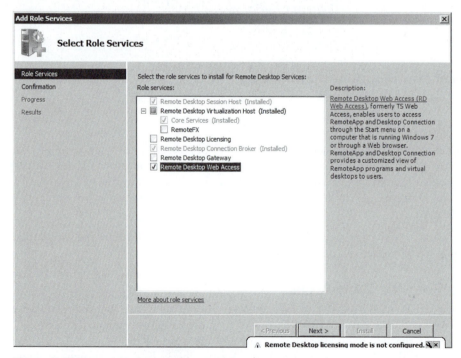

Figure 7-13 Remote Desktop Web access selected

Source: Microsoft Virtual Machine Manager 2008 R2 SP1, Windows Server 2008 R2 SP1

Click Add Required Role Services, click Next three times, record the Default RD Web access site, and click Install.

RD Web access requires configuration. To begin, click Start, point to Administrative Tools, point to Remote Desktop Services, and click Remote Desktop Web Access Configuration. Figure 7-14 shows the first page of the remote access Web site. You can ignore the Web site security warning and proceed to the Web site.

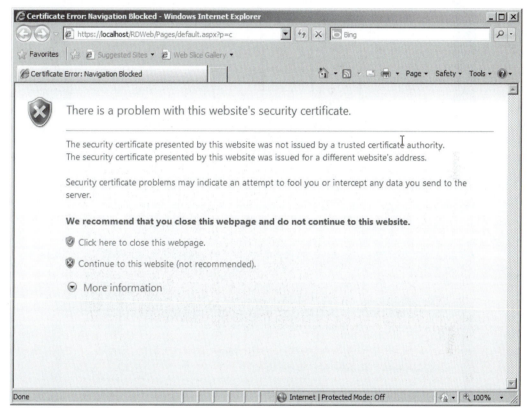

Figure 7-14 Remote access Web site

Source: Microsoft Virtual Machine Manager 2008 R2 SP1, Windows Server 2008 R2 SP1

Figure 7-15 shows the logon window for the Remote Desktop Services default connection. Because all three computers are local, click This is a private computer.

After you sign in, the Web page used to tie to the RD connection broker appears. Figure 7-16 shows the completed Web page used to identify the RD connection broker.

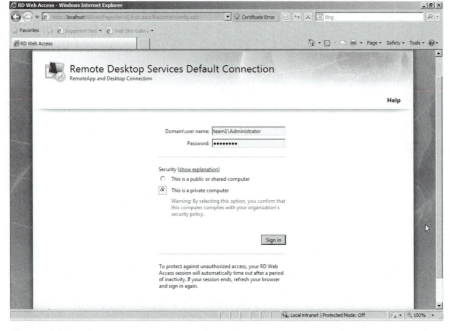

Figure 7-15 Logon window for Remote Desktop Services default connection

Source: Microsoft Virtual Machine Manager 2008 R2 SP1, Windows Server 2008 R2 SP1

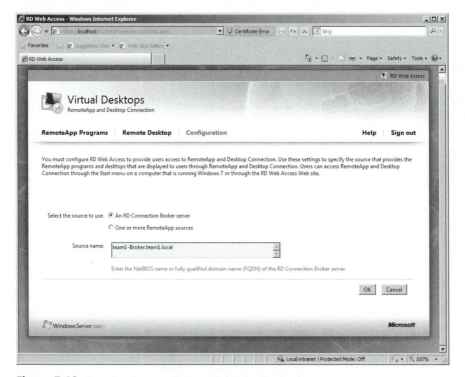

Figure 7-16 Completed connection to RD connection broker

Source: Microsoft Virtual Machine Manager 2008 R2 SP1 and Internet Explorer, on Windows Server 2008 R2 SP1

Configuring RD Services

After you install the four Remote Desktop services, use the Remote Desktop Connection Manager to configure the services to work together. You configure the Remote Desktop services from the virtual machine created for the RD connection broker.

To open the connection manager, click Start, point to Administrative Tools, point to Remote Desktop Services, and click Remote Desktop Connection Manager. To start the configuration, click Configure Virtual Desktops in the right pane, and click Next. Enter the server name for the host computer running Hyper-V, which serves as the RD virtualization host. Click Add (see Figure 7-17). Click Next to continue.

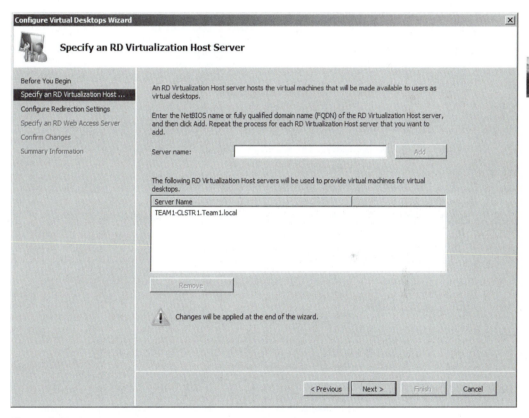

Figure 7-17 Specifying RD virtualization host server

Source: Microsoft Virtual Machine Manager 2008 R2 SP1, Windows Server 2008 R2 SP1

To configure redirection settings, enter the name of your CLTSR1 server as the server name, clear the Do not automatically configure check box, and click Next. Figure 7-18 shows the completed redirection settings.

Enter team1-clstr1.team1.local for the RD Web access server, click Next, and click Apply. Figure 7-19 shows the entry for the RD Web access server.

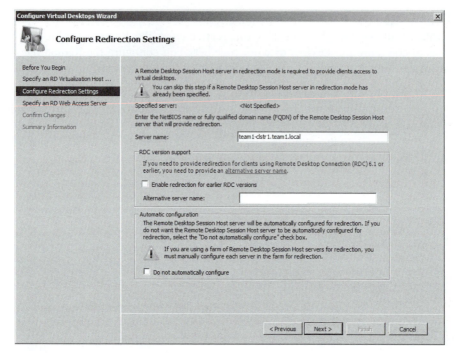

Figure 7-18   Completed redirection settings

Source: Microsoft Virtual Machine Manager 2008 R2 SP1, Windows Server 2008 R2 SP1

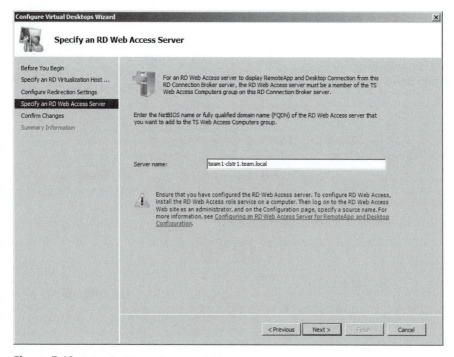

Figure 7-19   Entry for RD Web access server

Source: Microsoft Virtual Machine Manager 2008 R2 SP1, Windows Server 2008 R2 SP1

ACTIVITY

Activity 7-1: Installing the Virtual Machine for the RD Connection Broker

Time Required: 45 minutes

Objective: Install the RD connection broker.

Description: In this activity, your team installs the virtual machine to be used by the RD connection broker. First, you create the virtual network for the management network on the two host computers. You install a copy of Windows Server 2008 R2 SP1 on a new virtual machine. You then add Remote Desktop Services and the RD connection broker on the new Broker virtual machine.

Table 7-1 provides the team member assignments for this activity.

Team Member	Steps	Host Computer
1	1-16	MGMT, CLSTR1, CLSTR2
2	17-31	CLSTR1
3	32-37	
1	38-53	

Table 7-1 Team member assignments for Activity 7-1

© Cengage Learning 2014

1. Switch the KVM switch to port 1.

2. Turn on the power and log on to your MGMT server with a username of **Team1\ Administrator**, substituting your team name for **Team1**. Enter a password of **P@ssw0rd**.

3. Switch the KVM switch to port 2.

4. Turn on the power and log on to your CLSTR1 server with a username of **Team1\ Administrator**, substituting your team name for **Team1**. Enter a password of **P@ssw0rd**.

5. To discover the physical adapter used by the management network, click the **Network** icon on the taskbar, click **Open Network and Sharing Center**, click **Change adapter settings**, hover your mouse over the physical network adapter for the management network, and record the physical adapter name. Close the Network Connections window.

6. To start Hyper-V Manager, double-click the **Hyper-V Manager** icon on the desktop.

7. To create a virtual network, click **Virtual Network Manager** in the right pane, click **Add**, and enter **Management Virtual** over the text "New Virtual Network." Click the **External** arrow, click the **network adapter** recorded in Step 5, click **OK**, and click **Yes**.

8. Repeat Steps 3 through 7 for the CLSTR2 server, which is on switch port 3.

9. Switch the KVM switch to port 2.

10. To update the files in Windows Server, click **Start**, click **Control Panel**, click the **View by arrow**, click **Small icons**, click **Windows Update**, and click **Check for updates**.

11. When the list appears, click **Install,** click **I accept the license terms,** and click **Finish.**

12. Wait for the download and installation to complete.

13. If you are prompted to install Internet Explorer, click Don't Install.

14. When prompted that some updates were not installed, click **Restart now.**

15. Wait for the remaining updates to be installed.

16. Log on to your CLSTR1 server with a username of Team1\Administrator, substituting your team name for Team1. Enter a password of P@ssw0rd.

17. If necessary, open the Hyper-V Manager console by double-clicking the **Hyper-V Manager** icon on the desktop.

18. To create the virtual machine for the RD connection broker, click **New** in the Actions pane, click **Virtual Machine,** click **Next,** and enter **Broker.** Click **Next,** enter **768** in the Memory text box, and click **Next.** Click the **Connection** arrow, click **Management Virtual,** and click **Next.** Review the virtual disk to be created, click **Next,** click **Install an operating system from a boot CD/DVD-ROM,** click **Image file (.iso),** and click **Browse.** Double-click **Local Disk (C:),** double-click **ISOFiles,** click **Windows Server 2008 R2 SP1,** click **Open,** and click **Next.** Review the summary information, and click **Previous** if necessary to return to previous windows and correct any mistakes. Click **Finish** when you are done.

19. Wait for the virtual machine and virtual hard disk to be created.

20. To ensure that the Broker virtual machine starts when the CLSTR1 host computer is restarted, right-click **Broker,** and click **Settings.** Click **Automatic Start Action,** and click **Always start this virtual machine automatically.** Click **Automatic Stop Action,** and click **Shut down the guest operating system.** Click **OK.**

21. To connect to the virtual machine, right-click **Broker,** click **Connect,** click the **Action** menu in the Virtual Machine Connection window, and then click **Start.**

22. When the regional settings window appears, verify the selections for language, time, currency, and keyboard. Make corrections as needed, and then click **Next.**

23. Click the **Install now** link.

24. To indicate which version to install, click **Windows Server 2008 R2 Standard (Full Installation),** and then click **Next.**

25. When the license terms window appears, check **I accept the license terms,** and then click **Next.**

26. Click the **Custom (advanced)** icon.

27. Click **Disk 0 Unallocated Space,** and then click **Next.**

28. Wait for Windows to copy and expand files, install features and updates, and restart the computer to complete the installation.

29. Wait while Windows prepares to start for the first time and then prepares the computer for use.

30. When prompted that the user password must be changed before logging on for the first time, click **OK.** Enter **P@ssw0rd** in the New password text box, press **Tab,** enter **P@ssw0rd** in the Confirm password text box, press **Enter,** and then click **OK.**

When the Set Network Location window appears, click Work and then click Close.

31. To set the time zone, click the **Set time zone** link. If necessary, click the **Change time zone** button, click the appropriate time zone, and click **OK**. Click the **Change date and time** button, change the time, and then click **OK** twice.

32. To determine the IP configuration for your Broker computer, locate the team number assigned by your instructor in Table 7-2. This row contains the IP configuration.

Team#	IP Address	Subnet Mask	Default Gateway	DNS Server Address
1	192.168.0.171	255.255.255.0	192.168.0.1	192.168.0.111
2	192.168.0.181	255.255.255.0	192.168.0.1	192.168.0.121
3	192.168.0.191	255.255.255.0	192.168.0.1	192.168.0.131
4	192.168.0.201	255.255.255.0	192.168.0.1	192.168.0.141
5	192.168.0.211	255.255.255.0	192.168.0.1	192.168.0.151
6	192.168.0.221	255.255.255.0	192.168.0.1	192.168.0.161

Table 7-2 IP configurations for Broker server

© Cengage Learning 2014

It is very important that you use the correct IP addresses for your classroom network. Ask your instructor if an alternative IP addressing scheme will be used in your classroom.

33. To view the local area connections, click **Configure networking**, and right-click **Local Area Connection**. Click **Properties**, clear the **Internet Protocol Version 6 (TCP/IPv6)** check box, click **Internet Protocol Version 4 (TCP/IPv4)**, and then click **Properties**. Click **Use the following IP Address**, enter the IP address you identified in Step 32 in the IP address text box, and then press **Tab** twice; the subnet mask will appear in the Subnet mask text box. Next, enter the default gateway you identified in Step 32, press **Tab** twice, and enter the preferred DNS server address from Step 32. Click **OK**, and click **Close**. Close the Network Connections window.

34. To name the virtual machine, click **Provide computer name and domain**, click **Change**, and enter *Team1*-**Broker** as the Computer name, substituting your team name for *Team1*. Click **Domain**, and enter *Team1*.**local** as the Domain name, substituting your team name for *Team1*. Click **OK**, and then log on with a username of *Team1*\ **Administrator**, substituting your team name for *Team1*. Enter a password of **P@ssw0rd**.

35. Wait for the message that welcomes you to the domain.

36. Click **OK** twice, click **Close**, and then click **Restart Now**.

37. Wait for the virtual machine to restart.

38. Click **Action**, click **Ctrl+Alt+Delete**, click **Switch User**, click **Other User**, and log on with a username of *Team1\Administrator*, substituting your team name for *Team1*. Enter a password of **P@ssw0rd**.

39. To switch to the Server Manager window, click **Do not show this window at logon**, and then close the window.

40. If your school uses volume keys, click **Activate Windows**, ask your instructor to enter the product key, and press **Enter**. Click **Close**.

41. If your school does not use volume keys, click **Activate Windows**, enter the product key provided by your instructor, and press **Enter**. Click **Close**.

42. Wait for Windows to be activated.

43. To add the RD connection broker host, click **Roles** in the left pane of Server Manager, click **Add Roles**, and click **Next**. Click the **Remote Desktop Services** check box, and click **Next**. Click **Role Services**, click **OK**, click the **Remote Desktop Connection Broker** check box, click **Next**, and click **Install**.

44. Wait for the installation to be completed. Review the installation results, and click **Close**.

45. To configure the TS Web Access Computers group, click **Start**, point to **Administrative Tools**, and then click **Computer Management**.

46. Expand **Local Users and Groups**, and then click **Groups**. Double-click **TS Web Access Computers**. Click **Add** and then click **Advanced**.

47. Click **Object Types**. Click the **Computers** check box, and then click **OK**.

48. Enter **team** in the Starts with Name text box, click **Find Now**, and click *TEAM1-BROKER*, substituting your team name for *TEAM1*. Press **Ctrl** and then click *TEAM1-CLSTR1*, substituting your team name for *TEAM1*. Click **OK** three times.

49. To configure the Session Broker computers, first double-click **Session Broker Computers**. Click **Add**, and then click **Advanced**.

50. Click **Object Types**. Click the **Computers** check box, and then click **OK**.

51. Enter **team** in the Starts with Name text box, click **Find Now**, and click *TEAM1-CLSTR1*, substituting your team name for *TEAM1*. Click **OK** three times.

52. Minimize the Broker on Local Host – Virtual Machine connection window.

53. Remain logged on for future lab activities.

Activity 7-2: Installing the Remaining Remote Desktop Role Services

Time Required: 30 minutes

Objective: Install the remaining Remote Desktop role services.

Description: In this activity, your team completes the installation and configuration of the Remote Desktop roles on both the CLSTR1 host computer and the Broker virtual machine. Also, you install a certificate for the Web site.

Table 7-3 provides the team member assignments for this activity.

Team Member	Steps	Host Computer
1	1-7	MGMT, CLSTR1
2	8-10	CLSTR1
3	11-17	
1	18-28	
2	29-34	
3	35-50	MGMT, CLSTR1

Table 7-3   **Team member assignments for Activity 7-2**

© Cengage Learning 2014

1. Switch the KVM switch to port 1.

2. If necessary, log on to your MGMT server with a username of *Team1\Administrator*, substituting your team name for *Team1*. Enter a password of **P@ssw0rd**.

3. To open Active Directory Domain Services, click **Start**, point to **Administrative Tools**, and click **Active Directory Users and Computers**. Click **Users**, click the **Action** menu, point to **New**, and click **Group**. Enter **DesktopUsers** as the Group name, click **OK**, and close the Active Directory Users and Computers window.

4. Switch the KVM switch to port 2.

5. If necessary, log on to your CLSTR1 server with a username of *Team1\Administrator*, substituting your team name for *Team1*. Enter a password of **P@ssw0rd**.

6. To start installing the RD virtualization host on the CLSTR1 server, click **Roles** in the left pane of Server Manager on the CLSTR1 server, click **Add roles** in the right pane, and click **Next**. Click the **Remote Desktop Services** check box, click **Role Services**, click **Remote Desktop Virtualization Host**, click **Next**, and click **Install**.

7. Wait for the installation to be completed. Review the installation results, and click **Close**.

8. To install the RD session host, expand **Roles**, click **Remote Desktop Services** in the left pane, scroll and click **Add Role Services** in the right pane, click the **Remote Desktop Session Host** check box, and click **Next** twice. Click **Require Network Level Authentication**, click **Next**, retain the **Configure later** setting, and click **Next**. Click **Add**, click **Advanced**, enter **desktop** in the Starts with text box, click **Find Now**, click **DesktopUsers**, and click **OK** twice. Click **Next** twice, review the installation selections, and click **Install**.

9. Wait for the installation to be completed. Review the installation results, and click **Close**.

10. To restart the server, click **Yes**. Wait for the host server to restart.

11. Log on to your CLSTR1 server with a username of *Team1\Administrator*, substituting your team name for *Team1*. Enter a password of **P@ssw0rd**. Click **Close** to close the wizard.

12. To install RD Web access, expand **Roles** in the left pane of Server Manager, click **Remote Desktop Services**, scroll and click **Add Role Services** in the right pane, and click the **Remote Desktop Web Access** check box. Click **Add Required Role Services**, click **Next** three times, record the default RD Web access site, and click **Install**.

13. Wait for the installation to be completed. Review the installation results, and click **Close**.

14. To open the RD Web access console, click **Start,** point to **Administrative Tools,** point to **Remote Desktop Services,** and click **Remote Desktop Web Access Configuration.**

15. Ignore the Web site security certificate warning, and click **Continue to this website (not recommended).**

16. Enter a domain\user name of **Team1\administrator** and a password of **P@ssw0rd.** Click **This is a private computer,** and click **Sign in.**

17. Click **An RD Connection Broker server,** and enter *Team1*-Broker.*Team1*.local over the text "localhost" in the Source name text box, substituting your team name for *Team1*. Click **OK.** Minimize the Internet Explorer window.

18. If necessary, open the Hyper-V Manager console by double-clicking the **Hyper-V Manager** icon on the desktop.

19. Click *Team1*-**Broker,** substituting your team name for *Team1*. Click **Connect.**

20. Click the **Action** menu, and click **Ctrl+Alt+Delete.** Log on to your Broker server with a username of *Team1***Administrator,** substituting your team name for *Team1*. Enter a password of **P@ssw0rd.**

21. To start the Remote Desktop Connection Manager, click **Start,** point to **Administrative Tools,** point to **Remote Desktop Services,** and click **Remote Desktop Connection Manager.**

22. Click **Configure Virtual Desktops** in the right pane, and click **Next.**

23. To name the RD virtualization host, enter *Team1*-clstr1.*Team1*.local as the server name, substituting your team name for *Team1*. Click **Add.** Click **Next.**

24. To configure redirection settings, enter *Team1*-clstr1.*Team1*.local as the server name, substituting your team name for *Team1*. Clear the **Do not automatically configure** check box, and click **Next.**

25. If necessary, click **Broker,** and enter *Team1*-clstr1.*Team1*.local as the name of the RD Web access server in the Server name text box, substituting your team name for *Team1*. Click **Next,** and then click **Apply.**

26. Clear the **Assign personal virtual desktop** check box, and then click **Finish.**

27. To change the Display name, click **Change** on the line that contains the Display name, enter **Virtual Desktops** over the text "Enterprise Remote Access," and click **OK.**

28. Minimize the Broker virtual machine, and return to the CLSTR1 host computer.

29. To open the Internet Information Services (IIS) console, click **Start,** point to **Administrative Tools,** and click **Internet Information Services (IIS) Manager.**

30. To view the server settings, click *TEAM1*-CLSTR1 (*TEAM1*\administrator), substituting your team name for *TEAM1*.

31. To request a certificate, double-click **Server Certificates,** click **Create Domain Certificate,** and enter *Team1*-clstr1.*Team1*.local as the Common name, substituting your team name for *Team1*. Enter your team name as the Organization, and enter **IT** as the Organizational unit. Enter your city/locality, your state/province, and your country/region code, and then click **Next.**

32. Enter *Team1*-TEAM1-MGMT-CA*Team1*-MGMT in the Specify Online Certification Authority text box, substituting your team name for *Team1*. Enter **Desktop Certificate** as the Friendly name, and click **Finish.**

33. When informed that the Certificate request was submitted to the online authority but was not issued, click **OK** and then click **Cancel.**

34. Minimize the Internet Information Services (IIS) Manager window.

35. To return to the MGMT host computer, switch the KVM switch to port 1.

36. To create a shared folder, click **Start,** and click *Team1*-MGMT, substituting your team name for *Team1*. Double-click **Local Disk (C:),** click **New folder,** enter **Certificates** over the text "New Folder," and press **Enter.** Right-click **Certificates,** point to **Share with,** click **Specific people,** click **Share,** and click **Done.** Close the Local Disk (C:) window.

37. To open the Certification Authority, click **Start,** point to **Administrative Tools,** and click **Certification Authority.** Expand *Team1*-*TEAM1*-MGMT-CA, substituting your team name for *Team1*.

38. To approve the request, click **Pending Requests,** right-click the request, point to **All Tasks,** and click **Issue.**

39. To convert the certificate to a binary file, click **Issued Certificates.** Right-click the **certificate,** point to **All Tasks,** and click **Export Binary Data.** Click **Save binary data to a file,** click **OK,** click **Local Disk (C:),** double-click **Certificates,** and click **Save.** Close the certsrv window.

40. To return to the CLSTR1 host computer, switch the KVM switch to port 2.

41. To copy the certificate, click **Start.** Enter ***Team1*-mgmt\\certificates** over the text "Search programs and files," substituting your team name for *Team1*. Click **Certificates,** right-click **Binary-Certificate,** click **Copy,** right-click **Documents** in the left pane, and then click **Paste.** Close the Certificates window.

42. Restore the Internet Information Services (IIS) Manager window.

43. To install the certificate, click **Complete Certificate Request** in the right pane, click the **Browse** button, click the **file extension** arrow, click ***.*,** click the **binary certificate,** and click **Open.** Enter **Desktop Certificate** as the Friendly name, and click **OK.**

44. To view the default Web site installation, expand **Sites,** and click **Default Web site.**

45. To add the binding to use SSL, click **Bindings** in the right pane, click **https,** click **Remove,** and click **Yes.** Click **Add,** click the **Type** arrow, click **HTTPS,** and enter the IP address for your CLSTR1 server. Click the **SSL certificate** arrow, click **Desktop Certificate,** click **OK,** and click **Close.**

46. To establish the logon identity for RD Web access to the Broker, expand *Team1*-CLSTR1 (*Team1*\\administrator), substituting your team name for *Team1*. Click **Application Pools,** right-click **RD WebAccess,** and click **Advanced Settings.**

47. Click the **Identity** box under Process Model, and then click the **Browse** button. Click **Custom Account,** and click **Set.** Enter *Team1*\\administrator as the user name, substituting your team name for *Team1*. Enter **P@ssw0rd** as the password, and enter **P@ssw0rd** again to confirm the password. Click **OK** three times.

48. Right-click *Team1*-CLSTR1 (*Team1*\\administrator), substituting your team name for *Team1*. Click **Stop.**

49. Wait for the IIS server to stop, and then click **Start.**

50. Remain logged on for future lab activities.

Configuring Personal Virtual Desktops

In this section, you install Windows 7 on the base virtual machine for future virtual machine deployments of VDI in the private cloud. You deploy a virtual machine and assign it as a virtual desktop.

Creating a Base Virtual Machine

In Chapter 5, you learned to create base virtual machines and store them in the library for future deployment. Prior to placing the machine in the library, you need to download a script provided by Microsoft to make a few adjustments to the Windows 7 operating system:

1. Enable the Remote Desktop.

2. Add security groups to the Remote Desktop Users group for users who will access virtual machines.

3. Enable Remote RPC on the virtual machine with the Registry Editor.

4. Give the RD virtualization host server the correct security permissions to orchestrate the virtual machine by running a batch file.

5. Create firewall exceptions for the Remote Desktop and Remote Service Management.

6. Copy and use a script to fix the RDP Virtualization Host Permissions.

Activity 7-3: Creating a Base Virtual Machine

Time Required: 60 minutes

Objective: Create the base virtual machine for future virtual desktops.

Description: In this activity, your team creates a base virtual machine image for future virtual desktop deployments. Prior to placing the virtual machine image in the library, you configure it for the remote desktop using a Visual Basic script.

Table 7-4 provides the team member assignments for this activity.

Team Member	Steps	Host Computer
1	1-15	MGMT, CLSTR1
2	16-23	CLSTR1
3	24-30	
1	31-35	
2	36-45	
3	46-51	

Table 7-4 Team member assignments for Activity 7-3

© Cengage Learning 2014

1. If necessary, switch the KVM switch to port 1.

2. If necessary, log on to your MGMT server with a username of *Team1\Administrator*, substituting your team name for *Team1*. Enter a password of **P@ssw0rd**.

3. If necessary, switch the KVM switch to port 2.

4. If necessary, log on to your CLSTR1 server with a username of *Team1*\Administrator, substituting your team name for *Team1*. Enter a password of **P@ssw0rd**.

5. Minimize the Server Manager.

6. If necessary, start Hyper-V Manager by double-clicking the **Hyper-V Manager** icon on the desktop of CLSTR1.

7. To start the New Virtual Machine Wizard, click *Team1*-**CLSTR1**, substituting your team name for *Team1*. Click **New** in the Actions pane, and then click **Virtual Machine**.

8. To name the new virtual machine, click **Specify Name and Location**, enter **BaseWin7** over the text "New Virtual Machine," and then click **Next**.

9. To assign memory for the new virtual machine, enter **768** over the 512, and then click **Next**.

10. To add a network adapter, click the **Connection** arrow, click **Management Virtual**, and then click **Next**.

11. To accept the default name for the virtual hard disk, click **Next**.

12. To connect the DVD drive to the virtual machine, click **Install an Operating System from a boot CD/DVD-ROM**, and then click **Next**.

13. Review the description, and then click **Finish**.

14. Insert the Windows 7 Enterprise DVD.

15. If the Autoplay window appears, close it.

16. To start the BaseWin7 client, click **Start** in the Actions pane.

17. To connect to the BaseWin7 client, click **Connect** in the Actions pane.

18. When the regional settings window appears, verify the language, time, currency, and keyboard. Make corrections as needed, and then click **Next**.

19. Click the **Install now** link.

20. When the license terms appear, check **I accept the license terms**, and then click **Next**.

21. Click the **Custom** (**advanced**) icon, and then click **Next**.

22. Wait for Windows to copy and expand files, install features and updates, and restart the computer to complete the installation.

23. Wait while Windows prepares to start for the first time and then prepares the computer for use.

24. Remove the Windows 7 Enterprise DVD.

25. When the Set Up Windows window appears, enter **LocalAdmin** in the Type a user name text box. Next, enter *TEAM1*-**BASEWIN7** in the Type a computer name text box, substituting your team name for *TEAM1*. When you finish, click **Next**.

26. Enter **P@ssw0rd** in the Type a password text box, re-enter the password in the next text box, enter **It's a Microsoft password** in the Type a password hint text box, and then click **Next**.

27. To delay the installation of updates, click **Ask me later**.

28. If necessary, click the **Change time zone** button and click the **appropriate time zone**. If necessary, change the time. When you finish, click **Next**.

29. Wait for Windows to complete the configuration.

When the Set Network Location window appears, click Work and then click Close.

30. To release the Windows 7 Enterprise DVD, click the **Media** menu, point to **DVD Drive**, and click **Uncapture D:**.

31. To determine the IP configuration for your BASEWIN7 computer, locate the team number assigned by your instructor in Table 7-5. This row contains the IP configuration.

It is very important that you use the correct IP addresses for your classroom network. Ask your instructor if an alternative IP addressing scheme will be used in your classroom.

Team#	IP Address	Subnet Mask	Default Gateway	DNS Server Address
1	192.168.0.172	255.255.255.0	192.168.0.1	192.168.0.111
2	192.168.0.182	255.255.255.0	192.168.0.1	192.168.0.121
3	192.168.0.192	255.255.255.0	192.168.0.1	192.168.0.131
4	192.168.0.202	255.255.255.0	192.168.0.1	192.168.0.141
5	192.168.0.212	255.255.255.0	192.168.0.1	192.168.0.151
6	192.168.0.222	255.255.255.0	192.168.0.1	192.168.0.161

Table 7-5 IP configurations for BASEWIN7 server

© Cengage Learning 2014

32. To view the local area connections, click the **Network** icon on the taskbar, click **Open Network and Sharing Center**, click **Change adapter settings**, and right-click **Local Area Connection**. Click **Properties**, clear the **Internet Protocol Version 6 (TCP/IPv6)** check box, click **Internet Protocol Version 4 (TCP/IPv4)**, and then click **Properties**. Click **Use the following IP Address**, enter the IP address you identified in Step 31 in the IP address text box, and then press **Tab** twice; the subnet mask will appear in the Subnet mask text box. Next, enter the default gateway you identified in Step 31, press **Tab** twice, and enter the preferred DNS server address from Step 31. Click **OK**, and click **Close**. Close the Network Connections window.

33. To join the domain, click **Start**, right-click **Computer**, and click **Properties**. Click **Change settings**, click **Change**, click **Domain**, and enter *team1*.local for the domain, substituting your team name for *team1*. Click **OK**. Log on with a username of *Team1*\administrator, substituting your team name for *Team1*. Enter a password of **P@ssw0rd**.

34. When the welcome message appears, click **OK** twice, click **Close**, and click **Restart Now**.

35. Wait for the virtual machine to restart. Click **Action**, click **Ctrl+Alt+Delete**, click **Switch User**, and then click **Other User**. Log on with a username of *Team1*\administrator, substituting your team name for *Team1*. Enter a password of **P@ssw0rd**.

Ask your instructor for the location of the shared Scripts folder. Substitute the provided information for the \\ServerName\Scripts entry in Step 36.

36. To copy the Fix-RDP-Permissions, click **Start,** and enter ***ServerName**Scripts*,** substituting the information provided by your instructor. Double-click **Scripts,** right-click **Fix-RDP-Permissions.cmd,** and click **Copy.**

37. Click **Documents,** click **Organize,** and click **Paste.**

38. To open the Fix-RDP-Permissions.cmd file, click **Start,** click **All Programs,** and click **Accessories.** Right-click **Notepad,** and click **Run as administrator.** Click **File,** click **Open,** click the **Text Documents (*.txt)** arrow, click **All Files,** click **Fix-RDP-Permissions,** and click **Open.**

39. To edit the Fix-RDP-Permissions.cmd file, click **Edit,** and click **Replace.** Enter **contoso** in the Find What text box, and enter *Team1* in the Replace with text box, substituting your team name for *Team1.* Click **Replace All.** Enter **rdvh-srv** in the Find What text box, and enter *Team1*-**clstr1** in the Replace with text box, substituting your team name for *Team1.* Click **Replace All,** and click **Cancel.** Click **File** and click **Save As.** Double-click **Computer** and double-click **Local Disk (C:).** Click the **Text Documents (*.txt)** arrow, click **All Files,** and click **Save.** Close the Notepad and Libraries windows.

40. To start the Registry Editor, click **Start,** click **All Programs,** click **Accessories,** right-click **Command Prompt,** and click **Run as administrator.** Enter **start regedit,** and press **Enter.**

41. To change the key, expand **HKEY_LOCAL_MACHINE, System,** expand **CurrentControlSet,** expand **Control,** scroll, and click **Terminal Server.** Right-click **AllowRemoteRPC,** click **Modify,** click **Decimal,** enter **1,** and click **OK.** Close the Registry Editor window.

42. To configure the RDP Virtualization Host RDP permissions, enter **CD ** and press **Enter.** Enter **Fix-RDP-Permissions** and press **Enter.** If you are asked whether you want to continue this operation, press **Y** and press **Enter.** Scroll through the Command Prompt window. If you see any ReturnValues that are not zero, contact your instructor. Otherwise, close the Command Prompt window.

43. To create firewall exceptions for RDP and Remote Service Management, click **Start,** click **Control Panel,** click the **View by** arrow, and click **Small icons.** Click **Windows Firewall,** and click **Allow a program or feature through Windows Firewall.** Scroll and click **Remote Desktop,** click **Home/Work(Private),** and click **Public** for Remote Desktop. Scroll and click **Remote Service Management.** Click **Home/Work(Private)** for Remote Service Management, click **Public** for Remote Service Management, and click **OK.** Close the Control Panel window.

44. To shut down the BaseWin7 virtual machine, click the **Action** menu in the Virtual Machine Connection window, click **Shut Down,** and then click the **Shut Down** button.

45. Wait for the virtual machine to stop.

46. Switch the KVM switch to port 1.

47. To open the Virtual Machine Manager console, double-click the **SCVMM Admin Console** icon on the desktop.

48. Click the **Virtual Machines** bar in the lower-left corner.

49. To store the BaseWin7 virtual machine in the library, click **BaseWin7,** scroll and click **Store in library,** and click **Next.** Click **Browse,** click **MSSCVMMLibrary,** click **OK,** click **Next,** and click **Store.**

50. Wait for the job to be completed, and close the Jobs window.

51. Remain logged on for future lab activities.

Assigning Personal Desktops

Personal virtual desktops are assigned to one person, and are preferable when you want to create an experience like that of using a desktop computer in which the user can customize the virtual machine. Users have the freedom to run a personal virtual desktop from the Start menu or a Web browser.

When you assign a personal virtual desktop using the RD connection broker, the user does not need to know the name or IP address of the virtual machine. This information is handled automatically for the user. A link is provided in RD Web access, and a link is added to the user's Start menu on computers that run Windows 7.

To assign a personal virtual desktop, open the RD Connection Manager on the RD connection broker, expand RD Virtualization Host Servers, and open the Assign Personal Virtual Desktop Wizard. Work through the wizard to assign the desktop to a user account for the Personal Virtual Desktop.

To link the virtual desktop to an existing virtual machine, click the Virtual machine arrow, and then click the virtual machine name, as shown in Figure 7-20. Click Next, and then confirm the assignment by clicking Assign. To assign an additional virtual desktop, click Continue; otherwise, click Cancel.

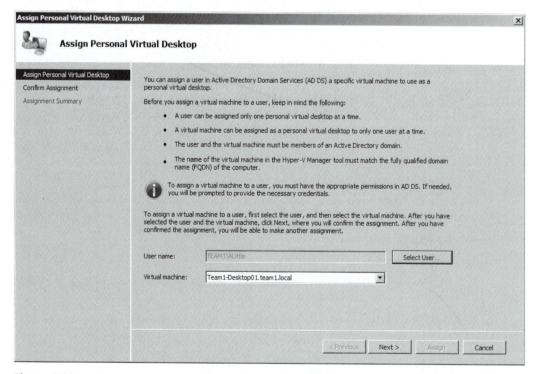

Figure 7-20 Assigning virtual machine to personal virtual desktop

Source: Microsoft Virtual Machine Manager 2008 R2 SP1, Windows Server 2008 R2 SP1

To access the virtual desktop, click Start, point to All Programs, click RemoteApp and Desktop Connections, click Virtual Desktops, click My Desktop, and click Connect. Figure 7-21 shows a connection to a virtual desktop. The RD connection broker wakes the virtual machine from its saved state and completes the connection. The desktop background is turned off during remote connections, which reduces the amount of data transferred from the host computer and the client.

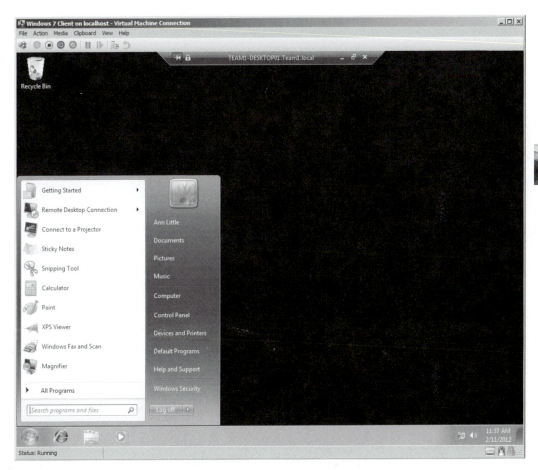

Figure 7-21 Connection to virtual desktop session

Source: Microsoft Virtual Machine Manager 2008 R2 SP1, Internet Explorer, Windows 7 Enterprise, Windows Server 2008 R2 SP1

To close the session, click the X on the right side of the blue bar at the top of the screen, and click OK. The virtual desktop is placed in a saved state.

Activity 7-4: Creating a Personal Desktop

Time Required: 30 minutes

Objective: Create a personal desktop.

Description: In this activity, your team creates a personal virtual desktop for a user.

Table 7-6 provides the team member assignments for this activity.

Team Member	Steps	Host Computer
1	1-15	MGMT, CLSTR1
2	16-22	CLSTR1
3	23-33	
1	34-40	MGMT
2	41-49	

Table 7-6 Team member assignments for Activity 7-4

© Cengage Learning 2014

NOTE

If you need to repeat the steps in this activity, use a new name for the user and virtual machine.

1. If necessary, switch the KVM switch to port 1.

2. If necessary, log on to your MGMT server with a username of **Team1\Administrator**, substituting your team name for **Team1**. Enter a password of **P@ssw0rd**.

3. If necessary, switch the KVM switch to port 2.

4. If necessary, log on to your CLSTR1 server with a username of **Team1\Administrator**, substituting your team name for **Team1**. Enter a password of **P@ssw0rd**.

5. Switch the KVM switch to port 1.

6. To open the Active Directory Users and Computers window, click **Start**, point to **Administrative Tools**, and click **Active Directory Users and Computers**.

7. To begin creating a user named Ann Little, expand **Team1.local**, substituting your team name for **Team1**. Click **Users**, click the **Action** menu, point to **New**, and click **User**.

8. Enter **Ann** in the First name text box, enter **Little** in the Last name text box, enter **ALittle** in the User logon name text box, and click **Next**.

9. Enter **P@ssw0rd** as the password, enter **P@ssw0rd** in the Confirm password text box, clear the **User must change password at next logon** check box, click **User cannot change password**, and click **Password never expires**. Click **Next**, and click **Finish**.

10. To add the user to the DesktopUsers group, right-click **Ann Little**, click **Add to a group**, click **Advanced**, and enter **Desktop** in the Name Starts with text box. Click **Find Now**, click **DesktopUsers**, and click **OK** three times.

11. Close the Active Directory Users and Computers window.

12. If necessary, open the Virtual Machine Manager by double-clicking the **SCVMM Admin Console** icon on the desktop.

13. To create a virtual machine, click the **Virtual Machines** bar, click **New virtual machine**, and click **Browse**. Click **BaseWin7**, click **OK**, click **Next**, and enter **Team1-Desktop01**.

Team1.local as the Virtual machine name, substituting your team name for *Team1*. Click **Next** three times, and click *Team1-clstr1.Team1*.local, substituting your team name for *Team1*. Click **Next** twice, click the **Virtual Network** arrow, click **Management Virtual**, click **Next** twice, and click **Create**.

14. Wait for the virtual machine to be created, and then close the Jobs window.

15. Switch the KVM switch to port 2.

16. If necessary, open the Hyper-V Manager console by double-clicking the **Hyper-V Manager** icon on the desktop.

17. To start and connect to the virtual machine, click *Team1-Desktop01.Team1*.local, substituting your team name for *Team1*. Click **Start**, and then click **Connect** in the right pane.

18. Click the **Action** menu, click **Ctrl+Alt+Delete**, and log on with a username of *Team1*\ **Administrator**, substituting your team name for *Team1*. Enter a password of **P@ssw0rd**.

19. To determine the IP configuration for your *Team1-Desktop01.Team1*.local computer, locate the team number assigned by your instructor in Table 7-7. This row contains the IP configuration.

 It is very important that you use the correct IP addresses for your classroom network. Ask your instructor if an alternative IP addressing scheme will be used in your classroom.

Team#	IP Address	Subnet Mask	Default Gateway	DNS Server Address
1	192.168.0.173	255.255.255.0	192.168.0.1	192.168.0.111
2	192.168.0.183	255.255.255.0	192.168.0.1	192.168.0.121
3	192.168.0.193	255.255.255.0	192.168.0.1	192.168.0.131
4	192.168.0.203	255.255.255.0	192.168.0.1	192.168.0.141
5	192.168.0.213	255.255.255.0	192.168.0.1	192.168.0.151
6	192.168.0.223	255.255.255.0	192.168.0.1	192.168.0.161

Table 7-7 IP configurations for *Team1-Desktop01.Team1*.local client

© *Cengage Learning 2014*

20. To view the local area connections, click the **Network** icon on the taskbar, click **Open Network and Sharing Center**, click **Change adapter settings**, and right-click **Local Area Connection**. Click **Properties**, clear the **Internet Protocol Version 6 (TCP/IPv6)** check box, click **Internet Protocol Version 4 (TCP/IPv4)**, and then click **Properties**. Click **Use the following IP Address**, enter the IP address you identified in Step 19 in the IP address text box, and then press **Tab** twice; the subnet mask will appear in the Subnet mask text box. Next, enter the default gateway you identified in Step 19, press **Tab** twice, and enter the preferred DNS server address from Step 19. Click **OK**, and click **Close**. Close the Network Connections window.

For any adapter setting that appears in the Local Area Connection window before you enter settings, you may need to reenter the setting by repeating Step 20.

21. To unjoin the domain, click **Start**, right-click **Computer**, click **Properties**, click **Change settings**, and click **Change**. Click **Workgroup**, enter **WORKGROUP**, and then click **OK**. Click **OK** three more times, click **Close**, and then click **Restart Now**.

22. When the welcome message appears, click **OK** twice, click **Close**, and click **Restart Now**.

23. Log on with a username of **LocalAdmin**. Enter a password of **P@ssw0rd**. To join the team1.local domain, click **Start**, right-click **Computer**, click **Properties**, click **Change settings**, and click **Change**. Enter *TEAM1*-**DESKTOP01** as the Computer name, substituting your team name for *TEAM1*. Click **Domain**, and then enter *Team1*.**local** as the Domain name, substituting your team name for *Team1*. Click **OK**. Log on with a username of *Team1***administrator**, substituting your team name for *Team1*. Enter a password of **P@ssw0rd**.

24. When the Computer Name/Domain Changes message appears, click **OK** twice, click **Close**, and click **Restart Now**.

25. Wait for the virtual machine to restart.

26. Click the **Action** menu, and then click **Ctrl+Alt+Delete**. Click **Switch User**, click **Other User**, and log on with a username of *Team1***ALittle**, substituting your team name for *Team1*. Enter a password of **P@ssw0rd**.

27. To set up the Remote Desktop, click **Start**, right-click **Computer**, click **Properties**, and click **Remote Settings**. Log on with a username of *Team1***administrator**, substituting your team name for *Team1*. Enter a password of **P@ssw0rd**. Click **Allow connections only from computers running Remote Desktop with Network Level Authentication (more secure)**. Click **Select Users**, click **Add**, and click **Advanced**. Enter **Ann** in the Starts with text box, click **Find Now**, click **Ann Little**, and click **OK** four times. Close the Control Panel window.

28. To shut down the virtual machine, click **Start**, click **Shut Down**, and click **Shut Down**. Close the Virtual Machine Viewer window.

29. Return to the Broker virtual machine.

30. If necessary, open the Remote Desktop Connection Manager. Click **Start**, point to **Administrative Tools**, point to **Remote Desktop Services**, and click **Remote Desktop Connection Manager**.

31. To start the Assign Personal Virtual Desktop Wizard, expand **RD Virtualization Host Servers**, click **Personal Virtual Desktops**, and click **Assign Personal Desktops to users** in the right pane.

32. To assign the personal virtual desktop, click **Select User**, click **Advanced**, enter **Ann** in the Name Starts with text box, click **Find Now**, click **Ann Little**, and click **OK** twice. Click the **Virtual machine** arrow, and click *Team1*-**Desktop01.***Team1*.**local**, substituting your team name for *Team1*. Click **Next** and then click **Assign**. Clear the **Assign another virtual machine to another user** check box, and then click **Finish**.

33. If necessary, click **Show in RemoteApp and Desktop Connections** in the right pane.

34. Switch the KVM switch to port 1.

35. If necessary, open the Hyper-V Manager console by double-clicking the **Hyper-V Manager** icon on the desktop.

36. To start the Windows 7 client, click **Windows 7 Client**, click **Start**, and click **Connect**.

37. Click the **Action** menu, and then click **Ctrl+Alt+Delete**. Click **Switch User**, click **Other User**, and log on with a username of **alittle@***team1***.local**, substituting your team name for *team1*. Enter a password of **P@ssw0rd**.

38. If you receive the message, "The security database on the server does not have a computer account for this workstation trust relationship", place the Windows 7 client in a WORKGROUP and then rejoin the domain.

39. To set up a connection to the virtual desktop, click **Start**, click **Control Panel**, click the **View by** arrow, click **Small icons**, and click **RemoteApp and Desktop Connections**. Click **Set up a new connection with RemoteApp and Desktop Connections**, and enter **https://***Team1***-clstr1.***Team1***.local/rdweb/feed/webfeed.aspx**, substituting your team name for *Team1*. Click **Next** twice, and click **Finish**. Close the Control Panel window.

40. To test a connection to the virtual desktop, click **Start**, point to **All Programs**, click **RemoteApp and Desktop Connections**, click **Virtual Desktops**, click **My Desktop**, and click **Connect**. Enter **P@ssw0rd** as the password and click **OK**.

 If you see a message that remote logins are currently disabled, configure the CLSTR1 server to accept logins. Click Start, right-click Command Prompt, and click Run as administrator. Enter Start Regedit. Expand HKEY_Local Machine, expand SYSTEM, expand Currentcontrolset, and expand Control. Scroll down and click Terminal Server, right-click TSServerDrainMode, click Modify, enter 0, and click OK. Restart the CLSTR1 server.

41. To close the remote connection, click the **X** on the right side of the blue bar at the top of the screen, and then click **OK**.

42. To test the connection through the Web browser, click **Start**, point to **All Programs**, and click **Internet Explorer**.

43. If the Welcome window appears, click **Next**, click **No, don't turn on**, click **Next**, click **Use express settings**, and then click **Finish**.

44. Enter **https://***Team1***-clstr1.***Team1***.local/rdweb**, substituting your team name for *Team1* in the address bar. When you finish, press **Enter**.

45. When the yellow bar appears with the request to add an add-on, click the yellow message, click **Run Add-on**, and click **Run**. (If you are using Internet Explorer 8, click **Allow**.) Maximize the Internet Explorer window. If necessary, click **Continue to this web site (not recommended)**.

46. Enter a domain\user name of *Team1***\alittle**, substituting your team name for *Team1*. Enter a password of **P@ssw0rd**. Click **This is a private computer**, and then click **Sign in**.

47. Click **My Desktop**, and click **Connect**. Enter **P@ssw0rd** as the password, and click **OK**.

48. To close the remote connection, click the **X** on the right side of the blue bar at the top of the screen, and click **OK**.

49. To shut down the Windows 7 client virtual machine, click the **Action** menu, click **Shut Down**, and click **Shut Down**.

50. Remain logged on for future lab activities.

Using Virtual Machine Pools

In the previous section, you configured the RD virtualization host so that each user was assigned a unique virtual desktop. Another option is to redirect users to a shared pool of identically configured virtual machines, where a virtual desktop is assigned dynamically. This option works best for casual remote users who frequently run the same application. When the user closes the session, the virtual machine reverts to the previous state and discards any changes because the user is running a snapshot for the virtual machine.

When a user requests a virtual desktop in the pool, the RD connection broker will first check to see if the user has a disconnected session in the pool. If the user has a disconnected session, the user is reconnected to the same virtual desktop. If the user does not have a disconnected session, a virtual desktop in the pool is assigned to the user dynamically.

With virtual machine pools, there is no relationship between the pool and the server where it is located. A virtual machine pool can be on a single server or it can occupy multiple servers. Because the virtual machine pool does not have to be located on a single server, you can add capacity to the pool by adding new servers to the private cloud.

You prepare a pooled virtual machine just as you prepared the virtual desktop in the previous section, but an additional step is needed. You must keep pooled virtual machines in a pristine state by enabling a **rollback** that discards any changes made by the user while working on the virtual machine. To enable the rollback, you create a snapshot for each virtual machine and rename it RDV_RollBack. When the virtual machine host agent puts the virtual machine in the saved state, it restores the snapshot. The rollback occurs when the user logs off the virtual machine.

To prepare the virtual machine to run in a virtual machine pool, complete the following steps:

1. Open the Hyper-V Manager console.

2. Under Virtual machines, right-click the running virtual machine and then click Snapshot.

3. Wait until the snapshot is created.

4. Locate the snapshot in the folder for the virtual machine.

5. Rename the snapshot RDV_Rollback.

6. Rename the virtual machine hard disk file as RDV_Rollback.

To create a virtual machine pool, click Start, point to Administrative Tools, point to Remote Desktop Services, and click Remote Desktop Connection Manager. Right-click RD Virtualization Host Servers, and click Refresh. Right-click RD Virtualization Host Servers, and click Create Virtual Desktop Pool. The Create Virtual Desktop Pool Wizard appears, as shown in Figure 7-22.

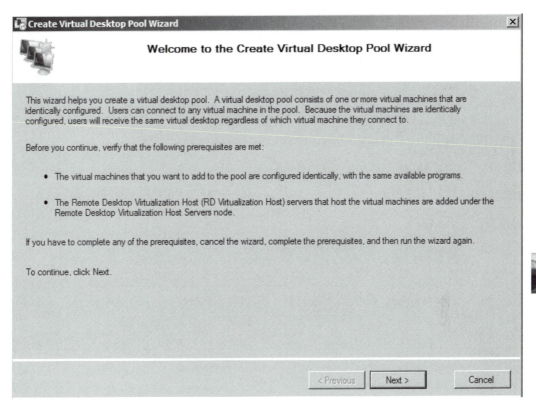

Figure 7-22 Create Virtual Desktop Pool Wizard

Source: Microsoft Virtual Machine Manager 2008 R2 SP1, Windows Server 2008 R2 SP1

The wizard contains some good advice. First, all the virtual machines should be identical, or the user's experience will vary depending on which virtual machine is connected. You met the second requirement shown in the window by placing the virtual machines on the host computer that runs the RD virtualization host. Click Next to advance to the next window.

To add virtual machines to the pool, scroll to locate the first virtual machine, press and hold the Ctrl key, and click each virtual machine you want to add, as shown in Figure 7-23. Click Next to continue.

Next, enter a display name and a Pool ID for the virtual desktop pool. The display name is visible to users, but the Pool ID is not. Figure 7-24 shows the completed Set Pool Properties window. Click Next.

Figure 7-25 shows the configuration results. In this example, two virtual machines are placed on the RD virtualization host. Users will see that the pool is identified as Windows 7 Pool on their client computers; the pool is managed under the name VMPool. After reviewing the results, click Finish.

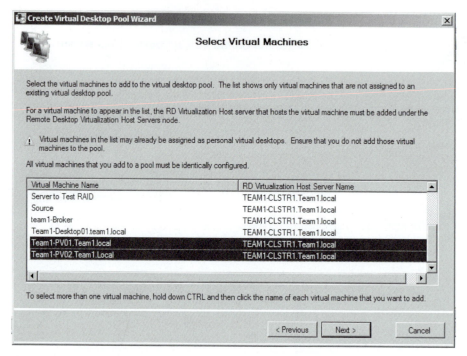

Figure 7-23 Virtual machines selected for virtual desktop pool

Source: Microsoft Virtual Machine Manager 2008 R2 SP1, Windows Server 2008 R2 SP1

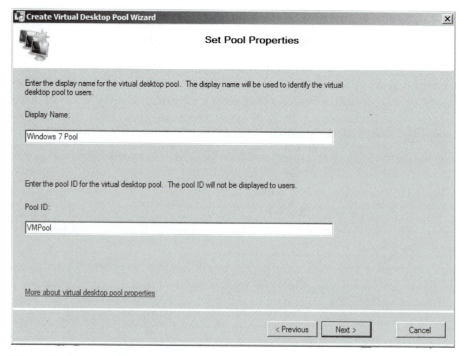

Figure 7-24 Completed pool properties

Source: Microsoft Virtual Machine Manager 2008 R2 SP1, Windows Server 2008 R2 SP1

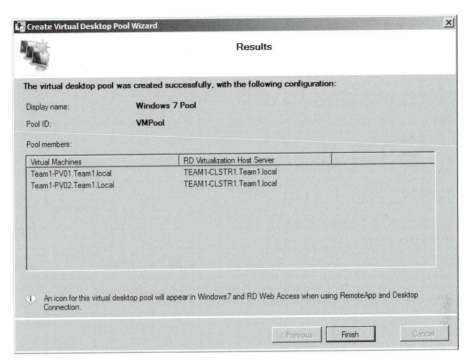

Figure 7-25 Successful creation of virtual desktop pool

Source: Microsoft Virtual Machine Manager 2008 R2 SP1, Windows Server 2008 R2 SP1

Configuring Roaming Profiles and Folder Redirection

Roaming user profiles and folder redirection help users work with VDI in the private cloud. The basic elements of a user's workspace are the configuration settings in the user's profile and the default location for saving data. A **roaming user profile** allows users to log on and have a consistent desktop experience, such as having applications remember toolbar positions and preferences, or having a desktop appearance that stays the same. **Folder redirection** moves the storage location for user files, such as moving the Documents folder from the virtual machine profile to a file server.

The user's roaming profile is initially defined as configuration settings with saved documents for the work environment in the virtual desktop. For example, a user's changes to application layouts and menu bars are preserved in the profile. One change you should make is to configure the user policy to store documents using folder redirection. This reduces the size of the profile, resulting in quicker virtual desktop loads.

Working with Roaming Profiles

A local profile is created the first time a user logs on. All profiles are created from a "default profile," which is provided by the RD session host. This new profile is created in a folder named after the user's login name.

Roaming profiles are stored on a network share on the host computer that is running Active Directory. For virtual machines that are domain members, first look for the profile in the share. If the profile is not there, use the default profile on the host computer.

To implement roaming profiles:

1. Create a network share such as \\team1-clstr1\Profiles to store the roaming profiles.

2. Configure the user accounts to use roaming profiles in Active Directory Users and Computers.

3. Have each user log on and create the roaming profile.

When the user is configured to use roaming profiles, the following events occur the first time the user logs on to the virtual desktop:

1. The user profile service creates a profile folder in the specified path, such as \\Team1-MGMT\Profiles.

2. The user profile service copies the default profile on the virtual machine to give the user a profile.

3. When the user logs off, the user profile service copies the profile to the user's profile folder that was created in Step 1.

To store profiles, you provide specific share and security permissions. Table 7-8 defines the sharing permissions for the Profiles folder. Table 7-9 lists the NTFS permissions for the Profiles folder.

User Account	Default Permissions	Minimum Permissions Required
Everyone	Read only	No permissions
Security group of users who need to put data on share	N/A	Full Control

Table 7-8   Share permissions for the Profiles folder

© Cengage Learning 2014

User Account	Minimum Permissions Required
Creator Owner	Full Control, Subfolders and Files Only
Administrator	None
Security group of users who need to put data on share	List Folder/Read Data, Create Folders/Append Data – This Folder Only
Everyone	No permissions
Local System	Full Control, This Folder, Subfolders and Files

Table 7-9   NTFS permissions for the Profiles folder

© Cengage Learning 2014

To specify the folder to store the profiles, use the Active Directory Users and Computers Console. To open the console, click Start, point to Administrative Tools, and click Active Directory Users and Computers. Locate the Virtual Desktop user. For example, to open the Properties window for Ann Little, right-click Ann Little, click Properties, and click the Profile tab. Enter the location of the profile, followed by %username%. The operating system will replace %username% with the actual username. Figure 7-26 shows a completed profile entry. After completing the entry, click OK. If you enter the profile in the format of \\team1-mgmt\users\profile\%username%, you can copy and paste the string for each user. This process saves time when you are completing numerous entries.

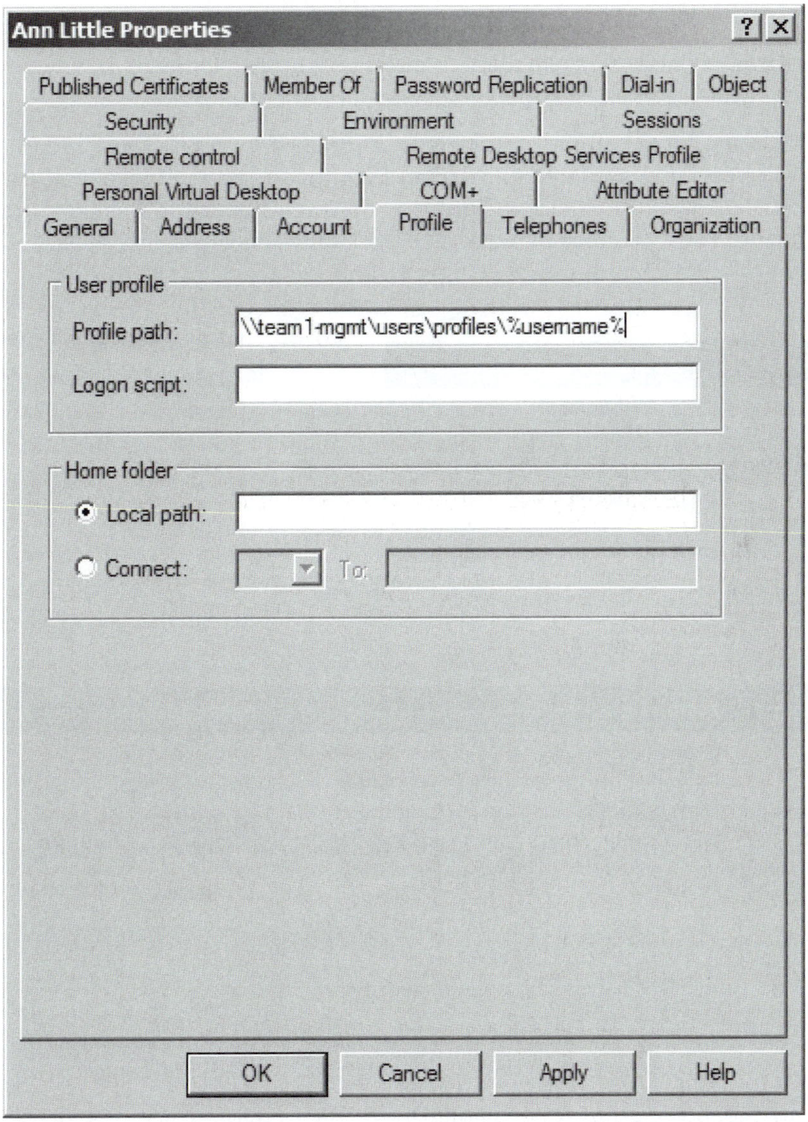

Ann Little Properties

| Published Certificates | Member Of | Password Replication | Dial-in | Object |

Security — Environment — Sessions

Remote control — Remote Desktop Services Profile

Personal Virtual Desktop — COM+ — Attribute Editor

General | Address | Account | Profile | Telephones | Organization

User profile

Profile path: `\\team1-mgmt\users\profiles\%username%`

Logon script:

Home folder

○ Local path:

○ Connect: ___ To: ___

[OK] [Cancel] [Apply] [Help]

Figure 7-26 User profile entered for virtual desktop user Ann Little

Source: Windows Server 2008 R2 SP1

Working with Folder Redirection

Redirecting user data folders to a network share speeds user logons and logoffs. By default, user folders such as Documents and Desktop are stored in the user's profile, but you can change this behavior by creating a pointer to the network share where the data actually resides. Users then use files in their personal folders, but the files are retrieved and stored on the network share.

To redirect personal folders:

1. Create a network share with the prescribed permissions.

2. Create an organizational unit (OU) that contains the user accounts for Remote Desktop users.

3. Create a Group Policy to invoke folder redirection for the identified users. A **Group Policy** specifies which actions the operating system allows or imposes.

You create a Group Policy to redirect folders to a specified location. The Group Policy will automatically create the destination folders, such as a user's individual Application Data, Desktop, or Documents folders, with the permissions applied to the parent folder. See Table 7-10 for the Share permissions and Table 7-11 for the NTFS permissions.

Security Group	Share Permission
Everyone	Full Control
Administrators	Full Control
System	Full Control

Table 7-10 Share permissions for the redirected folder

© Cengage Learning 2014

Security Group	Permissions	Apply to
Everyone	Create Folder/Append Data, List Folder/Read Data, Read Attributes, Traverse Folder/Execute File	This Folder Only
Creator Owner	Full Control	Subfolders and Files Only
System	Full Control	This Folder, Subfolders, and Files
Domain Admins	Full Control	This Folder, Subfolders, and Files

Table 7-11 NTFS permissions for the redirected folder

© Cengage Learning 2014

With the Share permissions and NTFS permissions, you establish which users have access to individual data files and folders. By creating the Group Policy for folder redirection, you direct the operating system to place user data on a network share. You use an OU to identify the users to which the policy applies.

To create an OU, use Active Directory Users and Computers. Figure 7-27 shows the menu you use to create an OU. To open the New Object window, right-click the domain name, point to New, and click Organizational Unit. Enter the name for the OU, and click OK.

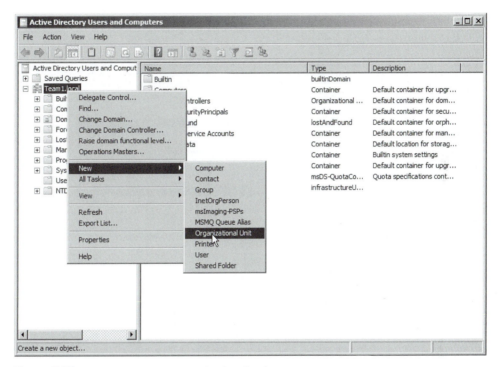

Figure 7-27 Menu to create an Organizational Unit

Source: Windows Server 2008 R2 SP1

The next task is to populate the OU with the user accounts. Click the first username, press and hold the Ctrl key, and click each remaining desktop user, as shown in Figure 7-28. Right-click a highlighted user account, click Move, click the OU name in the Move window, and click OK. The user accounts are now in the OU.

From the Group Policy Management console, you create group policies. The console is located under Administrative Tools. Expand the nodes, as shown in Figure 7-29, to locate the OU that contains the user accounts for the desktop users.

To start creating the folder redirection Group Policy, right-click the OU, and click "Create a GPO in this domain and link it here." In the New GPO window, enter the name of the Group Policy Object (GPO). In this case, enter Folder Redirection, and click OK. Figure 7-30 shows the completed entries for the folder redirection.

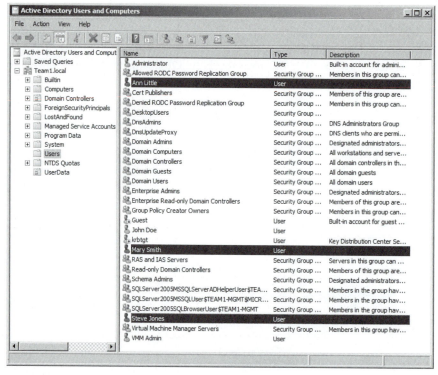

Figure 7-28   User accounts selected

Source: Windows Server 2008 R2 SP1

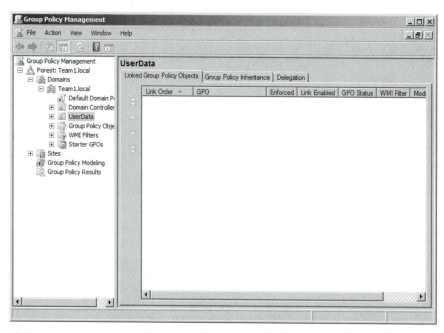

Figure 7-29   Group Policy Management console showing location of UserData OU

Source: Windows Server 2008 R2 SP1

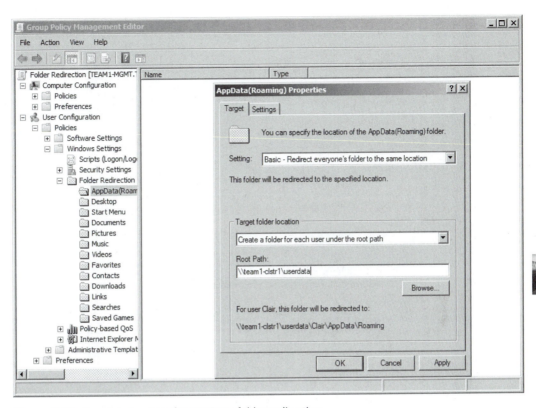

Figure 7-30 Completed entries for AppData folder redirection

Source: Windows Server 2008 R2 SP1

Choose the location of the redirected folder from the following options:

- *Follow the Documents folder*—Use this option for the Pictures, Music, and Videos folders.
- *Basic – Redirect everyone's folder to the same location*—The folder for all users will be redirected to the same share.
- *Advanced – Specify locations for various user groups*—Use this option when you want to specify shares for users by security group membership.

If you choose Basic for the location, you have three choices, depending on the folder:

- *Create a folder for each user under the root path*—Choose this option to have a folder created for each user under the share where the user will store files.
- *Redirect to the following location*—Use this option to force the Desktop and Start menus to the same folder.
- *Redirect to the local profile location*—Don't choose this option. You want to use profiles redirected to the network share.

Figure 7-31 shows the default redirection settings. By default, the user is granted exclusive rights to AppData(Roaming); in other words, only the user has access to folders and files. To permit the administrator to help manage these folders and correct any problems, clear

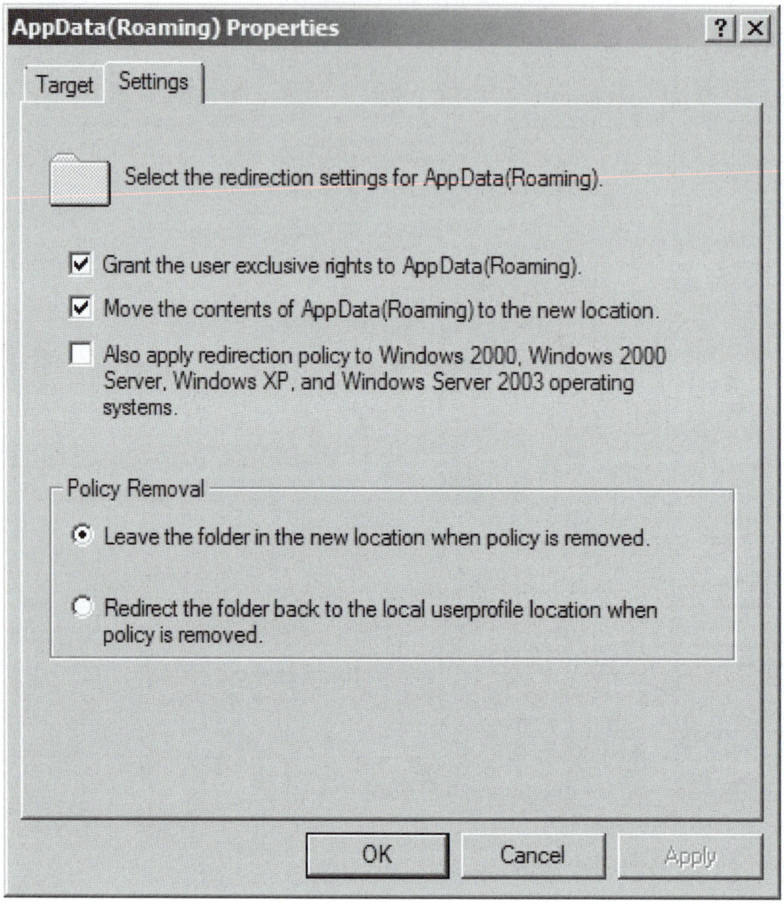

Figure 7-31 Default redirection settings

Source: Windows Server 2008 R2 SP1

the top check box. However, giving the administrator access to user files creates a potential security problem.

You should retain the selection of "Move the contents of AppData to the new location," which ensures that any existing data will be moved when the user logs off.

Follow the preceding process for any remaining folders that should be moved. If you anticipate that a folder might contain a limited number of files, you can leave the folder in the profile.

Before deploying your Group Policy solution, use the **Group Policy Modeling** tool to determine the effects of applying the various policy settings you configured. The tool simulates the effect of a Group Policy on a specified user and computer. The simulation is performed by a service that runs on Windows Server 2008 domain controllers. Figure 7-32 shows the results of a simulation. You will work with this tool in Activity 7-6.

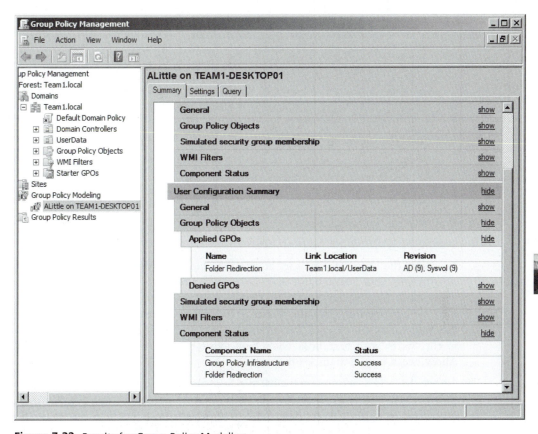

Figure 7-32 Results for Group Policy Modeling

Source: Windows Server 2008 R2 SP1

Activity 7-5: Working with Roaming Profiles

Time Required: 25 minutes

Objective: Work with roaming profiles.

Description: In this activity, your team works with roaming profiles. You create the profile share and set the proper permissions. You add the profile path to the user accounts for the desktop users. Next, you log on and log off the virtual desktops to create the initial profile. Then, you verify that the profiles were created.

Table 7-12 provides the team member assignments for this activity.

1. If necessary, switch the KVM switch to port 1.

2. If necessary, log on to your MGMT server with a username of *Team1***Administrator**, substituting your team name for *Team1*. Enter a password of **P@ssw0rd**.

3. If necessary, switch the KVM switch to port 2.

Team Member	Steps	Host Computer
2	1-10	MGMT
3	11-13	
1	14-22	

Table 7-12 Team member assignments for Activity 7-5

© Cengage Learning 2014

4. If necessary, log on to your CLSTR1 server with a username of **Team1\Administrator**, substituting your team name for **Team1**. Enter a password of **P@ssw0rd**.

5. Minimize the Server Manager.

6. Switch the KVM switch to port 1.

7. To create the shared folder for the profiles, click **Start**, and then click **Team1-MGMT**, substituting your team name for **Team1**. Double-click **Local Disk (C:)**, double-click **Users**, click **New folder**, and enter **Profiles** over the text "New folder." Right-click **Profiles**, click **Properties**, click the **Sharing** tab, and click **Advanced Sharing**. Click the **Share this folder** check box, click **Permissions**, click **Add**, and click **Advanced**. Enter **Desktop** in the Starts with text box, click **Find Now**, click **OK** twice, click the **Full Control Allow** check box, and click **OK** twice.

8. To set the NTFS permissions, click the **Security** tab, click **Advanced**, and click **Change Permissions**. Clear the **Include inheritable permissions for this object's parent** check box, click **Add**, click **Add** again, and click **Advanced**. Enter **Desktop** in the Starts with text box, click **Find Now**, and click **OK** twice. Click the **Apply to** arrow, click **This folder only**, click **List Folder/Read Data Allow**, click **Create Folders/Append Data Allow**, and click **OK**.

9. Click **Add**, click **Advanced**, and enter **Creator** in the Starts with text box. Click **Find Now**, click **CREATOR OWNER**, click **OK** twice, click the **Full Control Allow** check box, and click **OK**.

10. To remove unneeded security groups, click **Users (TEAM1\Users)**, and click **Remove**. If necessary, click **Users (TEAM1\Users)** again, and click **Remove**. Click **OK** twice, and click **Close**. Close the Users window.

11. To open the Active Directory Users and Computers window, click **Start**, point to **Administrative Tools**, and click **Active Directory Users and Computers**.

12. Right-click **Ann Little**, click **Properties**, click the **Profile** tab, and enter **\\Team1-mgmt \users\profiles\%username%** in the Profile path text box, substituting your team name for **Team1**. When you finish, click **OK**.

13. Close the Active Directory Users and Computers window.

14. If necessary, open the Hyper-V Manager console by double-clicking the **Hyper-V Manager** icon on the desktop.

15. If necessary, start the Windows 7 client. Click **Windows 7 Client**, click **Start**, and click **Connect**.

16. Click the **Action** menu, and then click **Ctrl+Alt+Delete**. Click **Switch User**, and then click **Other User**. Log on with a username of **ALittle@*Team1*.Local**, substituting your team name for *Team1*. Enter a password of **P@ssw0rd**.

17. To open the virtual desktop, click **Start**, point to **All Programs**, click **RemoteApp and Desktop Connections**, click **Virtual Desktops**, click **My Desktop**, and click **Connect**. Enter **P@ssw0rd** as the password, and click **OK**.

18. To log off the virtual desktop, click **Start** and click **Log off**.

19. To log off the Windows 7 client, click **Start** and click **Log off**.

20. To verify that the profile folder was created on the MGMT server, click **Start**, and click *Team1***MGMT**, substituting your team name for *Team1*. Double-click **Local Disk (C:)**, double-click **Users**, and double-click **Profiles**.

21. Verify that a folder was created, and then close the Profiles window.

22. Remain logged on for the next lab activity.

Activity 7-6: Working with Folder Redirection

Time Required: 25 minutes

Objective: Work with folder redirection.

Description: In this activity, your team explores folder redirection. You create the UserData share and set the proper permissions. You create an organizational unit for UserFolder and populate it with usernames. Using Group Policy Management, you create a Group Policy Object. You identify the folders that you redirect in the Group Policy Editor. Using the Group Policy Modeling Wizard, you verify that the Group Policy Object was configured correctly.

Table 7-13 provides the team member assignments for this activity.

1. If necessary, switch the KVM switch to port 1.

2. If necessary, log on to your MGMT server with a username of *Team1***Administrator**, substituting your team name for *Team1*. Enter a password of **P@ssw0rd**.

Team Member	Steps	Host Computer
2	1-14	MGMT
3	15-21	
1	22, 20-21	
2	23-25	
3	26-29	
3	30-32	
1	33-35	CLSTR1
2	36, 33-35	CLSTR2
	37, 33-35	MGMT

Table 7-13 Team member assignments for Activity 7-6

3. If necessary, switch the KVM switch to port 2.

4. If necessary, log on to your CLSTR1 server with a username of *Team1***Administrator**, substituting your team name for *Team1*. Enter a password of **P@ssw0rd**.

5. Minimize the Server Manager.

6. Switch the KVM switch to port 1.

7. To create the shared folder for the user data on the MGMT server, click **Start,** and click *Team1***-MGMT**, substituting your team name for *Team1*. Double-click **Local Disk (C:),** and double-click **Users.** Click **New folder,** enter **UserData** over the text "New folder," and press **Enter.** Right-click **UserData,** click **Properties,** click the **Sharing** tab, click **Advanced Sharing,** and click the **Share this folder** check box. Click **Permissions,** and then click the **Full Control Allow** check box.

8. Click **Add,** click **Advanced,** enter **Adm** in the Starts with text box, and click **Find Now.** Click **Administrators,** click **OK** twice, click the **Full Control Allow** check box, and click **Apply.**

9. Click **Add,** click **Advanced,** enter **SYSTEM** in the Starts with text box, and click **Find Now.** Click **OK** twice, click the **Full Control Allow** check box, click **Apply,** and click **OK** twice.

10. To set the NTFS permissions, click the **Security** tab, click **Advanced,** and click **Change Permissions.** Clear the **Include inheritable permissions for this object's parent** check box, and click **Add.** If necessary, click **Users (TEAM1\Users),** and click **Remove.**

11. Click **Everyone,** click **Edit,** click the **Apply to** arrow, and click **This folder only.** Retain the existing Allow settings, click **Create folders/Append Data Allow,** and click **OK.**

12. Click **Add,** click **Advanced,** enter **Creator** in the Starts with text box, and click **Find Now.** Click **CREATOR OWNER,** click **OK** twice, click the **Full Control Allow** check box, click **OK** three times, and click **Close.**

13. To create the UserFolder OU, click **Start,** point to **Administrative Tools,** and click **Active Directory Users and Computers.** Expand *Team1***.Local,** replacing *Team1* with your team name. Click **Action,** point to **New,** and click **Organizational Unit.** Enter **UserFolder** as the name and click **OK.**

14. To populate the UserFolder OU, click **Users.** Right-click **Ann Little,** click **Move,** click **UserFolder,** and click **OK.**

15. To open the Group Policy Management console, click **Start,** point to **Administrative Tools,** and click **Group Policy Management.**

16. To navigate to the UserFolder OU, expand **Forest:** *Team1***.local,** expand **Domains,** expand *Team1***.local,** and click **UserFolder.** Replace *Team1* with your team name.

17. To create a Group Policy Object, right-click **UserFolder,** click **Create a GPO in this domain and link it here,** enter **Folder Redirection** over the text "New Group: Policy Object," and click **OK.**

18. To edit the Folder Redirection GPO, expand **UserFolder,** right-click **Folder Redirection,** and click **Edit.**

19. To navigate to the Folder Redirection node, expand **Policies** under User Configuration, expand **Windows Settings,** and expand **Folder Redirection.**

20. To configure application data, right-click **AppData(Roaming)**, click **Properties**, click the **Setting** arrow, and click **Basic – Redirect everyone's folder to the same location**. Enter the Root Path **\\\Team1-MGMT\UserData**, substituting your team name for *Team1*. Click **Apply**, and click **Yes**.

21. To permit administrator access to the files for maintenance purposes, click the **Settings** tab, clear the **Grant the user exclusive rights to AppData(Roaming)** check box, click **OK**, and click **Yes**.

22. Repeat Steps 20 and 21 for the Desktop, Documents, and Downloads folders.

23. To configure the Pictures folder, right-click **Pictures**, click **Properties**, click the **Setting** arrow, and click **Follow the Documents folder**. Click **Apply**, click **Yes**, and click **OK**.

24. Repeat Step 23 for the Music and Videos folders.

25. Close the Group Policy Management Editor window.

26. To test the Group Policy in the Group Policy Management window, right-click **UserData**, click **Group Policy Modeling Wizard**, click **Next** twice, click **User**, click **Browse**, click **Advanced**, and enter **Ann** in the Name Starts with text box. Click **Find Now**, click **Ann Little**, and click **OK** twice. Click **Computer**, click **Browse**, click **Advanced**, enter **Team1** in the Name Starts with text box, click **Find Now**, click **Team1-Desktop01**, and click **OK** twice.

27. Click **Skip to the final page of this wizard without collecting additional data**, and click **Next**. Review the summary and click **Next**. Click **Finish**.

28. Wait for the report to be provided. Scroll, expand **Group Policy Objects**, and then click **Applied GPOs**. If necessary, expand **Group Policy Objects** by clicking the link on the right. Scroll down and click **Component Status**.

29. Review the component status and verify that the folder redirection was successful. Close the Group Policy Management window.

30. Return to the Windows 7 client.

31. To log off the virtual desktop, click **Start** and click **Log off**.

32. To log off the Windows 7 client, click **Start** and click **Log off**.

33. Switch the KVM switch to port 2.

34. To shut down the host computer, click **Start**, click the arrow next to **Log off**, click **Shut down**, click the **Option** arrow, click **Operating System: Reconfiguration (Planned)**, and then click **OK**. If necessary, click **Yes**.

35. Wait for the host computer to shut down.

36. If necessary, complete Steps 33 through 35 for CLSTR2, which is on KVM switch port 3.

37. Complete Steps 33 through 35 for MGMT, which is on KVM switch port 1.

Chapter Summary

■ Virtual Desktop Infrastructure (VDI) gives users the freedom to access their Windows desktops on a computer of their choice.

- The Remote Desktop role services implement VDI and give administrators a choice of using personal virtual desktops or pooled virtual desktops.

- Four services support the Remote Desktop (RD) role: the RD connection broker, which manages connections to sessions; the RD session host server, which manages user sessions; the RD virtualization host, which integrates with Hyper-V; and RD Web access, which provides a Web site for access to virtual desktops from Web browsers.

- A personal virtual desktop is a desktop assigned to a user. A pooled virtual desktop is a group of desktops available to a set of users on a temporary basis. You can configure each type of desktop as needed.

- Roaming user profiles and folder redirection help users work with VDI in the private cloud. Roaming user profiles are user settings for an operating system and applications that are retained between user sessions. Folder redirection is a policy that lets administrators redirect the path of a folder to a new location.

Key Terms

folder redirection   A policy that lets administrators redirect the path of a folder to a new location.

Group Policy   A policy that specifies which actions an operating system allows or imposes.

Group Policy Modeling   A Microsoft tool that predicts the effects of group policies for a specified user and computer.

orchestration   A Microsoft term for making a virtual machine ready for connection.

personal virtual desktop   A virtual machine hosted on an RD virtualization host server and assigned to a single user.

pooled virtual desktop   Virtual machines that are hosted on an RD virtualization host server and available to users defined in the pool.

RD connection broker   A service that provides users access to virtual desktops.

RD session host   A service that provides redirection to virtual desktops through the RemoteApp and Desktop Connections.

RD virtualization host   A service that integrates with Hyper-V to provide virtual machines by using the RemoteApp and Desktop Connections.

RD Web access   A service that provides Web browsers access to virtual desktops.

RemoteApp and Desktop Connections   A service that provides connections to virtual desktops and virtual machine pools.

roaming user profiles   User settings for an operating system and applications that are retained between user sessions.

rollback   Returning a virtual machine to a previously stored state.

thin clients   Limited-function devices designed to support access to VDI environments.

Virtual Desktop Infrastructure (VDI)   An environment in which users connect to virtual machines running in central servers.

Review Questions

1. ___VDI___ is a delivery model that enables users to connect with a computer of their choice to the virtual machines in the private cloud.

2. Existing personal computers that can be redeployed using secure versions of Windows 7 are called _____.

3. VDI offers which of the following solutions? (Choose all correct answers.)

    a.   local desktop sessions

    b.   personal virtual desktops

    c.   pooled virtual desktops

    d.   remote desktop sessions

4. When you configure ___RD Session Host___, the virtual machine discards changes and reverts to a previous state.

5. The _____ integrates with Hyper-V. _RD virtualization host_

6. The RD connection broker performs which of the following tasks? (Choose all correct answers.)

    a.   identifying the virtual machine

    b.   looking up the IP address for the virtual machine

    c.   communicating to the RD virtualization host to request that a virtual machine be made ready for communications

    d.   returning the IP address to the RD session host

    e.   monitoring sessions in the virtual desktop pool

    f.   redirecting a user to the existing session in a pool

7. The _____ prepares a virtual machine for a remote desktop connection when requested by the RD connection broker. _RD_

8. To connect to a personal virtual desktop, the user accesses _____ on the Start menu.

9. _____ makes it possible to put a virtual machine to sleep and wake it on request.

10. _____ enhances security by requiring that a user establish a session with the RD session host prior to logging on to the virtual machine.

11. The licensing options supported by the RD licensing server include _____. (Choose all correct answers.)

    a.   Per device

    b.   Per virtual machine

    c.   Per user

    d.   Configure later

    e.   Wait 120 days

12. To create a base virtual machine to be used as a future virtual desktop, you
    must _____. (Choose all correct answers.)

    a. enable the Remote Desktop

    b. add security groups to the Remote Desktop Users group for users who will access
       virtual machines

    c. enable Remote RPC on the virtual machine with the Registry Editor

    d. give the RD virtualization host server the correct security permissions to orchestrate
       the virtual machine by running a batch file

    e. create firewall exceptions for the Remote Desktop and Remote Service Management

13. Personal virtual desktops are assigned to _____ person(s).

14. To assign a virtual machine to an individual user, you _____. (Choose all
    correct answers.)

    a. access the RD Connection Manager

    b. use the Personal Virtual Desktop Wizard

    c. assign the user name

    d. link the user to an existing virtual machine

15. For the shared pool, _____ are assigned dynamically.

16. When the RD connection broker finds a disconnected session in the pool, it _____.

    a. places an error message in the event log

    b. shuts down the disconnected session to save memory

    c. reconnects to the same virtual desktop

    d. This cannot occur because the RD session host terminates all disconnected sessions.

17. To prepare a virtual machine to run in a virtual pool, you _____. (Choose all
    correct answers.)

    a. create a rollback

    b. create a snapshot

    c. locate the created file in the folder for the virtual machine and rename the file
       RDV_Rollback

    d. locate the created file in the folder for the virtual machine and rename the file
       RDV_Snapshot

    e. rename the virtual machine hard disk file as RDV_Rollback

    f. rename the virtual machine hard disk file as RDV_Snapshot

18. Basic user configuration settings are stored in the _____.

19. The user's first profile is created from the _____.

20. To implement folder redirection, you _____. (Choose all correct answers.)

    a. create a network share with the prescribed permissions

    b. create an organizational unit for Remote Desktop users

    c.   move the user accounts to the organizational unit

    d.   create a Group Policy to invoke folder redirection for the identified users

Case Projects

Case 7-1: Demonstrating VDI

You installed Remote Desktop Services for your organization's pilot of VDI. You have been asked to demonstrate VDI at the next TechShare meeting. Prepare a detailed outline for your presentation.

Case 7-2: Using Virtual Desktops

Your boss is concerned that VDI might cause lengthy logon times for users of virtual desktops. Prepare a one-page policy statement for user configurations of VDI.

Case 7-3: Using Thin Clients

Your boss is intrigued by the opportunity to use thin clients. Research the use of thin clients with VDI on the Internet. Prepare a one-page executive summary of your findings.

chapter 8

Implementing High Availability

After reading this chapter and completing the exercises, you will be able to:

- Describe high availability
- Configure iSCSI targets and clients
- Validate a cluster
- Configure failover clustering
- Enable a cluster shared volume

High availability is the implementation of operating systems technology in a private cloud that enables a computer to take over processing if a different computer fails. When a virtual machine has high availability, its downtime can be reduced. In many cases, downtime can be reduced enough that users of an application do not notice an outage. This chapter also explains how to configure an Internet Small Computer System Interface (iSCSI) for a storage area network (SAN), which permits clustered computers to share storage. Cluster validation determines that the proper resources are available to configure the cluster. By using a cluster shared volume, host computers use common storage without access conflicts.

High Availability

Businesses depend on information technology (IT) to increase the productivity of workers in their organizations. Managers must respond to situations in which something fails, employees are unable to work, and customers are not being served. In some cases, an IT failure could bring a business to a halt. High availability provides a technological solution when IT outages occur.

Private clouds require high availability. In Chapter 1, you learned about the following characteristics of the private cloud:

- *Server virtualization* is the use of software to simulate a physical computing environment and the use of virtual hardware on which you can install a number of operating systems (OSs) and interact with them. Server virtualization in the private cloud enables rapid provisioning—the addition of virtual machines to meet increased demands for processing online requests.

- *Storage virtualization* enables virtual machines to use data from a unified storage entity rather than individual disks, which makes the management of storage more flexible.

- *Clustering* connects multiple computers and makes them work as a unified system. Load balancing distributes processing across multiple servers. Redundancy is the ability of a cluster to respond gracefully to an unexpected hardware or software failure. Failover is the capability to switch to a redundant or standby server automatically when the active server fails.

In previous chapters, you implemented the following components:

- *Microsoft Hyper-V hypervisor* presents a virtual operating platform to guest operating systems and manages their execution.

- *Virtual machines* are guest operating systems executing in a virtualization environment.

- *Virtual hard disks* have the same contents as a physical hard disk drive, such as disk partitions and a file system. They are typically used as the hard disks of virtual machines.

- *Virtual network switches* work like a physical network switch, except that the switch is implemented in software.

- *Memory optimization* is implemented as dynamic memory by Hyper-V.
- *Processor optimization*, which also is implemented by Hyper-V, controls the number of logical processors that a virtual machine may acquire from the pool of available processor cores on the host computer.
- *Host computer performance monitoring* records key performance measures such as memory and processor counters.
- *Active Directory Domain Services (AD DS)* manages network resources.
- *Domain Name Service* is a resolution technique that enables users to locate network computers with a user-friendly name instead of an IP address.
- *Virtual Machine Manager (VMM)* controls a series of host computers and virtual machines from a central console.
- The *VMM server* is the central component of the VMM environment.
- The *VMM database* uses Microsoft SQL Server 2005 Express Edition SP3 to store configuration information.
- The *VMM administrator console* provides the interface to manage the VMM environment.
- *Windows PowerShell* runs scripts to perform management tasks for VMM.
- The *VMM library* is the central location for the building blocks needed to deploy virtual machines to the private cloud.
- *Hardware profiles* contain the most common hardware settings for a virtual machine.
- *Guest OS profiles* contain system configurations to ensure that operating systems are deployed consistently.
- *Templates* contain components, such as operating systems and applications, to speed the implementation of virtual machines in the private cloud.
- The *self-service portal* provides a mechanism for an Infrastructure as a Service (IaaS) model of a private cloud.
- *User roles* control access to the virtual machines accessed through the self-service portal.
- *Virtual Desktop Infrastructure (VDI)* gives users the freedom to access their virtual desktops on a computer of their choice.
- *Roaming profiles* and *folder redirection* allow users' settings and data files to follow them when working with virtual desktops.

In this chapter, you implement the following components to ensure high availability and finalize the implementation of the private cloud:

- iSCSI is an Internet Protocol (IP)-based storage networking solution that links data storage to host computers.
- A **failover cluster** is a group of host computers working together as a single system to ensure that private cloud applications and resources remain available to users and customers. Microsoft calls its solution the **Hyper-V cluster**.

- A **cluster shared volume (CSV)** is a Microsoft solution for the storage of virtual machines that are accessible across multiple host computers.

In Chapter 9, you will learn to manage the Hyper-V cluster for users of the private cloud. In the last chapter, you will learn how to use PowerShell scripts to automate routine management tasks for the private cloud.

Describing the iSCSI Storage Solution

iSCSI is an economical solution for storage in a private cloud environment. Microsoft provides the iSCSI server solution in Windows Storage Server 2008 R2. When the iSCSI software is installed on a Windows Server 2008 R2 server, it becomes accessible as a storage device using the iSCSI protocol. The protocol allows clients, called **initiators**, to send iSCSI commands to the target iSCSI storage device, as shown in Figure 8-1. **Targets** execute the command and return the data to the clients. The iSCSI protocol encapsulates SCSI commands in TCP/IP packets. An encapsulated packet is called a **Protocol Data Unit (PDU)**; it contains a header, the command, and a data segment.

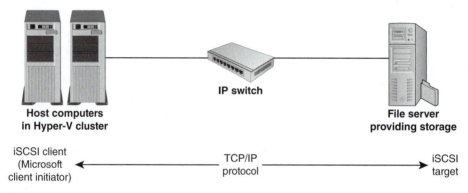

Figure 8-1 iSCSI protocols

© Cengage Learning 2014

Figure 8-2 shows a host computer that uses storage disk E. When connected with the iSCSI protocol, this disk appears to the operating system as resident (installed locally) to the computer, with read/write access at the block level. The disk controller in your host computer uses block-level access to read and write to the disks that are attached internally within the computer. These storage devices can be partitioned and formatted with Windows Server 2008 tools.

The host computers access the storage server with a logical unit number (LUN), which is a unique identifier used to designate a unit of storage. (See Figure 8-2.) In the Computer Management window, the host computer sees a local disk drive, storage disk E. On the storage server, this LUN was defined as a unit of storage, as represented by the black block. The iSCSI initiator/target pair manages communications between the host computer and the storage server.

Describing the Hyper-V Cluster

In Chapter 1, you learned about clustering, which increases a computer system's load balancing and redundancy. Load balancing distributes processing across multiple host

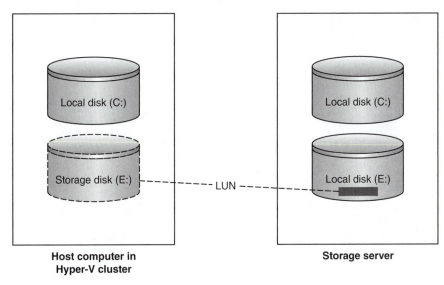

Figure 8-2 shows LUN access between host computer and storage server with labels: Local disk (C:), Storage disk (E:), LUN, Local disk (C:), Local disk (E:), Host computer in Hyper-V cluster, Storage server

Figure 8-2 LUN access between host computer and storage server

© Cengage Learning 2014

computers, which is important when you do not know how many requests to expect for a group of host computers or when the requests will arrive. Load balancing might allocate incoming requests evenly to all servers, or it might send requests to the next available host computer.

Redundancy and failover keep your system running smoothly when one of the components fails. Failover automation occurs using a "heartbeat" network of two host computers. Essentially, the second server monitors the first host computer and will immediately begin executing the functions of the first computer if it detects a failure.

When the Hyper-V cluster begins providing service to the user in the example shown in Figure 8-3, host computer #1 is running the virtual machine with the user application. This figure shows one virtual machine, but in reality, numerous virtual machines could be involved in this scenario. The host computers exchange heartbeat pulses and are aware of each other.

At some point, host computer #1 has developed difficulties and has almost stopped functioning. Host computer #1 stops sending regular heartbeat signals across the network to host computer #2. Figure 8-4 shows what happens in the brief interval just after host computer #1 stops sending signals.

Shortly after heartbeat signals stop arriving from host computer #1, host computer #2 begins taking over the functions of the virtual machine, as shown in Figure 8-5. Service is interrupted only for a short time and is not noticed by most users.

You use a similar process for scheduled downtime. For example, if a host computer is running correctly and is the current owner of the virtual machines, but software updates need to be applied to the host computer, you can move the virtual machines to another host computer so that the updates can be applied. You will learn to move virtual machines in Chapter 9.

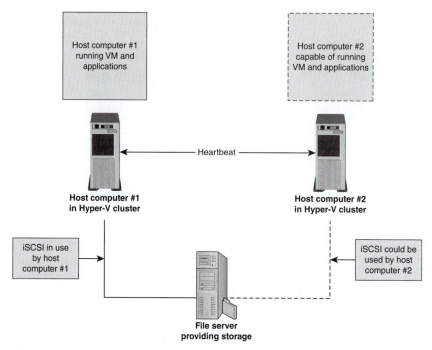

Figure 8-3 Host computers exchange heartbeat pulses

© Cengage Learning 2014

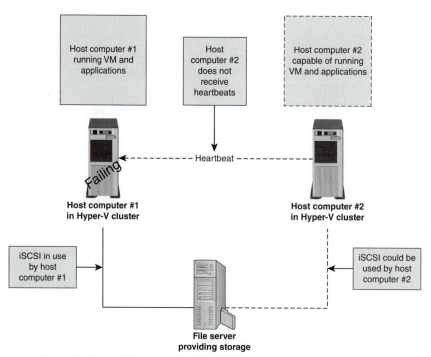

Figure 8-4 Host computer #1 does not receive heartbeat

© Cengage Learning 2014

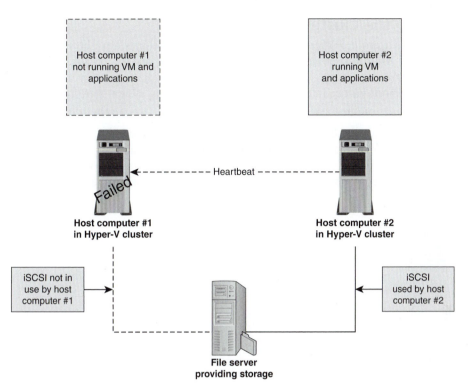

Figure 8-5 Host computer #2 takes over

© Cengage Learning 2014

A Hyper-V cluster has the following hardware requirements:

- *Servers*—The cluster has two to sixteen servers with identical hardware configurations: 64-bit architecture with virtualization technology and data execution protection, and 4 GB or more of memory.

- *Network adapters*—Four or more network adapters are required; each must be 1Gbit Ethernet or faster. At a minimum, separate network adapters must be dedicated to management, storage, heartbeat, and virtual machine functions. Additional adapters provide network redundancy.

- *Shared storage*—The storage should contain at least two separate volumes (LUNs): a witness disk for failover cluster communication and a second volume for the virtual hard disk files that are being shared between the cluster's host computers.

A Hyper-V cluster has the following software requirements:

- Windows Server 2008 R2 SP1 Enterprise or Windows Server 2008 R2 SP1 Datacenter on the host computers

- System Center Virtual Machine Manager 2008 R2 SP1

- A supported version of SQL Server 2005; VMM setup can install SQL Server 2005 Express Edition SP1

- iSCSI Software Target 3.3

Describing the Cluster Shared Volume

One requirement of the Hyper-V cluster is that virtual machines must be stored on local hard drives. Virtual machines cannot be started from network storage because the storage driver used on Windows operating systems during initial OS loading can only access local storage. iSCSI storage meets this requirement because the operating system perceives that the storage is local.

A second requirement is that each host computer uses a unique LUN, as shown in Figure 8-6. This requirement makes it difficult to move a virtual machine among host computers. For example, moving a virtual machine between LUNs requires a migration from one LUN to the other. The time lapse for this move would prohibit failover within clustered hosts.

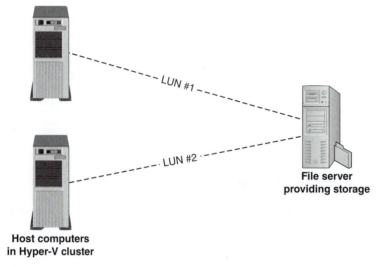

**Host computers
in Hyper-V cluster**

Figure 8-6 One LUN per host computer

© Cengage Learning 2014

The Microsoft solution to this predicament is called the cluster shared volume (CSV). A volume configured as a CSV can be accessed by all the host computers of a Hyper-V cluster. Each host computer can access and manage files on the volume. Therefore, different host computers can host different virtual machines that all have virtual hard disk files on the same volume. Figure 8-7 shows a single LUN shared by two host computers in the Hyper-V cluster.

With a CSV, the path appears to be on the system drive of the host computer as the C:\ClusterStorage folder. However, the contents are the same when viewed from any host computer in the Hyper-V cluster. The volume is owned by one host computer. Some operations, such as opening a file, can be performed only by the volume owner. To enable this type of access, a request for the operation is communicated to the owning host computer. Block mode data read/writes can be performed by any host computer in the cluster, which provides common storage for virtual machines. Common storage is a requirement for high availability when a virtual machine may be placed on any host computer or migrated to any host.

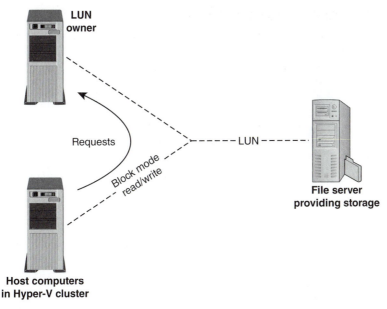

Figure 8-7 LUN shared by two host computers

© Cengage Learning 2014

Configuring iSCSI Targets and Clients

iSCSI Software Target 3.3 is a Microsoft solution for shared storage. From this point, it will simply be called the Software Target. The Software Target creates a virtual SAN environment running on the Windows Server 2008 R2 platform. You save money by using a server's internal hard drives. The Software Target is ideally suited for development and training environments.

Wizards make configuring iSCSI an easy task. Use the virtual hard disk wizard to create virtual hard disks, which provide storage for each LUN. With the iSCSI target wizard, you identify a connection and specify which host computers and virtual machines are authorized to use it. From the Microsoft iSCSI Software Target console, you link the LUNs to the targets.

Once the Software Target is installed on a virtual machine, special consideration is required when placing the virtual hard disks. The passthrough disk allows the virtual machine to manage the physical hard disk; using this disk is better for the virtual machine's performance than placing virtual hard drives directly on the host computer. Also, using this disk means that you can avoid placing the Software Target's virtual hard disks in the virtual machine's hard disk files, which results in poor performance.

Installing the Software Target

To begin installing the Software Target, you execute the Microsoft Installer iscsitarget file in ISCSI_Software_Target_33.iso. Refer to Activity A-1 in Appendix A for instructions on preparing this .iso file. Figure 8-8 shows the opening screen.

Figure 8-8 Welcome screen for Software Target installation

Source: Microsoft Windows Server 2008 R2 SP1

After you click Next, the license agreement appears. To advance to the Destination Folder window, click Next. In this window, as shown in Figure 8-9, you can browse to the location where you want to install the Software Target files.

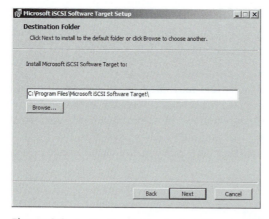

Figure 8-9 Destination folder for installing the Software Target

Source: Microsoft iSCSI Software Target 3.3, Windows Server 2008 R2 SP1

After selecting the destination folder, click Next. The window that appears gives you the option to join the Customer Experience Improvement Program (CEIP). You learned about the CEIP in Chapter 4.

Click Next to advance to the Microsoft Update options, as shown in Figure 8-10. By default, the updates are not downloaded and installed.

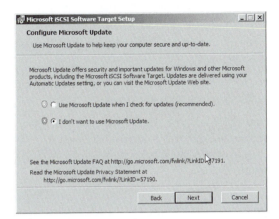

Figure 8-10 Microsoft Update options

Source: Microsoft iSCSI Software Target 3.3, Windows Server 2008 R2 SP1

After you click Next, the Ready to install window appears, as shown in Figure 8-11. Click Install to start installing the Software Target.

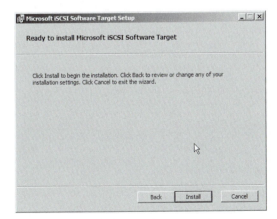

Figure 8-11 Software Target installation

Source: Microsoft iSCSI Software Target 3.3, Windows Server 2008 R2 SP1

The installation of the Software Target does not open port 3260 in the Windows firewall. You enable communications for this port in Activity 8-3.

Creating iSCSI Targets

The Software Target creates storage devices as iSCSI virtual disks with files in .vhd format. After the initiator connects to the target, these virtual disks appear as locally attached hard disks to the host computer.

You configure two iSCSI virtual disks for your private cloud implementation:

- *Witness*—A special disk used to make decisions if host computers lose communication with each other
- *Virtual machines*—Shared storage for all virtual machines deployed to the two host computers in the cluster

You can set the size of the Witness disk to be as small as 1 gigabyte (GB). The remaining disk space is allocated for the virtual machines and future expansion.

You manage the iSCSI environment from the Microsoft iSCSI Software Target console, as shown in Figure 8-12. To open this console, click Start, point to Administrative Tools, and click Microsoft iSCSI Software Target. You define iSCSI targets by clicking iSCSI Targets, and you define virtual hard disks by clicking Devices.

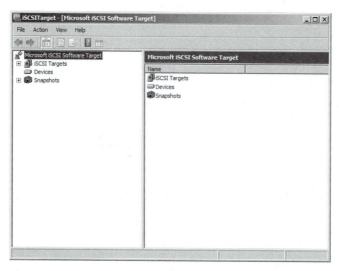

Figure 8-12 iSCSI Software Target console

Source: Microsoft iSCSI Software Target 3.3, Windows Server 2008 R2 SP1

To start the virtual hard disk wizard for the Witness disk, right-click Devices and then click Create Virtual Disk. The wizard appears, as shown in Figure 8-13.

Click Next to advance to the next window, and then enter a file name for the Witness disk. In Figure 8-14, the disk is Disk E:, which is named E:\WitnessDisk.vhd. You must type the .vhd extension. You will create the E: drive in Activity 8-4.

Figure 8-13 Create Virtual Disk Wizard

Source: Microsoft iSCSI Software Target 3.3, Windows Server 2008 R2 SP1

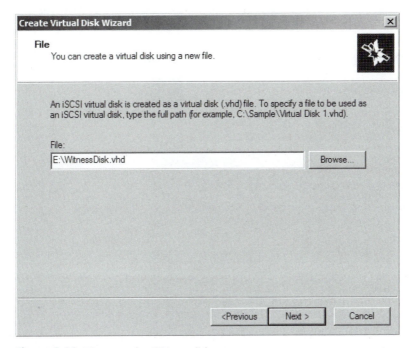

Figure 8-14 File name for Witness disk

Source: Microsoft iSCSI Software Target 3.3, Windows Server 2008 R2 SP1

Click Next to enter the disk size. The Witness virtual disk only needs to be 1 GB, as shown in Figure 8-15. You must enter the size in megabytes. Recall that 1,024 MB equals 1 GB.

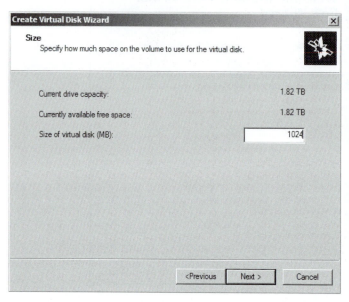

Figure 8-15 Disk size for Witness disk

Source: Microsoft iSCSI Software Target 3.3, Windows Server 2008 R2 SP1

Enter a description of the Witness disk, and then click Next. Figure 8-16 shows a typical description.

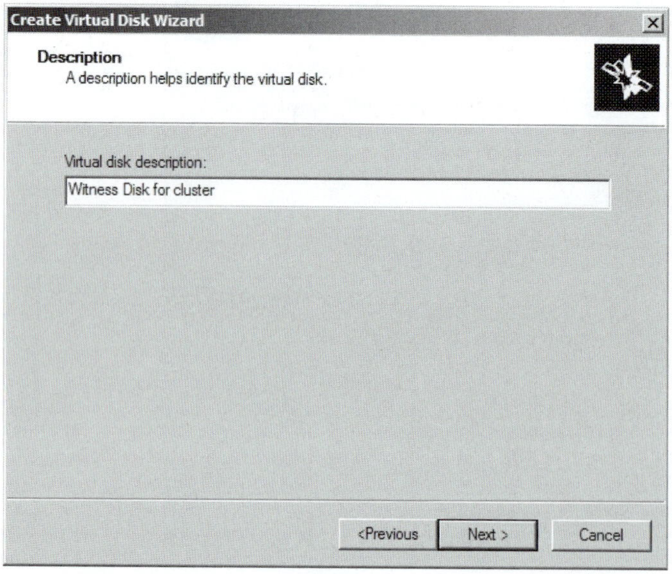

Figure 8-16 Witness disk description

Source: Microsoft iSCSI Software Target 3.3, Windows Server 2008 R2 SP1

Figure 8-17 shows the targets that have access to the Witness disk. You can specify these targets after they are created. For now, click Next to skip this window, and then click Finish to close the wizard.

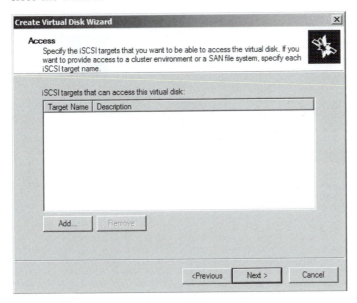

Figure 8-17 Targets with access to Witness disk

Source: Microsoft iSCSI Software Target 3.3, Windows Server 2008 R2 SP1

To start the iSCSI target wizard, right-click iSCSI Targets in the Software Target console, and then click Create iSCSI Target. After viewing the welcome message, click Next to identify the iSCSI target, as shown in Figure 8-18. Click Next to go to the next window.

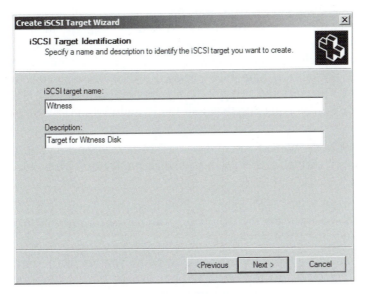

Figure 8-18 Identification for iSCSI target

Source: Microsoft iSCSI Software Target 3.3, Windows Server 2008 R2 SP1

Click the Advanced button to enter an identifier for each iSCSI initiator, as shown in Figure 8-19. This identifier is the IP address of each client that connects to the target.

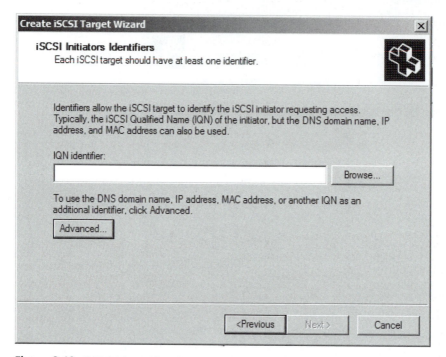

Figure 8-19 iSCSI initiator identifiers

Source: Microsoft iSCSI Software Target 3.3, Windows Server 2008 R2 SP1

In the Advanced Identifiers window, you identify the clients that will access the target. You can use a DNS domain name, an IP address, or a MAC address. In Activity 8-4, you will set the two cluster servers on the 192.168.10.0 network as 192.168.10.101 and 192.168.10.102. To add each IP address, click Add, click the Identifier type arrow, click IP Address, enter the address, and then click OK. When entering the second IP address, click Yes to indicate that the two host computers are in a cluster. Figure 8-20 shows two IP addresses entered. After specifying all the IP addresses, click Next and then click Finish.

To link the Witness target to the Witness virtual disk, click Devices, right-click Virtual Disk 0, click Assign/Remove Target, click Add, click Witness, and click OK twice. These windows are shown in Figure 8-21.

To open the iSCSI initiator, click Start, point to Administrative Tools, and click iSCSI Initiator. The first time you open the iSCSI initiator, the message shown in Figure 8-22 appears. Click Yes to start the iSCSI service.

Figure 8-23 shows the iSCSI initiator properties. The window appears when you open the iSCSI initiator. On the Targets tab, use the Target text box to enter the IP address of the iSCSITarget server where you configured your software target.

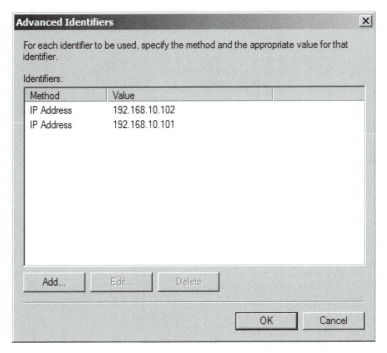

Figure 8-20 iSCSI client IP addresses

Source: Microsoft iSCSI Software Target 3.3, Windows Server 2008 R2 SP1

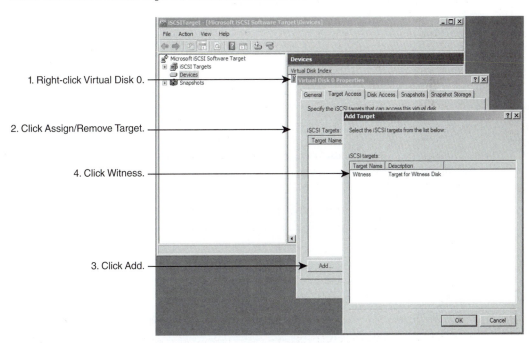

Figure 8-21 Windows to add Witness target to Witness virtual disk

Source: Microsoft iSCSI Software Target 3.3, Windows Server 2008 R2 SP1

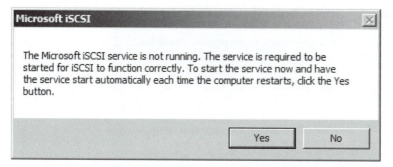

Figure 8-22 Message that appears when iSCSI initiator is started the first time

Source: Microsoft iSCSI Software Target 3.3, Windows Server 2008 R2 SP1

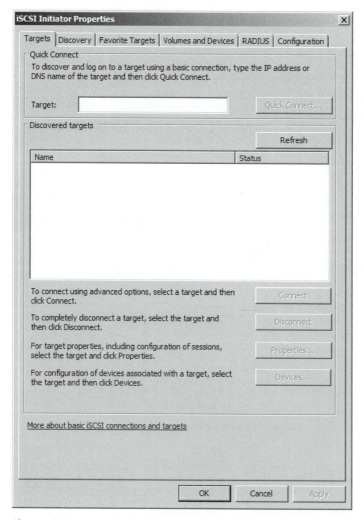

Figure 8-23 iSCSI initiator properties

Source: Microsoft iSCSI Software Target 3.3, Windows Server 2008 R2 SP1

After you click Quick Connect, a window appears with the targets. Click Done. Figure 8-24 shows the two targets created on the iSCSITarget server. The **iSCSI Qualified Name (IQN)** allows hardware and software vendors to manage their own iSCSI name spaces. The format for the IQN is the literal prefix "iqn," followed by the date (in yyyy-mm format) when the naming authority took ownership of the domain, the reversed domain name of the authority (in this example, com.microsoft), and a string to identify the target. To place each target in the Favorite Targets list, click the target, click Connect, and click OK.

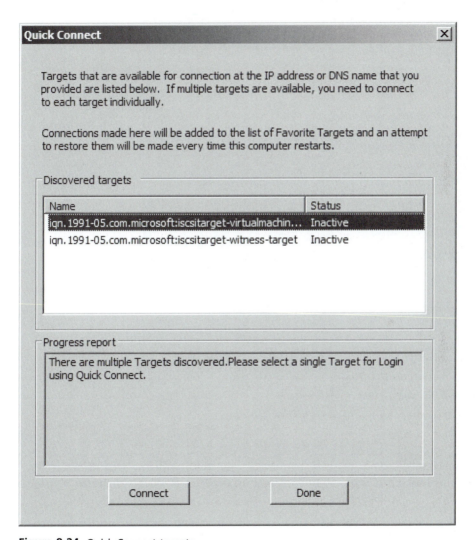

Figure 8-24 Quick Connect targets

Source: Microsoft iSCSI Software Target 3.3, Windows Server 2008 R2 SP1

To link the targets to the .vhd files, click the Volumes and Devices tab and then click Auto Configure. The mount points for the volumes appear in the Volume list, as shown in Figure 8-25.

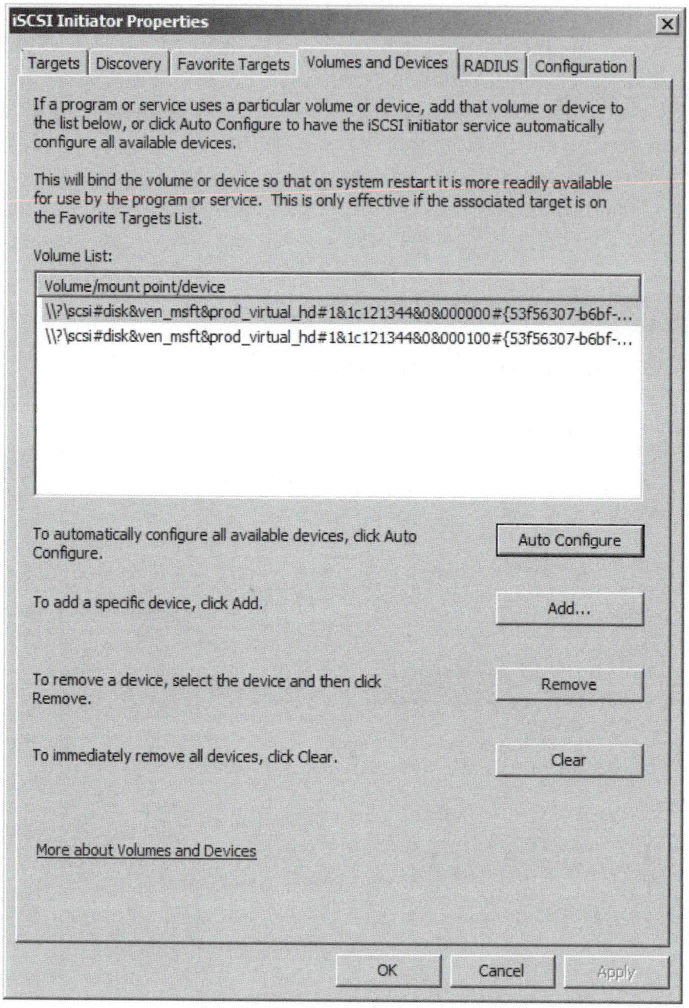

Figure 8-25 Volume list

Source: Microsoft iSCSI Software Target 3.3, Windows Server 2008 R2 SP1

To complete the setup of these two disks, you work with the Disk Management tool. To open this tool, click Start, point to Administrative Tools, click Computer Management, and then click Disk Management. The two disks appear, as shown in Figure 8-26.

To bring the disks online, right-click each disk icon and click Online. To initialize the disks, right-click each disk icon, click Initialize Disk, and then click OK. To create a volume and format it, right-click each unallocated area, click New Simple Volume, click Next three times, enter a volume name over New Volume, click Next, and click Finish. The quick format feature enables you to format a disk in less than a minute.

In Activity 8-4, you will configure the two virtual hard disks with the appropriate targets and client access.

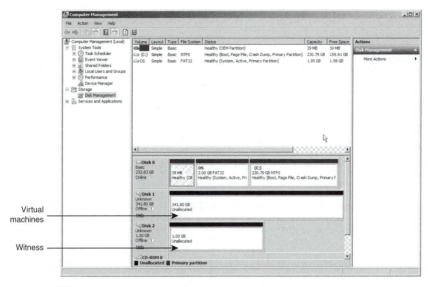

Virtual machines

Witness

Figure 8-26 Disk Management tool with two disks displayed

Source: Microsoft Windows Server 2008 R2 SP1

Activity 8-1: Cabling the Storage Network

Time Required: 10 minutes

Objective: Cable the three servers for the storage network.

Description: In this activity, your team will cable the three servers to form the storage network. Pay attention to the steps to make future activities easier. Table 8-1 provides the team member assignments for this activity.

Team Member	Steps	Host Computer
1	1–2	CLSTR1
2	3–4	CLSTR2
3	5–6	MGMT

Table 8-1 Team member assignments for Activity 8-1

© Cengage Learning 2014

Do not place network cables in the servers or switches until you are instructed to do so in each activity.

NOTE

1. Locate the CLSTR1 server.

2. Connect a green cable between the top available RJ45 connector on the CLSTR1 server and port 1 of a 5-port network switch.

> You are adding the CLSTR1, CLSTR2, and MGMT servers to complete the storage network.

3. Locate the CLSTR2 server.

4. Connect a green cable between the top available RJ45 connector on the CLSTR2 server and port 2 of the 5-port network switch.

5. Locate the MGMT server.

6. Connect a green cable between the top available RJ45 connector on the MGMT server and port 3 of the 5-port network switch.

Activity 8-2: Configuring the Storage Network Adapters

Time Required: 30 minutes

Objective: Configure the network adapters for the storage network.

Description: In this activity, your team identifies, enables, and configures a network adapter in each host computer for the storage network. Also, you copy the iSCSI Software Target file into the library. Pay attention to the steps to make future activities easier.

Table 8-2 provides the team member assignments for this activity.

Team Member	Steps	Host Computer
1	1–9	MGMT
2	10–18	CLSTR1
3	19, 10–18	CLSTR2
1	20–28	MGMT

Table 8-2   **Team member assignments for Activity 8-2**

© Cengage Learning 2014

1. If necessary, switch the KVM switch to port 1.

2. If necessary, log on to your MGMT server with a username of *Team1\Administrator*, substituting your team name for *Team1*. Enter a password of **P@ssw0rd**.

3. To view the local area connections, right-click the network icon on the taskbar, click **Open Network and Sharing Center**, and then click **Change adapter settings**.

4. To enable the local area connection that is currently not being used, right-click the local area connection's Disabled message, and then click **Enable**.

5. If the Local Area Connection message changes, continue with Step 8.

6. To disable the local area connection that is not currently available, right-click the local area connection identified in Step 5, and then click **Disable**.

7. Repeat Steps 4 through 6 for the remaining unused network adapter.

If you cannot locate the new active network adapter, ask your instructor for help.

8. To enter the IP configuration, right-click the active local area connection you located in Step 5. Click **Properties**, clear the **Internet Protocol Version 6 (TCP/IPv6)** check box, click **Internet Protocol Version 4 (TCP/IPv4)**, and then click **Properties**. Click **Use the following IP Address**, enter **192.168.10.100** in the IP address text box, and then press **Tab** twice; the subnet mask will appear in the Subnet mask text box. Press **Tab** twice, click **OK** twice, and then click **Close**.

It is very important that you use the correct IP addresses for your classroom network. Ask your instructor if an alternative IP addressing scheme will be used in your classroom.

9. Right-click the active local area connection, click **Rename**, enter **Storage**, and then press **Enter**. Close the Network Connections window.

10. Switch the KVM switch to port 2.

11. If necessary, log on to your CLSTR1 server with a username of *Team1***Administrator**, substituting your team name for *Team1*. Enter a password of **P@ssw0rd**.

12. To view the local area connections, right-click the network icon on the taskbar, click **Open Network and Sharing Center**, and then click **Change adapter settings**.

13. To enable the local area connection that is currently not being used, right-click the local area connection's Disabled message, and then click **Enable**.

14. If the Local Area Connection message changes, continue with Step 17.

15. To disable the local area connection that is not currently available, right-click the local area connection identified in Step 13, and then click **Disable**.

16. Repeat Steps 13 through 15 for the remaining unused network adapter.

If you cannot locate the new active network adapter, ask your instructor for help.

17. To enter the IP configuration, right-click the active local area connection you located in Step 14. Click **Properties**, clear the **Internet Protocol Version 6 (TCP/IPv6)** check box, click **Internet Protocol Version 4 (TCP/IPv4)**, and then click **Properties**. Click **Use the following IP Address**, enter **192.168.10.101** in the IP address text box, and then press **Tab** twice; the subnet mask will appear in the Subnet mask text box. Press **Tab** twice, click **OK**, and then click **Close**.

18. To rename the active local area connection, right-click it, click **Rename**, enter **Storage**, and then press **Enter**. Close the Network Connections window.

19. Repeat Steps 10 through 18 for the CLSTR2 server on KVM switch port 3, using 192.168.10.102 for the IP address.

20. Switch the KVM switch to port 1.

 Your instructor will provide the location of the server that contains the iSCSI_Software_Target_33.iso file. Instructions for producing the file are in Activity A-1 of Appendix A. Substitute your classroom name for servername and sharename in Step 21.

21. To locate the iSCSI Software Target .iso file, click **Start**, enter ***servername**sharename***, and then press **Enter**.

22. When the Explorer window appears for the server, right-click the filename of the iSCSI Software Target file, and then click **Copy**.

23. To open the SCVMM Admin Console, double-click the icon on the desktop.

24. Click the **Library** bar in the lower-left corner of the console window, right-click **MSSCVMMLibrary**, click **Explore**, right-click **ISOFiles**, and click **Paste**.

25. To create the virtual network for the Storage network adapter, click the **Hosts** bar in the lower-left corner of the console window, expand **All Hosts**, and then right-click **TEAM1-MGMT**, substituting your team name for *TEAM1*. Click **Properties**, click the **Networking** tab, click **Add** in the menu bar, and enter **Storage** over New Virtual Network #0. Click **Physical network adapter**, click **Add**, click the **Host network adapter** arrow, click the physical adapter, and click **OK**. Click **Yes**, click **OK**, and then click **Yes**.

26. Close the Windows Explorer windows.

27. To refresh the library, click the **Library** bar, click **MSSCVMMLibrary**, and click **Refresh** in the Actions pane.

28. Remain logged on for future lab activities.

Activity 8-3: Deploying Windows Server 2008

Time Required: 60 minutes

Objective: Deploy a virtual machine for the iSCSI target.

Description: In this activity, your team deploys a virtual machine with Windows Server 2008 R2 SP1 on the MGMT server for the iSCSI target installation. You will configure the virtual machine to support the storage network, link to the iSCSI Software Target in the hardware profile, and add the passthrough disk for iSCSI storage. Table 8-3 provides the team member assignments for this activity.

1. If necessary, switch the KVM switch to port 1.

2. If necessary, log on to your MGMT server with a username of *Team1***Administrator**, substituting your team name for *Team1*. Enter a password of **P@ssw0rd**.

3. If necessary, open the VMM administrator console by double-clicking **SCVMM Admin Console** on the desktop.

Team Member	Steps	Host Computer
1	1–16	MGMT
2	17–25	
3	26–34	
1	35–45	
2	46–51	
3	52–64	

Table 8-3 Team member assignments for Activity 8-3

© Cengage Learning 2014

4. To view the future passthrough disk, click **Start**, point to **Administrative Tools**, click **Computer Management**, and click **Disk Management**.

5. Verify that Disk 1 is offline. If Disk 1 is online, right-click the **Disk 1** icon and click **Offline**.

6. Close the Computer Management window.

7. To open the New Virtual Machine Wizard, click the **Virtual Machines** bar in the lower-left corner of the console window, and click **New virtual machine** in the Actions pane.

8. To select an existing template, click **Use an existing template or virtual hard disk**. Click **Browse**, expand the Name column by dragging the bar on the right, click **Blank Disk - Large**, click **OK**, and then click **Next**.

9. To identify the virtual machine, enter **iSCSITarget** in the Virtual machine name text box, enter **Install Windows Server 2008 R2 SP1 for future iSCSI** in the Description text box, and then click **Next**.

10. To update the hardware profile, click **Processor**, click the processor type for the MGMT server, click **Memory**, and then click **Dynamic**. Enter **1024** over 65536. Click **Virtual DVD drive**, click **Existing image file**, and then click **Browse**. Click the Windows Server 2008 R2 SP1 file, click **OK**, and then click **Next** twice.

11. To place the virtual machine on the MGMT server, click *TEAM1*-MGMT.Team1.Local, substituting your team name for *TEAM1*. Then click **Next** twice.

12. To connect the network adapter, click the **Virtual Network** arrow, click **Management Virtual**, and click **Next**.

13. To specify the Windows server edition, click the arrow next to **Specify the operating system you will install in the virtual machine**, click **64-bit edition of Windows Server 2008 R2 Enterprise**, and then click **Next**.

14. To view the PowerShell script, click **View Script**, click **Format** in the Notepad window, click **Word Wrap**, examine the script, and close the Notepad window.

15. Review the Summary window, and then click **Previous** if necessary to return to a previous window and change a setting. When you are satisfied with the settings, click **Create**.

8

16. Wait for the virtual machine to be completed, and close the Jobs window.

Ignore the message that Virtual Machine Manager cannot locate the boot or system volume.

17. To connect to the virtual machine, click **iSCSITarget,** click **Start,** and then click **Connect to virtual machine.**

18. When the regional settings window appears, verify the selections for language, time, currency, and keyboard. Make corrections as needed, and then click **Next.**

19. Click the **Install now** link.

20. To indicate which version to install, click **Windows Server 2008 Enterprise (Full Installation)**, and then click **Next.**

21. When the license terms appear, check **I accept the license terms**, and then click **Next.**

22. Click the **Custom (advanced)** icon.

23. Click **Disk 0 Unallocated Space**, and then click **Next.**

24. Wait for Windows to copy and expand files, install features and updates, and restart the computer to complete the installation.

25. Wait while Windows prepares to start for the first time and then prepares the computer for use.

26. When prompted that the user password must be changed before logging on the first time, click **OK**. Enter **P@ssw0rd** in the New password text box, press **Tab,** enter **P@ssw0rd** in the Confirm password text box, press **Enter,** and then click **OK**.

When the Set Network Location window appears, click Work and then click Close.

27. To set the time zone, click the **Set time zone** link. If necessary, click the **Change time zone** button, click the appropriate time zone, click the **Change date and time** button, change the time, and then click **OK** twice.

28. To determine the IP configuration for your iSCSITarget computer, locate the team number assigned by your instructor in Table 8-4. This row contains the IP configuration.

It is very important that you use the correct IP addresses for your classroom network. Ask your instructor if an alternative IP addressing scheme will be used in your classroom.

29. To enter the IP configuration, click **Configure Networking,** and then right-click the active local area connection. The other connection(s) should indicate that the network cable is unplugged. Click **Properties,** clear the **Internet Protocol Version 6 (TCP/IPv6)** check box, click **Internet Protocol Version 4 (TCP/IPv4),** and then click **Properties.**

Team#	IP Address	Subnet Mask	Default Gateway	DNS Server Address
1	192.168.0.114	255.255.255.0	192.168.0.1	192.168.0.111
2	192.168.0.124	255.255.255.0	192.168.0.1	192.168.0.121
3	192.168.0.134	255.255.255.0	192.168.0.1	192.168.0.131
4	192.168.0.144	255.255.255.0	192.168.0.1	192.168.0.141
5	192.168.0.154	255.255.255.0	192.168.0.1	192.168.0.151
6	192.168.0.164	255.255.255.0	192.168.0.1	192.168.0.161

Table 8-4 IP configurations for iSCSITarget server

© Cengage Learning 2014

Click **Use the following IP Address**, enter the IP address you identified in Step 28 in the IP address text box, and then press **Tab** twice; the subnet mask will appear in the Subnet mask text box. Next, enter the default gateway you identified in Step 28, press **Tab** twice, and enter the preferred DNS server from Step 28. Click **OK**, and then click **Close**.

30. To rename the active local area connection, right-click it, click **Rename**, enter **Management**, and then press **Enter**. Close the Network Connections window.

31. If your school is using volume keys, click **Activate Windows**, ask your instructor to enter the product key, and press **Enter**. Click **Close**.

32. If your school is not using volume keys, click **Activate Windows**, enter the product key provided by your instructor, and press **Enter**. Click **Close**.

33. Click **Provide computer name and domain**, click **Change**, enter **iSCSITarget** in the Computer name text box, click **OK** twice, click **Close**, and then click **Restart Now**.

34. Wait for the virtual machine to restart.

35. To log on, click **Ctrl-Alt-Del**, enter **P@ssw0rd** for the password, and press **Enter**.

36. To switch to the Server Manager window, check **Do not show this window at logon**, and then close the Initial Configuration Tasks window.

37. To join the domain, click **Change System Properties**, click **Change**, click **Domain**, and enter **Team1.local**, substituting your team name for **Team1** in the domain name. When you finish, click **OK**.

38. Log on with a username of **Team1\Administrator**, substituting your team name for **Team1**. Enter a password of **P@ssw0rd**.

39. Wait for the Welcome message, and click **OK** twice. Click **Close** and click **Restart Now**.

40. Wait for the virtual machine to restart.

41. To switch users, click **Ctrl-Alt-Del**, click **Switch User**, and click **Other User**.

42. Log on with a username of **Team1\Administrator**, substituting your team name for **Team1**. Enter a password of **P@ssw0rd**.

43. Wait for the desktop to appear, and then minimize the Virtual Machine Viewer window.

44. To shut down the virtual machine, click **Shut down** in the Actions pane, and click **Yes**.

45. Wait for the virtual machine to shut down.

46. To view the hardware configuration, right-click **iSCSITarget** in the middle pane, click **Properties**, and click **Hardware Configuration**.

47. To link to the iSCSI Software Target, click **Virtual DVD Drive**, click **Browse**, click **iSCSI_Software_Target_33.iso**, and click **OK**.

48. To add a SCSI hard disk, click **SCSI Adapter** in the menu bar.

49. To add the passthrough disk, click **Disk** in the menu bar, click the **Channel** arrow, click **SCSI 0 ID 0**, click the **Pass through to physical drive on host** option button, click the **Pass through to physical drive on host** arrow, and click **\\.\PHYSICALDRIVE1**.

50. To add the Storage network adapter, click **Network Adapter** in the menu bar, click **Synthetic network adapter**, click the **Connected to** option button, click the **Connected to** arrow, and then click **Storage**.

51. To set the startup and shutdown for the virtual machine, click the **Actions** tab, click the **Action when physical server starts** arrow, click **Always automatically turn on the virtual machine**, click the **Action when physical server stops** arrow, click **Shut down guest OS**, and then click **OK**.

52. To start and connect to the virtual machine, click **iSCSITarget**, click **Start**, and then click **Connect to virtual machine**.

53. To log on, click **Ctrl-Alt-Del**. Log on with a username of *Team1***Administrator**, substituting your team name for *Team1*. Enter a password of **P@ssw0rd**.

54. To configure the network adapter for the Storage network, click **View Network Connections** in the Server Manager, and then right-click the local area connection. Click **Properties**, clear the **Internet Protocol Version 6 (TCP/IPv6)** check box, click **Internet Protocol Version 4 (TCP/IPv4)**, and then click **Properties**. Click **Use the following IP Address**, enter **192.168.10.103** in the IP address text box, and then press **Tab** twice; the subnet mask will appear in the Subnet mask text box. Click **OK**, and then click **Close**.

55. To rename the active local area connection, right-click it, click **Rename**, enter **Storage**, and then press **Enter**. Close the Network Connections window.

56. To create the volume for the passthrough disk, click **Start**, point to **Administrative Tools**, click **Computer Management**, expand **Storage**, and click **Disk Management**.

If you do not see Disk 1, ask your instructor for help.

57. To bring the disk online, right-click the **Disk 1** icon, and click **Online**.

58. If a volume exists, right-click the allocated area for Disk 1, click **Delete Volume**, and click **Yes**.

59. To create a volume and format the disk, right-click the unallocated area, click **New Simple Volume**, click **Next** four times, and click **Finish**.

60. Wait for the formatting to be completed.

61. To rename the volume, right-click **New Volume**, click **Properties**, enter **Storage** over New Volume, and click **OK**.

62. To enable the port for iSCSI packets, click **Start**, point to **Administrative Tools**, click **Windows Firewall with Advanced Security**, and click **Inbound Rules**. Scroll and right-click **iSCSI Service (TCP-In)**, click **Enable Rule**, and then close the window.

63. Close the Computer Management window.

64. Remain logged on to the MGMT server with the iSCSITarget virtual machine running.

Activity 8-4: Configuring iSCSI Storage Access

Time Required: 45 minutes

Objective: Configure the virtual disks, targets, and clients for the storage network.

Description: In this activity, your team configures iSCSI storage access. You will install the Software Target, and then you will create the two virtual hard disks for the Witness disk and virtual machines. Next, you create the targets and assign clients. The last task is to link the targets and virtual hard disks. Pay attention to the steps to make future activities easier.

Table 8-5 provides the team member assignments for this activity.

Team Member	Steps	Host Computer
1	1–10	MGMT
2	11–17	
3	18, 12–17	
1	19–24	
2	25, 19–24	
3	26–27	
1	28–40	CLSTR1
2	41–52	CLSTR2

Table 8-5 Team member assignments for Activity 8-4

© Cengage Learning 2014

1. If necessary, switch the KVM switch to port 1.

2. If necessary, log on to your MGMT server with a username of **_Team1_\Administrator**, substituting your team name for _Team1_. Enter a password of **P@ssw0rd**.

3. If necessary, log on to your iSCSITarget virtual machine with a username of **_Team1_\Administrator**, substituting your team name for _Team1_. Enter a password of **P@ssw0rd**.

4. To start the iSCSI Software Target installation, click **Start,** click **Computer,** double-click **DVD Drive (D:), DVD_ROM,** double-click **X64,** and double-click **iscsitarget.**

5. When the Microsoft iSCSI Software Target Setup window appears, click **Next.**

6. Click **I accept the terms in the License Agreement,** and then click **Next.**

7. Review the destination folder, and click **Next** twice.

8. Review the Configure Microsoft update, click **Next,** and click **Install.**

9. Wait for the installation to be completed, and then click **Finish.**

10. Close Windows Explorer.

11. To open the Microsoft iSCSI Software Target, click **Start,** point to **Administrative Tools,** and click **Microsoft iSCSI Software Target.**

12. To start the Create Virtual Disk Wizard, right-click **Devices,** and click **Create Virtual Disk.**

13. In the Welcome window, click **Next.**

14. To name the .vhd file, enter **E:\WitnessDisk.vhd** in the File text box, and click **Next.**

15. To specify the disk size, enter **1024** in the Size of virtual disk (MB) text box, and click **Next.**

16. Enter **Witness for cluster** in the Virtual disk description text box, and click **Next.**

17. Click **Next** to permit the target to be specified later, and then click **Finish.**

18. Repeat Steps 12 through 17 for E:\VirtualMachines.vhd. Enter **400,000** MB as the size and **Virtual Machines for cluster** as the description.

 Increase the file sizes for E:\VirtualMachines.vhd to fit the size of the E: drive on your MGMT server. Leave approximately 20% for expansion and additional LUNs.

19. To start the Create iSCSI Target Wizard, right-click **iSCSI Targets** and then click **Create iSCSI Target.** Enter **Witness** as the iSCSI target name.

20. In the Welcome window, click **Next.**

21. To identify the iSCSI target, enter **Witness** in the iSCSI target name text box, enter **Witness for cluster** in the Description text box, and click **Next.**

22. To add a target, click **Advanced,** click **Add,** click the **Identifier type** arrow, click **IP Address,** enter **192.168.10.101** in the Value text box, and click **OK.**

23. To add another target, click **Add,** click the **Identifier type** arrow, click **IP Address,** enter **192.168.10.102** in the Value text box, and click **OK.** Click **Yes** and click **OK.**

24. Click **Next** and then click **Finish.**

25. Repeat Steps 19 through 24, but enter **VirtualMachines** as the iSCSI target name and **Virtual machines for cluster** in the Description text box.

26. To link the Witness virtual disk to the target, click **Devices** in the left pane, right-click **Virtual Disk 0,** click **Assign/Remove Target,** click **Add,** click **Witness,** and then click **OK** twice.

27. To link the Virtual Machines virtual disk to the target, right-click **Virtual Disk 1,** click **Assign/Remove Target,** click **Add,** click **VirtualMachines,** and then click **OK** twice.

28. Switch the KVM switch to port 2.

29. If necessary, log on to your CLSTR1 server with a username of *Team1***Administrator**, substituting your team name for *Team1*. Enter a password of **P@ssw0rd**.

30. To start the iSCSI initiator, click **Start**, point to **Administrative Tools**, click **iSCSI Initiator**, and click **Yes**.

31. To connect to the iSCSITarget server, enter **192.168.10.103** for the target, and click **Quick Connect**.

32. Wait for the connection and click **Done**.

If you do not see the two discovered targets, contact your instructor.

33. To bring the first IQN into the discovered targets, click the first IQN, click **Connect**, and then click **OK**.

34. Repeat Step 33 for the second IQN. Click **Done**.

35. To link the two discovered targets to the virtual hard disks, click the **Volumes and Devices** tab, click **Auto Configure**, and click **OK**.

36. To open the Disk Management tool, click **Start**, point to **Administrative Tools**, click **Computer Management**, and then click **Disk Management**.

37. To bring the first disk online, right-click the **Disk 1** icon and click **Online**.

38. To initialize the disk, right-click the **Disk 1** icon, click **Initialize Disk**, and then click **OK**.

If the initialization takes too long, you may need to disable the off-load adapter settings. Ask your instructor for assistance.

39. To create a volume and format it, right-click the unallocated area, click **New Simple Volume**, click **Next** three times, enter **Virtual Machines** over Volume Label, click **Next**, and click **Finish**.

The quick format feature enables you to format a disk in less than a minute.

40. Repeat Steps 37 through 39 for Disk 2, and enter **Witness** as the volume name.

41. Switch the KVM switch to port 3.

42. If necessary, log on to your CLSTR2 server with a username of *Team1***Administrator**, substituting your team name for *Team1*. Enter a password of **P@ssw0rd**.

43. To start the iSCSI initiator, click **Start**, point to **Administrative Tools**, click **iSCSI Initiator**, and click **Yes**.

44. To connect to the iSCSITarget server, enter **192.168.10.103** for the target, and click **Quick Connect**.

45. Wait for the connection and click **Done**.

If you do not see the two discovered targets, contact your instructor.

46. To bring the first IQN into the discovered targets, click the first IQN, click **Connect**, and then click **OK**.

47. Repeat Step 46 for the second IQN. Click **Done**.

48. To link the two discovered targets to the virtual hard disks, click the **Volumes and Devices** tab, click **Auto Configure**, and click **OK**.

49. To open the Disk Management tool, click **Start**, point to **Administrative Tools**, click **Computer Management**, and then click **Disk Management**.

50. To bring the first disk online, right-click the **Disk 1** icon and click **Online**.

51. To bring the second disk online, right-click the **Disk 2** icon and click **Online**.

The volumes were created and formatted on CLSTR1.

52. Remain logged on for future lab activities.

Activity 8-5: Enabling the Heartbeat Network

Time Required: 30 minutes

Objective: Cable the two cluster servers for the heartbeat network.

Description: In this activity, your team will cable two servers to form the heartbeat network. You will also enable and configure the network adapters for the heartbeat network. Pay attention to the steps to make future activities easier. Table 8-6 provides the team member assignments for this activity.

Team Member	Steps	Host Computer
3	1–2	CLSTR1
2	3–4	CLSTR2
1	5–11	CLSTR1
2	12, 5–11, 13	CLSTR2

Table 8-6   **Team member assignments for Activity 8-5**

Do not place network cables in the servers or switches until you are instructed to do so in each activity.

1. Locate the CLSTR1 server.

2. Connect a red cable between the available RJ45 connector on the CLSTR1 server and port 1 of a 5-port network switch.

You are adding the CLSTR1 and CLSTR2 servers to complete the heartbeat network.

3. Locate the CLSTR2 server.

4. Connect a red cable between the available RJ45 connector on the CLSTR2 server and port 2 of the 5-port network switch.

5. If necessary, switch the KVM switch to port 2.

6. If necessary, log on to your CLSTR1 server with a username of *Team1***Administrator**, substituting your team name for *Team1*. Enter a password of **P@ssw0rd**.

7. To view the local area connections, right-click the network icon on the taskbar, click **Open Network and Sharing Center**, and then click **Change adapter settings**.

8. To enable the local area connection that is currently not being used, right-click the local area connection's Disabled message, and then click **Enable**.

If you cannot locate the new active network adapter, ask your instructor for help.

9. To enter the IP configuration, right-click the active local area connection. Click **Properties**, clear the **Internet Protocol Version 6 (TCP/IPv6)** check box, click **Internet Protocol Version 4 (TCP/IPv4)**, and then click **Properties**. Click **Use the following IP Address**, enter **192.168.20.101** in the IP address text box, and then press **Tab** twice; the subnet mask will appear in the Subnet mask text box. Click **OK**, and then click **Close**.

10. To rename the active local area connection, right-click it, click **Rename**, enter **Heartbeat**, and then press **Enter**.

11. To disable the Test network, right-click **Local Area Connection 5**, which is the Test network. Click **Disable**, and then close the Network Connections window.

12. Repeat Steps 5 through 11 for CLSTR2 on KVM switch port 3, using an IP address of 192.168.20.102.

13. Remain logged on for future lab activities.

Validating the Cluster

With the cluster validation wizard, you run a set of focused tests on the two host computers that you intend to use as nodes in the cluster. Cluster validation tests the underlying hardware and software to verify that failover clustering can be supported. Cluster validation includes the following tasks and tests:

- *Cluster configuration*—Validate critical cluster configuration settings.

- *Inventory tests*—Provide an inventory of the hardware, software, and configuration settings on the host computers, and information about the storage.

- *Network tests*—Validate that networks have the correct settings to support clustering.

- *Storage tests*—Validate that the storage is functioning correctly and supports the required functions of the cluster.

- *System configuration tests*—Validate that the system software and configuration settings are compatible across servers.

To start the validation, click Start, point to Administrative Tools, and then click Failover Cluster Manager. Figure 8-27 shows the Failover Cluster Manager window; click the Validate a Configuration link to start the validation wizard.

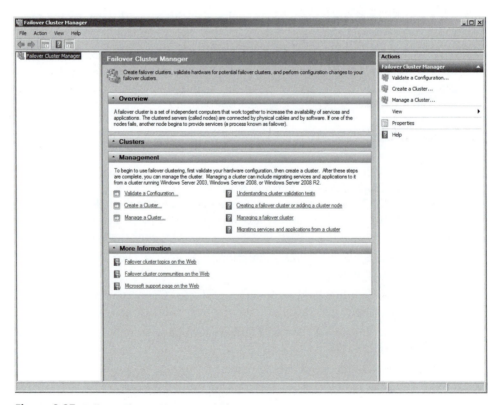

Figure 8-27 Failover Cluster Manager window

Source: Microsoft Failover Cluster Manager, Windows Server 2008 R2 SP1

Figure 8-28 shows the window where you identify servers for the cluster. You placed the host computer names in Active Directory when they joined the domain. You learn how to find these host computer names in Activity 8-7. Click Next to go to the next window.

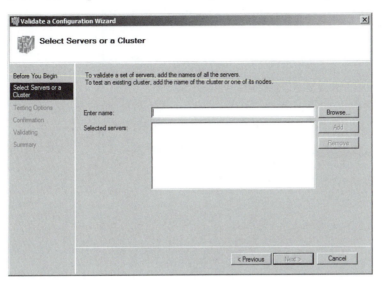

Figure 8-28 Identifying servers for clusters

Source: Microsoft Failover Cluster Manager, Windows Server 2008 R2 SP1

You can run all of the tests or select one or more tests. (See Figure 8-29.) If you click Run only tests I select, you will select individual tests, which is appropriate when you need to run diagnostics to resolve a problem in a particular area. Because this is the initial validation, you will run all of the tests, which is the default option. Click Next to go to the next window.

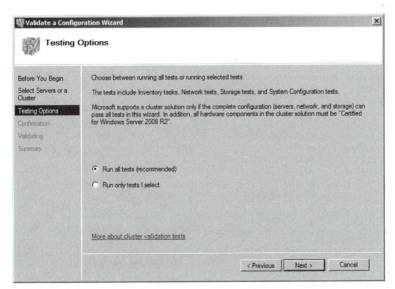

Figure 8-29 Testing Options window

Source: Microsoft Failover Cluster Manager, Windows Server 2008 R2 SP1

From the Confirmation window shown in Figure 8-30, you review the tests to be performed by scrolling the test list. To continue, click Next.

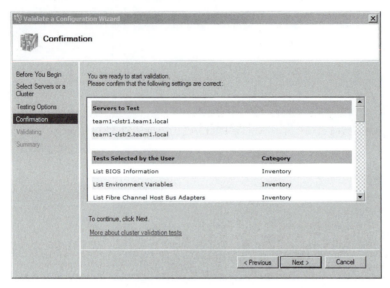

Figure 8-30 Test confirmation window

Source: Microsoft Failover Cluster Manager, Windows Server 2008 R2 SP1

Figure 8-31 shows the running log that you can review to see the progress of the validation tests. Many tests run **asynchronously,** or independently of each other, which results in faster completion.

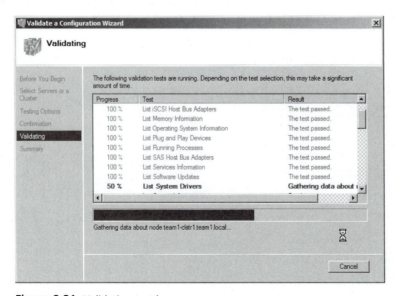

Figure 8-31 Validation test log

Source: Microsoft Failover Cluster Manager, Windows Server 2008 R2 SP1

After the tests are completed, a summary appears, as shown in Figure 8-32. To see the report, click View Report. The report can exceed 100 pages; you should view it in Internet Explorer.

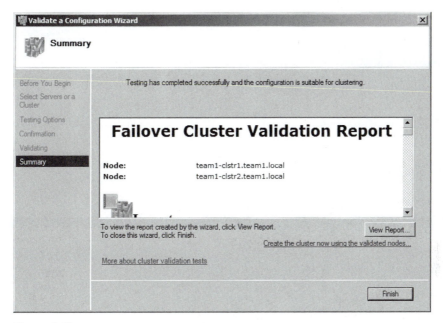

Figure 8-32 Validation summary window

Source: Microsoft Failover Cluster Manager, Windows Server 2008 R2 SP1

Figure 8-33 shows a validation report in which all four categories of tests were completed successfully. Four icons might be displayed in the report. Table 8-7 explains each icon. All tests must pass with a green check mark, or in some cases a yellow triangle (warning).

Scroll through the Internet Explorer window to see more detail, as shown in Figure 8-34. The list of tests for each test category appears.

To see additional details, drill down by clicking the link for a test. For example, Figure 8-35 shows the results of the Validate IP Configuration test. Invalid IP configurations can cause the validation to fail.

You need to review the areas that did not pass. If you completed all of the previous lab activities correctly, the validation tests will be successful. The following checklist includes possible problems that you might need to resolve:

1. IP configurations are invalid; this is a major cause of failures.

2. Network hardware is not cabled correctly, or network adapters are not enabled.

3. Test networks are not disabled.

4. The virtual machine with the iSCSI service is not started.

5. Port 3260 is not enabled in the Windows firewall on the iSCSITarget virtual machine.

6. Local storage volumes on cluster machines for the Witness disks or virtual machines are not formatted.

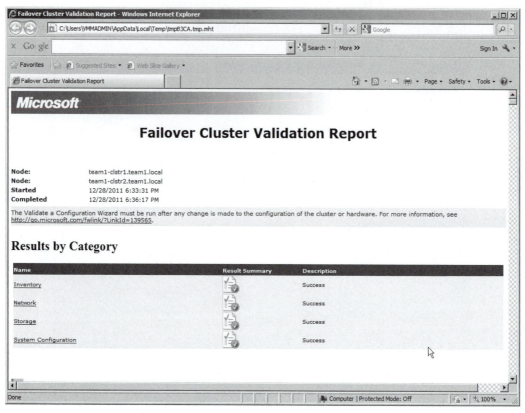

Figure 8-33 Validation report

Source: Microsoft Failover Cluster Manager, Windows Server 2008 R2 SP1

Report Icon	Explanation of Symbol
	The corresponding validation test passed, as indicated by a green circle with a white checkmark.
	The corresponding validation test produced a warning, which is indicated by an exclamation mark within a yellow triangle. The test results might not meet the recommended best practices, and should be reviewed.
	The corresponding validation test failed, as indicated by a red circle with a white X. You must correct the problem.
	The corresponding validation test was canceled, as indicated by a red bar symbol. This result occurs when the test depended on another test that was not completed successfully.

Table 8-7 Validation report icons

© Cengage Learning 2014

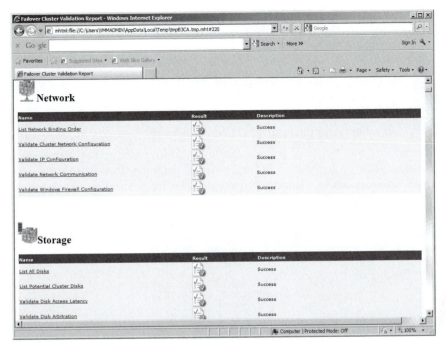

Figure 8-34 Lists of tests for test categories

Source: Microsoft Failover Cluster Manager, Windows Server 2008 R2 SP1

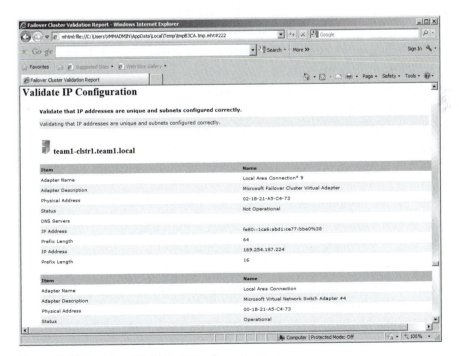

Figure 8-35 Results of Validate IP Configuration test

Source: Microsoft Failover Cluster Manager, Windows Server 2008 R2 SP1

After correcting any problems, you must rerun the cluster validation until all tests pass. A passing test is indicated by a green check mark or a yellow triangle in some cases.

Activity 8-6: Adding the Failover Clustering Feature

Time Required: 15 minutes

Objective: Add the failover clustering feature.

Description: In this activity, your team will add the failover clustering feature to all of the host servers and then restart the iSCSITarget virtual machine. Pay attention to the steps to make future activities easier. Table 8-8 provides the team member assignments for this activity.

Team Member	Steps	Host Computer
1	1–7	MGMT
2	8, 4–7	CLSTR1
3	9, 4–7	CLSTR2
1	10–12	MGMT

Table 8-8   Team member assignments for Activity 8-6

© Cengage Learning 2014

1. If necessary, switch the KVM switch to port 1.

2. If necessary, log on to your MGMT server with a username of *Team1***Administrator**, substituting your team name for *Team1*.

3. Enter a password of **P@ssw0rd**.

4. Restore the Server Manager.

5. To open the Add Features Wizard, click **Features** in the left pane, and then click **Add Features** in the right pane.

6. To add the failover clustering feature, click the **Failover Clustering** check box, click **Next**, and click **Install**.

7. Wait for the installation to be completed, and then click **Close**.

8. Repeat Steps 4 through 7 for CLSTR1, which is on KVM switch port 2.

9. Repeat Steps 4 through 7 for CLSTR2, which is on KVM switch port 3.

10. Switch the KVM switch to port 1.

11. If necessary, connect to the virtual machine that provides storage. Click the **Virtual Machines** bar in the lower-left corner of the console window, and then click **iSCSITarget** on *Team1*-MGMT, substituting your team name for *Team1*. Click **Start**, and then click **Connect to virtual machine**.

12. Remain logged on for future lab activities.

Activity 8-7: Validating the Cluster

Time Required: 45 minutes

Objective: Validate the cluster.

Description: In this activity, your team validates the cluster to determine if the hardware and software are ready to be configured as a cluster. Pay attention to the steps to make future activities easier. Table 8-9 provides the team member assignments for this activity.

Team Member	Steps	Host Computer
2	1–4	MGMT
3	5–8	
1	9–12	

Table 8-9 Team member assignments for Activity 8-7

© Cengage Learning 2014

1. If necessary, switch the KVM switch to port 1.

2. If necessary, log on to your MGMT server with a username of *Team1***Administrator**, substituting your team name for *Team1*. Enter a password of **P@ssw0rd**.

3. To open the Failover Cluster Manager, click **Start**, point to **Administrative Tools**, and click **Failover Cluster Manager**.

4. To start the cluster validation, click the **Validate a Configuration Wizard** link. Read the introductory message and click **Next**.

5. To add the cluster servers, click **Browse**, click **Advanced**, enter **TEAM** in the Name text box, and click **Find Now**. Click *TEAM1*-**CLSTR1**, substituting your team name for *TEAM1*. Press and hold **Ctrl**, click *TEAM1*-**CLSTR2**, and then click **OK** twice. Click **Next**.

6. To run all of the tests, click **Next**.

7. To accept the settings, click **Next**.

8. Wait for the validation to be completed, and then click **View Report**.

9. Review the report to locate any problem areas.

10. Resolve any open issues and repeat Steps 4 through 9 if necessary.

If you cannot resolve the open issues, contact your instructor.

11. Close the Internet Explorer window.

12. Remain logged on for future lab activities.

Configuring Failover Clustering

In a previous section of this chapter, "Describing the Hyper-V Cluster," you learned that a heartbeat is used to determine when a virtual machine failover occurs from one host computer to a second host. The concept of a **quorum** is related to failover.

If you have been an officer in a club or professional organization, you know that a certain percentage of voting members must be present to conduct business. This percentage is known as a quorum. In the failover cluster, a quorum must be present for the cluster to function. Each host computer in the cluster that communicates with other host computers has a vote. If a disk witness or file share witness is available, it will get a vote. Microsoft defines four quorum modes:

- *Node Majority*—Each available host computer that is in communication can vote. The cluster functions only when it has more than half the votes (a majority).

- *Node and Disk Majority*—Each host computer plus a witness disk in cluster storage can vote, whenever they are available and in communication. The cluster functions only when more than half the votes are available.

- *Node and File Share Majority*—Each host computer plus a file share witness created by the administrator can vote, whenever they are available and in communication. The cluster functions only when it has more than half the votes (a majority).

- *No Majority: Disk Only*—The cluster has a quorum if one host computer is available and in communication with a specific disk in the cluster storage.

This textbook defines a two-node cluster. Therefore, the quorum configuration will be a Node and Disk Majority, which is the default selection for a cluster that has an even number of host computers. The Create a Cluster Wizard places a copy of the cluster configuration database on the Witness disk and on each host computer. A Node and Disk Majority quorum means that the host computers and the Witness disk each contain copies of the cluster configuration, and that the cluster has a quorum as long as a majority (two out of three) of these copies are available.

Configuring the failover cluster is similar to the cluster validation you completed in Activity 8-7. To start configuring the failover cluster, click the Create a Cluster Wizard link in the Failover Cluster Manager. Select the two servers as you did during the cluster validation. Refer back to Figure 8-28 and Activity 8-7 if necessary. To continue, click Next.

Figure 8-36 shows the completed configuration for the Team1 cluster. Enter a name for the cluster and an IP address to be created for use by the cluster.

After clicking Next, review the confirmation and click Next to agree. The wizard then completes the cluster. Click View Report to see the details. You will create the cluster in the next activity.

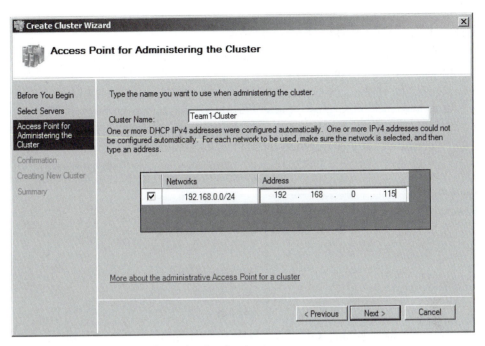

Figure 8-36 Completed configuration for the cluster

Source: Microsoft Failover Cluster Manager, Windows Server 2008 R2 SP1

Activity 8-8: Creating the Failover Cluster

Time Required: 30 minutes

Objective: Create the failover cluster.

Description: In this activity, your team will create the failover cluster. Pay attention to the steps to make future activities easier. Table 8-10 provides the team member assignments for this activity.

Team Member	Steps	Host Computer
3	1–5	MGMT
2	6–8	
1	9–13	

Table 8-10 Team member assignments for Activity 8-8

© Cengage Learning 2014

1. If necessary, switch the KVM switch to port 1.

2. If necessary, log on to your MGMT server with a username of *Team1\Administrator*, substituting your team name for *Team1*. Enter a password of **P@ssw0rd**.

3. If necessary, open the Failover Cluster Manager. Click **Start**, point to **Administrative Tools**, and click **Failover Cluster Manager**.

4. To create the cluster, click the **Create a Cluster Wizard** link. Read the introductory message and click **Next**.

5. To add the cluster servers, click **Browse**, click **Advanced**, enter **TEAM** in the Name text box, and click **Find Now**. Click *TEAM1*-CLSTR1, substituting your team name for *TEAM1*. Press and hold **Ctrl**, click *TEAM1*-CLSTR2, and then click **OK** twice. Click **Next**.

6. To determine the configuration details for your cluster, locate the team number assigned by your instructor in Table 8-11. This row contains the configuration details.

Team#	Cluster Name	IP Address
1	Team1-Cluster	192.168.0.115
2	Team2-Cluster	192.168.0.125
3	Team3-Cluster	192.168.0.135
4	Team4-Cluster	192.168.0.145
5	Team5-Cluster	192.168.0.155
6	Team6-Cluster	192.168.0.165

Table 8-11 Cluster configurations for each team

© Cengage Learning 2014

It is very important that you use the correct IP addresses for your classroom network. Ask your instructor if an alternative IP addressing scheme will be used in your classroom.

7. To enter the cluster configuration, enter the name you identified in Step 6 in the Cluster Name text box, click **Click here to type an address**, enter the IP address you identified in Step 6, and then click **Next**.

8. Review the confirmation window and click **Next**.

9. Wait for the cluster to be created.

10. Click **Next** to review the summary.

11. To view the details, click **View Report**.

Note that the quorum appears as Node and Disk Majority.

12. Close the Internet Explorer window and click **Finish**.

13. Remain logged on for future lab activities.

Enabling a Cluster Shared Volume

You use the Failover Cluster Manager to enable cluster shared volumes (CSVs). Once the CSV feature has been enabled, a new CSV node will appear in the Failover Cluster Manager. This node provides a place to identify which disks should be enabled as supporting CSV. Only empty disks can be enabled; the console does not permit you to enable a disk resource that contains virtual machines. Once the volumes are created, you migrate virtual machines to CSV-enabled disks. When migrating these virtual machines, enable each for high availability.

When you enable CSVs, the new default storage location for virtual machines changes to various subfolders under C:\ClusterStorage. This location is on the system drive of your host computers, but it is not the actual location of the virtual hard disk files. CSV uses information stored on the root drive of every host computer in a cluster to determine ownership of files on the disk resource, and it operates as a set of pointers to the actual data in your iSCSI storage. Figure 8-37 shows a warning message that appears when CSVs are enabled. You could corrupt the data in the C:\ClusterStorage folder by accessing it with Windows Explorer.

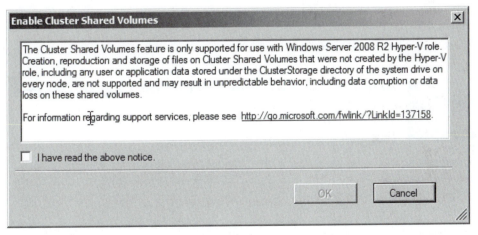

Figure 8-37 Warning message that appears when CSVs are enabled

Source: Microsoft Failover Cluster Manager, Windows Server 2008 R2 SP1

You will add the volumes in the SAN in Activity 8-9. After the volumes are managed as CSVs, they are marked as reserved in the Disk Management window, as shown in Figure 8-38. You cannot use Windows Explorer to move virtual machines to the C:\ClusterStorage folder. You will learn how to migrate virtual machines in Chapter 9.

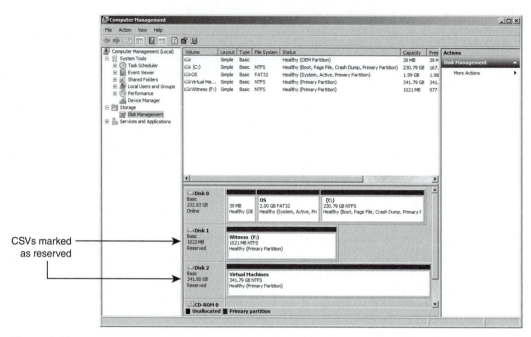

Figure 8-38 CSVs marked as reserved

Source: Microsoft Windows Server 2008 R2 SP1

Activity 8-9: Creating the Cluster Shared Volume

Time Required: 20 minutes

Objective: Create the cluster shared volume.

Description: In this activity, your team will create the cluster shared volume. You will observe the CSV disks using the Disk Management tool. Pay attention to the steps to make future activities easier. Table 8-12 provides the team member assignments for this activity.

Team Member	Steps	Host Computer
1	1–4	MGMT
2	5–7	
3	8–12	CLSTR1
1	13, 8–12	CLSTR2
2	14–16	CLSTR1
3	17, 14–16	CLSTR2
1	18, 14–16	MGMT

Table 8-12 Team member assignments for Activity 8-9

© Cengage Learning 2014

1. If necessary, switch the KVM switch to port 1.

2. If necessary, log on to your MGMT server with a username of *Team1***Administrator**, substituting your team name for *Team1*. Enter a password of **P@ssw0rd**.

3. If necessary, open the Failover Cluster Manager. Click **Start**, point to **Administrative Tools**, and click **Failover Cluster Manager**.

4. To create the cluster shared volume, click the **Enable Cluster Shared Volumes Wizard** link. Read the warning message, click **I have read the above notice**, and click **OK**.

Note that Cluster Shared Volumes now appears under Nodes in the Failover Cluster Manager.

5. To view the cluster shared volumes, expand *Team1*-**Cluster.***Team1*.**local**, substituting your team name for *Team1*. Click **Cluster Shared Volumes**.

6. To add disks to the cluster shared volume, click **Add storage** in the Actions pane, make sure that the **Cluster Disk** check box is selected, and then click **OK**.

7. To verify the storage allocations, click **Storage**, and then expand the entry under Cluster Shared Volumes.

8. Switch the KVM switch to port 2.

9. If necessary, log on to your CLSTR1 server with a username of *Team1***Administrator**, substituting your team name for *Team1*. Enter a password of **P@ssw0rd**.

10. To open the Disk Management tool, click **Start**, point to **Administrative Tools**, click **Computer Management**, and then click **Disk Management**.

11. Verify that Disk 1 and Disk 2 are marked as Reserved.

You should see C:\ClusterStorage\Volume1 as the folder location on the local hard drive for the CLSTR1 and CLSTR2 host computers.

12. Right-click the operating system partition on Disk 0, click **Explore**, and double-click **ClusterStorage**. Note that the Volume 1 folder exists. Close the ClusterStorage and Computer Management windows.

13. Repeat Steps 8 through 12 for CLSTR2, which is on KVM switch port 3.

14. Switch the KVM switch to port 2.

15. To shut down the host computer, click **Start**. If necessary, click the arrow next to **Log off**. Click **Shut down**, click the **Option** arrow, click **Operating System: Reconfiguration (Planned)**, and then click **OK**. If necessary, click **Yes**.

16. Wait for the host computer to shut down.

17. Complete Steps 14 through 16 for CLSTR2, which is on KVM switch port 3.

18. Complete Steps 14 through 16 for MGMT, which is on KVM switch port 1.

Chapter Summary

- When a virtual machine has high availability, its downtime can be reduced. In many cases, downtime can be reduced enough that users of an application do not notice an outage.

- This chapter is the pivotal chapter of this textbook. All of the tools for the private cloud became available. In future chapters, you will learn to deploy and manage the private cloud for the user community.

- You must complete a number of tasks to implement high availability for the private cloud:

  - Cable and configure the storage network.

  - Implement the iSCSI Software Target to provide a virtual SAN for the Witness disk and storage for virtual machines.

  - Cable and configure the heartbeat network.

  - Validate the cluster configuration to determine that the proper resources are available to configure the cluster.

  - Implement the cluster so that if a host computer fails, another can take over.

  - Implement cluster shared volumes so host computers can use common storage without access conflicts.

Key Terms

asynchronous   In operating systems, refers to a process that operates independently of other processes.

cluster shared volume (CSV)   A shared disk containing an NTFS volume that is made accessible for read and write operations by all host computers within a Windows Server failover cluster. The CSV was first introduced in Windows Server 2008 R2 for use with the Hyper-V role.

failover cluster   A group of host computers that work together to increase the availability of virtual machines and applications.

high availability   Groups of host computers that support virtual machines that can be used reliably with a minimum of downtime.

Hyper-V cluster   A Microsoft implementation of a failover cluster.

initiator   In iSCSI storage, a client that issues commands for services from the iSCSI target.

iSCSI Qualified Name (IQN)   A unique name that identifies an iSCSI target.

No Majority: Disk Only   A quorum configuration in which one node is available; this node is in communication with a specific disk in the cluster storage.

Node and Disk Majority   A quorum configuration used when an even number of nodes have available shared storage.

Node and File Share Majority   A quorum configuration that is recommended if you have an even number of nodes and shared storage is not available.

Node Majority   The recommended quorum configuration if you have an odd number of nodes.

Protocol Data Unit (PDU)   In iSCSI storage communications, an encapsulated TCP/IP packet that contains SCSI commands.

quorum   In a failover cluster, the number of host computers that must be present for the cluster to function.

target   In iSCSI storage, a server that responds to commands for services from the iSCSI client.

Review Questions

1. _high availability_ is the implementation of operating systems technology so that if a virtual machine fails, another can take over for it.

2. Which of the following business needs does high availability meet? (Choose all correct answers.)

   a. Sensitivity to situations in which employees cannot do their work

   b. A computer failure that could keep customers from purchasing items on the company's Web site

   c. A computer failure that could cause business activities to come to a halt

   d. Job opportunities for IT personnel

3. _____ enables virtual machines to use data from a unified storage entity.

4. Which of the following are made available by clustering? (Choose all correct answers.)

   (a.) load balancing

   (b.) redundancy

   c. storage

   d. failover

5. _initiator_ send SCSI commands to the target storage device.

6. The iSCSI _____ contains a header with a command and a data segment.

7. When connected with the iSCSI protocol, _____. (Choose all correct answers.)

   a. the disk appears to the operating system as being installed locally

   b. read/write access is at the file level

   c. read/write access is at the block level

   d. the devices can be partitioned and formatted by the Windows Server 2008 tools

8. _____ distributes processing across multiple host computers.

9. _____ is the capability to switch to a standby server without operator intervention.

8

10. Which of the following are requirements of operating system disks for virtual machines prior to the use of CSV in the Hyper-V cluster? (Choose all correct answers.)

    a. Virtual machines can be started from shared storage.

    b. Virtual machines must be started from local storage.

    c. Each host computer requires a unique LUN for each virtual machine.

    d. Virtual machines can be migrated between host computers.

11. A volume that is configured as a/an _____ can be accessed by all of the host computers in the Hyper-V cluster.

12. Which of the following are characteristics of a cluster shared volume? (Choose all correct answers.)

    a. The path appears on the host computer as C:\ClusterSharedVolume.

    b. The path appears on the host computer as C:\ClusterStorage.

    c. The volume is owned by one host computer.

    d. Block read/write access is performed by any host computer in the cluster.

13. With the _iSCSI target_ wizard, you specify which host computers are authorized to connect to the iSCSI targets.

14. You can identify the iSCSI clients that can access the target by which of the following methods? (Choose all correct answers.)

    a. DNS domain names

    b. IP addresses

    c. IP subnets

    d. MAC addresses

15. The components of the iSCSI Qualified Name (IQN) include _____ . (Choose all correct answers.)

    a. The literal prefix "iqn"

    b. The date in mm-yyyy format

    c. The date in yyyy-mm format

    d. The domain name of the authority

    e. The reversed domain name of the authority

    f. A string to identify the target

16. The Microsoft Software Target uses port _____ for communication between the initiator and client.

    a. 25

    b. 80

    c. 443

    d. 3260

17. The cluster validation test verifies which of the following categories? (Choose all correct answers.)

   a. Inventory
   b. Network
   c. Storage
   d. System configuration

18. The validation report shows which of the following icons? (Choose all correct answers.)

   a. Passed
   b. Warning
   c. Information
   d. Failed
   e. Canceled

19. Microsoft defines which of the following quorum modes? (Choose all correct answers.)

   a. Node Majority
   b. Node and Disk Majority
   c. Node and File Share Majority
   d. No Majority: Node Only
   e. No Majority: Disk Only

20. The default quorum for an even number of host computers is _____ .

Case Projects

Case 8-1: Describing High Availability

Your supervisor has asked you to mentor the new network administrator. You are implementing a high-availability solution for the Web sales application. Identify a list of topics that you plan to discuss. Include descriptions for each topic.

Case 8-2: Describing Cluster Shared Volumes

You are asked to make a presentation at the next TechShare meeting. Prepare a one-page summary on cluster shared volumes.

Case 8-3: Troubleshooting Cluster Validation

When you view the Cluster Evaluation report, you see the following error:

Network interfaces TEAM1-CLSTR1.Team1.local - Local Area Connection 5 and TEAM1-CLSTR2.Team1.local - Local Area Connection 5 are on the same cluster network, yet either address fe80::3cd0:8425:1ee5:1da2%20 is not reachable from fe80::f583:1f5c:2d7e:5bc3%22 or the ping latency is greater than the maximum allowed 500 milliseconds

What will you do to resolve the problem? Research this problem on the Internet and prepare a one-page report that identifies the steps you will take to solve this problem.

chapter 9

Managing High-Availability Clusters

After reading this chapter and completing the exercises, you will be able to:

- Monitor high-availability clusters
- Migrate virtual machines
- Back up and recover the VMM environment
- Troubleshoot high-availability clusters

In the previous chapter, you finished creating a private cloud. In this chapter, you will learn the skills for day-to-day management of software that supports the private cloud. As an administrator, you have the responsibility of maintaining availability for the cloud, which requires monitoring high-availability clusters. Management tasks also include moving virtual machine files between various storage locations. To achieve load balancing, you will migrate virtual machines between host computers. To protect the VMM environment, you must learn to back up and restore data files that support the private cloud. When problems occur with high-availability clusters, you must troubleshoot and correct the problems.

Monitoring High-Availability Clusters

In Chapter 8, you learned that information technology (IT) meets business needs by providing high-availability clusters to minimize situations in which outages might occur. As a system administrator, you have the responsibility of monitoring this environment to maximize uptime for the private cloud.

Earlier in this textbook, you installed two Microsoft managers that provide monitoring tools. The Failover Cluster Manager provides tools that monitor the health of the failover cluster. Virtual Machine Manager includes tools that provide insight into the virtual machine environment.

Monitoring with the Failover Cluster Manager

In Chapter 8, you used the Failover Cluster Manager to validate the hardware and software in the cluster and then to create the cluster. In this chapter, you use the same tool to monitor resources in the cluster.

To open the Failover Cluster Manager, click Start, point to Administrative Tools, and click Failover Cluster Manager. If you are using this tool for the first time, you must select a cluster to manage, as shown in Figure 9-1. Enter the cluster name, substituting your team name for Team1, and click OK.

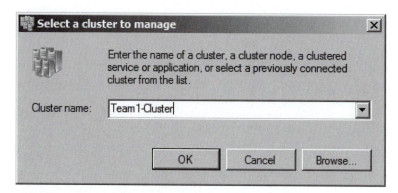

Figure 9-1 Selecting a cluster to manage

Source: Microsoft Failover Cluster Manager, Windows Server 2008 R2 SP1

To see the entries in the left pane, expand each node. Figure 9-2 shows the Failover Cluster Manager with expanded nodes. The summary information provides a high-level view of the cluster.

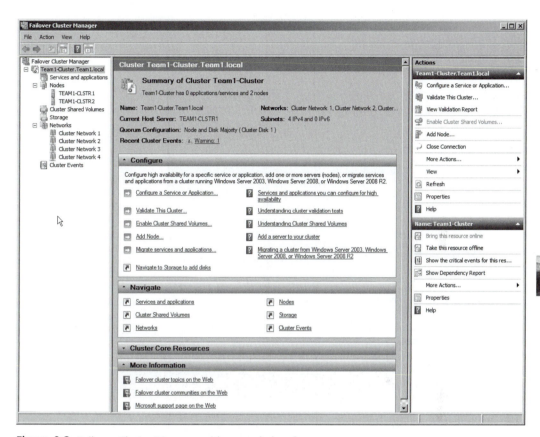

Figure 9-2 Failover Cluster Manager with expanded nodes

Source: Microsoft Failover Cluster Manager, Windows Server 2008 R2 SP1

Click Cluster Events in the left pane to see recent activities related to the cluster. Figure 9-3 shows cluster events that have occurred in the last 24 hours, including the date and time of the event, the reporting host computer (Node), the event ID, and the task category. Click the event entry to see more details.

Because no virtual machines have met the requirements for high availability, the Services and applications node in the left pane is empty. You will migrate and configure virtual machines later in this chapter, in the section called "Migrating Storage and Virtual Machines."

The Nodes view in the left pane shows the host computers in the cluster. To see detailed information for TEAM1-CLSTR1, click its name in the left pane and then click Detailed view for TEAM1-CLSTR1 in the right pane. To see more detail, as shown in Figure 9-4, expand each network connection.

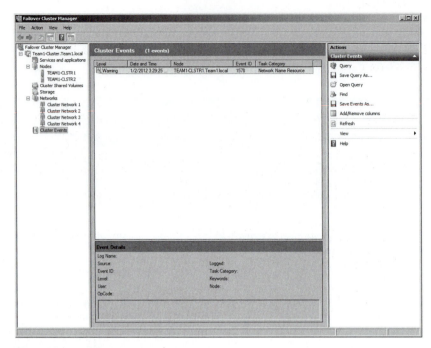

Figure 9-3 List of cluster events

Source: Microsoft Failover Cluster Manager, Windows Server 2008 R2 SP1

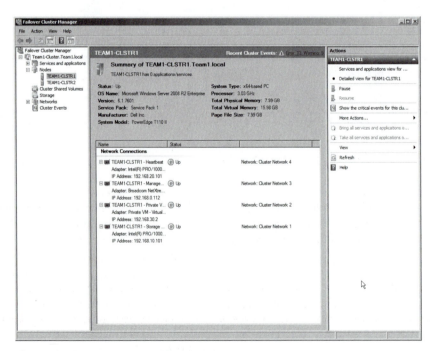

Figure 9-4 Detailed view for TEAM1-CLSTR1

Source: Microsoft Failover Cluster Manager, Windows Server 2008 R2 SP1

Figure 9-5 shows the cluster shared volumes. Only the storage for virtual machines is configured as a cluster shared volume. In the figure, the current owner of the cluster shared volume is TEAM1-CLSTR2. While TEAM1-CLSTR1 can read and write data blocks, requests for other operations are made to the current owner, TEAM1-CLSTR2.

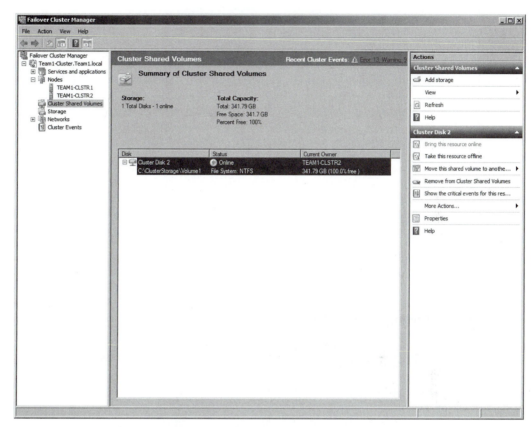

Figure 9-5 Cluster shared volumes

Source: Microsoft Failover Cluster Manager, Windows Server 2008 R2 SP1

The storage allocations are shown in Figure 9-6. These allocations appear when you click Storage in the left pane. Cluster Disk 1 is the Witness disk in the quorum, which is not shown in the cluster shared volumes (see Figure 9-5). The status for both disks is Online. If a disk has a status of Redirected Access, read/write access to that volume is being redirected over the network to another host computer in the cluster that still has direct access to the storage supporting the cluster shared volume. This recovery mode prevents the loss of all connectivity to storage. If a disk has Redirected Access status, you need to evaluate the situation and migrate virtual machines to other host computers in the cluster that are not having connectivity problems.

To view the configurations in your networks, expand the Networks node in the left pane, click the cluster network to investigate, and expand the network connections. Figure 9-7

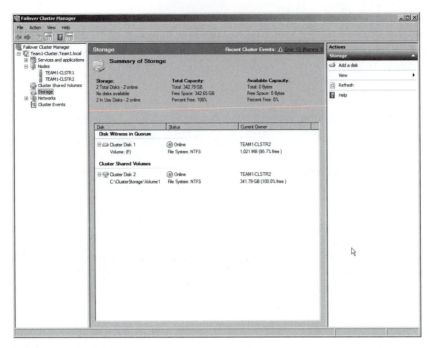

Figure 9-6 Storage allocations

Source: Microsoft Failover Cluster Manager, Windows Server 2008 R2 SP1

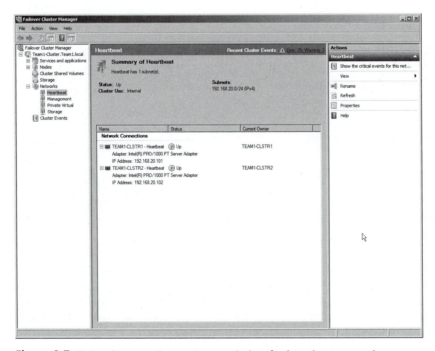

Figure 9-7 Network connections summary window for heartbeat network

Source: Microsoft Failover Cluster Manager, Windows Server 2008 R2 SP1

shows the connections for the Heartbeat network. To identify your networks, you will name the network connections in Activity 9-1. By viewing a network configuration, you can confirm the status of the network connection and the assigned IP addresses. Because of the way Windows Server 2008 allocates network devices, physical cables may not connect to the same network adapter on each host computer. To work around this problem, in Chapter 8 you inserted one network cable at a time and determined which network adapter Windows Server 2008 had detected.

The last node in the left pane shows the cluster events. You can select the events to display by clicking Query in the right pane. By default, Critical, Error, and Warning messages are selected. You can click the Informational check box to add routine operational information. You can select the dates of interest by clicking the From date arrow, and clicking a start date. This query is shown in Figure 9-8.

Cluster Events Filter

Select the criteria for which you want to display events.

Nodes:
- ☑ TEAM1-CLSTR1.Team1.local
- ☑ TEAM1-CLSTR2.Team1.local

Event Logs:
- ☐ Application
- ☐ Forwarded Events
- ☐ Hardware Events
- ☐ Internet Explorer
- ☐ Key Management Service
- ☐ Microsoft-IIS-Configuration/Operational
- ☐ Microsoft-Windows-API-Tracing/Operational

☑ Read only cluster events from the System log

Level: ☑ Critical ☑ Error ☑ Warning ☑ Informational ☐ Verbose

Event IDs:

Enter ID numbers and/or ID ranges separated by comma. To exclude criteria, type a minus sign first. For example: 1, 3, 5-99, -76

From: Events On | 4/ 1/2012 | 3:33:15 PM

To: Last Event | 4/ 9/2012 | 3:34:45 PM

[Reset] [OK] [Cancel]

Figure 9-8 Cluster Events Filter window showing criteria for cluster events

Source: Microsoft Failover Cluster Manager, Windows Server 2008 R2 SP1

Figure 9-9 shows the warnings and errors that have occurred over the last 24 hours. You need to check this view daily.

Cluster Events Filter   ✕

Select the criteria for which you want to display events.

Nodes:
☑ TEAM1-CLSTR1.Team1.local
☑ TEAM1-CLSTR2.Team1.local

Event Logs:
☐ Application
☐ Forwarded Events
☐ Hardware Events
☐ Internet Explorer
☐ Key Management Service
☐ Microsoft-IIS-Configuration/Operational
☐ Microsoft-Windows-API-Tracing/Operational

☑ Read only cluster events from the System log

Level: ☑ Critical   ☑ Error   ☑ Warning
          ☑ Informational   ☐ Verbose

Event IDs:

Enter ID numbers and/or ID ranges separated by comma. To exclude criteria, type a minus sign first. For example: 1, 3, 5-99, -76

From: Events On ▼   4/ 8/2012 ▼   3:33:15 PM
To: Last Event ▼   4/ 9/2012 ▼   3:40:27 PM

Reset   OK   Cancel

Figure 9-9 Cluster Events Filter window showing events of last 24 hours

Source: Microsoft Failover Cluster Manager, Windows Server 2008 R2 SP1

Activity 9-1: Monitoring the Cluster

Time Required: 20 minutes

Objective: Monitor the status of the cluster with the Failover Cluster Manager.

Description: In this activity, your team will investigate each node in the left pane of the Failover Cluster Manager. To facilitate future activities with the four network connections, you will rename them. If you encounter errors that need resolution, refer to the section on troubleshooting later in this chapter. Pay attention to the steps to make future activities easier.

Table 9-1 provides the team member assignments for this activity.

Team Member	Steps	Host Computer
1	1-6	MGMT
2	7-9	
3	10-11	
1	12, 10-11	
2	13-17	
3	18-19	
1	20, 18-19, 21	

Table 9-1 Team member assignments for Activity 9-1

© Cengage Learning 2014

1. Switch the KVM switch to port 1.

2. Log on to your MGMT server with a username of *Team1\Administrator*, substituting your team name for *Team1*. Enter a password of **P@ssw0rd**.

3. To open Virtual Machine Manager, double-click **SCVMM Admin Console** on the desktop.

4. If necessary, start the iSCSITarget virtual machine. Click **Virtual Machines**, click **iSCSITarget**, and click **Start** in the right pane.

5. To open the Failover Cluster Manager on the MGMT server, click **Start**, point to **Administrative Tools**, and click **Failover Cluster Manager**.

6. If you are using the Failover Cluster Manager for the first time, click **Manage a Cluster** in the **Actions** pane, and then enter the cluster name *Team1*-**Cluster.***Team1*.**local**, substituting your team name for *Team1*. Click **OK**.

7. To view the summary of the cluster, click *Team1*-**Cluster.***Team1*.**local**, substituting your team name for *Team1*.

8. To view the recent cluster events, click the blue link after Recent Cluster Events.

9. To view the event details, click the entries of interest and read the details at the bottom.

10. To view the summary for the CLSTR1 host computer, expand **Nodes**, and click *TEAM1*-**CLSTR1**, substituting your team name for *TEAM1*. Click **Detailed view for** *TEAM1*-**CLSTR1** and expand each network connection.

If CLSTR1 is the owner of the cluster disks, you will see information for the cluster disks.

11. Verify that each resource is online.

12. Repeat Steps 10 and 11 for the CLSTR2 host computer.

13. To view the summary of the cluster shared volumes, expand **Cluster Shared Volumes** in the left pane.

14. Verify that the status is Online.

15. To view the storage summary, expand **Storage**, and then expand each **Cluster Disk**.

16. Verify that the status is Online.

17. To view the network summary, expand **Networks**.

18. Click **Cluster Network 1** and expand the Network connections. Verify that the information is correct in the Status and Cluster Use fields in the upper-center section. Review the details for host computers.

19. To rename the cluster network, click **Cluster Network 1**. Using Table 9-2, look up the subnet, enter the network connection name over "Cluster Network 1," and press **Enter**.

Subnets	Network Connection
192.168.0.0	Management
192.168.10.0	Storage
192.168.20.0	Heartbeat
192.168.30.0	Private VM

Table 9-2 Names for subnets

© Cengage Learning 2014

20. Repeat Steps 18 and 19 for the remaining cluster networks.

21. Remain logged on for future lab activities.

Monitoring with Virtual Machine Manager

While Failover Cluster Manager is your first choice for monitoring the cluster, VMM also offers useful tools to manage many aspects of the virtualization environment. These tools are available in the Administration view of the VMM administrator console.

Click the Administration bar in the lower-left corner of the console window to view the VMM monitoring options. Figure 9-10 shows the Overview pane, which displays the current status of the host computers, virtual machines, recent jobs, and library resources. The Overview pane is color-coded to draw your attention to problem areas.

The rest of this section describes each node in the left pane of the VMM Administration view. For example, when you click General, you can determine and restore the settings for the areas indicated in the center pane in Figure 9-11. For example, double-clicking Placement Settings displays a window in which you can set your preferences for virtual machine placement.

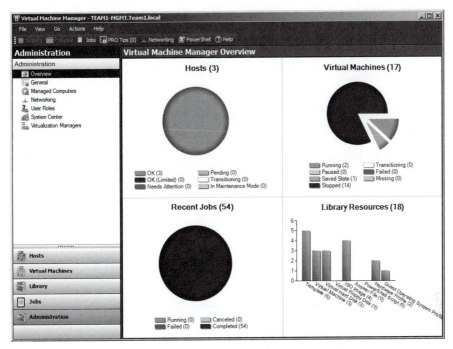

Figure 9-10 VMM Administration view showing overview of virtualization environment

Source: Microsoft Virtual Machine Manager 2008 R2 SP1, Windows Server 2008 R2 SP1

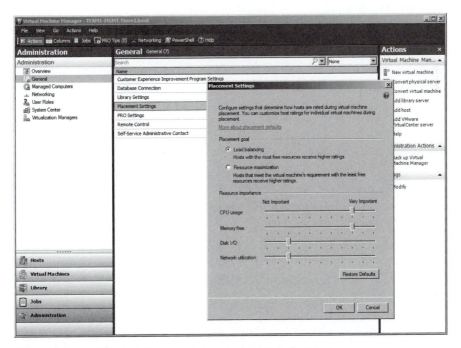

Figure 9-11 VMM Administration view showing General settings

Source: Microsoft Virtual Machine Manager 2008 R2 SP1, Windows Server 2008 R2 SP1

Click Managed Computers in the left pane to list the host computers that are managed by VMM. Figure 9-12 shows the three host computers and the status of the VMM agents. You can use this information to determine if there is a problem with an agent.

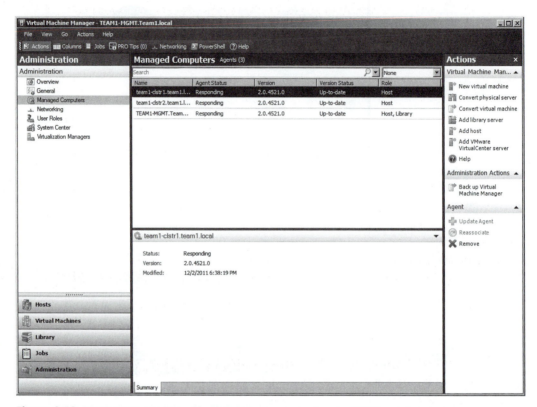

Figure 9-12 VMM Administration view showing managed computer VMM agent status

Source: Microsoft Virtual Machine Manager 2008 R2 SP1, Windows Server 2008 R2 SP1

Click Networking to see the MAC address range for assignment to virtual network devices. You probably will not need to change these settings.

Figure 9-13 shows the role members for the Administrator role. You use User Roles to control which tasks a user can perform in the virtual environment. For example, User Roles are used with the Web portal environment, which you learned about in Chapter 6.

The System Center is used with the **System Center Operations Manager (SCOM)**, which Microsoft describes as a cross-platform data center management system for operating systems and hypervisors. SCOM requires additional hardware resources, which means it is beyond the scope of this textbook.

The Virtualization Manager brings the VMware VirtualCenter server into the VMM environment, which permits host computers running VMware ESX to be managed by VMM. **VMware VirtualCenter** is the VMware product that manages VMware ESX host computers. The product is beyond the scope of this textbook.

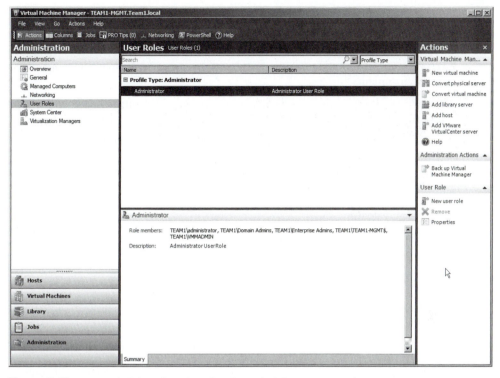

Figure 9-13 VMM Administration view showing Administrator user role

Source: Microsoft Virtual Machine Manager 2008 R2 SP1, Windows Server 2008 R2 SP1

Activity 9-2: Monitoring the Virtualization Environment

Time Required: 20 minutes

Objective: Monitor the status of the virtualization environment with VMM.

Description: In this activity, your team will investigate nodes in the left pane of the VMM Administration view. If you encounter errors that need resolution, refer to the section on troubleshooting later in this chapter. Pay attention to the steps to make future activities easier.

Table 9-3 provides the team member assignments for this activity.

Team Member	Steps	Host Computer
3	1-6	MGMT
2	7-9	

Table 9-3 Team member assignments for Activity 9-2

© Cengage Learning 2014

1. If necessary, switch the KVM switch to port 1.

2. If necessary, log on to your MGMT server with a username of *Team1\Administrator*, substituting your team name for *Team1*. Enter a password of **P@ssw0rd**.

3. If necessary, open Virtual Machine Manager by double-clicking **SCVMM Admin Console** on the desktop.

4. If necessary, click the **Administration** bar in the lower-left corner, and then click the **Overview** node. Examine the pie graphs for summary information about the virtualization environment.

5. Click the **General** node, and then double-click **Customer Experience Improvement Program Settings**. Review the settings.

6. Repeat Step 5 to examine the remaining entries in the middle pane of the General node.

7. To determine the VMM agent status on the host computers, click the **Managed Computers** node.

8. To determine the role members for the Administrator role, click **User Roles**, and then click **Administrator**.

9. Remain logged on for future lab activities.

Migrating Storage and Virtual Machines

With failover clusters, you have two choices when moving a virtual machine from one cluster host computer to another: Quick Storage Migration and live migration.

Quick Storage Migration

Quick Storage Migration (QSM) enables you to migrate a running virtual machine from one storage location to another. QSM can move the virtual disks of a running machine regardless of the storage type, with minimal downtime. You can select any storage type that is available to VMM, including local storage or SANs.

To begin the QSM process, VMM takes a snapshot of the running virtual machine, which creates a differencing disk (see Figure 9-14). All disk write operations from this point go to

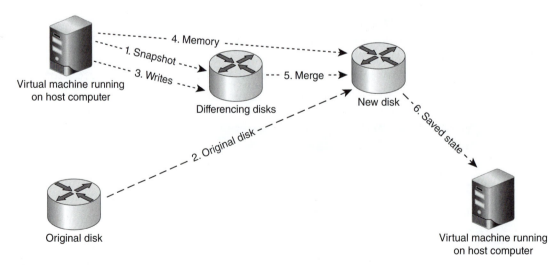

Figure 9-14 Steps for Quick Storage Migration

the differencing disk, while the original disk becomes read-only. VMM uses the Background Intelligent Transfer Service (BITS) to copy the original disk to the new location. This copy represents the bulk of the transfer; the virtual machine continues to run. Once the copy of the original disk is complete, the virtual machine is placed in a saved state. The memory is copied to the new location. A merge combines the original disk, snapshot, disk writes, and memory in the new location. Once all of the elements are transferred, VMM exports and then imports the virtual machine on the same host computer to make the final changes to the virtual machine configuration file.

To start the Quick Storage Migration, open the Virtual Machines view in the VMM administrator console, and then locate and click the existing virtual machine on the host computer, as shown in Figure 9-15.

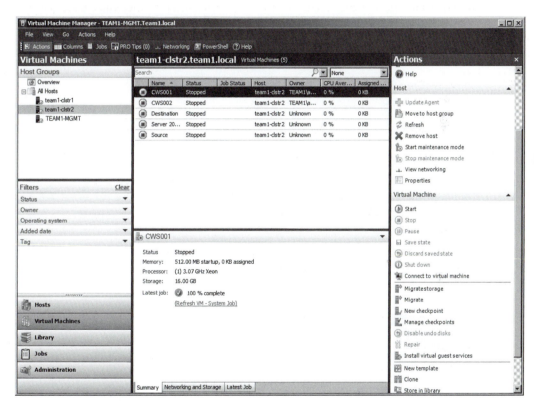

Figure 9-15 Starting Quick Storage Migration

Source: Microsoft Virtual Machine Manager 2008 R2 SP1, Windows Server 2008 R2 SP1

Next, scroll and click Migratestorage in the right pane. The Migrate Virtual Machine Wizard appears. Find the new location for the virtual machine by clicking Browse in the Select Path window. An example of the completed window is shown in Figure 9-16. In the Select Destination Folder window, expand ClusterStorage, and then click Volume1, as shown in Figure 9-17. The C:\ClusterStorage\Volume1 folder then will be used to locate the files on the cluster shared volumes on the iSCSI SAN. Click OK to return to the Select Path window, which now shows the target location. Click the virtual disks you want to move, as shown in Figure 9-16, and click Next.

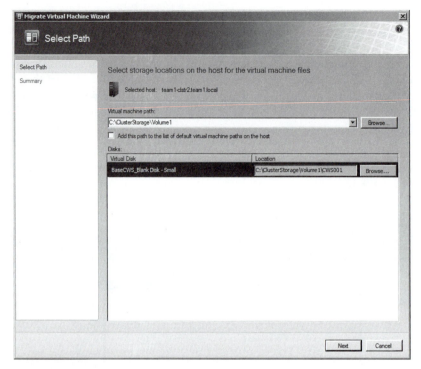

Figure 9-16 Completed Select Path window

Source: Microsoft Virtual Machine Manager 2008 R2 SP1, Windows Server 2008 R2 SP1

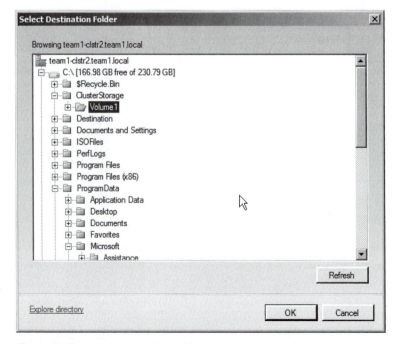

Figure 9-17 Select Destination Folder window

Source: Microsoft Virtual Machine Manager 2008 R2 SP1, Windows Server 2008 R2 SP1

Figure 9-18 shows the summary of the migration. Notice that the Source host and Destination host are the same. You are changing the location of the virtual machine's files, not the ownership of the virtual machine. Click Move to start the job.

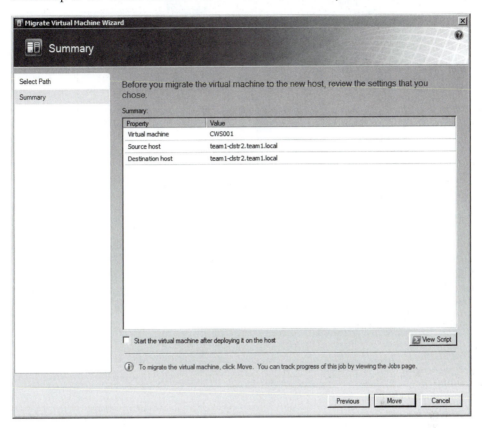

Figure 9-18 Migration summary

Source: Microsoft Virtual Machine Manager 2008 R2 SP1, Windows Server 2008 R2 SP1

Because the destination path is a cluster shared volume, QSM marks the virtual machines with a High Availability label. For virtual machines with storage on the cluster shared volume, high availability should be enabled. When virtual machines are configured with high availability, they can participate in a live migration.

If the virtual machine is stopped, QSM works faster because the virtual hard disk is moved directly to the host computer; the snapshot and merge are not required.

Live Migration

Live migration moves running virtual machines from one host computer to another. You use live migration to balance loads between host computers or to move a virtual machine off a host computer when you perform maintenance on the host. Figure 9-19 shows a live migration in which the cluster copies the memory being used by the virtual machine from the current host computer to another host. Next, the cluster copies the virtual machine's files to the other host computer. When the transition to the other host computer occurs, the memory and state information is already in place for the virtual machine. The transition is usually fast enough that a client using the virtual machine does not lose the network connection.

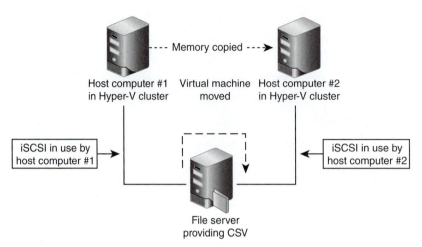

Figure 9-19 Live migration of a virtual machine

© Cengage Learning 2014

Live migrations are performed from the Failover Cluster Manager. To open it, click Start, point to Administrative Tools, and click Failover Cluster Manager. To start the live migration process, click *Team1*-Cluster.*Team1*.Local in the left pane, substituting your team name for *Team1*. Expand Services and applications. Figure 9-20 shows the virtual machines that have high availability. To select a virtual machine for migration, click its

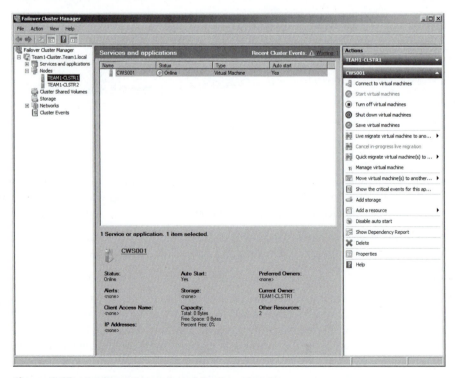

Figure 9-20 Virtual machine selected for live migration

Source: Microsoft Failover Cluster Manager, Windows Server 2008 R2 SP1

name in the left pane. In the example, the current owner of CWS001 is TEAM1-CLSTR1. Click Live migrate virtual machine to another (see Figure 9-21), and click the Live migrate to node (where the other host computer is displayed). Live migration with cluster shared volumes is almost instantaneous because no transfer of disk ownership is needed. The cluster copies the memory being used by the virtual machine from the current host computer to another host.

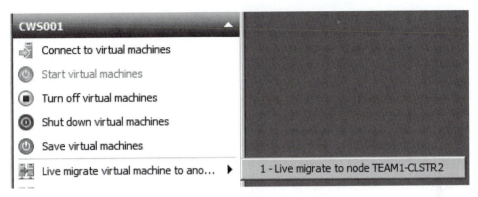

Figure 9-21 Destination host machine selected for live migration

Source: Microsoft Failover Cluster Manager, Windows Server 2008 R2 SP1

The live migration occurs so quickly that users will not be aware that the running virtual machine was moved. Figure 9-22 shows the migration in progress after the destination was clicked; in this example, 16% of the virtual machine has been migrated.

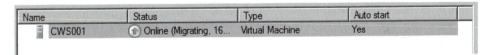

Figure 9-22 Live migration of virtual machine in progress

Source: Microsoft Failover Cluster Manager, Windows Server 2008 R2 SP1

Certain conditions apply when you perform a live migration. For example, a host computer in a cluster can participate as the source or destination computer in only one live migration at a time. However, if a migration fails, the virtual machine continues to operate on the source host computer with no disruption.

Activity 9-3: Moving Virtual Machines to the Cluster Shared Volume

Time Required: 20 minutes

Objective: Move a virtual machine to another host computer.

Description: In this activity, your team migrates stopped virtual machines to the cluster shared volume for storage. Pay attention to the steps to make future activities easier.

Table 9-4 provides the team member assignments for this activity.

Team Member	Steps	Host Computer
2	1-11	MGMT
3	12, 4-10	
1	13, 4-10	
2	14-20	
3	21, 14-19	
1	22, 14-19	
	23-26	
	27, 25-26	
	28, 25-26	

Table 9-4   Team member assignments for Activity 9-3

© Cengage Learning 2014

1. If necessary, switch the KVM switch to port 1.

2. If necessary, log on to your MGMT server with a username of *Team1\Administrator*, substituting your team name for *Team1*. Enter a password of **P@ssw0rd**.

3. If necessary, open Virtual Machine Manager. Click **Start**, and then click **SCVMM Admin Console**.

4. Click the **Virtual Machines** bar in the lower-left corner of the console window.

5. If CWS001 is not running, continue with Step 9.

6. Click **Connect to virtual machine** in the Actions pane.

7. If necessary, log on by clicking **Ctrl-Alt-Del**. Enter a password of **P@ssw0rd**.

8. To shut down the virtual machine, click **Start**, click the arrow next to Log off, click **Shut down**, click the **Option** arrow, click **Operating System: Reconfiguration (Planned)**, and then click **OK**.

9. Confirm that CWS001 is selected and stopped, and then click **Install virtual guest services**.

10. Wait for the job to be completed, and then close the Jobs window if necessary.

11. Repeat Steps 4 through 10 for CSW002.

12. Repeat Steps 4 through 10 for CWS003 and CWS004.

13. Repeat Steps 4 through 10 for CWS005 and CWS006.

14. Click **CWS001**.

15. To open the storage migration wizard, scroll and then click **Migrate storage** in the right pane.

16. To specify the new location for the virtual machine, click **Browse** next to the Virtual machine path arrow, expand **ClusterStorage**, click **Volume1**, and click **OK**.

17. Click the virtual hard disk you want to move, and click **Next**.

18. Review the Summary window, and then click **Previous** if necessary to return to a previous window and change a setting. When you are satisfied with the settings, click **Move**.

19. Verify that the job was completed successfully, and then close the Jobs window.

20. Repeat Steps 14 through 19 for CWS002.

21. Repeat Steps 14 through 19 for CWS003 and CWS004.

22. Repeat Steps 14 through 19 for CWS005 and CWS006.

23. If necessary, open the Failover Cluster Manager. Click **Start**, point to **Administrative Tools**, and click **Failover Cluster Manager**.

24. Expand **Services and applications** in the left pane.

25. Click **Configure a Service or Application** in the right pane, click **Next**, scroll and then click **Virtual Machine**, click **Next**, click **CWS001** and **CWS002**, and then click **Next** twice.

26. Click **View Report**. Examine the report, close the Internet Explorer window, and click **Finish**.

27. Repeat Steps 25 and 26 for CWS003 and CWS004.

28. Repeat Steps 25 and 26 for CWS005 and CWS006.

29. Remain logged on for future lab activities.

Activity 9-4: Using Live Migration

Time Required: 20 minutes

Objective: Migrate a running virtual machine to another host computer.

Description: In this activity, your team performs a live migration of running virtual machines to the other host computer in the cluster. Pay attention to the steps to make future activities easier.

Table 9-5 provides the team member assignments for this activity.

Team Member	Steps	Host Computer
1	1-6	MGMT
2	7, 5-6	
3	8, 5-6	
1	9, 5-6	
2	10-11	
3	12, 10-11	
1	13, 10-11	
2	14, 10-11	
3	15-16, 10-11	

Table 9-5 Team member assignments for Activity 9-4

© Cengage Learning 2014

1. If necessary, switch the KVM switch to port 1.

2. If necessary, log on to your MGMT server with a username of *Team1*\Administrator, substituting your team name for *Team1*. Enter a password of **P@ssw0rd**.

3. If necessary, open the Failover Cluster Manager. Click **Start,** point to **Administrative Tools,** and click **Failover Cluster Manager.**

4. If necessary, click ***Team1*-Cluster.*Team1*.local** in the left pane, substituting your team name for *Team1.* Expand **Services and applications.**

5. Click **CWS001** in the left pane, and then click **Start virtual machines** in the Actions pane.

6. Wait for the virtual machine to start.

7. Repeat Steps 5 and 6 for CWS002.

8. Repeat Steps 5 and 6 for CWS003 and CWS004.

9. Repeat Steps 5 and 6 for CWS005 and CWS006.

10. Click **CWS001** in the left pane, click **Live migrate virtual machine to another,** and click the **Live migrate to** node (where the other host computer is displayed).

11. Wait for the migration to be completed.

12. Repeat Steps 10 and 11 for CWS002.

13. Repeat Steps 10 and 11 for CWS003.

14. Repeat Steps 10 and 11for CWS004.

15. Repeat Steps 10 and 11for CWS005.

16. Repeat Steps 10 and 11for CWS006.

17. Remain logged on for future lab activities.

Backing up and Recovering the VMM Environment

Protecting the Hyper-V virtualization environment includes backing up the VMM database, the library server, and the VMM server. Backup and recovery are familiar tasks for server administrators.

Backing up the SQL Database

Because the main location for VMM information is the SQL database, you should include this database in your backup plans. From the VMM administrator console, you start the backup by selecting the Administration view and then the General node. In the right pane, click Back up Virtual Machine Manager. Enter the path to the folder to store the SQL server backup, as shown in Figure 9-23. Click OK to start the backup. The backup occurs rapidly with no progress displays.

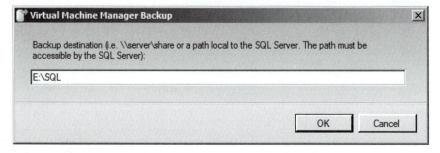

Figure 9-23 Backup destination with backup path entered

Source: Microsoft Virtual Machine Manager 2008 R2 SP1, Windows Server 2008 R2 SP1

Backing up the Library Server

The VMM library server is a file server that hosts the MSSCVMMLibrary share. To back up the library server, you use the Windows Server Backup feature in Windows Server 2008. You will install this feature in Activity 9-7. Figure 9-24 shows the initial Server Backup window.

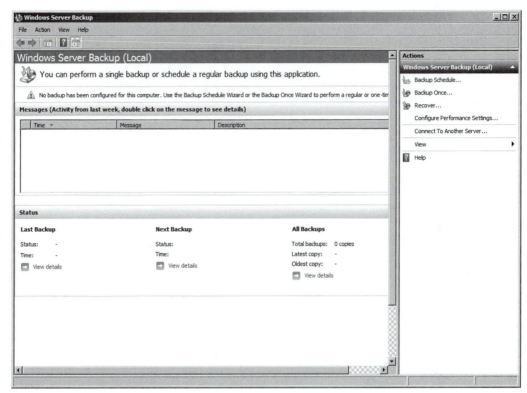

Figure 9-24 Windows Server Backup window

Source: Microsoft Windows Server Backup, Windows Server 2008 R2 SP1

To schedule a backup with the Backup Schedule Wizard, click Backup Schedule in the right pane and click Next to advance to the Select Backup Configuration window. Because you are backing up only the contents of the MSSCVMMLibrary, click Custom as shown in Figure 9-25, and then click Next.

To add items to the backup, click Add Items, expand Local Disk (C:), expand Program Data, and click the Virtual Machine Manager Library Files check box, as shown in Figure 9-26. Click OK to return to the Select Items for Backup window. Figure 9-27 shows the completed selection. Click Next to advance to the next window and specify the backup time.

You can schedule the backup to occur at a fixed time each day (see Figure 9-28) or more than once a day. You might select multiple backups during the day if you are creating the library building blocks. For example, you could select backups every four hours during the work day: 7:00 AM, 11:00 AM, 3:00 PM, and 7:00 PM. To schedule these backups, scroll and click 7:00 AM, click Add, click 11:00 AM, click Add, and so on. If you need to make a

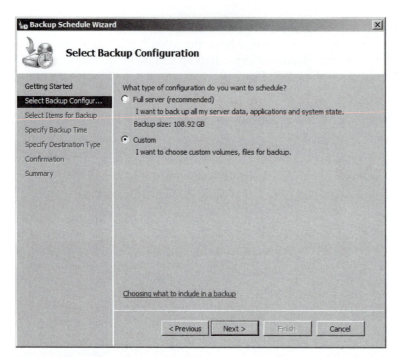

Figure 9-25 Select Backup Configuration window with Custom backup selected

Source: Microsoft Windows Server Backup, Windows Server 2008 R2 SP1

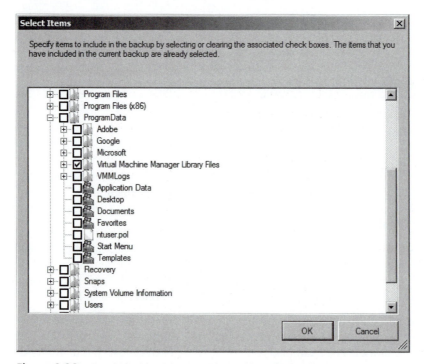

Figure 9-26 Virtual Machine Manager library files selected for backup

Source: Microsoft Windows Server Backup, Windows Server 2008 R2 SP1

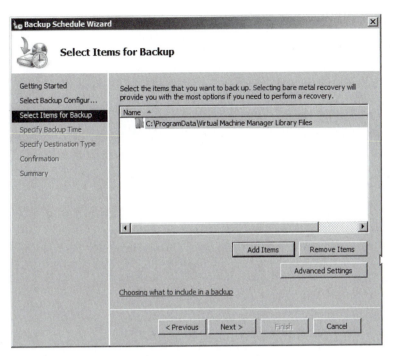

Figure 9-27 Completed selection for MSSCVMMLibrary

Source: Microsoft Windows Server Backup, Windows Server 2008 R2 SP1

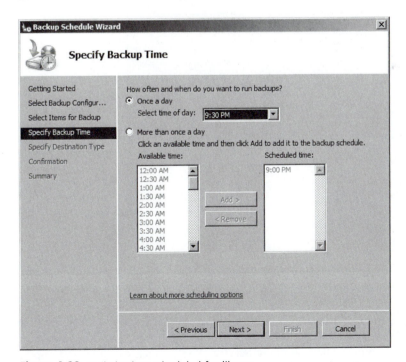

Figure 9-28 Daily backup scheduled for library

Source: Microsoft Windows Server Backup, Windows Server 2008 R2 SP1

correction, click the erroneous time in the Scheduled time list and click Remove. Click Next to advance to the next window and select the destination volume.

Figure 9-29 shows the three destination types you can select:

- *Back up to a hard disk that is dedicated for backups (recommended)*—For this option, you install a hard disk to use only for backups. For example, if you have a 250-GB drive for the operating system, a 1-TB hard drive would be a good choice for the backup drive. This backup drive is dedicated to the Windows Server Backup feature.
- *Back up to a volume*—This is a good choice when you need to place backups generated by more than one backup system (for example, the SQL database backup and Windows Server Backup). This option also is a good choice for backups to a SAN.
- *Back up to a shared network folder*—Use this option to make single-copy backups in which the current backup overlays the previous backup.

If you are backing up to a volume, you can choose from two volume types: a local drive or a local DVD burner. If you have free space on another server, you can choose to back up to a shared folder (see Figure 9-29). You will back up to an iSCSI SAN in Activity 9-7. The Windows Server Backup feature will not permit backups to magnetic tape.

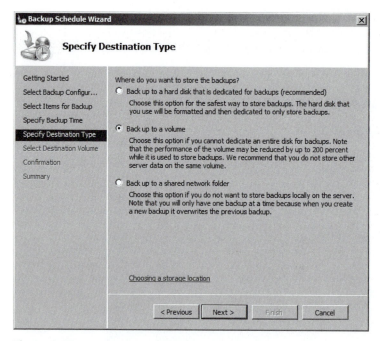

Figure 9-29 Specifying a destination type for backups

Source: Microsoft Windows Server Backup, Windows Server 2008 R2 SP1

Click Next to advance to the next window and select the destination volume. Figure 9-30 shows the volume selected for the backup files. The Windows Server Backup feature backs up files using the **Volume Shadow Copy Service** (VSS), which captures and copies files for backup on running systems. A shadow copy is a snapshot of a file that duplicates the file data at an instant in time.

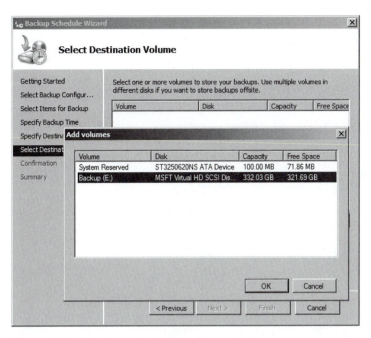

Figure 9-30 Selecting a destination volume for backups

Source: Microsoft Windows Server Backup, Windows Server 2008 R2 SP1

Figure 9-31 shows the Summary window for the backup. Click Previous if necessary to return to a previous window and change a setting. When you are satisfied with the settings, click Close.

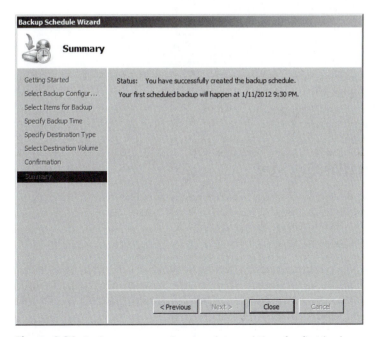

Figure 9-31 Backup summary showing date and time for first backup

Source: Microsoft Windows Server Backup, Windows Server 2008 R2 SP1

Scheduled backups will continue until you choose to stop them. To remove a backup from the schedule, click Backup Schedule in the right pane of Windows Server Backup, and then click Stop backup, as shown in Figure 9-32. Click Next and then click Close.

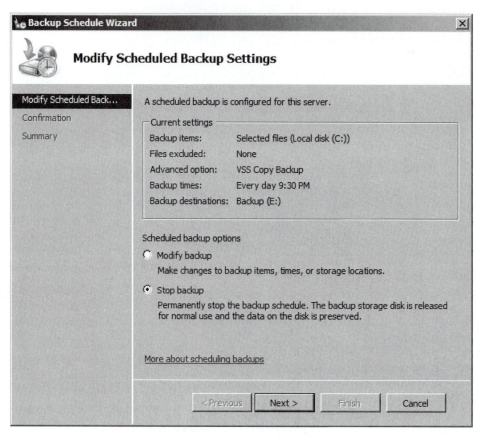

Figure 9-32 Deleting a scheduled backup

Source: Microsoft Windows Server Backup, Windows Server 2008 R2 SP1

Backing up the VMM Server

Creating a full backup of the VMM server is the best way to prepare it for a possible catastrophic failure. Again, you use the Windows Server Backup feature in Windows Server 2008. With a full system backup, you can recover individual files, folders, or entire volumes. The only drawback is the time and size of the backup, which can be considerable.

To back up the VMM server, start Windows Server Backup, as you did for the library backup described in the preceding section. Figure 9-33 shows the Full server option selected. You then schedule the time for the backup, as shown earlier in Figure 9-28. You should schedule the backup during a period of low activity, such as 3:00 AM.

Click Next to specify a backup destination. If you chose the full server backup, the destination options are different from backing up particular files and folders (see Figure 9-34).

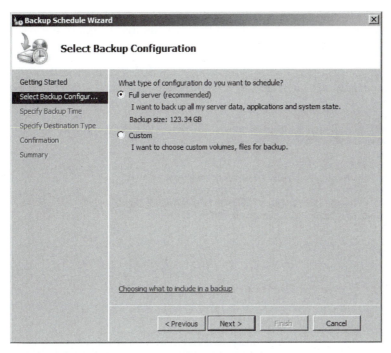

Figure 9-33 Full server option selected for backups

Source: Microsoft Windows Server Backup, Windows Server 2008 R2 SP1

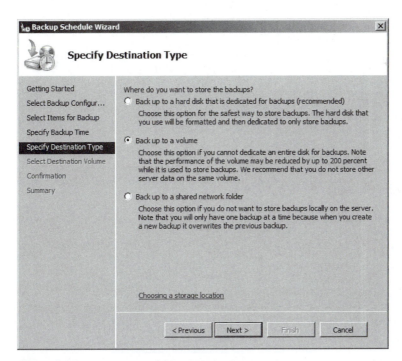

Figure 9-34 Three options for backup destination

Source: Microsoft Windows Server Backup, Windows Server 2008 R2 SP1

Because the hardware configuration has free space only on a volume, click the Back up to a volume option. Click Next to select the destination volume (see Figure 9-30). Click Backup (E:) and then click OK.

A caution message appears (see Figure 9-35) because a full server backup captures all of the volumes on the VMM server, including the destination volume. Click OK to exclude the Backup (E:) volume.

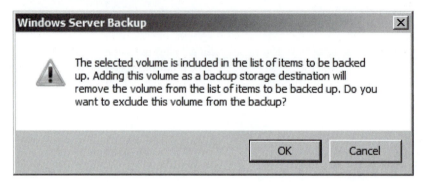

Figure 9-35 Destination volume included in list of items to be backed up

Source: Microsoft Windows Server Backup, Windows Server 2008 R2 SP1

Click Next to advance to the Confirmation window, as shown in Figure 9-36. Review the Confirmation window, and then click Previous if necessary to return to a previous window and change a setting. When you are satisfied with the settings, click Finish.

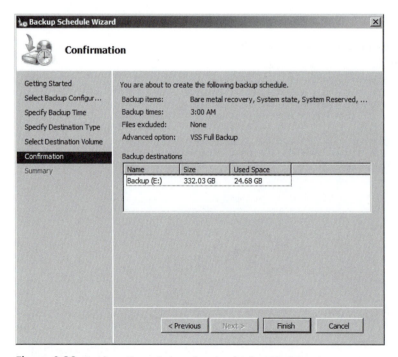

Figure 9-36 Confirmation window showing backup choices

Source: Microsoft Windows Server Backup, Windows Server 2008 R2 SP1

Notice in the figure that Windows Server Backup provides the option to create a backup that can be used to restore the operating system and applications to a **bare metal server**—a server that either has no operating system or requires that you replace the operating system and all applications. To select the bare metal recovery option, start Windows Server Backup, advance to the Select Backup Configuration window, as shown in Figure 9-25, and then click Custom. In the Select Items window, click the Bare metal recovery check box. In the Specify Destination Type window, select the local hard drive where you want to place the image, and then proceed with the Backup once scenario.

Use the Windows Server installation DVD to place the operating system and applications on the bare metal server. Start as if you were installing Windows Server 2008. When the Install Now window appears, select the Repair your server link and select the image that you previously created. Due to hardware limitations, a full description of the creation and restoration of a bare metal image is beyond the scope of this textbook.

Activity 9-5: Configuring iSCSI Storage Access

Time Required: 20 minutes

Objective: Configure the virtual disks, targets, and clients for the backup disk.

Description: In this activity, your team configures iSCSI storage access. You begin by creating the Backup virtual hard disk. Next, you create the target and assign the client. The last task is to link the target and virtual hard disk. Pay attention to the steps to make future activities easier.

Table 9-6 provides the team member assignments for this activity.

Team Member	Steps	Host Computer
3	1-9	MGMT
1	10-17	
2	18-24	
3	25-28	
1	29-30	

Table 9-6 Team member assignments for Activity 9-5

© Cengage Learning 2014

1. If necessary, switch the KVM switch to port 1.

2. If necessary, log on to your MGMT server with a username of *Team1\Administrator*, substituting your team name for *Team1*. Enter a password of **P@ssw0rd**.

3. If necessary, open Virtual Machine Manager. Click **Start**, and then click **SCVMM Admin Console**.

4. If necessary, start and connect to the virtual machine. Click **iSCSITarget**, click **Start**, and then click **Connect to virtual machine**.

5. If necessary, log on by clicking **Ctrl-Alt-Del**. Enter a password of **P@ssw0rd**.

6. To open the Microsoft iSCSI Software Target, click **Start**, point to **Administrative Tools**, and click **Microsoft iSCSI Software Target**.

7. To start the Create Virtual Disk Wizard, right-click **Devices**, and click **Create Virtual Disk**.

8. In the Welcome window, click **Next**.

9. To name the .vhd file, enter **E:\Backup.vhd** in the File text box, and click **Next**.

In Activity 8-4, you were asked to leave approximately 20% of the drive for expansion and additional LUNs. If sufficient space is not available for the Backup.vhd file, contact your instructor.

10. To specify the size of the virtual disk, view the amount shown in the Currently available free space field, calculate the number in megabytes, enter the number in the Size of virtual disk (MB) text box, and click **Next**.

11. Enter **Backup Disk for VMM** in the Virtual disk description text box, and click **Next**.

12. Click **Next** to permit the target to be specified later, and then click **Finish**.

13. To start the Create iSCSI Target Wizard, right-click **iSCSI Targets**, and click **Create iSCSI Target**.

14. In the Welcome window, click **Next**.

15. To identify the iSCSI target, enter **Backup** in the iSCSI target name text box, enter **Backup Disk for VMM** in the Description text box, and click **Next**.

16. To add a target, click **Advanced**, click **Add**, click the **Identifier type** arrow, click **IP Address**, enter **192.168.10.100** in the Value text box, and click **OK** twice.

17. Click **Next** and then click **Finish**.

18. To link the Backup virtual disk to the target, click **Devices**, right-click **Virtual Disk 2**, click **Assign/Remove Target**, click **Add**, click **Backup**, and then click **OK** twice.

19. Minimize the Virtual Machine Viewer window.

20. To start the iSCSI initiator, return to the MGMT host computer, click **Start**, point to **Administrative Tools**, click **iSCSI Initiator**, and click **Yes**.

21. To connect to the iSCSITarget server, enter **192.168.10.103** for the target, and click **Quick Connect**.

22. Wait for the connection to be completed, and click **Done**.

If you do not see the discovered targets, contact your instructor.

23. To bring the first IQN into the discovered targets, click the first IQN, click **Connect**, and then click **OK**.

24. To link the discovered target to the virtual hard disk, click the **Volumes and Devices** tab, click **Auto Configure**, and click **OK**.

 Do not complete the following steps on Disk 0 or Disk 1.

25. To open the Disk Management tool, click **Start**, point to **Administrative Tools**, click **Computer Management**, and then click **Disk Management**.

26. To bring Disk 2 online, right-click the **Disk 2** icon, and then click **Online**.

27. To initialize the disk, right-click the **Disk 2** icon, click **Initialize Disk**, and then click **OK**.

28. To create a volume and format it, right-click the unallocated area, click **New Simple Volume**, click **Next** three times, enter **Backup** over "New Volume," click **Next**, and click **Finish**.

 The quick format feature enables you to format a disk in less than a minute.

29. To create a folder for the SQL backup, right-click in the allocated area, click **Explore**, click **New folder**, enter **SQL** over "New Folder," and press **Enter**.

30. Close the Windows Explorer and Disk Management windows.

31. Remain logged on for future lab activities.

Activity 9-6: Backing up the VMM SQL Database

Time Required: 5 minutes

Objective: Back up the VMM SQL database.

Description: In this activity, your team backs up the VMM SQL database. Pay attention to the steps to make future activities easier.

Table 9-7 provides the team member assignments for this activity.

Team Member	Steps	Host Computer
3	1-5	MGMT
1	6-8	

Table 9-7 Team member assignments for Activity 9-6

© Cengage Learning 2014

1. If necessary, switch the KVM switch to port 1.

2. If necessary, log on to your MGMT server with a username of *Team1\Administrator*, substituting your team name for *Team1*. Enter a password of **P@ssw0rd**.

3. If necessary, open Virtual Machine Manager. Click **Start**, and then click **SCVMM Admin Console**.

4. Click the **Administration** bar in the lower-left corner of the console window, and then click **General** in the left pane.

5. Click **Back up Virtual Machine Manager** in the right pane. Enter **E:\SQL** in the Backup destination text box, and click **OK**.

6. To verify that the backup was completed, click **Start**, click **MGMT**, double-click **Backup (E:)**, and double-click **SQL**.

7. Verify that a file was created today, and then close the SQL window.

8. Remain logged on for future lab activities.

Activity 9-7: Backing up the Library Server

Time Required: 15 minutes

Objective: Back up the library server.

Description: In this activity, your team practices backing up files on the library server. To save class time, you will back up only a portion of the available files. Normally, you would back up the entire VMM library. Pay attention to the steps to make future activities easier.

Table 9-8 provides the team member assignments for this activity.

Team Member	Steps	Host Computer
1	1-9	MGMT
2	10-16	

Table 9-8   Team member assignments for Activity 9-7

© Cengage Learning 2014

1. If necessary, switch the KVM switch to port 1.

2. If necessary, log on to your MGMT server with a username of *Team1***Administrator**, substituting your team name for *Team1*. Enter a password of **P@ssw0rd**.

3. Maximize the Server Manager by clicking the **Server Manager** icon on the taskbar. The icon displays a grey server and toolbox.

4. To add Windows Server Backup, scroll down and click **Add Features** in the right pane, scroll and then click the **Windows Server Backup Features** check box, click **Next**, and click **Install**.

5. Wait for the installation to be completed, and then click **Close**.

6. Click **Start**, point to **Administrative Tools**, and click **Windows Server Backup**.

7. Wait for Windows Server Backup to locate the backup database and display the status.

8. To start an unscheduled backup, click **Backup Once** in the right pane, click **Next**, click **Custom**, and click **Next**.

9. To add items to the backup, click **Add Items**, expand **Local Disk (C:)**, and then expand **ProgramData**. Expand **Virtual Machine Manager Library Files**, click the **BaseCWS** check box, and click the **ISOFiles** check box. Click **OK**, and then click **Next**.

10. Verify that Local drives is selected, and then click **Next**.

11. If necessary, click the **Backup destination** arrow, click **Backup (E:)**, and then click **Next**.

12. To start the backup, click **Backup**.

13. Wait for the shadow copy to be created.

14. Wait for the data to be transferred.

15. Verify that the Status column reports a successfully completed backup, and then click **Close**.

16. Remain logged on for future lab activities.

Activity 9-8: Recovering Files on the Library Server

Time Required: 15 minutes

Objective: Recover a file from the library backup.

Description: In this activity, your team practices recovering files from a previous backup to the library server. To save class time, you will recover only a single file. Normally, you might recover the entire VMM library. Pay attention to the steps to make future activities easier.

Table 9-9 provides the team member assignments for this activity.

Team Member	Steps	Host Computer
1	1-8	MGMT
2	9-13	
3	14-15	

Table 9-9 Team member assignments for Activity 9-8

© Cengage Learning 2014

1. If necessary, switch the KVM switch to port 1.

2. If necessary, log on to your MGMT server with a username of *Team1\Administrator*, substituting your team name for *Team1*. Enter a password of **P@ssw0rd**.

3. Click **Start**, point to **Administrative Tools**, and click **Windows Server Backup**.

4. Wait for Windows Server Backup to locate the backup database and display the status.

5. To start a recovery, click **Recover** in the right pane, and then click **Next**.

6. To select the date for the backup, click the last blue highlighted date, and then click **Next**.

7. Retain the Files and Folders option, and click **Next**.

8. Wait for the backup catalog to be read and then expand *TEAM1*-MGMT, substituting your team name for *TEAM1*.

9. Expand **Local Disk (C:)**, expand **ProgramData**, expand **Virtual Machine Manager Library Files**, expand **BaseCWS**, click **en-windows_server_2008_R2_SP1**, and then click **Next**.

10. Review the recovery destination options, and then review the recovery options under "When the wizard finds items in the backup that are already in the recovery destination."

11. To replace the file, click **Overwrite the existing versions with the recovered versions,** and click **Next.**

12. To start the recovery, click **Recover.**

13. Wait for the data to be transferred.

14. Verify that the Status column reports a successfully completed recovery, and then click **Close.** Close the Windows Server Backup window.

15. Remain logged on for future lab activities.

Troubleshooting High-Availability Clusters

A high-availability cluster has numerous components that are designed to make your private cloud more efficient and productive. It is critical to know how to troubleshoot this environment and maximize uptime. This section covers what you need to understand about troubleshooting, and it introduces common tools used to provide data about the virtualization environment.

Six-Step Troubleshooting Plan

You sometimes troubleshoot problems as you go about your daily activities. For example, it might be time to watch your favorite Tuesday night television show. You pick up the remote control and press the power button, but your flat-screen TV does not display an image. The troubleshooting process begins as soon as you ask yourself, "*What happened?*"

You need a systematic process that solves the problem. If you don't have a process that you prefer, you can use the following six steps:

1. *Define the problem*—Write a one-sentence definition of the problem. For example, "The flat screen does not display an image."

2. *Gather information to solve the problem*—What information is available through observation or testing? For example, is the flat screen plugged in?

3. *Research the solution*—Depending on your experience with resolving problems, you have a number of choices. You could use the troubleshooting guide that came with your TV, or you could perform a Web search to try to solve the problem.

4. *Develop an action plan*—Formulate a set of steps to resolve the problem. For example, is the indicator on the surge protector green? Is the TV plugged in? Can it be turned on manually? Is the infrared receiver blocked? Is it time to replace the battery in the remote?

5. *Execute the action plan*—Carry out each step in the plan. Work your way through the list until the problem is resolved.

6. *Test to see if the problem is resolved*—Continue with the action plan until the problem is resolved. When an image is displayed on your TV, the problem has been corrected.

The six-step plan provides a systematic solution to resolve problems in high-availability clusters.

Monitoring with Event Viewer

Event Viewer is the primary tool in Windows Server 2008 for monitoring your virtualization environment. You can use Event Viewer to gather information when you realize that you have a problem, but it is better to monitor your host computers and virtual machines in Event Viewer before problems occur.

To open the program, click Start, point to Administrative Tools, and click Event Viewer. You also can open the program by clicking the Diagnostics node in the left pane of Server Manager.

Figure 9-37 shows an event that occurred in Hyper-V when the MGMT server was shut down. Numerous logs are maintained by Windows Server 2008; expand the nodes in the left pane to locate the desired log. To see the details for an event, double-click the event in the center pane. You will use Event Viewer in Activity 9-9.

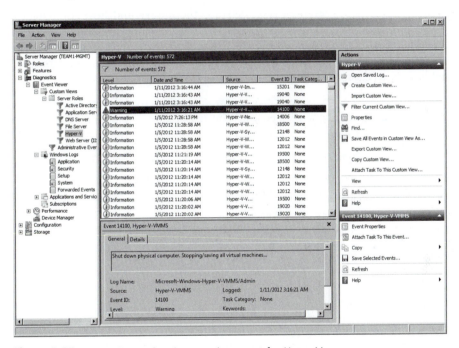

Figure 9-37 Event Viewer showing warning event for Hyper-V

Source: Microsoft Event Viewer, Windows Server 2008 R2 SP1

In your previous classes, you used the following Windows logs:

- *Applications*—Logs events from applications
- *Security*—Displays audited security events
- *Setup*—Includes events related to operating system installation and the installation and removal of roles or features
- *System*—Records events related to the operating system

Another useful node is Custom Views. The Server Roles node under Custom Views lists events for a selected server role. Figure 9-37 shows events for the Hyper-V role. The Administrative Events node shows all critical, error, and warning events, but excludes Informational events.

Monitoring Performance

In Chapter 3, you used Performance Monitor to examine the operation of the host computer and the running virtual machines. In Chapter 8, you installed the iSCSI Software Target, which provides additional counters to monitor performance. You will use these counters in Activity 9-10.

Troubleshooting VMM Installation Issues

To help identify common problems with VMM, use the Virtual Machine Manager Configuration Analyzer (VMMCA). The VMMCA analyzes the VMM server, Windows-based hosts, and hypervisor-based hosts. You ran the VMMCA in Chapter 4 prior to installing VMM. Refer to Chapter 4 for instructions on running the VMMCA.

Analyzing Network Problems with Network Monitor

If the quality of the network connection between the library and host computers is insufficient, a virtual machine might take too long to deploy. Also, network quality affects the live migration of virtual machines. If you suspect that network quality is a problem, Microsoft Network Monitor 3 becomes an important tool. Network Monitor is a **protocol analyzer** that enables you to capture, view, and analyze network data.

When analyzing traffic with Network Monitor, you need to monitor both the source and destination ends of the network connection. You might get acceptable results when analyzing only the source or destination, but you get a clearer picture by analyzing both.

By design, Network Monitor can only see frames received by or sent from the host computer.

Figure 9-38 shows the initial window for Network Monitor 3.4. To select the Storage network to analyze, scroll and clear all of the networks shown in Figure 9-39 except for Storage.

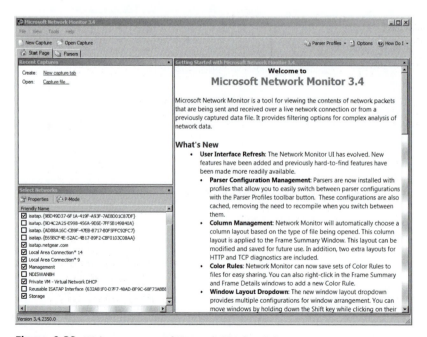

Figure 9-38 Welcome screen of Network Monitor 3.4

Source: Microsoft Network Monitor 3.4, Windows Server 2008 R2 SP1

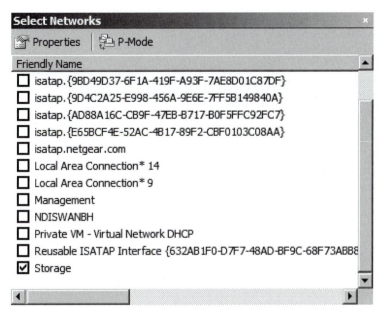

Figure 9-39 Storage network selected for monitoring

Source: Microsoft Network Monitor 3.4, Windows Server 2008 R2 SP1

To start a capture of network data, click New Capture and then click Start. To stop a capture, click Stop. Figure 9-40 shows handshake traffic between CLSTR1 and CLSTR2. More than 200 packets were captured during a 24-second trace.

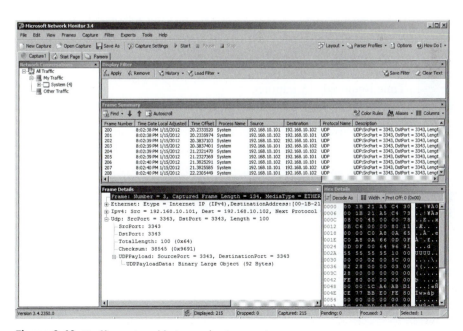

Figure 9-40 Traffic captured between host computers

Source: Microsoft Network Monitor 3.4, Windows Server 2008 R2 SP1

To see a frame's details, double-click it in the Frame Summary pane. To see the details of a UDP packet, expand the appropriate items, as shown in Figure 9-41. The figure shows healthy traffic between the two clustered host computers.

```
Frame Details                                                                    x
  Frame: Number = 3, Captured Frame Length = 134, MediaType = ETHER
  Ethernet: Etype = Internet IP (IPv4),DestinationAddress:[00-1B-21
  Ipv4: Src = 192.168.10.101, Dest = 192.168.10.102, Next Protocol
  Udp: SrcPort = 3343, DstPort = 3343, Length = 100
      SrcPort: 3343
      DstPort: 3343
      TotalLength: 100 (0x64)
      Checksum: 38545 (0x9691)
      UDPPayload: SourcePort = 3343, DestinationPort = 3343
          UDPPayloadData: Binary Large Object (92 Bytes)
```

Figure 9-41 Frame Details pane with UDP packet displayed

Source: Microsoft Network Monitor 3.4, Windows Server 2008 R2 SP1

Using Cluster Validation Tests for Troubleshooting

You can use the Validate a Configuration Wizard to troubleshoot a failover cluster and choose tests based on the problems you see. Before running the wizard, you must shut down any running virtual machines and take the cluster shared volumes offline.

You will use the Validate a Configuration Wizard to test your failover cluster in Activity 9-12.

Activity 9-9: Monitoring with Event Viewer

Time Required: 15 minutes

Objective: Monitor system health with Event Viewer.

Description: In this activity, your team uses Event Viewer to examine the health of the host computers in your private cloud. Pay attention to the steps to make future activities easier.

Table 9-10 provides the team member assignments for this activity.

Team Member	Steps	Host Computer
1	1-11	MGMT
2	12, 5-11	
3	13, 5-11	
1	14-17	
2	18-22	

Table 9-10 Team member assignments for Activity 9-9

1. If necessary, switch the KVM switch to port 1.

2. If necessary, log on to your MGMT server with a username of *Team1***Administrator**, substituting your team name for *Team1*. Enter a password of **P@ssw0rd**.

3. Maximize the Server Manager.

4. To open Event Viewer, click **Diagnostics** in the left pane, and double-click **Event Viewer**.

5. To locate the Systems log, expand **Event Viewer** in the left pane, expand **Windows Logs**, and click **System**.

6. Scroll and click a message of your choice.

7. To see the details of the message, double-click it, and then click the **Details** tab. Expand the **System** node in the event properties.

8. Review the details and click **Close**.

9. To filter events, click **Filter Current Log** in the Actions pane, click the **Warning** and **Error** check boxes, and click **OK**.

10. Scroll and then click a message that contains an Error level. To see the details, double-click the message and click the **Details** tab.

11. Review the details and click **Close**.

12. Repeat Steps 5 through 11 using an item in the Application log.

13. Repeat Steps 5 through 11 using an item in the Security log.

14. To see event messages for Hyper-V, expand **Custom Views** in the left pane, expand **Server Roles**, and click **Hyper-V**.

15. Scroll and click a message of your choice.

16. To see the details of the message, double-click it, and then click the **Details** tab.

17. Review the details and click **Close**.

18. To see event messages for VM Manager, expand **Applications and Services Logs** in the left pane, and click **VM Manager**.

19. Scroll and click a message of your choice.

20. To see the details of the message, double-click it, and then click the **Details** tab.

21. Review the details and click **Close**.

22. Remain logged on for future lab activities.

Activity 9-10: Monitoring Performance

Time Required: 15 minutes

Objective: Monitor system performance of the ISCSITarget virtual machine.

Description: In this activity, your team practices using Performance Monitor to examine the performance of iSCSI storage in your private cloud. Pay attention to the steps to make future activities easier.

Table 9-11 provides the team member assignments for this activity.

Team Member	Steps	Host Computer
1	1-6	MGMT
2	7-9	
3	10-14	
1	15-17	
2	18-19	

Table 9-11 Team member assignments for Activity 9-10

© Cengage Learning 2014

1. If necessary, switch the KVM switch to port 1.

2. If necessary, log on to your MGMT server with a username of *Team1\Administrator*, substituting your team name for *Team1*. Enter a password of **P@ssw0rd**.

3. If necessary, open Virtual Machine Manager. Click **Start**, and then click **SCVMM Admin Console**.

4. To connect to the iSCSITarget virtual machine, click **All Hosts**, click **iSCSITarget**, and click **Connect to virtual machine** in the Actions pane.

5. If necessary, log on by clicking **Ctrl-Alt-Del**. Enter a password of **P@ssw0rd**.

6. Maximize the Server Manager.

7. To open Performance Monitor, expand **Diagnostics** in the left pane, expand **Performance**, expand **Monitoring Tools**, and double-click **Performance Monitoring.**

8. To add a performance counter, click the **Add Counters** button, which looks like a green plus sign. Scroll and then expand **iSCSI Target**, click **# Pending Requests**, and click **Add.**

9. To add another counter, click **# Sessions**, and click **Add.**

10. To determine the virtual disk for the virtual machines, click the **ISCI Target** icon on the taskbar. The icon displays a blue computer screen with a connection indicator. Expand **iSCSITargets**, click **Virtual Machines**, and view the Virtual Disk Index.

11. Minimize the iSCSITarget window.

12. Scroll and expand **iSCSI Target Disks**, click **Avg. Disk Bytes/Transfer**, click the Index you viewed in Step 10, and click **Add.**

13. To add another counter, click **I/O Bytes/sec**, click the Index you viewed in Step 10, and click **Add.**

14. Review the counters and click **OK.**

15. To scale the # Pending Requests counter, right-click the **# Pending Requests** counter below the graph, observe the line color, and then click **Scale Selected Counters.**

16. To observe the scaled value, point to the line color you observed in Step 15.

17. Repeat Steps 15 and 16 for the remaining counters.

18. Observe the changes on the graph for five minutes.

To see the statistics for a counter, click the counter at the bottom of the graph.

19. Remain logged on to the virtual machine for future activities.

Activity 9-11: Monitoring Network Traffic

Time Required: 15 minutes

Objective: Monitor network traffic for the Storage network.

Description: In this activity, your team monitors network traffic on the Storage network. Pay attention to the steps to make future activities easier.

Table 9-12 provides the team member assignments for this activity.

Team Member	Steps	Host Computer
3	1-11	MGMT
1	12-18	CLSTR1
2	19-25	
3	26-35	MGMT

Table 9-12 Team member assignments for Activity 9-11

© Cengage Learning 2014

1. If necessary, switch the KVM switch to port 1.

2. If necessary, log on to your MGMT server with a username of *Team1\Administrator*, substituting your team name for *Team1*. Enter a password of **P@ssw0rd**.

3. To open Internet Explorer, click **Start** and then click **Internet Explorer**.

4. To locate the Microsoft Network Monitor download, enter **download network monitor 3** in the search box, and then press **Enter**.

5. Click the **Download Microsoft Network Monitor 3.4** link.

6. To download Network Monitor 3.4, click the **NM34_x64.exe DOWNLOAD** link, and click **Save** twice.

7. To install Network Monitor 3.4 on the MGMT server, click **Run** twice, click **Yes**, and then click **Next**. Click **I accept the terms in the License Agreement**, click **Next**, click **Typical**, and then click **Install**.

8. Wait for the setup to be completed, and then click **Finish**.

9. Wait for Windows to configure the network parsers, which will require longer than the indicated time.

10. To log off the MGMT server, click **Start**, and then click **Log off**.

11. Log on to your MGMT server with a username of *Team1***Administrator**, substituting your team name for *Team1*. Enter a password of **P@ssw0rd**.

12. Switch the KVM switch to port 2.

13. If necessary, log on to your CLSTR1 server with a username of *Team1***Administrator**, substituting your team name for *Team1*. Enter a password of **P@ssw0rd**.

14. Click **Start**, and then enter *Team1*-**mgmt**\ in the search box, substituting your team name for *Team1*. Press **Enter**, double-click **Users**, double-click **Administrator**, double-click **Downloads**, and then double-click **NM34_x64**.

15. To install Network Monitor 3.4 on the CLSTR1 server, click **Run**, click **Yes**, and click **Next**. Click **I accept the terms in the License Agreement**, click **Next** twice, click **Typical**, and then click **Install**.

16. Wait for the setup to be completed, and then click **Finish**.

17. Wait for Windows to configure the network parsers, which will require longer than the indicated time.

18. Close the Downloads window.

19. To start Network Monitor, double-click **Microsoft Network Monitor 3.4** on the desktop.

20. If this is the first time you have opened Microsoft Network Monitor 3.4, clear the **Periodically check for updates when Network Monitor starts** check box, and then click **No**.

21. To monitor only the Storage network, scroll and clear all of the check boxes but **Storage** in the Select Networks pane.

22. To start a capture of network data, click **New Capture** on the menu bar, and then click **Start**.

23. Wait for 30 seconds, and then click **Stop** on the menu bar.

24. To see the details for a frame, double-click one in the Frame Summary pane.

25. Close the Microsoft Network Monitor 3.4 window. Click **No** to discard the capture file.

26. Switch the KVM switch to port 1.

27. If necessary, log on to your MGMT server with a username of *Team1***Administrator**, substituting your team name for *Team1*. Enter a password of **P@ssw0rd**.

28. Repeat Steps 19 through 23 for the MGMT server.

29. To see the details of an iSCSI packet, scroll and double-click a packet with a protocol name of ISCSI.

30. To view additional packets, click **Start**.

31. To filter packets, right-click an iSCSI protocol in a frame, click **Add 'Protocol Name' to Display Filter**, and click **Apply**.

32. Wait for 30 seconds, and then click **Stop** on the menu bar.

33. To see the details for a frame, double-click one in the Frame Summary pane.

34. Close the Microsoft Network Monitor 3.4 window. Click **No** to discard the capture file.

35. Remain logged on for future lab activities.

Activity 9-12: Using Cluster Validation Tests

Time Required: 30 minutes

Objective: Use the Validate a Configuration Wizard to troubleshoot a failover cluster.

Description: In this activity, your team runs the Validate a Configuration Wizard to trouble-shoot the health of a cluster. You shut down all of the virtual machines except for iSCSITarget, and you take the cluster shared volume offline. Pay attention to the steps to make future activities easier.

Table 9-13 provides the team member assignments for this activity.

Team Member	Steps	Host Computer
1	1-6	MGMT
2	7-10	
3	11-16	
1	17-19	
2	20-22	CLSTR1
3	23, 20-22	CLSTR2
1	24, 20-22	MGMT

Table 9-13 Team member assignments for Activity 9-12

© Cengage Learning 2014

1. If necessary, switch the KVM switch to port 1.

2. If necessary, log on to your MGMT server with a username of *Team1*\Administrator, substituting your team name for *Team1*. Enter a password of **P@ssw0rd**.

3. If necessary, open the VMM console by double-clicking **SCVMM Admin Console** on the desktop.

4. Click the **Virtual Machines** bar in the lower-left corner of the console window, and then click **All hosts** in the left pane.

5. To shut down the CWS001 virtual machine, click **CWS001**, click **Shut down** in the right pane, and then click **Yes**.

6. Repeat Step 5 for any remaining running virtual machines except for the iSCSITarget.

If you stop the iSCSITarget virtual machine, all storage-related tests will fail.

7. To open the Failover Cluster Manager console, click **Start**, point to **Administrative Tools**, and click **Failover Cluster Manager.**

8. Expand *Team1*-Cluster.*Team1*.local, substituting your team name for *Team1*.

9. To take the cluster shared volume offline, click **Cluster Shared Volumes** in the left pane, click **Take this resource offline**, and click **Take this Cluster Shared Volume offline**.

10. Wait for the resource to be taken offline.

11. To open the Validate a Configuration Wizard, click **Failover Cluster Manager**, and click **Validate a Configuration** in the right pane.

12. To select the cluster to validate, click **Next**, click **Browse**, and click **Advanced**. Enter **team** in the Name text box, click **Find Now**, and click *TEAM1*-CLUSTER, substituting your team name for *TEAM1*. Click **OK** twice.

13. Verify that the CLSTR1 and CLSTR2 host computers were selected, and click **Next**.

14. To run all of the tests, click **Next** twice.

15. Wait for the validation to be completed, and then click **View Report**.

 Because the cluster shared volume is offline, you can safely ignore the messages related to its resource status.

16. Close Internet Explorer, and then click **Finish**.

17. To bring the cluster shared volume online, click **Cluster Shared Volumes** in the left pane, and click **Bring this resource online**.

18. Return to the Virtual Machine Manager window. Click the **Virtual Machines** bar in the lower-left corner of the console window, and then click **All hosts** in the left pane.

19. To shut down the iSCSITarget virtual machine, click **iSCSITarget**, click **Shut down** in the right pane, and then click **Yes**.

20. Switch the KVM switch to port 2.

21. To shut down the host computer, click **Start**, click the arrow next to **Log off**, click **Shut down**, click the **Option** arrow, click **Operating System: Reconfiguration (Planned)**, and then click **OK**. If necessary, click **Yes**.

22. Wait for the host computer to shut down.

23. Complete Steps 20 through 22 for CLSTR2, which is on KVM switch port 3.

24. Complete Steps 20 through 22 for MGMT, which is on KVM switch port 1.

Chapter Summary

- Maintaining availability of the private cloud requires the monitoring of high-availability clusters.

- To deploy virtual machines, you move their files between the various storage locations.

- To achieve load balancing, you migrate virtual machines between host computers.

- To protect the VMM environment, you must back up and restore data files that support the private cloud.

- When problems occur with high-availability clusters, you must troubleshoot the problems and correct them.

Key Terms

bare metal server   A server that either has no operating system or requires that you replace the operating system and all applications.

live migration   The process of moving a running virtual machine from one host computer to another without interrupting the user.

protocol analyzer   A network tool for identifying, analyzing, and diagnosing communications problems.

Quick Storage Migration (QSM)   A Microsoft tool that moves a virtual machine from one storage location to another while the virtual machine may be running.

System Center Operations Manager (SCOM)   A Microsoft product for comprehensive monitoring of a private cloud.

VMware VirtualCenter   A VMware product for comprehensive monitoring of a private cloud.

Volume Shadow Copy Service (VSS)   A Microsoft feature that allows volume backups to be performed while applications on a system continue to write to the volumes.

Review Questions

1. The _____ is used to monitor resources in a failover cluster.

2. The Services and applications node in the Failover Cluster Manager contains _____.

   a. virtual hard disks used by applications and services

   b. virtual machines that have met the requirements for high availability

   c. applications running on the host computers

   d. services running on the host computers

   e. virtual machines that have not met the requirements for high availability

3. Shared storage for virtual machines is configured on the iSCSI SAN as _____.

4. The _____ error indicates that read/write access to a volume is being redirected over the network to another host computer in the cluster.

5. When using the Networks view in the Failover Cluster Manager to set up networks in this textbook, which networks appear? (Choose all correct answers.)

   a. Management

   b. Server

   c. Heartbeat

   d. Storage

   e. Private Virtual

   f. Windows Management Interface

6. Which graphs appear in the Administration view of the VMM administrator console? (Choose all correct answers.)

   a. Hosts

   b. Recent Jobs

   c. Virtual Machines

   d. Networks

   e. Library Resources

   f. User Roles

7. _____ control which tasks a user can perform in the virtual environment.

   a. User actions

   b. User permissions

   c. User roles

   d. Account roles

8. _____ enables the migration of a virtual machine from one storage location to another.

9. _____ moves running virtual machines from one host computer to another.

10. The maximum number of simultaneous live migrations for a single host computer _____.

   a. depends on the number of networks

   b. is one

   c. is unlimited

   d. is configurable from the VMM console

   e. is configurable from the Failover Cluster Manager

11. The main location for VMM information is the _____.

12. The VMM library server is a/an _____ that hosts the MSSCVMMLibrary share.

13. Which of the following destination types are defined in Windows Server Backup? (Choose all correct answers.)

   a. Back up to a hard disk that is dedicated for backups.

   b. Back up to a magnetic tape that is dedicated for backups.

   c. Back up to a volume.

   d. Back up to a shared network folder.

   e. Back up to a DVD that is dedicated for backups.

14. Creating a/an _____ of the VMM server is the best way to back up the server.

15. The six suggested steps to solve a problem include which of the following? (Choose all correct answers.)

    a. Define the problem.

    b. Gather information to solve the problem.

    c. Use intuition.

    d. Run diagnostic tools.

    e. Develop an action plan.

    f. Execute the action plan.

    g. Test to see if the problem is resolved.

    h. Research the solution.

16. You can use _____ to gather information about a virtualization event and stop a potential problem before it occurs.

17. The Windows logs consist of which of the following? (Choose all correct answers.)

    a. Applications

    b. Administrative events

    c. Security

    d. Setup

    e. System

18. To help identify common problems in the VMM environment, run the _____.

19. Microsoft Network Monitor is a/an _____ that enables you to capture, view, and analyze network data.

20. You can use the _____ to troubleshoot a failover cluster.

Case Projects

Case 9-1: Resolving a Problem with Local Disks

You use the Disk Management tool to view the local disk associated with the cluster shared volume for virtual machine storage, and you notice that the volume is offline. Develop an action plan to bring the volume online. Use the Internet to research possible causes and solutions to the problem.

Case 9-2: Differences between Quick Storage Migration and Live Migration

You have received an e-mail from a classmate who wants to know the difference between Quick Storage Migration and live migration. What will you tell him in your response?

Case 9-3: Planning for Backup

Your boss has asked you to review the existing backup plan for the virtualization environment. She wants you to submit a checklist of the items you would review. Prepare the checklist.

chapter 10

Managing the Private Cloud with PowerShell

After reading this chapter and completing the exercises, you will be able to:

- Describe the PowerShell environment
- Install the Hyper-V PowerShell Management Library
- Manage virtual machines with PowerShell
- Create scripts to manage the private cloud

Starting with the installation of Virtual Machine Manager (VMM) in Chapter 4, you looked at the PowerShell scripts that VMM uses to accomplish tasks in the private cloud. In this chapter, you learn to use PowerShell to manage the private cloud. PowerShell is a new Windows command-line shell designed especially for server administrators. The Power-Shell Management Library for Hyper-V R2, which currently includes 80 functions, allows you to manage a variety of components. When you need to perform repetitive tasks, you can create scripts in PowerShell to manage the private cloud. Some tasks, such as rapid provisioning, can be performed only in PowerShell.

Describing the PowerShell Environment

You have worked from the command prompt in previous chapters, and probably in previous courses. For example, you have used the DIR command to get a listing of the folders and files in the current directory. When you enter a command such as START REGEDIT, the Start command loads the Registry editor and turns control over to it. When you complete your task, you close the Registry editor and return control to the command prompt. When working from the command prompt, you interact with the Windows Server 2008 command shell.

The command shell is a separate software program that provides direct communication between you and the operating system. When you enter a command, the command interpreter executes it, requests that the operating system perform the task for you, and displays text output on the screen. The command shell of the Windows server operating system uses the command interpreter CMD.EXE, which translates user input into a form that the operating system understands.

PowerShell is a new Windows command-line shell designed especially for server administrators. From the Windows PowerShell interactive prompt, you can enter commands or invoke scripts. Scripts provide the ability to repeat commands in a scripting environment. Unlike the command prompt, which accepts and returns text, PowerShell is built on top of the .NET Framework, and accepts and returns .NET Framework objects. The **.NET Framework** (pronounced *dot net*) is a software environment that runs primarily in Windows. It includes a large library and supports several programming languages, including PowerShell. This fundamental change in the environment brings entirely new tools into the management of Windows server roles.

The .NET Framework uses objects. As an example of an object, consider a bicycle. All real-world objects share two characteristics: state and behavior. A bicycle's state includes current gear ratio, current pedal cadence, current speed, and current direction. Bicycles also have behaviors, such as changing gear ration, changing pedal cadence, applying brakes, and rotating handle bars. The state of an object is its data, and the behavior of an object is its methods. When you use an object, you pass along the data and the methods that can be used to transform the data.

PowerShell Cmdlets

PowerShell introduces the concept of a cmdlet (pronounced *command-let*) or small command. These single-function command-line tools are built into PowerShell. You can use each cmdlet separately, but their power is realized when you chain these simple tools in sequence to perform complex tasks. PowerShell includes more than 100 basic cmdlets. The PowerShell command prompt is shown in Figure 10-1.

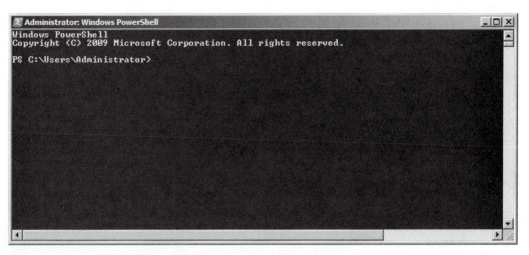

Figure 10-1 The PowerShell command prompt

Source: Microsoft Windows PowerShell, Windows Server 2008 R2 SP1

Many of your favorite commands will work in PowerShell. Consider the DIR command that you have used with the regular command prompt. Figure 10-2 shows the results of using the DIR command in PowerShell. It is interesting to see how PowerShell interprets this command. If you enter Get-Alias DIR, you see that PowerShell uses Get-ChildItem to produce the output. To see the entire alias list, enter get-alias. When you enter this command in Activity 10-1, you will also see some of your favorite Windows and UNIX commands. The get-alias command is a quick way to learn equivalent PowerShell commands for commands you learned when working with other shells.

Figure 10-2 Using the DIR command from the command shell in PowerShell

Source: Microsoft Windows PowerShell, Windows Server 2008 R2 SP1

PowerShell Verbs and Nouns

As an example of a basic cmdlet, consider Get-Date, as shown in Figure 10-3. Like all cmdlets, Get-Date is constructed from a verb and a noun and may be followed by qualifying information that is used to customize the actions of the cmdlet.

Figure 10-3 Get-Date cmdlet

Source: Microsoft Windows PowerShell, Windows Server 2008 R2 SP1

The verb and noun are separated by a hyphen. As in any language, a verb conveys action. Table 10-1 describes some verbs that you might encounter when working with PowerShell.

Verb	Description
Get	Retrieves a resource
Set	Creates or replaces data for a resource
Copy	Copies a resource to another container; also renames a resource
Out	Sends data out of the environment
New	Creates an empty resource that is not associated with any content
Add	Adds a resource to a container; paired with Remove
Remove	Deletes a resource from a container; paired with Add
Clear	Sets the contents to the null value
Import	Creates a resource from a file
Select	Locates a resource in a container
Show	Makes a resource visible to the user
Test	Verifies the operation of a resource

Table 10-1 Standard PowerShell verbs

© Cengage Learning 2014

Cmdlets are named as verb/noun pairs. Table 10-2 lists some verb/noun pairs you might encounter when working with PowerShell.

Noun	Cmdlet	Description
Alias	Get-Alias	Returns alias names for cmdlets
ChildItem	Get-ChildItem	Gets child items, which are contents of a folder or registry key
Command	Get-Command	Retrieves basic information about a command
Computer	Stop-Computer	Stops (shuts down) a computer
Content	Set-Content	Puts content in the item
Counter	Import-Counter	Imports performance counter log files
Date	Set-Date	Sets the system date on the host system
EventLog	Get-EventLog	Gets event log data
History	Clear-History	Deletes entries from the session history
Item	New-Item	Creates a new item in a namespace
ItemProperty	Clear-ItemProperty	Removes the property value from a property
Location	Set-Location	Sets the current working directory
Module	Import-Module	Adds a module to the session
Object	New-Object	Creates a new .NET object
Path	Test-Path	Returns true if the path exists; otherwise, returns false
Process	Stop-Process	Stops a running process
Service	Start-Service	Starts a stopped service

Table 10-2 Examples of verb/noun pairs in PowerShell

© Cengage Learning 2014

Using `Get-Help` with a Cmdlet

To be successful with PowerShell, you need to learn to work with the `Get-Help` command, which provides information about a cmdlet. For example, to see information about the `Get-Date` cmdlet, enter `Get-Help Get-Date`. The results are shown in Figure 10-4.

If you learn better by seeing examples, you can add the `-example` switch and run the cmdlet shown in Figure 10-5. A **switch** controls the action of the cmdlet. Using the `-example` switch provides real examples and helps reduce the learning curve for PowerShell.

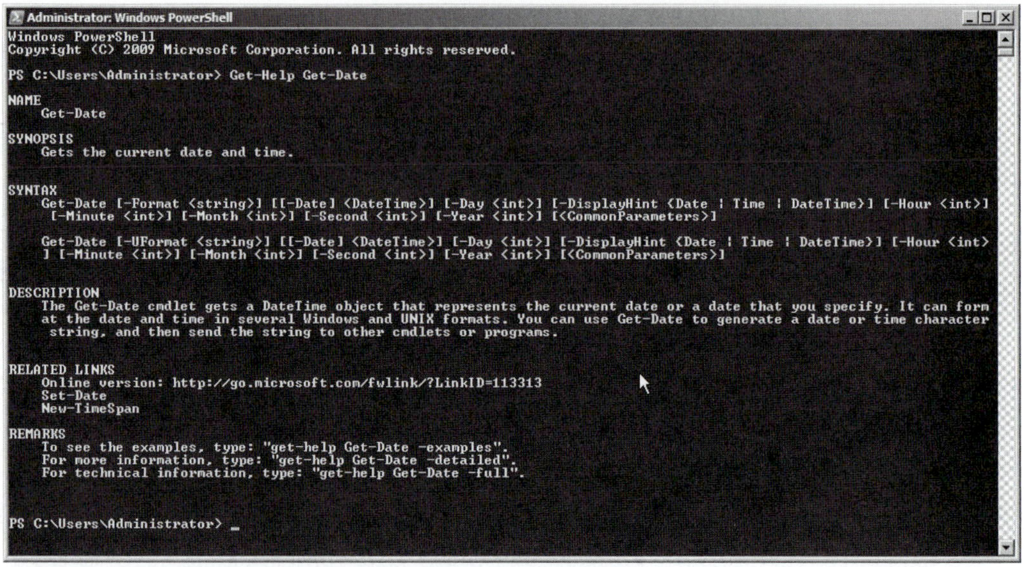

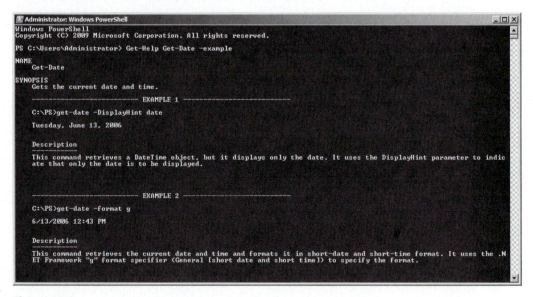

Figure 10-4 `Get-Help` command used with `Get-Date` cmdlet

Source: Microsoft Windows PowerShell, Windows Server 2008 R2 SP1

Figure 10-5 `Get-Help Get-Date` command used with `-example` switch

Source: Microsoft Windows PowerShell, Windows Server 2008 R2 SP1

If you need more information, you can use the `-detailed` switch, as shown in Figure 10-6.

When you are not sure about the results of a command, the `-full` switch provides technical information that might help you correct the problem. Figure 10-7 shows the results of using the `-full` switch.

You can use the `-example`, `-detailed`, and `-full` switches with most cmdlets. This provides a consistent approach when you learn to use the PowerShell cmdlets.

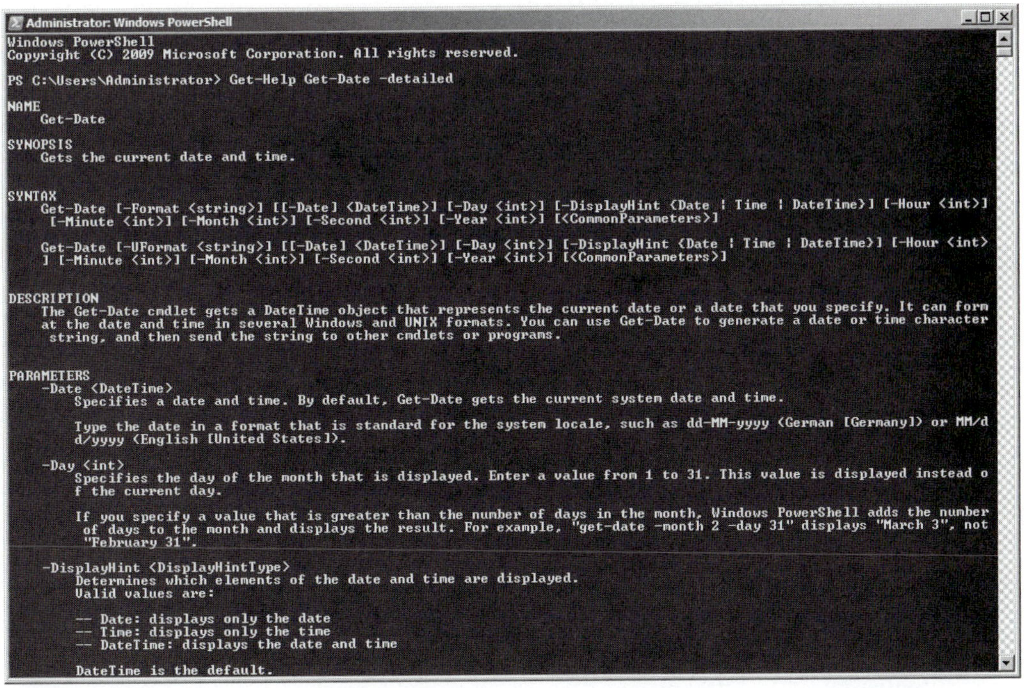

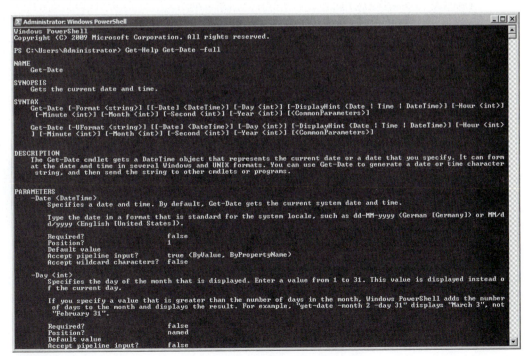

Figure 10-6 `Get-Help Get-Date` command used with `-detailed` switch

Source: Microsoft Windows PowerShell, Windows Server 2008 R2 SP1

10

Figure 10-7 `Get-Help Get-Date` command used with `-full` switch

Source: Microsoft Windows PowerShell, Windows Server 2008 R2 SP1

PowerShell is not case sensitive. In the cmdlets used so far, the first letter of each word was capitalized to match the PowerShell documentation. However, any of the following cases will work:

```
Get-Date
get-date
GET-DATE
```

Although PowerShell is not case sensitive, it requires proper syntax and spelling. When you enter a cmdlet in the wrong syntax or misspell a word, a red message appears and indicates that something is wrong.

A tool that you can use to enter long commands correctly is **tab autocomplete**. To use this tool to complete a noun, type the first few characters and then press the Tab key. For example, you can type `Get-PSSe` and press Tab to get `Get-PSSession`. Then type `C` and press Tab to get `Configuration`, which completes the cmdlet name `Get-PSSessionConfiguration`. You must enter the minimum number of characters to complete the noun before you press Tab.

Another handy tool that saves typing is the up arrow key. You have used this tool in the regular command prompt to cycle back through your history of commands and locate a previously used command. To reuse the command after you have located and selected it, press Enter. Of course, you can also use the left arrow key or Backspace key to edit the command.

Using Parameters

Parameters allow you to modify the information that a cmdlet returns. When you run a cmdlet, the results contain properties and values that correspond to the nouns in your cmdlets. Parameters allow you finer control over the properties that PowerShell returns in the resulting table. Parameters are unique to the nouns in your cmdlet. For example, Figure 10-8 shows the `-name` parameter used with `dir` to show the alias for the `dir` command.

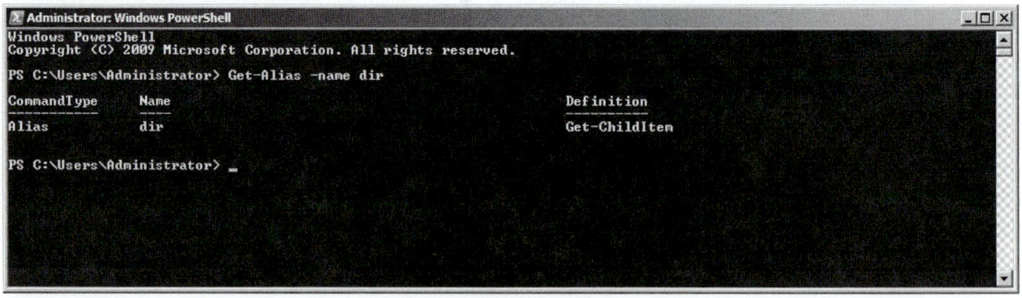

Figure 10-8 `Get-Alias` command used with `-name` parameter

Source: Microsoft Windows PowerShell, Windows Server 2008 R2 SP1

The `-name` parameter is a keyword parameter that you explicitly specify in the cmdlet: `Get-Alias -name dir`. You do not need to use the keyword. `Get-Alias dir` returns the same results. When there is more than one keyword, you enter the parameters in the order of the keywords for the cmdlet. These are known as **positional parameters**.

You need to remember two things when using positional parameters. First, you need to know the correct position of the parameter when you enter the cmdlet syntax. Second, not all parameters are positional. Some are named parameters, and you must use the keyword. Figure 10-9 shows an example of each type.

```
Administrator: Windows PowerShell                                               _ □ ×
Windows PowerShell
Copyright (C) 2009 Microsoft Corporation. All rights reserved.

PS C:\Users\Administrator> Get-Alias -name dir

CommandType     Name                                      Definition
---------       ----                                      ----------
Alias           dir                                       Get-ChildItem


PS C:\Users\Administrator> Get-Alias dir

CommandType     Name                                      Definition
---------       ----                                      ----------
Alias           dir                                       Get-ChildItem


PS C:\Users\Administrator>
```

Figure 10-9 `Get-Alias` command used with and without `-name` parameter

Source: Microsoft Windows PowerShell, Windows Server 2008 R2 SP1

Using Wildcards

You have used wildcards such as `*.*` (known as *star dot star*) and `???` when working with the regular command prompt. PowerShell supports the use of these wildcards and one more: a pair of brackets, which find a range of characters. Table 10-3 describes the PowerShell wildcard characters and their uses.

Wildcard	Usage
`*`	Matches any string of characters starting where you place the `*`. For example, if you type `g*`, you find anything that starts with the letter *g*.
`?`	Matches a single character according to where you place the `?`. For example, you could enter `r??k` to return *rick*, *rock*, or *rook*.
`[ ]`	Allows you to specify a range of characters. For example, `[k-s]ick` could return *kick*, *lick*, *pick*, or *sick*. Or, you could be more specific and enter `[kps]ick`, which could return *kick*, *pick*, or *sick*.

Table 10-3 Wildcards and their uses

© Cengage Learning 2014

Figure 10-10 shows the aliases that start with the letter *m*, which appear when you search with an *m* and the `*` wildcard. This search would be handy if you could not remember an alias but you knew it started with *m*.

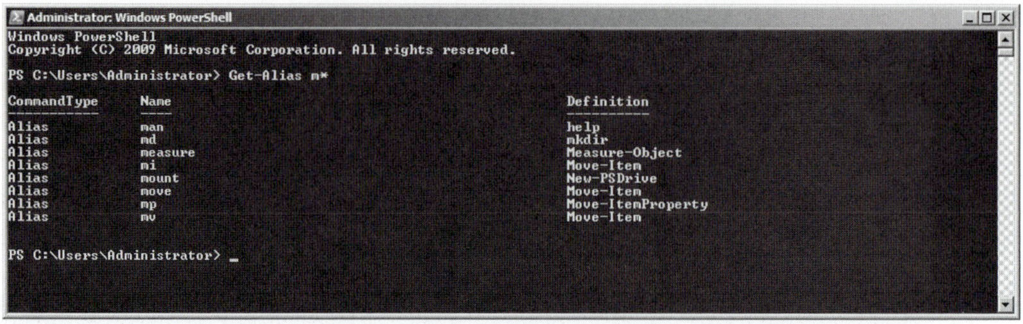

Figure 10-10 `Get-Alias` command used with `m*` wildcard

Source: Microsoft Windows PowerShell, Windows Server 2008 R2 SP1

Working with Properties

Properties have two parts in PowerShell: property names and property values. Property names are column headings, and property values are the data shown below the headings. For example, in Figure 10-11, the `Get-ChildItem` property names are `Mode`, `LastWriteTime`, `Length`, and `Name`. The property values are shown in the rows below the heading names.

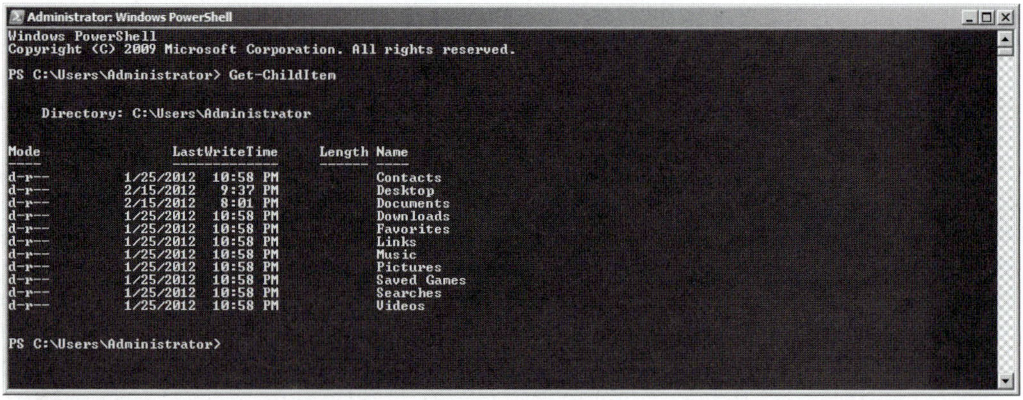

Figure 10-11 `Get-ChildItem` property names

Source: Microsoft Windows PowerShell, Windows Server 2008 R2 SP1

Think of these property values as being read-only. While you cannot directly use properties in your PowerShell commands, you can control the properties shown as output. For example, enter `Get-ChildItem -name` to list the names of the directory items.

Using Aliases and Creating Your Own

Aliases are shortcuts that let you use shorter commands in PowerShell. Because of these aliases, most of the commands you use in other command prompt windows work in PowerShell. For example, PowerShell uses `Get-ChildItem` to display directory listings, but you can get the same information by using the `dir` command or the UNIX `ls` command.

To see a list of the 130 built-in aliases available in PowerShell, enter `Get-Alias`. To see information about an alias—for example, `dir`—enter `Get-Help dir`, as shown in Figure 10-12.

```
Administrator: Windows PowerShell
Windows PowerShell
Copyright (C) 2009 Microsoft Corporation. All rights reserved.

PS C:\Users\Administrator> Get-Help dir

NAME
    Get-ChildItem

SYNOPSIS
    Gets the items and child items in one or more specified locations.

SYNTAX
    Get-ChildItem [[-Path] <string[]>] [[-Filter] <string>] [-Exclude <string[]>] [-Force] [-Include <string[]>] [-Name
    ] [-Recurse] [-UseTransaction] [<CommonParameters>]

    Get-ChildItem [-LiteralPath] <string[]> [[-Filter] <string>] [-Exclude <string[]>] [-Force] [-Include <string[]>] [
    -Name] [-Recurse] [-UseTransaction] [<CommonParameters>]

DESCRIPTION
    The Get-ChildItem cmdlet gets the items in one or more specified locations. If the item is a container, it gets the
    items inside the container, known as child items. You can use the Recurse parameter to get items in all child cont
    ainers.

    A location can be a file system location, such as a directory, or a location exposed by another provider, such as a
    registry hive or a certificate store.
```

Figure 10-12 Getting help for the `dir` alias

Source: Microsoft Windows PowerShell, Windows Server 2008 R2 SP1

You can also create new aliases to make PowerShell responsive to the way you want to work. If you find that you are entering the same long cmdlets repeatedly, create an alias.

To create a new alias, use the `New-Alias` cmdlet. One cmdlet that you will use frequently is `Get-Help`; the letters `gh` are a good candidate for an alias for `Get-Help`. Figure 10-13 shows how to create the `gh` alias, followed by two tests to verify that `gh` was created properly.

```
Administrator: Windows PowerShell
Windows PowerShell
Copyright (C) 2009 Microsoft Corporation. All rights reserved.

PS C:\Users\Administrator> New-Alias gh Get-Help
PS C:\Users\Administrator> Get-Alias gh

CommandType     Name                                Definition
-----------     ----                                ----------
Alias           gh                                  Get-Help

PS C:\Users\Administrator> gh New-Alias

NAME
    New-Alias

SYNOPSIS
    Creates a new alias.
```

Figure 10-13 Creating and testing the `gh` alias for `Get-Help`

Source: Microsoft Windows PowerShell, Windows Server 2008 R2 SP1

Working with the Pipe Operator

You might have used the `more` command in a regular command prompt to page through a large file. In a command such as `dir | more`, you use the pipe operator (|) to pass the output to the `more` command.

Piping cmdlets together is called **pipelining**, in which you take the output of one cmdlet and pass it to the next cmdlet. For example, if you were running low on disk space and needed to find the largest files in a folder, you could enter the series of commands shown in Figure 10-14.

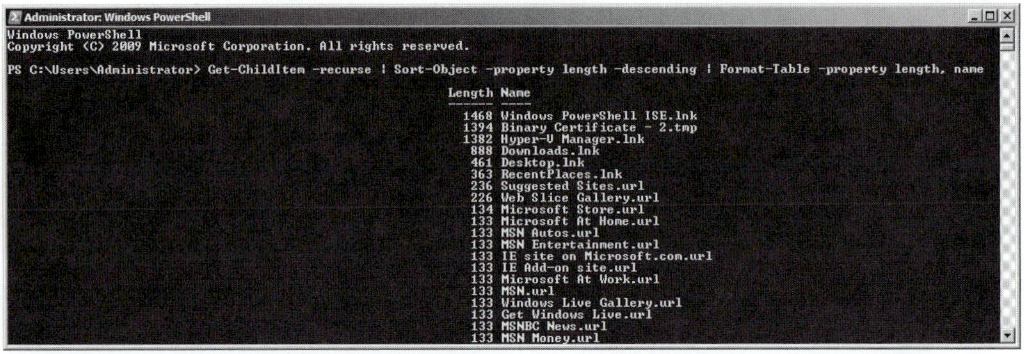

Figure 10-14 Using piped cmdlets to list largest files in a folder

Source: Microsoft Windows PowerShell, Windows Server 2008 R2 SP1

The `Get-Childitem -recurse` command creates a table of file properties for the current folder and subfolders. This table is piped to the `Sort-Object` cmdlet, where the table is sorted in descending order for the length property. The sorted table is piped to the `Format-Table` cmdlet, where the table is formatted and output to the screen. Notice that the object-based nature of PowerShell allows you to work with any parameters of a particular object—in this case, length and name. The pipe routes the tables automatically and correctly, providing consistency with little effort on your part.

Working with PowerShell Output

The previous section explained how to pipe between commands. In this section, you learn about cmdlets that control output and how the pipe operator is used with them.

The pipe operator is typically used with the following types of commands:

- *Sorting*—Arranging a table in a particular order
- *Filtering*—Selecting items to remain in a table after filtering out unwanted items using the `Where-Object` cmdlet
- *Formatting*—Making the output look more pleasing
- *Redirecting*—Sending output to a file

The only cmdlet you need to learn in order to sort tables is `Sort-Object`. You also need to know the parameters of an object to sort the table. For example, if you want to sort a table of filenames, run the following command:

`Get-ChildItem | Sort-Object -property name`

If you want to page through the sorted output, add `| more` to the end of the previous command:

`Get-ChildItem | Sort-Object -property name | more`

In some situations, you might need to see only a part of the complete table. If so, you can use PowerShell's filtering capabilities with the `Where-Object` cmdlet. To use this cmdlet, you need to learn two concepts. First, you need to be familiar with the automatic variable $_., which consists of a dollar sign, underscore, and dot. This variable refers to the current object in the pipeline. For example, $_.Length refers to the length parameter in Get_ChildItem, where the container is a directory. Second, you need to know the comparison operators defined in Table 10-4.

Operator	Definition
-eq	Equals, which is used for finding identical values
-ne	Not equals, which includes values that are not identical
-gt	Greater than
-ge	Greater than or equal to
-lt	Less than
-le	Less than or equal to
-like	Matching operator that uses the * wildcard operator
-contains	Allows you to see whether an identical value exists in a list of values
-notlike	Allows you to identify the value that does not match
-notmatch	Allows you to find the values of a string that do not match
-notcontains	Allows you to find the values in a list that do not match

Table 10-4 Comparison operators used with Where-Object

© *Cengage Learning 2014*

In an earlier example, you used the Get-ChildItem cmdlet to obtain the largest files in a folder. If you want your output to exclude the directories, which have a length of zero, you can add Where-Object {$_.Length -gt 0} to the previous cmdlets:

Get-ChildItem -recurse | **Where-Object {$_.Length -gt 0}** | Sort-Object -property length -descending | Format_table -property length, name

You have seen an example of the Format-Table cmdlet, which is one of the formatting options available in PowerShell. Two other options are available as well. Table 10-5 describes these three formatting choices.

Cmdlet	Usage
Format-List	Controls which properties are displayed in a list
Format-Wide	Creates a wide table with one column for each property
Format-Table	Outputs data in a table format

Table 10-5 Formatting options

© *Cengage Learning 2014*

The results of almost any PowerShell cmdlet can be sent or redirected to a file. You can redirect output in several different types of files, including CSV for spreadsheets, HTML, or text files. Table 10-6 shows the types of output you can use with PowerShell.

Out **cmdlets**	Description
Out-File	Creates a text file
Out-GridView	Creates a grid in a separate window that you can sort and filter
Out-Host	Displays the results in the PowerShell session (default option)
Out-Null	Deletes the output
Out-Printer	Sends output to a connected printer
Out-String	Outputs the results in an array of strings, which is useful for setting up variables for scripting operations
Export-CSV	Outputs a file in CSV format

Table 10-6   File output options

© Cengage Learning 2014

Working with PowerShell Input

If you need to work with numerous entries in PowerShell, it is easier to enter the lines first in the Notepad text editor. To input the lines in the text file, use the Get-Content cmdlet. If you need to create two or more objects per line, a better alternative is to enter the lines in a spreadsheet program and save the file in the **comma-separated values (CSV)** format. To input a CSV formatted file, use the Import-CSV cmdlet, as shown in Figure 10-15.

Figure 10-15   Inputting files into PowerShell with Get-Content and Import-CSV

Source: Microsoft Windows PowerShell, Windows Server 2008 R2 SP1

Reasons to Learn PowerShell

You need to learn PowerShell for several reasons:

1. *It's here to stay*—For example, PowerShell version 2 is prominently displayed on the taskbar in Windows Server 2008 R2.
2. *Most Microsoft products will eventually use it*—You have used PowerShell since Chapter 4, starting with Virtual Machine Manager. Virtually all current Microsoft

server products can be managed through PowerShell. If you become proficient in Power-Shell, you can manage most of Microsoft's newer products.

3. *It can make your job easier*—You can automate routine tasks. For example, creating 100 user roles for the self-service portal might take hours to complete if you do it manually. With a PowerShell script, you can complete the task with less effort.

4. *Many GUIs are PowerShell front ends*—Microsoft has been designing GUIs for various products that are actually front-end interfaces to PowerShell. One example is the Virtual Machine Manager console, in which the GUI actually generates a PowerShell script to complete your requested task.

5. *Microsoft certification exams contain PowerShell questions*—Microsoft has been adding questions about PowerShell to its virtualization exams. While you do not necessarily have to know the full command syntax, you do need to know which command you should use in a given situation.

6. *Microsoft considers it important*—The single most important skill you will need as a Windows administrator in the coming years is proficiency with Windows PowerShell.

7. *If you do not learn it, someone else will*—Given the intense competition for IT jobs, you need every edge you can get. Your chances for advancement might improve by knowing PowerShell.

Activity 10-1: Learning About PowerShell

Time Required: 45 minutes

Objective: Investigate cmdlets in PowerShell.

Description: In this activity, your team will learn useful cmdlets in PowerShell. Table 10-7 provides the team member assignments for this activity.

Team Member	Steps	Host Computer
1	1-24	MGMT
2	25, 5-24	
3	26, 5-24, 27	

Table 10-7 Team member assignments for Activity 10-1

© *Cengage Learning 2014*

1. Switch the KVM switch to port 1.

2. Log on to your MGMT server with a username of *Team1***Administrator**, substituting your team name for *Team1*. Enter a password of **P@ssw0rd**.

3. To open PowerShell, click the **PowerShell** icon on the taskbar. The icon contains the Greek sigma symbol.

4. To create an alias for the Get-Service cmdlet, enter **New-Alias gs Get-Service** and press **Enter**.

5. To verify that the gs alias exists, enter **Get-Alias gs** and press **Enter**.

6. To see a list of services, enter gs and press **Enter**.

7. To get help for the Get-Service cmdlet, enter **Get-Help gs** and press **Enter**.

To reuse a command, press the up arrow.

8. To get detailed help for the Get-Service cmdlet, enter **Get-Help gs -detailed** and press **Enter**.

9. To get detailed help for the Get-Service cmdlet while pausing the screen between pages, enter **Get-Help gs -detailed | more** and press **Enter**. Press the Spacebar to advance to the next page.

10. To see a list of services, enter gs and press **Enter**.

11. To see a list of services whose names start with *W*, enter **gs W*** and press **Enter**.

12. To see a list of services whose display names start with *Windows*, enter the following command and press **Enter**:

    gs -DisplayName Windows*

13. To see a list of services with *.Net* in the name, enter **gs -DisplayName *.net*** and press **Enter**.

14. To see a list of services starting with *Net* in the name, enter **gs net*** and press **Enter**.

15. To see a list of services sorted by name, enter the following command and press **Enter**:

    gs | Sort-Object -property name | more

To stop the output on the screen, press Ctrl+C.

16. To see a list of services in which the status is Stopped and the services are sorted by name, enter the following command and press **Enter**:

    gs | Where-Object {$_.Status -eq "Stopped"} | Sort-Object -property name | more

17. To see services in a formatted list in which the status is Stopped and the services are sorted by name, enter the following command and press **Enter**:

    gs | Where-Object {$_.Status -eq "Stopped"} | Sort-Object -property name | Format-List

18. To see services in a wide-formatted list in which the status is Stopped and the services are sorted by name, enter the following command and press **Enter**:

    gs | Where-Object {$_.Status -eq "Stopped"} | Sort-Object -property name | Format-Wide

19. To see a list of services in a formatted table in which the status is Stopped and the services are sorted by name, enter the following command on one line, and then press **Enter**:

```
gs | Where-Object {$_.Status -eq "Stopped"} | Sort-Object
-property name | Format-Table
```

20. To display the stopped services, enter the following command and press **Enter**:

```
gs | Where-Object {$_.Status -eq "Stopped"}
```

21. To create an output file of the stopped services, enter the following command on one line and then press **Enter**:

```
gs | Where-Object {$_.Status -eq "Stopped"} | Out-File Services.txt
```

22. To get the text within the Services.txt file, enter **Get-Content Services.txt** and press **Enter**.

23. To create a CSV output file of the stopped services, enter the following command on one line and then press **Enter**:

```
gs | Where-Object {$_.Status -eq "Stopped"} | Export-CSV Services.csv
```

24. To view the text within the Services.csv file, enter the following command and then press **Enter**. Close the window when you finish.

```
Import-CSV Services.csv
```

25. Team member 2 should repeat Steps 5 through 24.

26. Team member 3 should repeat Steps 5 through 24.

27. Remain logged on for future lab activities.

Using the Windows PowerShell Integrated Scripting Environment (ISE)

To make PowerShell easier to use, Microsoft provides the Integrated Scripting Environment (ISE), which you install from Server Manager. You add this feature in Activity 10-2.

To open the ISE, double-click the Windows PowerShell ISE icon. You will place this icon on the desktop in Activity 10-2. The ISE has three panes, as shown in Figure 10-16: Scripting, Output, and Command. Starting at the bottom, the Command pane is similar to the PowerShell command prompt that you have already used. The difference is that the output from entered commands appears in the Output pane.

Also, the output of scripts appears in the Output pane as you run them in the ISE. Because the ISE is a GUI tool, you can use the familiar cut, copy, and paste features. The output window is scrollable, which makes it easy to work with larger numbers of output lines. To clear the output pane, click the Clear Output Pane button, which looks like a blue squeegee. This button and others are identified in Figure 10-17.

The top pane shown in Figure 10-17 is the Scripting pane, and is the most useful. The ISE's true power is that it helps you enter and update PowerShell commands easily. Although you can edit commands and scripts in Notepad and then run them in PowerShell command

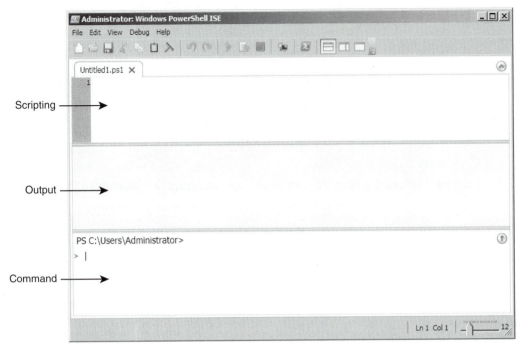

Figure 10-16   ISE with three panes identified

Source: Microsoft Windows PowerShell ISE, Windows Server 2008 R2 SP1

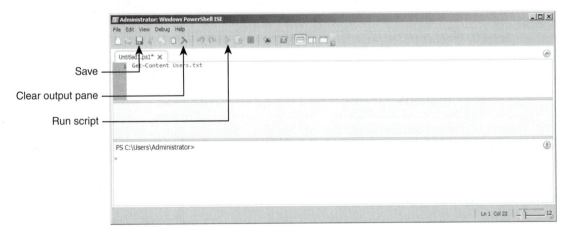

Figure 10-17   ISE and menu buttons

Source: Microsoft Windows PowerShell ISE, Windows Server 2008 R2 SP1

windows, it is much easier to do everything in one place. An added bonus is that you can work with up to eight sessions at the same time, which is particularly useful when you want to borrow some commands from a previous session. To run commands or a script, press the F5 key or Run Script button. To get help for the command you just entered, press the F1 key or Help button.

Figure 10-18 shows a command you entered in Activity 10-1 to display stopped services. The command is shown in the Scripting pane, and the command output is shown in the Output pane.

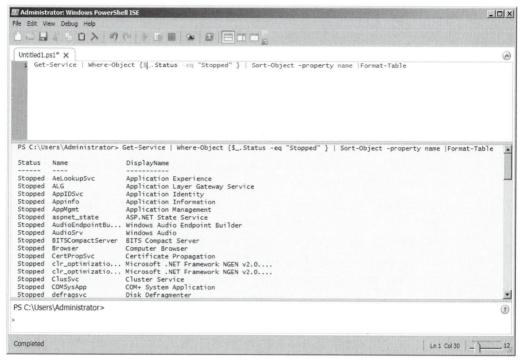

Figure 10-18 ISE showing command and output

Source: Microsoft Windows PowerShell ISE, Windows Server 2008 R2 SP1

Activity 10-2: Working with the ISE

Time Required: 30 minutes

Objective: Work with the ISE.

Description: In this activity, your team installs and works with the ISE. You progressively create a long command in a series of steps. Table 10-8 provides the team member assignments for this activity.

Team Member	Steps	Host Computer
1	1-12	MGMT
2	13, 6-12	
3	14, 6-12, 15	

Table 10-8 Team member assignments for Activity 10-2

© Cengage Learning 2014

1. If necessary, switch the KVM switch to port 1.

2. If necessary, log on to your MGMT server with a username of *Team1\Administrator*, substituting your team name for *Team1*. Enter a password of **P@ssw0rd**.

3. To add the ISE, restore the Server Manager window, click **Features** in the left pane, and click **Add Features** in the right pane. Scroll and then click the **Windows PowerShell Integrated Scripting Environment (ISE)** check box, read the feature description, click **Next,** and click **Install.**

4. Wait for the installation to be completed, and click **Close.**

5. To add a desktop icon for the ISE, click **Start,** enter **ise** in the **Search programs and files** text box, right-click **Windows PowerShell ISE,** point to **Send to,** and click **Desktop (create shortcut).**

6. To open the ISE, double-click the **Windows PowerShell ISE** icon on the desktop.

7. To view the help for `Get-Service`, enter **Get-Service**, click within `Get-Service`, and press the **F1** key. Close the Help window.

8. To see a list of services sorted by name, add | **Sort-Object -property name** to the command you entered in Step 7, and press the **F5** key.

9. Scroll through the window to see the start of the list.

10. To see a list of services in a formatted table in which the status is Stopped and the services are sorted by name, add | **Format-Table** to the previous command, and press the **F5** key.

11. Scroll through the window to see the start of the table.

12. Close the ISE window.

13. Team member 2 should repeat Steps 6 through 12.

14. Team member 3 should repeat Steps 6 through 12.

15. Remain logged on for future lab activities.

Installing the PowerShell Management Library for Hyper-V

PowerShell can be enhanced by the addition of a product-specific library. You can download the PowerShell Management Library for Hyper-V R2 from Microsoft's open source project site. This library, which currently has 80 functions, allows you to manage a variety of components, including the following:

- Virtual machine configuration and state
- Virtual hard disks
- Virtual floppy disks
- Virtual CD/DVD images
- Virtual network adapters

- Virtual network switches
- Snapshots

The Hyper-V PowerShell Management Library is available as a free download from the CodePlex site. **CodePlex** is an open source project hosting Web site from Microsoft that allows shared development of open source software. Developers use the site to share projects and ideas. The PowerShell Management Library for Hyper-V was developed by James O'Neill and others at Microsoft.

You can download the management library from *http://PShyperv.codeplex.com/* and place it in a folder for the PowerShell Hyper-V files. A suggested location is C:\PSHyperV. The file is in Zip format, and because it comes from the Internet, you need to unblock the file so it installs properly. Otherwise, you must contend with a message each time you work with the library. To unblock the Zip file, right-click it, click Properties, and click Unblock. The developers provide a script file to install the library. You will install the Hyper-V Management Library in Activity 10-3.

Using PowerShell Profiles

The Windows PowerShell profile is simply a script or text file that runs each time Windows PowerShell starts. You can use the profile to set up your Windows PowerShell environment. Two items enable you to use PowerShell more easily:

- `Set-ExecutionPolicy unrestricted -force`—This command allows the Hyper-V library to run without displaying annoying security warnings because the files came from the Internet.
- `$hosts="`*Team1-Clstr1*`","`*Team1-Clstr2*`"`—This variable starts with a dollar sign and provides the host computer names, which prevents the need for repetitive entry of the computer names. Remember to substitute your team name.

You set the profiles for the Windows PowerShell and Windows PowerShell ISE in Activity 10-3.

Activity 10-3: Installing the Hyper-V Management Library

Time Required: 45 minutes

Objective: Install the PowerShell Management Library for Hyper-V.

Description: In this activity, your team installs the PowerShell Management Library for Hyper-V. You download the library from the CodePlex site, prepare the files for installation, and run the script that installs the library. You create profiles to set up an environment to use the library within the PowerShell command prompt and ISE.

Table 10-9 provides the team member assignments for this activity.

Team Member	Steps	Host Computer
1	1-12	MGMT
2	13-20	
3	21-30	

Table 10-9 Team member assignments for Activity 10-3

© Cengage Learning 2014

1. If necessary, switch the KVM switch to port 1.

2. If necessary, log on to your MGMT server with a username of *Team1*\Administrator, substituting your team name for *Team1*. Enter a password of **P@ssw0rd**.

3. To create the PowerShell folder, click **Start**, click **MGMT**, and double-click **Local Disk (C:)**. Click **New Folder**, enter **PSHyperV** over the text "New folder," and press **Enter**.

4. To open Internet Explorer, click **Start**, and then click **Internet Explorer**.

5. To download the PowerShell module, enter **http://PShyperv.codeplex.com/** in the Address bar, and click the **Downloads** tab. Click **PSHyperV.zip** under the first Recommended Download. Click **Save**, click **Local Disk (C:)**, double-click **PSHyperV**, and click **Save**.

6. Wait for the download to be completed, and click **Close**.

7. Return to the PowerShellHyperV folder. Right-click **PSHyperV**, click **Properties**, and click **Unblock**. Click **OK**.

If you do not unblock the file, you will see a security alert when you work with the module.

8. To extract the files, right-click **PSHyperV**, and click **Extract All**. Note the folder where the files will be extracted, and click **Extract**.

9. To open a command prompt, click **Start**, right-click **Command Prompt**, and click **Run as administrator**.

10. To go to the folder where PSHyperV was extracted, enter the following command and press **Enter**:

    `cd \PSHyperV\PSHyperv`

11. To run the installation script, enter **install** and press **Enter**.

12. When prompted, press **Enter** three times, click **Yes**, and click **OK**. Press **Ctrl+C**, enter **y**, and press **Enter**. Close the Command Prompt window.

13. To open the PowerShell session in administrator mode, right-click the **PowerShell** icon on the taskbar, and click **Run as administrator**.

14. To see the path to the profile, enter **$profile** and press **Enter**.

15. To create an empty profile file, enter the following command and press **Enter**:

    `New-Item -path $profile -itemtype file -force`

16. To open Notepad and the profile file, enter **notepad $profile**, and press **Enter.**

17. To set the execution policy, enter the following command and press **Enter:**

```
Set-ExecutionPolicy unrestricted -force
```

18. To create an array variable with the host computer names, enter the following command and press **Enter.** Substitute your team name for *Team1.*

```
$hosts="Team1-Clstr1","Team1-Clstr2"
```

19. To save the profile file, click **File,** and click **Save.** Close the Notepad window.

20. Close the Windows PowerShell window.

21. To open the PowerShell session in administrator mode, right-click the **PowerShell** icon on the taskbar, and click **Run as administrator.**

22. To open the ISE, double-click the **Windows PowerShell ISE** icon on the desktop.

23. To open the existing profile, click **File,** click **Open,** double-click **WindowsPowerShell,** click **Microsoft.Powershell_profile,** and click **Open.**

24. To create a new profile for use in the ISE, enter the following command in the bottom pane and press **Enter:**

```
new-item -type file -path $profile -force
```

25. To open the ISE profile that was created, click **File,** click **Open,** click **Microsoft.PowershellISE_profile,** and click **Open.**

26. To copy the lines in the existing profile, click the **Microsoft.Powershell_profile** tab, click **Edit,** click **Select All,** click **Edit,** and click **Copy.**

27. To paste the lines to the ISE profile, click the **Microsoft.PowershellISE_profile** tab, click **Edit,** and click **Paste.**

28. To save the new profile, click **File** and click **Save.**

29. Enter **$hosts** in the bottom pane and press **Enter.** Verify that the two hosts are listed.

30. Remain logged on for future lab activities.

Managing Virtual Machines with the Hyper-V Management Library

With the Hyper-V Management Library, you can perform tasks more efficiently. You can execute a one-line command on several virtual machines to quickly perform a task that would require numerous "points and clicks" in the GUI. The cmdlets described in this section provide information about host computers and virtual machines, control the state of virtual machines, and enable you to work with virtual machine properties.

Obtaining Information about a Virtual Machine

The management library has a number of cmdlets that determine the status of virtual machines on a given host computer. To save time when working with these cmdlets, you created an **array variable** named $hosts in the previous section to hold the two names of the host computers. To see the names of the host computers and the running virtual machines, enter the commands shown in Figure 10-19.

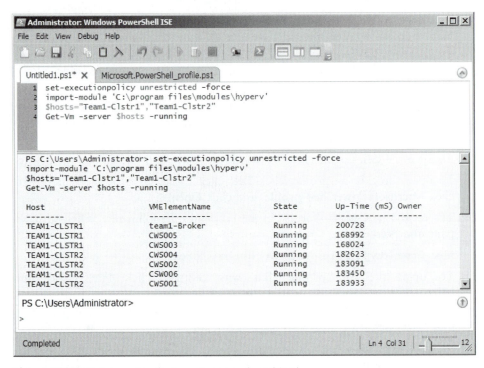

Figure 10-19 Script used to find running virtual machines

Source: Microsoft Windows PowerShell ISE, Windows Server 2008 R2 SP1

Use the `Get-VM -server $hosts -running` command to obtain a list of running virtual machines on the cluster servers. Other options are available to help you find different information. To learn more about a command, use the `Get-Help` cmdlet.

Table 10-10 provides a list of `Get` cmdlets you can use with virtual machines, along with the more useful properties returned by each cmdlet. These cmdlets work for commands entered in the following format:

`Get-XXX [VMName] -server $hosts`

where *XXX* represents the cmdlet and `[VMName]` represents one or more virtual machine names. For example, you use the wildcard `CWS*` in place of `[VMName]` to represent the six virtual machines running in the private cloud, as shown in Figure 10-20. Use the `-server $Hosts` notation to specify the host computers and locate the virtual machines.

You work with the `Get` cmdlets in Activity 10-4.

Cmdlet	Properties Returned for One or More Virtual Machines
Get-VM	VMHost, VMElementName, State, Uptime, Owner
Get-VMSummary	VMElementName, CPUCount, UpTimeFormatted, IpAddress, EnabledState, MemoryUsage
Get-VMSettingData	VMElementName, BootOrder, Created
Get-VMMemory	VMElementName, DynamicEnabled, VirtualQuantity, Limit, Reservation, Weight, Buffer
Get-VMCPUCount	VMElementName, Quantity, Limit, Reservation, Weight, Cores/Socket, SocketCount
Get-VMProcessor	VMName, SpeedMHz, Load %
Get-VMDiskController	VMElementName, ElementName
Get-VMDisk	VMElementName, ControllerName, DiskPath
Get-VMNIC	VMElementName, Switch

Table 10-10 **Cmdlets that provide information about virtual machines**

© Cengage Learning 2014

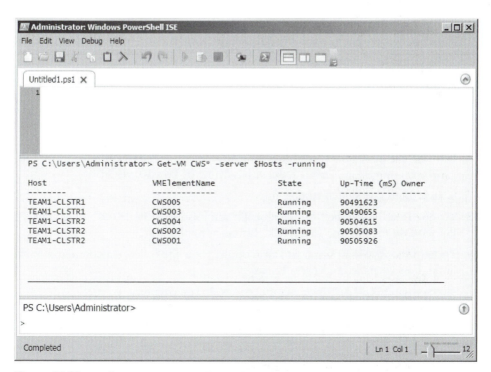

Figure 10-20 ISE showing `Get-VM` cmdlet with wildcard for finding virtual machine names

Source: Microsoft Windows PowerShell ISE, Windows Server 2008 R2 SP1

Activity 10-4: Working with the Hyper-V Library Get Cmdlets

Time Required: 45 minutes

Objective: Practice using the Get cmdlets in the Hyper-V library.

Description: In this activity, your team practices using the Get cmdlets in the Hyper-V library. You examine information about the virtual machines running in the private cloud. Table 10-11 provides the team member assignments for this activity.

Team Member	Steps	Host Computer
1	1-15	MGMT
2	16, 8-15	
3	17, 8-15	

Table 10-11   Team member assignments for Activity 10-4

© Cengage Learning 2014

1. If necessary, switch the KVM switch to port 1.

2. If necessary, log on to your MGMT server with a username of *Team1*\Administrator, substituting your team name for *Team1*. Enter a password of **P@ssw0rd**.

3. Switch the KVM switch to port 2.

4. Log on to your CLSTR1 server with a username of *Team1*\Administrator, substituting your team name for *Team1*. Enter a password of **P@ssw0rd**.

5. Switch the KVM switch to port 3.

6. Log on to your CLSTR2 server with a username of *Team1*\Administrator, substituting your team name for *Team1*. Enter a password of **P@ssw0rd**.

7. Switch the KVM switch to port 1.

8. To open the PowerShell ISE session in administrator mode, right-click the **PowerShell ISE** icon on the desktop, and click **Run as administrator**.

9. To load the Hyper-V Management module, enter the following command at the prompt in the bottom pane, and press **Enter**:

```
import-module 'c:\program files\modules\hyperv'
```

If the Hyper-V Management library is loaded more than once per PowerShell session, the management commands will produce an invalid class error.

10. To discover which virtual machines are running, enter the following command at the prompt in the bottom pane, and press **Enter**:

    `Get-VM -server $Hosts -running`

11. To see only the CWS virtual machines, press the up arrow, insert **CWS*** between Get-VM and -server in the previous command, and then press **Enter**.

To modify a previous command, press the up arrow and edit the line.

12. To see the VM summary information, enter the following command at the prompt in the bottom pane, and press **Enter**:

    `Get-VMSummary CWS* -server $Hosts`

13. To see the output in grid format, modify the previous command at the prompt in the bottom pane, and then press **Enter**. The modified command is shown below. When you finish, close the gridview window.

    `Get-VMSummary CWS* -server $Hosts | Out-Gridview`

14. Repeat Step 12 for the following cmdlets: Get-VMSettingData, Get-VMMemory, Get-VMCPUCount, Get-VMProcessor, Get-VMDiskController, Get-VMDisk, and Get-VMNIC.

15. Close the ISE window.

16. Repeat Steps 8 through 15. Enter the cmdlets from the MGMT server.

17. Repeat Steps 8 through 15. Enter the cmdlets from the MGMT server.

18. Remain logged on for further lab activities.

Working with the Properties of a Virtual Machine

You can use the eight commands shown in Table 10-12 to change the state or resources for one or more virtual machines. The Start-VM, Stop-VM, and Save-VM cmdlets work the same way as they work in Hyper-V. The Set-VMState cmdlet sets virtual machines in the running, stopped, or suspended (paused) state. For an orderly shutdown, use Invoke-VMShutdown. The Set-VM, Set-VMMemory, and Set-VMCPUCount cmdlets mirror the equivalent Get cmdlets listed in Table 10-10. You work with the Set cmdlets in Activity 10-5. You work with the Test cmdlets in Activity 10-6.

Cmdlet	Action for One or More Virtual Machines
Start-VM	Puts the virtual machine in the Running state
Stop-VM	Puts the virtual machine in the Stopped state
Save-VM	Puts the virtual machine in the Suspended (saved) state
Set-VMState	Sets the virtual machine state to Running, Stopped, Suspended
Invoke-VMShutdown	Instructs the OS to begin an orderly shutdown
Set-VM	Provides options for name, notes, boot order, start-up, shutdown, and recovery
Set-VMMemory	Sets the memory resources allocated
Set-VMCPUCount	Sets the CPU resources allocated
Test-Admin	Checks to see if the current session has administrator privileges
Test-VHD	Tests the working state of a disk
Test-VMHeartbeat	Tests to see if the VM is alive
Test-Path	Determines whether all elements of a path exist
Test-Connection	Pings one or more computers
Test-ComputerSecureChannel	Tests and repairs the secure channel between the local computer and its domain

Table 10-12   Cmdlets that work with the state or resources of one or more virtual machines

© Cengage Learning 2014

Activity 10-5: Working with a Hyper-V Library `Set` Cmdlet

Time Required: 45 minutes

Objective: Practice using a `Set` cmdlet in the Hyper-V library.

Description: In this activity, your team practices using a `Set` cmdlet in the Hyper-V library to change the state of virtual machines. Table 10-13 provides the team member assignments for this activity.

Team Member	Steps	Host Computer
1	1-16	MGMT
2	17, 9-16	
3	18, 9-16, 19	

Table 10-13   Team member assignments for Activity 10-5

© Cengage Learning 2014

1. If necessary, switch the KVM switch to port 1.

2. If necessary, log on to your MGMT server with a username of *Team1\Administrator*, substituting your team name for *Team1*. Enter a password of **P@ssw0rd**.

3. If necessary, switch the KVM switch to port 2.

4. If necessary, log on to your CLSTR1 server with a username of *Team1\Administrator*, substituting your team name for *Team1*. Enter a password of **P@ssw0rd**.

5. If necessary, switch the KVM switch to port 3.

6. If necessary, log on to your CLSTR2 server with a username of *Team1\Administrator*, substituting your team name for *Team1*. Enter a password of **P@ssw0rd**.

7. Switch the KVM switch to port 1.

8. To start the Virtual Machine Manager with the virtual machines for CLSTR1, double-click the **SCVMM Admin Console** icon on the desktop. Click the **Virtual Machines** bar in the lower-left corner, expand **Self Service**, and click *Team1-clstr1*, substituting your team name for *Team1*.

9. To open the PowerShell ISE session in administrator mode, right-click the **PowerShell ISE** icon on the desktop, and click **Run as administrator**.

10. To load the Hyper-V Management module, enter the following command at the prompt in the bottom pane, and press **Enter**:

    ```
    import-module 'c:\program files\modules\hyperv'
    ```

 If the Hyper-V Management library is loaded more than once per PowerShell session, the management commands will produce an invalid class error.

11. To start the source and destination virtual machines on CLSTR1, enter the following command at the prompt in the bottom pane. Substitute your team name for *Team1*. When you finish, press **Enter**.

    ```
    Start-Vm source,destination -server Team1-clstr1 -wait
    ```

12. To verify progress, return to the Virtual Machine Manager window.

13. To shut down the source and destination virtual machines on CLSTR1, enter the following command at the prompt in the bottom pane. Substitute your team name for *Team1*. When you finish, press **Enter**, and then click **Yes to All**.

    ```
    Invoke-VMShutdown source,destination -server Team1-clstr1
    ```

14. To verify progress, return to the Virtual Machine Manager window.

15. To view the memory allocations for the source and destination virtual machines on CLSTR1, enter the following command at the prompt in the bottom pane. Substitute your team name for *Team1*. When you finish, press **Enter**.

    ```
    Get-VMMemory source,destination -server Team1-clstr1
    ```

16. To set dynamic memory allocations for the source and destination virtual machines on CLSTR1, enter the following command at the prompt in the top pane. Substitute your team name for *Team1*. When you finish, press **Enter**.

    ```
    Get-VM source,destination -server Team1-clstr1 | Set-VMMemory
    -limit 1GB -buffer 20 -weight 5000 -dynamic
    ```

17. Repeat Steps 9 through 16 for CLSTR2. Enter the cmdlets from the MGMT server.

18. Repeat Steps 9 through 16 for CLSTR1. Enter the cmdlets from the MGMT server.

19. Remain logged on for future lab activities.

Activity 10-6: Working with Hyper-V Library `Test` Cmdlets

Time Required: 45 minutes

Objective: Practice using the `Test` cmdlets in the Hyper-V library.

Description: In this activity, your team practices using the `Test` cmdlets in the Hyper-V library. Table 10-14 provides the team member assignments for this activity.

Team Member	Steps	Host Computer
1	1-12	MGMT
2	13, 8-12	
3	14, 8-12, 15	

Table 10-14 Team member assignments for Activity 10-6

© Cengage Learning 2014

1. If necessary, switch the KVM switch to port 1.

2. If necessary, log on to your MGMT server with a username of *Team1***Administrator**, substituting your team name for *Team1*. Enter a password of **P@ssw0rd**.

3. If necessary, switch the KVM switch to port 2.

4. If necessary, log on to your CLSTR1 server with a username of *Team1***Administrator**, substituting your team name for *Team1*. Enter a password of **P@ssw0rd**.

5. If necessary, switch the KVM switch to port 3.

6. If necessary, log on to your CLSTR2 server with a username of *Team1***Administrator**, substituting your team name for *Team1*. Enter a password of **P@ssw0rd**.

7. Return to the MGMT server. To start the Virtual Machine Manager with the virtual machines for CLSTR1, double-click the **SCVMM Admin Console** icon on the desktop. Click the **Virtual Machines** bar in the lower-left corner, expand **Self Service**, and click *Team1*-**clstr1**, substituting your team name for *Team1*.

8. To open the ISE, double-click the **Windows PowerShell ISE** icon on the desktop.

9. To load the Hyper-V Management library, enter the following command and press **Enter**:

   `import-module 'C:\program files\modules\hyperv'`

If the Hyper-V Management library is loaded more than once per PowerShell session, the management commands will produce an invalid class error.

10. To see if the virtual machines on CLSTR1 are alive, enter the following command at the prompt in the bottom pane (substituting your team name for *Team1*), and press **Enter**:

   `Test-VMHeartbeat source,destination -server Team1-clstr1`

11. To test the working state of the VHDs for the source and destination virtual machines on CLSTR1, enter the following command at the prompt in the bottom pane (substituting your team name for *Team1*), and press **Enter**:

    Test-VHD source,destination -server *Team1*-clstr1

12. Close the Windows PowerShell ISE window.

13. Repeat Steps 8 through 12 for CLSTR2. Enter the cmdlets from the MGMT server.

14. Repeat Steps 8 through 12 for CLSTR1. Enter the cmdlets from the MGMT server.

15. Remain logged on for future lab activities.

Creating Scripts to Manage the Private Cloud

When you need to perform repetitive tasks, you can create scripts in PowerShell.

Creating Scripts to Manage Self-Service Users

Another powerful feature of PowerShell is that you can pipe the cmdlets by property. Consider this command from Activity 10-5:

```
Get-VM source,destination -server Team1-clstr1 | Set-VMMemory -limit 1GB
-buffer 20 -weight 5000 -dynamic
```

The `Get-VM` cmdlet identifies the source and destination virtual machines that run on the Team1-clstr1 server. The `Set-VMMemory` cmdlet works with the properties passed to it. To see the properties passed from `Get-VM source,destination -server Team1-clstr1`, you run only the first cmdlet. The output is shown in Figure 10-21. The Hosts and VMElement-Name property values are piped to the `Set-VMMemory` cmdlet.

Now that you know the property values, you could set up the properties and values in a spreadsheet. The column headings would be Hosts and VMElementName; two rows would describe

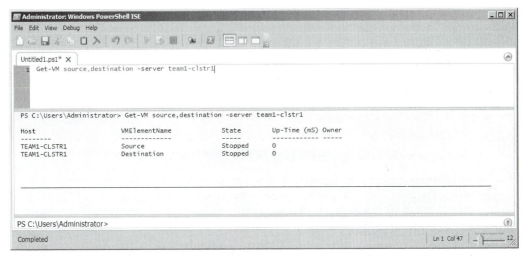

Figure 10-21 Properties passed by `Get-VM` cmdlet

Source: Microsoft Windows PowerShell ISE, Windows Server 2008 R2 SP1

the hosts and virtual machines. By knowing the property names, you can build a spreadsheet, import it, and pipe it to a cmdlet. This technique allows you to create hundreds of items quickly.

One repetitive task for which this technique would be effective is the creation of numerous new users in Active Directory. For example, you could add the user account for John Doe to Active Directory using the following command:

```
New-ADUser -Name "JDoe" -SamAccountName "JDoe"
-GivenName "John" -Surname "Doe" -DisplayName "John Doe"
-Path 'CN=Users,DC=Team1,DC=local'
-AccountPassword (ConvertTo-SecureString "P@ssw0rd" -AsPlainText -force)
```

Recall that each property is preceded by a hyphen. For example, `-GivenName` is the given or first name, `-Surname` is the last name, and so on. The `-SamAccountName` is the username used to log on. The `-Path` property provides the organizational unit and domain name to place the created user account. A secure password is created for `-AccountPassword` by the conversion code placed after the property.

The items that change for each user are `Name`, `SamAccountName`, `GivenName`, `Surname`, and `DisplayName`. These items would become column headings for the spreadsheet. Figure 10-22 shows a completed spreadsheet for four new users. You will import the spreadsheet and pipe it to the `New-ADUser` command to create the user accounts, as explained in Activity 10-7.

	A	B	C	D	E	F	G	H
1	Name	SamAccountName	GivenName	Surname	DisplayName			
2	FDunn	FDunn	Frank	Dunn	Frank Dunn			
3	REspinosa	REspinosa	Ruben	Espinosa	Ruben Espinosa			
4	JHagan	JHagan	Joan	Hagan	Joan Hagan			
5	DHawk	DHawk	Dave	Hawk	Dave Hawk			
6								
7								
8								
9								

Figure 10-22 Spreadsheet used to input to `Add-ADUser` command

Source: Microsoft Excel 2010

The next task is to create a self-service user role for each user, which will require you to capture the script, as explained in Activity 10-7. You can view the script in Notepad and save the PowerShell script for further analysis. Figure 10-23 shows the changes that need to be made the "generalize" the script:

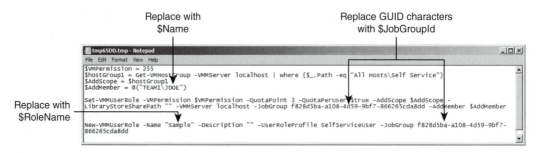

Figure 10-23 Captured self-service role script

Source: Microsoft Notepad, Windows Server 2008 R2 SP1

- The user's name needs to replace JDoe.
- Create a role name by attaching the characters *Role_* to the user name.
- Generate a Globally Unique Identifier (GUID) for the JobGroup to enable tracking of the commands within the script.

To create the `RoleName`, concatenate the characters to `$UserName` and place the result at `$RoleName`:

```
$RoleName = "Role_" + $UserName
```

To create the GUID, you must create a new GUID object:

```
$JobGroupID = [Guid]::NewGuid().ToString()
```

To process each user name, you need to introduce a new construct—`foreach`—which allows each line to be processed. To get started, use the `Import-CSV` cmdlet to place the file's contents at `$Users`. The column headings are objects, and PowerShell takes care of the necessary conversions. Each line can now be processed by the cmdlets that you place between the braces { }. The first command within the braces pulls the name for each user and places the value at `$Username`.

```
$Users = Import-CSV SelfServiceUsers.csv
foreach($Row in $Users) {
$UserName = $Row.Name
    <Cmdlets go here>
}
```

Figure 10-24 shows the completed script. You complete the generalized script in Activity 10-7.

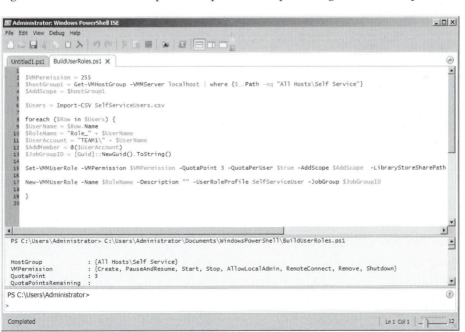

Figure 10-24 Completed self-service role script with generalizations

Source: Microsoft Windows PowerShell ISE, Windows Server 2008 R2 SP1

Activity 10-7: Creating Self-Service User Roles

Time Required: 30 minutes

Objective: Create self-service user roles.

Description: In this activity, your team practices creating self-service roles. First, you will copy the SelfServiceUsers.csv spreadsheet file to the MGMT server. Next, you will create a short script to import the users and pipe them to the `New-ADUser` cmdlet to create user accounts.

Table 10-15 provides the team member assignments for this activity.

Team Member	Steps	Host Computer
1	1-10	MGMT
2	11-19	
3	20-29	
1	30-39	
2	40-42	

Table 10-15 Team member assignments for Activity 10-7

© Cengage Learning 2014

To complete this activity, you need to create the spreadsheet with the four users shown in Figure 10-22. You must save the spreadsheet in CSV format.

1. If necessary, switch the KVM switch to port 1.

2. If necessary, log on to your MGMT server with a username of *Team1***Administrator**, substituting your team name for *Team1*. Enter a password of **P@ssw0rd**.

3. If necessary, switch the KVM switch to port 2.

4. If necessary, log on to your CLSTR1 server with a username of *Team1***Administrator**, substituting your team name for *Team1*. Enter a password of **P@ssw0rd**.

5. If necessary, switch the KVM switch to port 3.

6. If necessary, log on to your CLSTR2 server with a username of *Team1***Administrator**, substituting your team name for *Team1*. Enter a password of **P@ssw0rd**.

7. Switch the KVM switch to port 1.

8. If necessary, start the Virtual Machine Manager by double-clicking the **SCVMM Admin Console** icon on the desktop.

9. To access the USB drive that contains the spreadsheet file, click **Start**, double-click **MGMT**, and double-click the name of the USB drive. Right-click the name of the spreadsheet file, and click **Copy**.

10. To place the file in the Administrators folder, double-click **Local Disk (C:)**, double-click **Users**, double-click **Administrator**, click **Organize**, and click **Paste**. Close the Windows Explorer windows.

11. To open the ISE, double-click the **Windows PowerShell ISE** icon on the desktop.

12. To test the import of the spreadsheet file, enter **Import-CSV c:\users\administrator\ SelfServiceUsers.csv** in the bottom pane, and press **Enter**.

13. Enter `Import-Module ActiveDirectory` in the top pane and press **Enter**.

14. Enter the following script in the top pane. Type the entire command on one line. When you finish, press **Enter**.

    ```
    Import-CSV c:\users\administrator\SelfServiceUsers.csv | New-ADUser
    -Path 'CN=Users,DC=Team1,DC=local' -AccountPassword (ConvertTo-
    SecureString "P@ssw0rd" -AsPlainText -force)
    ```

15. To save the script file, click **File**, click **Save As**, enter **CreateSelfServiceUserAccounts.PS1** over the text "Untitled1," and then click **Save**.

16. To run the script, press the **F5** key.

17. Review the middle pane. Return to the top pane and make corrections as needed.

18. To determine that the user accounts were created, enter `Get-AdUser -identity dhawk` in the bottom pane and press **Enter**.

19. Verify that the properties are listed for David Hawk, the last user processed.

20. To load the Virtual Machine Manager snap-in, enter the following command in the top pane, and then press **Enter**.

    ```
    Add-PSSnapin 'Microsoft.SystemCenter.VirtualMachineManager'
    ```

21. To create the script file for the new user role, return to Virtual Machine Manager, click the **Administration** bar in the lower-left corner, and click **User Roles** in the left pane. Click **New user role** in the right pane, enter **Sample** as the User role name, and click **Next**. Click **Add**, enter **Jdoe** in the **Enter the object names to select** text box, click **Check Names**, click **OK**, and click **Next**. Check the **Self Service** check box, and click **Next**. Click the **Only selected actions** button, clear the **Checkpoint** check box, and click **Next**. Click the **Allow users to create new virtual machines** check box, click **Add**, click **SSDeploy**, and click **OK**. Click the **Set Quota for deployed virtual machines** check box, change the **Maximum quota points allowed for this user role** to 3, and click **Next** twice.

22. To view and save the script, click **View Script**, click **File**, and click **Save As**. Click the **Save as type** arrow, click **All Files**, enter **CapturedRoleScript.PS1** as the filename, and click **Save**.

23. Return to the Create User Role Wizard, click **Cancel**, and click **Yes**.

24. Return to the ISE, click **File**, click **Open**, click **CapturedRoleScript**, and click **Open**.

 To help modify the captured script, refer back to Figure 10-24 for the finished BuildUserRoles.PS1 script.

25. Click the line beneath the $AddScope line, and press **Enter** twice.

26. To add the command line that imports the user's names, enter the following command and press **Enter**:

    $Users = Import-CSV c:\users\administrator\SelfServiceUsers.csv

27. To add the command line that loops through $Users, enter the following command and press **Enter**:

    foreach ($Row in $Users) {

28. To add the command line that pulls the name for each user, enter **$UserName = $Row. Name** and press **Enter**.

29. To add the command line that creates the $RoleName by concatenating the characters *Role_* to $UserName, enter **$RoleName = "Role_" + $UserName**, and press **Enter**.

30. To add the command line that creates $UserAccount, enter the following command, substituting your team name for *Team1*. When you finish, press **Enter**.

    $UserAccount = "Team1\" + $Username

31. To add the command line that creates $AddMember, enter the following command and press **Enter**:

    $AddMember = @($UserAccount)

32. To add the line that generates the GUID for $JobGroupID, enter the following command and press **Enter**:

    $JobGroupID = [Guid]::NewGuid().ToString()

33. To replace the first GUID, scroll through the Set-VMMUserRole line to the right, delete the GUID characters, and enter **$JobGroupID**.

34. To replace the string "Sample" with the generated role name, scroll through the New-VMMUserRole line to the right, enter **$RoleName** over the word "Sample," and press **Enter**.

35. To replace the second GUID, scroll through the New-VMMUserRole line to the right, delete the GUID characters, and enter **$JobGroupID**.

36. To close the foreach { line, enter a closing **}** and press **Enter**.

37. To save the file, click **File**, click **Save As**, enter **BuildUserRoles.PS1** over the text "CapturedRoleScript," and then click **Save**.

38. To run the script, press the **F5** key.

39. Review the middle pane. Return to the top pane and make corrections as needed.

40. To verify that the self-service user roles were created, enter **Get-VMMUserRole Role_DHawk**, and press **Enter**.

41. Scroll down and review the middle pane.

42. Remain logged on for future lab activities.

Rapidly Provisioning Virtual Machines

Rapid provisioning speeds up the creation of virtual machines, and permits you to "prestage" a copy of the virtual hard disk prior to creating the virtual machine on the host computer. You cannot perform this task from the Virtual Machine Manager GUI; you must use

PowerShell. The time needed to copy the virtual hard disk is reduced because a copy over the local area network is faster than a Background Intelligent Transfer Service (BITS) copy, which uses less than the available bandwidth.

During rapid provisioning, you basically do everything that the GUI would do, with one exception—you add an extra cmdlet:

```
Move-VirtualHardDisk -Bus 0 -LUN 0 -IDE -Path $VHDName
```

This cmdlet signifies that you are moving a previously created virtual hard disk with a virtual machine. The `-Bus`, `-LUN`, and `-IDE` parameters match up with the virtual hard disk settings for the virtual machine and link up the VHD file for the virtual machine in place of the blank VHD, which was specified in the template.

Table 10-16 identifies the items that you provide to the cmdlets to deploy the virtual machine.

Parameter	Description	Example
$VMName	Virtual machine name for the current virtual machine	CWS007
$HostName	Host computer name for the current deployment	Team1-CLSTR1.Team1.local
$VHDName	Path and name for the virtual hard disk file	C:\ClusterStorage\Volume1\CWS007\ CWS007_Disk_1.vhd
$VMMServer	Management server name	Team1-MGMT.Team1.local
$OwnerID	Logon name	Team1\Administrator
$PATH	Location of virtual machine folders	C:\ClusterStorage\Volume1

Table 10-16 Variables to deploy a virtual machine

© Cengage Learning 2014

To load the cmdlets needed by the script, enter the following line:

```
Add-PSSnapin 'Microsoft.SystemCenter.VirtualMachineManager'
```

The next two lines must be updated each time the script is run. To deploy the CWS007 virtual machine on the CLSTR1 host computer, use the following lines, substituting your team name for *Team1*:

```
$VMName = "CWS007"
$Hostname = "Team1-Clstr1.Team1.Local"
```

The next three statements you enter establish values for later cmdlets:

```
$VHDName = "C:\ClusterStorage\Volume1\" + $VMName + "\BASECWS_Disk_1.vhd"
$VMMServer="Team1-MGMT.Team1.Local"
$OwnerID = "Team1\Administrator"
```

To track and tie the cmdlets together, use a GUID. To create the GUID, enter the following cmdlet:

```
$JobGuid = [System.Guid]::NewGuid().ToString()
```

To enable the script to connect to the VMM server and process commands, use the following cmdlet:

```
Get-VMMServer -ComputerName $VMMServer
```

Enter the following cmdlet to replace the blank hard disk in the template with the .vhd file for the BaseCWS virtual machine in the VMM library:

```
Move-VirtualHardDisk -Bus 0 -LUN 0 -IDE -path $VHDName -JobGroup $JobGuid
```

To retrieve the template object for the BaseCWS from the VMM library, use the following cmdlet:

```
$Template = Get-Template | Where {$_.Name -eq "TemplateBaseCWS"}
```

The last command ties everything together and deploys the new virtual machine. Enter the following cmdlet on one line:

```
New-VM -Template $Template -Name $VMName
    -Description "Rapid Provision" -Owner $OwnerID
    -VMHost $VMHost -UseLocalVirtualHardDisks
    -SkipInstallVirtualizationGuestServices -Path $HostName
    -RunAsynchronously -JobGroup $JobGuid
```

Three switches require further explanation. The `-UseLocalVirtualHardDisks` switch informs the `New-VM` cmdlet that you prestaged the virtual hard disk file and a BITS copy is not required. Because the operating system, Windows Server 2008 R2, is enlightened, you use the `-SkipInstallVirtualizationGuestServices` switch to skip adding these services. The `-RunAsynchronously` switch permits multiple cmdlets to run concurrently, resulting in reduced run times.

Figure 10-25 shows the script in the ISE that deploys the virtual machine. As the script runs, you will see two sets of output: information relating to the connection to the VMM server and the creation of the virtual machine in the center pane.

To follow the progress of the submitted job, return to the Virtual Machine Manager window, click the Virtual Machines bar in the lower-left corner, click CWS007, and click the Latest Job tab, as shown in Figure 10-26. The job might appear to hesitate when the virtual machine is started for the first time. You can connect to the virtual machine and check the progress. Before use, you need to start the virtual machine and complete the remaining configuration tasks, such as verifying regional settings and configuring IP.

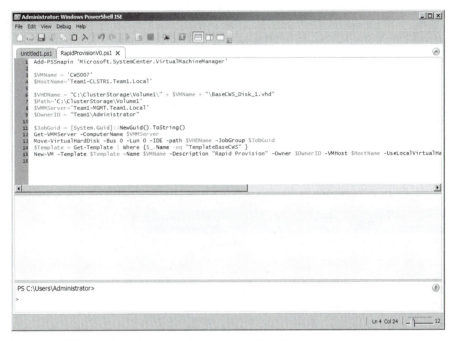

Figure 10-25 Rapid provisioning script as entered in ISE

Source: Microsoft Windows PowerShell ISE, Windows Server 2008 R2 SP1

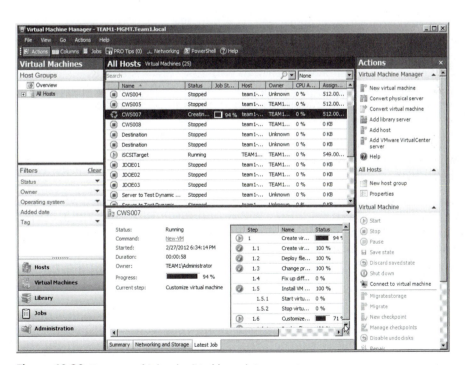

Figure 10-26 Progress of job submitted by script

Source: Microsoft Virtual Machine Manager 2008 R2 SP1, Windows Server 2008 R2 SP1

Activity 10-8: Creating a Script to Rapidly Provision Virtual Machines

Time Required: 120 minutes

Objective: Create a script to rapidly provision virtual machines.

Description: In this activity, your team practices creating scripts to rapidly provision virtual machines. First, you create a template that defines the hardware and guest operating system profiles. Next, you prestage the virtual hard disk file. Then, you create and test the script to rapidly provision the virtual machine.

Table 10-17 provides the team member assignments for this activity.

Team Member	Steps	Host Computer
1	1-14	MGMT
2	15-49	
3	50, 10-49	
	51, 10-49	
	52-54	
	55, 52-54	CLSTR2
	56, 52-54	MGMT

Table 10-17 Team member assignments for Activity 10-8

© Cengage Learning 2014

1. If necessary, switch the KVM switch to port 1.

2. If necessary, log on to your MGMT server with a username of *Team1\Administrator*, substituting your team name for *Team1*. Enter a password of **P@ssw0rd**.

3. If necessary, start the Virtual Machine Manager by double-clicking the **SCVMM Admin Console** icon on the desktop.

4. To create a library template for the BaseCWS virtual machine, click the **Library** bar in the lower-left corner, click **New template** in the right pane, and click **Browse**. Click **Blank Disk-Small**, click **OK**, and click **Next**. Enter **TemplateBaseCWS** as the Template name, and click **Next**. Click the **Hardware profile** arrow, click **HP_1N1VHD1G**, and click **Next**. Click the **Guest operating system profile** arrow, click **SP_W2K8R2SP1ENT**, and click **Next**. Click **Create**.

5. Wait for the script to be completed.

6. If necessary, switch the KVM switch to port 2.

7. If necessary, log on to your CLSTR1 server with a username of *Team1\Administrator*, substituting your team name for *Team1*. Enter a password of **P@ssw0rd**.

8. If necessary, switch the KVM switch to port 3.

9. If necessary, log on to your CLSTR2 server with a username of *Team1\Administrator*, substituting your team name for *Team1*. Enter a password of **P@ssw0rd**.

10. Switch the KVM switch to port 2.

11. To create a folder for the new virtual machine, click **Start**, click **CLSTR1**, and double-click **Local Disk (C:)**. Expand **ClusterStorage**, expand **Volume1**, click **New folder**, enter **CWS007** over the text "New Folder," and press **Enter**.

12. To copy the virtual machine hard disk file, click **Start**, and enter *Team1*-MGMT\ over the text "Search programs and files," substituting your team name for *Team1*. Click **MSSCVMMLibrary**, double-click **BaseCWS**, right-click **BaseCWS_disk_1.vhd**, click **Properties**, and click **Copy**.

13. To paste the virtual machine hard disk file, return to the Volume1 window, right-click **CWS007**, and click **Paste**.

14. Wait for the copy to be completed, and close the Windows Explorer windows.

15. Switch the KVM switch to port 1.

16. If necessary, start the Virtual Machine Manager by double-clicking the **SCVMM Admin Console** icon on the desktop.

17. To open the ISE, double-click the **Windows PowerShell ISE** icon on the desktop.

18. To load the cmdlets needed by the script, enter the following line and press **Enter**:

    ```
    Add-PSSnapin 'Microsoft.SystemCenter.VirtualMachineManager'
    ```

19. To specify the CWS007 virtual machine, enter **$VMName = "CWS007"** and press **Enter**.

20. To deploy the virtual machine on the *Team1*-Clstr1 host computer, enter the following command, substituting your team name for *Team1*. When you finish, press **Enter**.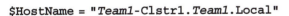

    ```
    $HostName = "Team1-Clstr1.Team1.Local"
    ```

21. To identify the virtual hard disk filename, enter the following command on one line, and then press **Enter**:

    ```
    $VHDName = "C:\ClusterStorage\Volume1\" + $VMName + "\BaseCWS_
    Disk_1.vhd"
    ```

22. To provide the path to the virtual machine folders, enter the following command on one line, and then press **Enter**:

    ```
    $PATH = "C:\ClusterStorage\Volume1"
    ```

23. To provide the name of the VMM server, enter the following command, substituting your team name for *Team1*. When you finish, press **Enter**.

    ```
    $VMMServer="Team1-MGMT.Team1.Local"
    ```

24. To provide the name for the virtual machine owner, enter the following command, substituting your team name for *Team1*. When you finish, press **Enter**.

    ```
    $OwnerID = "Team1\Administrator"
    ```

25. To create the GUID, enter the following command and press **Enter**:

    ```
    $JobGuid = [System.Guid]::NewGuid().ToString()
    ```

26. To enable the script to connect to the VMM server and process commands, enter the following command on one line, and then press **Enter**:

```
Get-VMMServer -ComputerName $VMMServer
```

27. To replace the blank hard disk in the template with the .vhd file, enter the following command on one line and press **Enter**:

```
Move-VirtualHardDisk -Bus 0 -LUN 0 -IDE -path $VHDName -JobGroup
$JobGuid
```

28. To retrieve the template object for BaseCWS from the VMM library, enter the following command on one line and press **Enter**:

```
$Template = Get-Template | Where {$_.Name -eq "TemplateBaseCWS"}
```

29. To deploy the virtual machine, enter the following command on one line, and then press **Enter**:

```
New-VM -Template $Template -Name $VMName
        -Description "Rapid Provision" -Owner $OwnerID
        -VMHost $HostName -UseLocalVirtualHardDisks
        -SkipInstallVirtualizationGuestServices
        -Path $Path -RunAsynchronously
        -JobGroup $JobGuid
```

30. To save the file, click **File**, click **Save As**, enter **RapidProvisionV0.PS1** over the text "Untitled1," and then click **Save**.

31. To run the script, press the **F5** key.

32. Review the middle pane. Return to the top pane and make corrections as needed.

33. To view the job's progress, return to the Virtual Machine Manager window, click the **Virtual Machines** bar in the lower-left corner, click **CWS007**, and click the **Latest Job** tab.

34. When the job has completed, close the job. Return to the Virtual Machines view in the Virtual Machine Manager.

35. To attach the network adapter, right-click **CWS007**, click **Properties**, and click the **Hardware Configuration** tab. Click **Network Adapter**, click the **Connected to** button, click the **Connected to** arrow, click **Private VM – Virtual Network**, and then click **OK**.

36. To start the virtual machine, click **Start** in the right pane, and click **Connect to virtual machine**.

37. To log on to the virtual machine, click **Ctrl-Alt-Del** on the menu bar, and then enter **P@ssw0rd** as the password.

38. To enter the IP configuration, click **Configure Networking**, and right-click **Local Area Connection**. Click **Properties**, clear the **Internet Protocol Version 6 (TCP/IPv6)** check box, and then click **OK**.

When the Set Network Location window appears, click Work, and then click Close.

39. If necessary, reset the IP configuration, right-click **Local Area Connection**, click **Diagnose**, and then click **Close**.

40. Close the Network Connections window.

41. To start Windows activation, click **Activate Windows**.

42. If your school uses volume license product keys, click **Product Key**, ask your instructor to enter the product key, and click **Next**. If your school uses product keys other than volume license keys, click **Product Key**, enter the product key provided by your instructor, and click **Next**.

43. Wait for Windows activation to be completed, and click **Close**.

44. Close the Virtual Machine viewer window, and then return to the Virtual Machine Manager window.

45. Right-click **CWS007**, click **Shut down**, and click **Yes**. Wait for the virtual machine to shut down.

46. To open the Failover Cluster Manager console, click **Start**, point to **Administrative Tools**, and click **Failover Cluster Manager**.

47. Expand *Team1*-**Cluster.***Team1***.Local**, substituting your team name for *Team1*. Click **Services and Applications**.

48. Click **Configure a Service or Application** in the right pane, and click **Next**. Scroll down and click **Virtual Machine**, click **Next**, click the **CWS007** check box, click **Next** twice, and click **Finish**.

49. To restart the virtual machine, click **CWS007**, and click **Start virtual machine** in the right pane.

50. Repeat Steps 10 through 49 for the RapidProvisionV1 script, deploying CWS008 on host computer CLSTR2. Enter the cmdlets from the MGMT server.

51. Repeat Steps 10 through 49 for the RapidProvisionV2 script, deploying CWS009 on host computer CLSTR1. Enter the cmdlets from the MGMT server.

52. Switch the KVM switch to port 2.

53. To shut down the host computer, click **Start**, click the arrow next to **Log off**, click **Shut down**, click the **Option** arrow, click **Operating System: Reconfiguration (Planned)**, and then click **OK**. If necessary, click **Yes**.

54. Wait for the host computer to shut down.

55. Complete Steps 52 through 54 for CLSTR2, which is on KVM switch port 3.

56. Complete Steps 52 through 54 for MGMT, which is on KVM switch port 1.

Chapter Summary

- PowerShell is a new Windows command-line shell designed especially for server administrators. You can use the features and components of PowerShell to perform the following tasks:
  - Install the PowerShell Management Library for Hyper-V, which currently includes 80 functions.

- Work with PowerShell cmdlet nouns and verbs.
- Use the pipe operator to string cmdlets and perform complex tasks.
- Work with PowerShell sorting, filtering, and formatting cmdlets.
- Input data in text and comma-separated variable formats.
- Access system information with Get cmdlets.
- Use the PowerShell Management Library for Hyper-V to manage virtual machines.
- Generalize scripts generated by Virtual Machine Manager.
- Create scripts to manage self-service users.
- Create scripts to rapidly provision virtual machines.

Key Terms

.NET Framework   A software environment that runs primarily in Microsoft Windows.

array variable   A fixed collection of variable elements that share the same data type and name.

CodePlex   Microsoft's open source project hosting Web site.

comma-separated values (CSV)   A file format in which columns of data are separated by commas.

parameters   In PowerShell, settings that are used to customize the actions of a cmdlet.

pipelining   In PowerShell, joining two or more cmdlets with the pipe operator (|).

positional parameters   Parameters that must be entered in a specific position within a cmdlet.

switch   In PowerShell, a command that provides controlling information to indicate that a cmdlet should take a particular action.

tab autocomplete   A common feature of command-line shells in which the shell automatically fills in partially typed commands.

Review Questions

1. _Powershell_ is a new Windows shell designed for use by server administrators.

2. The .NET Framework _____. (Choose all correct answers.)
   - a. is pronounced *dot net*
   - b. runs on numerous operating systems
   - c. runs primarily in Windows
   - d. supports several programming languages, including PowerShell
   - e. has a large library

3. PowerShell's equivalent of the DIR command is the _get-child item_ cmdlet.

4. Examples of PowerShell verbs include _____. (Choose all correct answers.)

   a. `Get`

   b. `Set`

   c. `Copy`

   d. `Paste`

   e. `Add`

   f. `Remove`

5. Examples of PowerShell verb/noun pairs include _____. (Choose all correct answers.)

   a. `Get-Alias`

   b. `Get-Command`

   c. `Import-Module`

   d. `New-Object`

   e. `Start-Service`

6. When using the `Get-Help` cmdlet, you can use which of the following switches? (Choose all correct answers.)

   a. `-example`

   b. `-verbose`

   c. `-detailed`

   d. `-full`

   e. `-technical`

7. Which of the following spellings would be valid in PowerShell? (Choose all correct answers.)

   a. `gEt-dATe`

   b. `Get-date`

   c. `GET-date`

   d. `Get-DATE`

   e. `GET-DATE`

   f. `GET-DAT`

8. By using the _____ feature, you can reduce the number of characters you type by pressing the Tab key.

9. Which of the following are valid wildcards? (Choose all correct answers.)

   a. `F*`

   b. `?un`

   c. `[FSP]un`

   d. `[F-P]un`

   e. `[F*P]un`

10. Use *pipe operator* to take the output of one cmdlet and pass it to the next cmdlet.

11. Which of the following cmdlets can you use between cmdlets to control output? (Choose all correct answers.)

    a. `Sort-Object`

    b. `Where-Object`

    c. `Filter-Object`

    d. `Object-Sort`

    e. `Get-Child`

12. Which of the following options format output? (Choose all correct answers.)

    a. `Format-List`

    b. `Format-Narrow`

    c. `Format-Table`

    d. `Format-Wide`

    e. `Format-Select`

    f. `Format-Column`

13. Which of the following options control screen output? (Choose all correct answers.)

    a. `Out-File`

    b. `Out-Spread`

    c. `Out-Host`

    d. `Out-Null`

    e. `Out-Printer`

    f. `Out-String`

14. Which of the following are reasons to learn PowerShell? (Choose all correct answers.)

    a. Microsoft considers it important.

    b. Most Microsoft products will eventually use it.

    c. You can automate routine tasks, which makes your job easier.

    d. Many GUIs are PowerShell front ends.

    e. Microsoft certification exams contain PowerShell questions.

15. To make PowerShell easier to work with, Microsoft provides a GUI called the _ISE_ _____.

16. _Codeplex_ _____ is an open source project hosting Web site from Microsoft.

17. You use a/an _____ to set up the PowerShell environment.

18. Which of the following are examples of cmdlets in the PowerShell Management Library for Hyper-V? (Choose all correct answers.)

   a. `Get-VM`

   b. `Set-VMMemory`

   c. `Get-Date`

   d. `Get-VMCPUCount`

   e. `Get-VMSummary`

   f. `Start-VM`

   g. `Stop-VM`

   h. `Clone-VM`

19. Use the _____ cmdlet to input files that have column names with rows of data.

20. _____ is an example of a task for deploying virtual machines that requires the use of PowerShell scripts.

Case Projects

CASE PROJECTS

Case 10-1: Reasons to Use PowerShell

You overhear a conversation about PowerShell before class between two of your classmates. One classmate says he can perform all needed tasks from the VMM GUI. The other is not as sure. They ask for your opinion. What will you say? Write a one-page summary of your opinion.

Case 10-2: Management Library for Hyper-V Presentation

You have been asked to give a short presentation about the use of James O'Neill's management library for Hyper-V. Prepare a one-page "cheat sheet" of relevant cmdlets used to manage virtual machines with the library.

Case 10-3: Migrating Virtual Machines from the Library

Using the generalization techniques in this chapter, prepare a script to migrate virtual machines using the Deploy Virtual Machine Wizard in the VMM Library view. You will need to create a virtual machine and place it in the library for migration.

Case 10-4: Modifying a Rapid Provisioning Script

Using the PowerShell input techniques of your choice, modify the script in Activity 10-8 to deploy two or more virtual machines while balancing the deployment between the two clustered host computers.

Author's Configuration

If you have wondered what hardware and software configurations the author used for this book, this appendix provides the details. Although your hardware may differ, you should be able to complete the activities in this book on similar hardware if you pay attention to the device details.

Hardware Overview

Figure A-1 shows the network diagram for a cloud station. The two clustered servers are shown in the box. Three 5-port gigabit switches provide for the Heartbeat, Management, and Storage networks. A firewall on the Private VM network isolates the virtual machines while providing NAT services. A third server provides support for a number of required roles: virtual machine management, Active Directory for account management, Web portal for student VM access, and a storage server to provide storage for the virtual machine files.

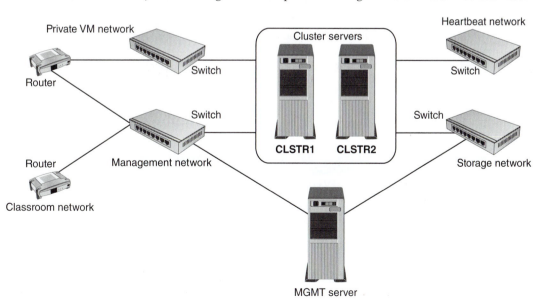

Figure A-1 Cloud station network diagram

© Cengage Learning 2014

To cluster the two servers, identical hardware must be used on both. The author leased two Dell servers with the specifications shown in Table A-1.

Dell PowerEdge 110 Mod 2 Server	
Processor	Intel® Pentium® G620 2.60 GHz, VT-x support
Memory	8 GB
Hard drive	250 GB, 7.2 K RPM SATA 3.5
DVD	16X DVD
Network (4 NICs)	One on-board single gigabit network adapter Three Broadcom 5722 1GbE Single Port NICs, PCIe-1

Table A-1 Cluster server hardware

© Cengage Learning 2014

For the third server (see Table A-2), the author used a server that was available from a previous project. A server such as the Dell PowerEdge 1900, with a single gigabit network adapter and a 2-TB SATA drive, should suffice for the third server.

Dell PowerEdge 1900 Server	
Processor	Two Intel ® Xeon E5310 processors with VT-x support
Memory	8 GB
Hard drive	250 GB 7.2 K RPM SATA 3.5 2 TB 7.2 K RPM SATA 3.5
DVD	16X DVD
Network (2 NICs)	Two on-board single gigabit network adapters

Table A-2 Hardware for third server

© Cengage Learning 2014

Table A-3 shows the network devices from the Netgear ProSafe line.

Network Devices	
Firewalls (2)	Two Netgear FVS318G ProSafe Gigabit VPN firewalls
Switches (3)	Three Netgear GS105 Desktop Switch ProSafe Gigabit
Switch	One Netgear ProSafe Plus GS105E switch with VLAN

Table A-3 Network devices

© Cengage Learning 2014

To simplify and correctly identify network connections, Ethernet cables of various colors were used. Table A-4 shows these cables.

Ethernet Cables	
Management network	Four blue cables
Storage network	Three green cables
Heartbeat network	Two red cables
Private VM network	Four yellow cables

Table A-4 Colored cables

© Cengage Learning 2014

To provide for a single LCD panel, keyboard, and mouse, which can be switched between the three servers, the author used an Iogear 4-port USB KVM switch with remote switching button.

Some versions of the RealTek Ethernet adapter cards reportedly have incompatibilities with Hyper-V. The Offload functions need to be disabled on each Virtual Machine Bus Network Adapter. For example, the following functions should be disabled: IPv4 Checksum Offload, Large Send Offload Version 2 (IPv4), Large Send Offload Version 2 (IPv6), TCP Checksum Offload (IPv4), TCP Checksum Offload (IPv6), UDP Checksum Offload (IPv4), and UDP Checksum Offload (IPv6).

To disable these functions, open the Network Connections window, right-click Local Area Connection, and click Properties. If the only selected item is the Microsoft Virtual network protocol, click Configure, and then click Advanced. In the next window, click each of the offload items, click the Value arrow, and click Disabled.

Software Overview

The two clustered servers require Windows Server 2008 R2 Enterprise edition with the appropriate roles. The third server also supports virtual machines for Windows Storage Server 2008 R2 and the Windows 7 client.

Table A-5 summarizes the software and roles installed on the two clustered servers.

Clustered Servers	
Operating system	Windows Server 2008 R2 Enterprise edition
Roles	Hyper-V Failover Cluster Management Cluster Shared Volumes
Agents	Virtual Machine Manager iSCSI configuration

Table A-5 Software and roles on clustered servers

© Cengage Learning 2014

Table A-6 summarizes the software and roles installed on the third server, which is the management server.

Management Server	
Operating system	Windows Server 2008 R2 Enterprise edition Windows Storage Server 2008 R2 Windows 7 Enterprise client Microsoft Office Microsoft Excel
Roles	Hyper-V Failover Cluster Management Active Directory DNS System Center Virtual Machine Manager 2008 R2 SP1 Internet Information Server Web portal

Table A-6 Software and roles on third server

© Cengage Learning 2014

Although it is not advisable to run application roles on the parent partition, you will for the purposes of performing the activities in this book. You will run Failover Cluster Management, Active Directory, DNS, Virtual Machine Manager 2008 R2, Internet Information Server, and the Web portal on the parent partition. Two virtual machines will support the Storage server and the Windows 7 Enterprise client.

Virtualization Overview

All three servers will be virtualized with Hyper-V. Each of the three servers will require roles to perform specific tasks.

The two clustered servers will require Windows server 2008 R2 Enterprise edition with the appropriate roles, including Hyper-V virtualization and Failover Cluster Management, as shown in Figure A-2.

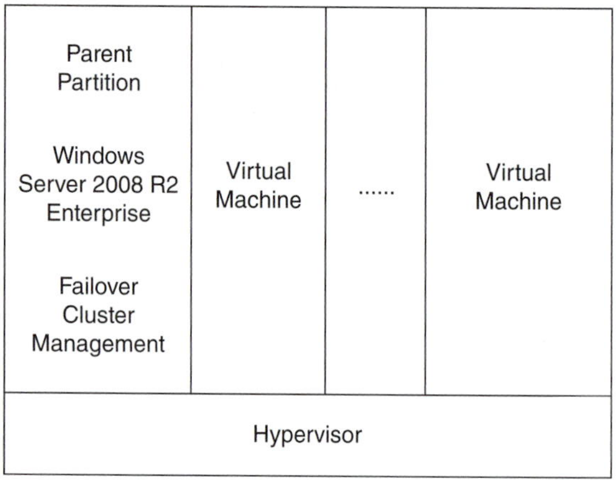

Figure A-2 Virtualization on clustered machines

© Cengage Learning 2014

The third server will also support virtual machines for Windows Storage Server 2008 R2 and the Windows 7 Enterprise client. The parent partition will require a number of roles to manage the three servers: Active Directory Domain Services (AD DS), Domain Name System (DNS), Virtual Machine Manager 2008 R2, Failover Cluster Management, and Internet Information Server. Figure A-3 shows these virtual machines.

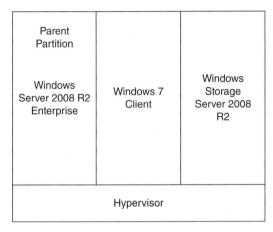

Figure A-3 Virtualization on management server

© *Cengage Learning 2014*

Network IP Configurations

Table A-7 provides the IP configurations for each of the servers.

TEAM1-CLSTR1

Network name	IP Address	Gateway	DNS
Management	192.168.0.112	192.168.0.1	192.168.0.1
Storage	192.168.10.101		
Heartbeat	192.168.20.101		
VM private	192.168.30.101	192.168.30.1	192.168.30.1

TEAM1-CLSTR2

Network name	IP Address	Gateway	DNS
Management	192.168.0.113	192.168.0.1	192.168.0.103
Storage	192.168.10.102		
Heartbeat	192.168.20.102		
VM private	192.168.30.102	192.168.30.1	192.168.30.1

TEAM1-MGMT

Network name	IP Address	Gateway	DNS
Management	192.168.0.111	192.168.0.1	192.168.0.103
Web portal	192.168.0.110	192.168.0.1	192.168.0.103
Storage	192.168.10.103		

TEAM1-CLUSTER

Network name	IP Address	Gateway	DNS
Management	192.168.0.100	192.168.0.1	192.168.0.103

TEAM1-Virtuals (on MGMT)

Virtual name	IP Address	Gateway	DNS
Windows 7	192.168.0.104	192.168.0.1	192.168.0.103
Storage	192.168.10.103	192.168.0.1	192.168.0.103

Table A-7   Network IP configurations

© Cengage Learning 2014

Budget

The budget for this project appears in Table A-8. The table illustrates the cost to set up one team station for three students. These costs were estimates at the time that research began for this book.

If you are using this hardware for multiple classes, you should use removable hard drives.

Quantity	Item	Cost Each	Extended Cost
3	Dell T110 Server	900	2,700
2	Netgear FVS318 ProSafe VPN Firewall	110	220
3	Netgear GS105 Desktop Switch ProSafe Gigabit	60	180
1	Netgear ProSafe Plus GS105E switch with VLAN	80	80
1	Iogear 4port KVM switch	45	45
1	LCD panel	220	220
1	CyberPower 1500 KVA	200	200
	Assorted cables	35	35
	Microsoft MSDN AA software	320/year	320
		Budgeted cost:	$4,000

Table A-8   Project budget

© *Cengage Learning 2014*

Using iSCSI Software Target 3.3

With Microsoft iSCSI Software Target 3.3, you provide storage that is accessible over a TCP/IP network. When used with Windows Server 2008 R2 SP1, Software Target provides shared block storage that appears on the host computer as a locally attached hard disk. You can use Software Target 3.3 to provide shared storage for Hyper-V and enable high availability and live migration in a private cloud. Microsoft touts Software Target as an economical solution suited for a development or training environment. Install the iSCSI_Software_Target_33.iso file in Windows Server 2008 R2 SP1 to provide access to the shared storage.

Activity A-1: Extracting iSCSI Software Target 3.3

Time Required: 10 minutes

Objective: Extract the iSCSI Target installer file.

Description: In this activity, you download Windows Storage Server 2008 R2 from the MSDN site and extract the iSCSI_Software_Target_33.iso file. To perform this activity, you must have access to a Microsoft Web site that offers MSDN. Also, you need to have DVD-burning software. These instructions are written for TechNet Plus and the DVDBURN program, which is part of the Windows Server 2003 Resource Kit. You need to make allowances for your own software environment.

The WSS2008R2+iSCSITarget33 .iso file may be available from sources other than the MSDN Web site. Other versions have not been tested.

1. Switch the KVM switch to port 1.

2. Log on to your MGMT server with a username of *Team1***Administrator**, substituting your team name for *Team1*. Enter a password of **P@ssw0rd**.

You need to have access to TechNet Plus, MSDN, or MSDN AA to download this software. These instructions are written for TechNet Plus.

3. To download Windows Storage Server 2008 R2, click **Start,** click **Internet Explorer,** enter **TechNet Plus** in the search box, and press **Enter.**

4. Sign in with your Windows Live ID and password. Click **Subscriber Downloads,** scroll and click **Browse Products A-Z,** click **W,** and click **Next.** Click **Windows Storage Server 2008 R2,** click **Download,** click **Allow,** and click **Transfer.**

If this is the first download, you must click the message bar to install the transfer manager.

5. Wait for the download to complete, and click **Close.**

Use .ISO burning software such as DVDBURN to burn the .ISO file to a DVD. DVDBURN is available in the Windows Server 2003 Resource Kit.

6. Insert the DVD, click **Open folder to view files,** double-click **WSS2008R2+iSCSITarget33,** click **Accept,** and click **Browse.** Expand *TEAM1*-MGMT, substituting your team name for *TEAM1*. Expand **Local Disk (C:),** click **ISOFiles,** click **OK,** and then click **Install.**

7. Wait for the files to be expanded.

Configuring Support Hardware and Software

The author used a Netgear FVS318G firewall to isolate the network for the virtual machines running on the CLSTR1 and CLSTR2 servers. The Netgear GS105E switch provides switching and VLAN tagging for the virtual machines. If your instructor uses another device, he or she will provide the equivalent instructions.

Figure B-1 shows the network diagram for a cloud station. The two clustered servers are shown in the box. Three 5-port gigabit switches provide for the Heartbeat, Management, and Storage networks.

This appendix provides instructions for setting up the firewall and switch for the network used by the private VM network. A firewall on the private VM network isolates the virtual machines while providing NAT services; the switch provides for future VLAN tagging.

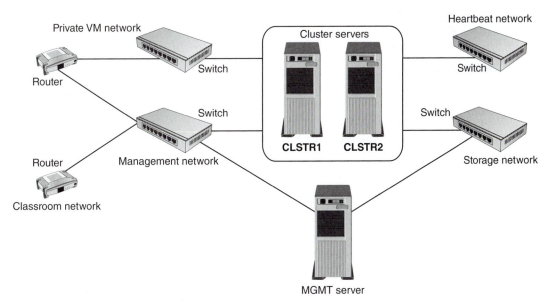

Figure B-1 Cloud station network diagram

© Cengage Learning 2014

Activity B-1: Configuring the Netgear FVS318G Firewall

Time Required: 10 minutes

Objective: Configure a Netgear FVS318G firewall with the CLSTR1 server.

Description: In this activity, you connect the firewall to the CLSTR1 server and configure the CLSTR1 server to access the firewall.

You should perform Activity B-1 before working through Chapter 2.

1. Locate the CLSTR1 server. If necessary, log off and shut down the CLSTR1 server.
2. Place a yellow cable between the bottom RJ45 connector and port 1 on the firewall.
3. Plug the power cord into the FVS318G firewall.
4. Wait one minute.
5. Turn on the power to the CLSTR1 server.
6. Switch the KVM switch to port 2.
7. Press **Ctrl+Alt+Delete**, and then log on to your CLSTR1 server with a username of **Administrator** and a password of **P@ssw0rd**.
8. To access the network connections, right-click the **Network** icon on the taskbar, click **Open Network and Sharing Center**, and click **Change adapter settings**.

Do not perform the following enabling steps on the network adapter for the Management network.

9. To enable the Ethernet adapter for the connection to the firewall, right-click the first **Local Area Connection**, and then click **Enable**.
10. If the adapter is enabled, an Identifying message appears. Continue with Step 14.
11. To disable the Ethernet adapter for the connection to the switch, right-click the first **Local Area Connection**, and then click **Disable**.
12. Repeat Steps 9 through 11 for Local Area Connection 2.
13. Repeat Steps 9 through 11 for Local Area Connection 3.

If you are unable to locate the connection for the firewall, contact your instructor.

14. Right-click the enabled local area connection.

15. Click **Properties**, clear the **Internet Protocol Version 6 (TCP/IPv6)** check box, click **Internet Protocol Version 4 (TCP/IPv4)**, and click **Properties**. Click the **Use the following IP Address** option button, enter **192.168.1.2** in the IP address text box, and press **Tab** twice. The Subnet mask appears in the Subnet mask text box. Click **OK**, and then click **Close**.

16. Minimize the Network Connections window.

17. To enable Web access for Internet Explorer, click **Start**, point to **Administrative Tools**, and click **Server Manager**. Scroll and then click the **Configure IE ESC** link, click **Off** for Administrators, and then click **OK**.

18. Close the Server Manager window.

19. To access the firewall, click **Start**, click **Internet Explorer**, enter **192.168.1.1** in the address bar, and then press **Enter**.

20. To log on to the firewall, enter **admin** in the User Name text box, and then enter **password** in the Password/Passcode text box, as shown in Figure B-2. Press **Enter**.

Figure B-2 Firewall logon

Source: Netgear FVS318G firewall

21. When the AutoComplete Passwords window appears, click **No**.

22. Click **Network Configuration**, and then click **LAN Settings**. Enter **192.168.30.1** in the IP Address text box, enter **192.168.30.2** as the Starting IP Address, and enter **192.168.30.100** as the Ending IP Address, as shown in Figure B-3. Scroll and then click **Apply**.

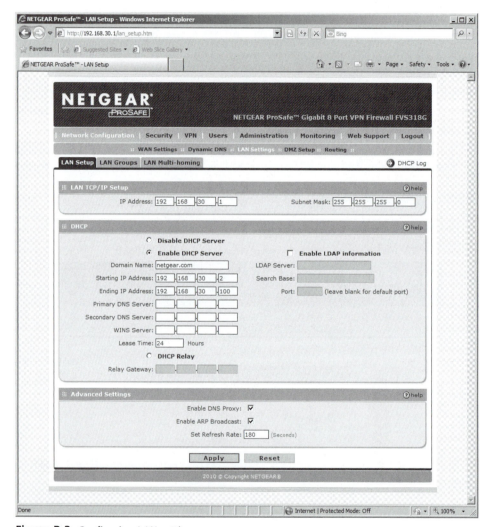

Figure B-3 Configuring LAN settings

Source: Netgear FVS318G firewall

23. Wait one minute for the firewall to IP address change to occur.

24. To change the IP address for the network adapter, maximize the Network Connections window, right-click the enabled local area connection, and click **Properties**. Click **Internet Protocol Version 4 (TCP/IPv4)**, click **Properties**, enter **192.168.30.2** in the IP address text box, click **OK**, and then click **Close**.

25. To access the firewall, click **Start**, click **Internet Explorer**, enter **192.168.30.1** in the address bar, and then press **Enter**.

26. To log on to the firewall, enter **admin** in the User Name text box, enter **password** in the Password/Passcode text box, and then press **Enter**.

27. When the AutoComplete Passwords window appears, click **No**.

28. Click **Monitoring**, click **Router Status**, and then verify that the LAN configuration agrees with the one shown in Figure B-4.

Figure B-4 Reviewing LAN settings

Source: Netgear FVS318G firewall

29. Close the Netgear ProSafe–DHCP log window, and then click **Log out**.

30. Right-click the enabled local area connection.

31. Click **Rename**, enter **Private VM**, and then press **Enter**.

32. Right-click the enabled local area connection, click **Properties**, and click **Internet Protocol Version 4 (TCP/IPv4)**. Click **Properties**, click the **Obtain an IP Address automatically** button, click **OK**, and then click **Close**.

33. Remove the yellow cable from the firewall. Place this cable in the Netgear GS105E switch port 5.

34. Use a new yellow cable to connect port 1 of the Netgear switch to port 1 of the FVS318G firewall.

35. Turn on the switch.

36. Use a new blue cable to connect port 4 of the management network switch to the WAN port of the FVS318G firewall.

37. Return to the Network Connections window.

38. Verify that the enabled network local area connection has a network identification.

39. Remain logged on for future activities.

Activity B-2: Cabling the CLSTR2 Server to the Netgear GS105E Switch

Time Required: 10 minutes

Objective: Cable the CLSTR2 server to the Netgear GS105E switch.

Description: In this activity, you connect the CLSTR2 server to the Netgear GS105E switch.

You should perform Activity B-2 before working through Chapter 2.

1. Locate the CLSTR2 server.

2. Place a yellow cable between the bottom RJ45 connector and port 2 on the Netgear GS105E switch.

3. Switch the KVM switch to port 3.

4. Press **Ctrl+Alt+Delete**, and then log on to your CLSTR2 server with a username of **Administrator** and a password of **P@ssw0rd**.

5. To access the network connections, right-click the **Network** icon on the taskbar, click **Open Network and Sharing Center**, and then click **Change adapter settings**.

Do not perform the following enabling steps on the network adapter for the Management network.

6. To enable the Ethernet adapter for the connection to the switch, right-click the first **Local Area Connection**, and then click **Enable**.

7. If the adapter is enabled, the Identifying message appears. Continue with Step 11.

8. To disable the Ethernet adapter for the connection to the switch, right-click the first **Local Area Connection**, and then click **Disable**.

9. Repeat Steps 6 through 8 for Local Area Connection 2.

10. Repeat Steps 6 through 8 for Local Area Connection 3.

If you are unable to locate the connection for the switch, contact your instructor.

11. Right-click the enabled local area connection.

12. Click **Rename**, enter **Private VM**, and then press **Enter**.

13. Remain logged on for future activities.

Activity B-3: Configuring the Netgear GS105E Switch for VLANs

Time Required: 10 minutes

Objective: Configure the Netgear GS105E switch with the CLSTR1 server for VLANs.

Description: In this activity, you connect the switch to the CLSTR1 server and configure the Netgear GS105E switch to use VLANs.

You should perform Activity B-3 before working through Chapter 6.

1. Locate the CLSTR1 server.

2. Insert the Netgear GS105E CD into the DVD drive.

3. Click **Run autorun.exe**, click **Install ProSafe Plus Utility**, and click **OK**.

4. Wait for the installation to complete, click **Next** five times, click **I Agree**, click **Install**, and then click **Finish**.

5. When the Adobe Air Setup window appears, click **I agree**, and click **Finish** twice.

6. If necessary, start the ProSafe Plus Configuration utility by double-clicking the **ProSafe Plus Utility** icon on the desktop.

7. To log on to the switch, click the button next to the GS105E for the 192.168.30.0 network, enter **password** for the password, and click **LOGIN**.

8. Click the **VLAN** tab, click **802.1Q**, click **Advanced**, click **Advanced 802.1Q VLAN Enable**, and click **Yes**.

9. Enter **02** in the VLAN ID text box, and click **Add**.

10. Click **VLAN Membership**, click the **VLAN Identifier** arrow, click **02**, click Ports **01** and **02**, and click **Apply**.

11. Review the settings and click **Quit**.

Activity B-4: Configuring the Netgear GS105E Switch to Remove VLANs

Time Required: 5 minutes

Objective: Configure the Netgear GS105E switch with the CLSTR1 server to remove VLANs.

Description: In this activity, you connect the switch to the CLSTR1 server and configure the Netgear GS105E switch to remove VLANs.

You should perform Activity B-4 before working through Chapter 6.

1. Locate the CLSTR1 server.

2. To start the ProSafe Plus Configuration Utility, double-click the **ProSafe Plus Utility** icon on the desktop.

3. To log on to the switch, click the button next to the GS105E for the 192.168.30.0 network, enter **password** for the password, and click **LOGIN**.

4. Click the **VLAN** tab, click **802.1Q**, click **Advanced**, click **Advanced 802.1Q VLAN Disable**, and click **Yes**.

5. Review the settings and click **Quit**.

Activity B-5: Downloading and Configuring the Script for the Virtual Desktop Configuration

Time Required: 15 minutes

Objective: Download and configure the script to fix the RDP permissions.

Description: In this activity, you download the Deploying Personal Virtual Desktops guide by using the Remote Desktop Web Access Step-by-Step Guide from Microsoft. Next, you locate the required script, copy it to Notepad, and then save the edited script to the Scripts folder.

You must complete these steps on a computer that is running Microsoft Word.

1. Locate the MGMT server.

2. To establish a folder for the configuration script on the MGMT server, click **Start**, click **Computer**, and double-click **Local Disk (C:)**. Click **New folder**, enter **Scripts** over the words "New folder," and press **Enter**.

3. To share the Scripts folder, right-click **Scripts**, and point to **Share with**. Click **Specific people**, click the **Add** arrow, click **Everyone**, click **Add**, and click **Share**.

4. When the folder is shared, click **Done.** Close the Local Disk (C:) window.

5. To open Internet Explorer, click the **Internet Explorer** icon on the taskbar.

6. When the Set Up Windows Explorer 8 window appears, click **Next,** click **No, don't turn on,** click **Next,** click **Use express settings,** and then click **Finish.**

7. To search for the required document, enter **Deploying Personal Virtual Desktops by using Remote Desktop Web Access Step-by-Step Guide** in the Bing search text box, and press **Enter.**

8. Click **Deploying Personal Virtual Desktops by using Remote Desktop Web Access Step-by-Step Guide.** Click **Download,** and then click **Open.**

9. To scroll to the last page, press **Ctrl+End.**

10. Locate the line that reads **At the command prompt, type the following commands:.**

11. To copy the script, click the first occurrence of **wmic,** and highlight the remaining indented lines through the line that reads **Net start term service.** Click **Edit,** and then click **Copy.**

12. To open Notepad, click **Start,** point to **All Programs,** and click **Accessories.** Right-click **Notepad,** click **Run as administrator,** and click **Yes.**

13. To paste the script into Notepad, click **Edit** and then click **Paste.**

14. Edit the lines to remove the punctuation on each line before the wmic or Net.

15. To save the script, click **File,** click **Save As,** click **Computer,** and double-click **Local Disk (C:).** Double-click **Scripts,** click the **Save as type** arrow, and click **All Files.**

16. Enter **Fix-RDP-Permissions.cmd** in the File name text box, and click **Save.**

Glossary

Actions pane In Hyper-V Manager, the pane where host and virtual machine actions are initiated.

Active Directory Certificate Services Role A Microsoft feature that lets you create and manage certificates used in software security systems.

Active Directory Domain Services (AD DS) A directory service from Microsoft that is part of the modern Windows Server family of operating systems, including Windows Server 2008.

array variable A fixed collection of variable elements that share the same data type and name.

assigned memory In Hyper-V, the amount of memory provided to a virtual machine.

asynchronous In operating systems, refers to a process that operates independently of other processes.

automatic start delay In Hyper-V, the number of seconds that the automatic start of a virtual machine is delayed when the host computer is started.

.avhd files Files used by Hyper-V to save snapshot images.

Background Intelligent Transfer Service (BITS) Microsoft communications software that maximizes the transfer of files between machines using idle network bandwidth.

bare metal server A server that either has no operating system or requires that you replace the operating system and all applications.

bottleneck A situation in which performance is limited by a single resource.

Certificate Authority Role service A Microsoft feature that issues digital certificates.

checkpoint An image of a virtual machine at a particular point in time. Checkpoints are very similar to snapshots, which you learned about in Chapter 3.

child partition In virtualization, the resident partition for a virtual machine.

client/server model A network architecture in which each computer or process on the network is either a client or a server. Clients rely on servers for resources, such as files, devices, and even processing power.

cloud computing A model that relies on sharing computing resources rather than having local servers or personal devices handle applications.

cluster shared volume (CSV) A shared disk containing an NTFS volume that is made accessible for read and write operations by all host computers within a Windows Server failover cluster. The CSV was first introduced in Windows Server 2008 R2 for use with the Hyper-V role.

clustering Connecting two or more computers so that they behave (or appear to behave) like a single computer.

cmdlets Small, task-oriented PowerShell commands.

CodePlex Microsoft's open source project hosting Web site.

comma-separated values (CSV) A file format in which columns of data are separated by commas.

CPU usage In Hyper-V, the reported percentage of CPU resources allocated to a virtual machine.

Customer Experience Improvement Program (CEIP) An optional Microsoft customer program that provides user data collected about the usage of a Microsoft product.

database schema The structure of a database defined in the language of the database.

differencing A parent/child pair of disks in which the parent disk is read-only and changes are written to the child disk.

domain A group of computers and devices on a network that are administered as a unit with rights and permissions.

domain controller A server that responds to security authentication requests in the Windows Server domain.

Domain Name Service (DNS) Microsoft terminology for the Domain Name System, an Internet service that translates a host name into an IP address.

dual-core processor A CPU that includes two complete execution cores per physical processor.

Dynamic Host Configuration Protocol (DHCP) An Internet protocol and service used to assign IP addresses dynamically to devices on a network.

dynamically expanding A disk that can grow from a minimum size to store additional data until the maximum size is reached.

emulated virtual device A device within an emulated hardware system that is emulated by software.

enlightenments A Microsoft term for implementations that reduce overhead and improve guest operating systems in virtual environments.

external virtual network A virtual network that permits virtual machines to access each other while accessing the host computer and external clients and servers.

failover The capability to switch to a redundant or standby server when the active server fails.

failover cluster A group of host computers that work together to increase the availability of virtual machines and applications.

fixed size A disk that is allocated at the maximum size.

folder redirection A policy that lets administrators redirect the path of a folder to a new location.

forest A Microsoft term for a collection of domain trees that share a common schema and have implicit trust relationships.

globally unique identifier (GUID) A unique reference number represented by a 32-character hexadecimal string.

Group Policy A set of rules that defines the settings and allowed actions for users and computers.

Group Policy Modeling A Microsoft tool that predicts the effects of group policies for a specified user and computer.

guests In virtualization, an operating system being run as a virtual machine.

hexa-core processor A CPU that includes six complete execution cores per physical processor.

high availability Groups of host computers that support virtual machines that can be used reliably with a minimum of downtime.

host In virtualization, the physical computer that supports the virtualization software.

HyperText Transfer Protocol (HTTP) A networking protocol for distributed, hypertext information systems.

HyperText Transfer Protocol Secure (HTTPS) A secure version of HTTP.

Hyper-Threading An Intel proprietary technology used to improve parallelization of computations (performing multiple tasks at once).

Hyper-V A hypervisor-based Windows Server virtualization platform included as a role in Windows Server 2008.

Hyper-V cluster A Microsoft implementation of a failover cluster.

hypervisor A software program that manages multiple operating systems on a single computer system.

indirect I/O model A model that allows virtual machines to be independent of specific types of hardware devices used on the physical server.

information pane In Hyper-V Manager, the pane where information is provided for virtual machines and snapshots.

Infrastructure as a Service (IaaS) A cloud computing service in which the service provider pays for servers, network equipment, storage, and backups. Customers pay only for the computing service, and they can build their own applications on the cloud.

initiator In iSCSI storage, a client that issues commands for services from the iSCSI target.

integration services Support for components that require a secure interface between a parent partition and child partition, such as heartbeat, shutdown, and time synchronization.

intelligent placement A Microsoft technique that identifies the best computer host to use for a deployed virtual machine.

internal virtual network A virtual network that permits virtual machines to access each other while accessing the host computer; external clients and servers are not accessed.

Internet Small Computer System Interface (iSCSI) A TCP/IP-based protocol for establishing and managing connections between IP-based storage devices, hosts, and clients.

iSCSI Qualified Name (IQN) A unique name that identifies an iSCSI target.

live migration The process of moving a running virtual machine from one host computer to another without interrupting the user.

load balancing The even distribution of processing across a computer network so that no single computer is overwhelmed.

logical processor A CPU that presents itself as multiple logical CPUs to the operating system so that it will schedule threads on all logical CPUs simultaneously as though they were independent processors.

logical unit number (LUN) A unique identifier used to designate a unit of computer storage.

logon authentication The process of identifying a user, typically based on a username and password.

maximum RAM In dynamic memory, the upper limit of RAM that the virtual machine is allowed to use.

memory balancer In Hyper-V, the process that allocates a memory resource to multiple running virtual machines.

memory buffer In dynamic memory, the amount of extra memory reserved for the guest in addition to the committed memory that the guest virtual machine requests from Hyper-V.

memory demand In Hyper-V, the reported memory requested by the virtual machine.

memory pressure In Hyper-V, the ratio of how much memory a virtual machine has to how much it wants.

memory status In Hyper-V, a field that indicates the memory condition of a running virtual machine.

memory weight In Hyper-V, a scheme to determine which virtual machine is next in line to receive an allocated amount of limited memory.

mouse release key A key combination that releases the mouse from a virtual machine's console window.

.NET Framework A library of software that provides access to operating system functions and runs primarily in Microsoft Windows.

Network Address Translation (NAT) An Internet standard that enables a LAN to use one set of IP addresses for internal traffic and a second set of addresses for external traffic.

network migration A procedure to move virtual machines between host computers.

network-attached storage (NAS) A network appliance that is dedicated to file sharing.

New Virtual Machine Wizard In Hyper-V Manager, the wizard that helps users create a virtual machine.

No Majority: Disk Only A quorum configuration in which one node is available; this node is in communication with a specific disk in the cluster storage.

Node and Disk Majority A quorum configuration used when an even number of nodes have available shared storage.

Node and File Share Majority A quorum configuration that is recommended if you have an even number of nodes and shared storage is not available.

Node Majority The recommended quorum configuration if you have an odd number of nodes.

Non-Uniform Memory Access (NUMA) A computer memory design used with multiprocessors in which the memory access time depends on the memory location relative to a processor.

orchestration A Microsoft term for making a virtual machine ready for connection.

organizational unit (OU) In Active Directory, the container that holds user and computer names and permits organization at the domain level.

parameters In PowerShell, settings that are used to customize the actions of a cmdlet.

parent partition The virtual machine that contains the Windows operating system after the Hyper-V role is added.

passthrough disk A disk that allows a virtual machine to access storage mapped directly to it without requiring the volume to be configured on the host computer.

performance baseline The level of performance you can reliably expect during typical usage and workloads; future performance is measured against the baseline.

Performance Monitor A Microsoft tool that reports data for internal counters used by the Windows operating system. Counter data is often shown in the form of a graph.

personal virtual desktop A virtual machine hosted on an RD virtualization host server and assigned to a single user.

Physical to Virtual (P2V) conversion A procedure to migrate an operating system and applications from a physical computer to a host computer as a virtual machine.

pipelining In PowerShell, joining two or more cmdlets with the pipe operator (|).

Platform as a Service (PaaS) A cloud computing service in which consumers create or acquire applications using programming languages and tools on a provider's cloud.

pooled virtual desktop Virtual machines that are hosted on an RD virtualization host server and available to users defined in the pool.

positional parameters Parameters that must be entered in a specific position within a cmdlet.

PowerShell A Microsoft scripting language used to provide system-oriented task management.

private cloud A cloud computing platform implemented within the corporate firewall of a private organization under the control of the IT department.

private virtual network A virtual network that permits virtual machines to access each other, but not to access external clients and servers or the host computer.

processor compatibility The ability to migrate virtual machines between Intel and AMD processors.

protocol analyzer A network tool for identifying, analyzing, and diagnosing communications problems.

Protocol Data Unit (PDU) In iSCSI storage communications, an encapsulated TCP/IP packet that contains SCSI commands.

quad-core processor A CPU that includes four complete execution cores per physical processor.

Quick Storage Migration (QSM) A Microsoft tool that moves a virtual machine from one storage location to another while the virtual machine may be running.

quorum In a failover cluster, the number of host computers that must be present for the cluster to function.

rapid provisioning The addition of virtual machines to meet increased demands for processing online requests.

RD connection broker A service that provides users access to virtual desktops.

RD session host A service that provides redirection to virtual desktops through the RemoteApp and Desktop Connections.

RD virtualization host A service that integrates with Hyper-V to provide virtual machines by using the RemoteApp and Desktop Connections.

RD Web access A service that provides Web browsers access to virtual desktops.

redundancy Duplication of server elements that provides alternatives in case of failure.

Redundant Array Independent Disk (RAID) An array of two or more disk drives that work together to improve fault tolerance and performance.

relative weight A Hyper-V setting that specifies how logical processors are allocated to a virtual machine when more than one virtual machine is running and the virtual machines compete for resources.

RemoteApp and Desktop Connections A service that provides connections to virtual desktops and virtual machine pools.

Remote Desktop Protocol (RDP) A Microsoft communications protocol that provides a graphical console to a remote client.

RemoteFX 3D video adapter A device to a virtual machine that provides a Windows Display Driver Model (WDDM) driver with support for DirectX 9.0c.

roaming user profiles User settings for an operating system and applications that are retained between user sessions.

role-based security A system of controlling user access to resources based on the user's role.

rollback Returning a virtual machine to a previously stored state.

SCSI controller An interface that connects to SCSI devices. Hyper-V uses the VMBus, which is much faster and requires less CPU overhead than an IDE controller.

Secure Sockets Layer (SSL) A protocol that allows Web browsers to communicate across a network without allowing eavesdropping.

Security ID (SID) A randomly generated, unique 96-bit number that serves as the prefix for user IDs and security groups.

self-service user role A role that grants users permission to create, operate, manage, store, and connect to their own virtual machines through the self-service portal of the System Center Virtual Machine Manager.

shared disk access The ability of a computer to access a device or information remotely from another computer.

snapshot In Hyper-V, an image of a virtual machine at a particular point in time.

Software as a Service (SaaS) A service that allows consumers to use a provider's applications running on a cloud infrastructure.

standard hardware system environment A consistent set of hardware provided by the virtualization program.

star rating A rating system developed by Microsoft to assist with the placement of virtual machines.

startup RAM The amount of RAM that Hyper-V always gives to a virtual machine.

storage area network (SAN) A high-speed subnetwork of shared storage devices.

storage virtualization A technology that treats storage as a single entity irrespective of the location of available physical media.

Surveyor pane In Hyper-V Manager, the pane that permits the selection of a host server.

switch In PowerShell, a command that provides controlling information to indicate that a cmdlet should take a particular action.

synthetic virtual devices Virtual devices implemented in software that function only with Hyper-V.

Sysprep A Microsoft tool that removes system-specific data from installed Windows operating systems.

System Center Operations Manager (SCOM) A Microsoft product for comprehensive monitoring of a private cloud.

System Center Virtual Machine Manager A role that enables centralized management of a virtual IT infrastructure.

system image A copy of a system that contains the operating system and related files, installed applications, and configuration preferences.

tab autocomplete A common feature of command-line shells in which the shell automatically fills in partially typed commands.

target In iSCSI storage, a server that responds to commands for services from the iSCSI client.

target memory A calculation by Hyper-V that indicates the ideal amount of memory for a running virtual machine.

thin clients Limited-function devices designed to support access to VDI environments.

thin provisioning The automated process of allocating the appropriate amount of server space at the appropriate time.

Virtual Desktop Infrastructure (VDI) An environment in which users connect to virtual machines running in central servers.

virtual LAN (VLAN) A network of computers that appear to be connected to a single, logical network segment, even though they may be located on different segments of a LAN.

Virtual Machine Connection A tool that supports access to a virtual machine's desktop or console.

virtual machine limit A Hyper-V setting that prevents a virtual machine from consuming an excessive amount of the available host's CPU resources.

Virtual Machine Manager (VMM) R2 SP1 A version of Microsoft's virtualization management software that is used in this textbook.

virtual machine reserve A Hyper-V setting that reserves a percentage of the host machine's overall CPU resources for the selected virtual machine.

Virtual Network Manager A tool in Hyper-V Manager that offers three types of virtual networks you can use for guest virtual machines and the host computer.

virtual network switch A software component of virtualization software. Virtual machines are connected to a virtual switch to allow communication between the machines.

Virtual to Virtual (V2V) conversion A procedure used to migrate an operating system and applications from a hypervisor, such as VMware ESX, to Microsoft Hyper-V.

virtualization The process of using software to simulate a physical environment and using virtual hardware on which you can install a number of operating systems (OSs) and interact with them.

Virtualization Service Client (VSC) A component that redirects device requests to VSPs in the parent partition via the VMBus. The process is transparent to the guest OS.

Virtualization Service Provider (VSP) A component that connects to the VMBus and handles device access requests from child partitions.

VLAN identifier (VLAN ID) A number that identifies the VLAN to which the frame belongs.

VLAN tagging A method of creating independent logical networks. A unique number called the VLAN ID identifies each VLAN.

VMBus A logical channel that enables communication between partitions in a Hyper-V environment.

VMware VirtualCenter A VMware product for comprehensive monitoring of a private cloud.

volume license A license needed when an organization purchases the contractual right to install the same operating system on multiple computers.

Volume Shadow Copy Service (VSS) A Microsoft feature that allows volume backups to be performed while applications on a system continue to write to the volumes.

Windows Communication Foundation (WCF) A Microsoft communications protocol that supports communication between services.

Windows Management Instrumentation (WMI) An extension of the Microsoft driver model that provides access to operating system components.

Windows Remote Management (WinRM) A Microsoft protocol that provides secure communication with remote clients.

Windows Server Failover Clustering Software designed to allow servers to work together as a computer cluster, which provides failover and increased availability of applications.

WS-Management protocol A public standard protocol for communication between devices.

Index